ELECTORAL CHANGE IN WESTERN DEMOCRACIES

Electoral Change in Western Democracies

Patterns and Sources
of
Electoral Volatility

Edited by
Ivor Crewe and David Denver

ST. MARTIN'S PRESS
New York

102639

Library of Congress Cataloging in Publication Data
Main entry under title:

Electoral change in western democracies.

   Includes index.
   1. Elections.   2. Comparative government.
I. Crewe, Ivor.   II. Denver, D.T.
JF1001.E39   1985   324.91812   84-40369
ISBN 0-312-24098-8

CONTENTS

Contents

Contents

LIST OF TABLES

List of Tables

List of Tables

List of Tables

List of Tables

List of Tables

List of Tables

List of Tables

LIST OF FIGURES

List of Figures

NOTES ON CONTRIBUTORS

Don Aitkin is Professor of Political Science in the Research School of Social Sciences at the Australian National University. His most recent books are Stability and Change in Australian Politics and (with Brian Jinks) Australian Political Institutions.

Percy Allum is Reader at the University of Reading. His field of research is West European and Italian politics and he is the author of Society and Politics in Post-War Naples and Italy: Republic Without Government?

Ole Borre is Professor of Political Sociology in the Institute of Political Science at the University of Aarhus, Denmark. He is the author of books (in Danish) on the Danish election surveys and on political sociology in general as well as numerous articles on voting behaviour, public opinion and protest behaviour in Denmark.

Ivor Crewe is a Professor in the Department of Government at the University of Essex. He was co-Director of the British Election Studies for 1974 and 1979 and is the author (with Bo Sarlvik) of Decade of Dealignment (1983).

David Denver is a Lecturer in the Department of Politics at the University of Lancaster. He is the author of numerous articles on parties and elections in Britain as a whole and Scotland in particular, and recently edited (with John Bochel and Allan Macartney) The Referendum Experience: Scotland 1979.

William H. Flanigan is Professor of Political Science at the University of Minnesota. His publications include (with Nancy H. Zingale) Political Behavior of the American Electorate and,

Notes on Contributors

most recently, Partisan Realignment and Analyzing Electoral History (both with Jerome M. Clubb and Nancy H. Zingale.

Gerard Grunberg is a Charge de Recherche in political science at the CNRS and at the Centre d'Etudes de la Vie Politique Francaise at the Fondation Nationale des Sciences Politiques in Paris. He is co-author of France de Gauche, Vote a Droite (1981) and L'Univers Politique Des Classes Moyennes (1983).

Christian Haerpfer is Senior Fellow in the Institute for Conflict Research, Vienna and Lecturer in Political Science at the University of Vienna. He is currently doing research on post-materialism and value change in Austria and on the political geography of the Austrian party system, on which he has published a number of articles.

Hans-Dieter Klingemann is Professor of Political Science at the Free University of Berlin. He has written numerous articles on aspects of elections and mass belief systems in West Germany. Most recently he has co-edited and contributed to Political Action (1979), Wahlen und Politisches System (1983) and Computerunterstutzte Inhaltsana-lyse in der Empirischen Sozialforschung. His current research interests include political representation in West Germany and the comparative study of mass belief systems and party manifestos.

Lawrence LeDuc is Professor of Political Science at the University of Windsor, Canada. He was co-Director of the Canadian National Election Studies in 1974, 1979 and 1980, and is co-author of the books Political Choice in Canada (1979) and Absent Mandate (1984).

Renato Mannheimer teaches Methods of Social Research at the Faculty of Political Science of the University of Milan. His recent publications include Mutamento Sociale e Comportamento Elettorale and Governanti in Italia.

Michael Marsh is a Lecturer in Political Science at Trinity College, Dublin. He has published articles on Irish and comparative politics covering the fields of political recruitment, electoral behaviour and political protest. He is currently involved in a cross-national research project on protest politics, and is completing a study of candidate appeal in Irish elections.

Anthony Mughan is a Lecturer in the Department of Politics at University College, Cardiff, and (from 1985) Senior Research Fellow in the Department of Political Science of the Australian National University. He is co-author, with R. D. McKinlay, of the recently published Aid and Arms to the Third World and is currently writing a study of turnout in British parliamentary elections.

Kees Niemoller is an Associate Professor in Political Science and Methodology at the University of Amsterdam and since 1979 has been a Study Director of the Dutch Parliamentary Election Study. He has recently published (with Cees van der Eijk) Electoral Change in the Netherlands (1983) and (with M. H. Leijenaar) several monographs and articles on women in politics.

Cees Van Der Eijk is an Associate Professor in Political Science and Methodology at the University of Amsterdam and since 1979 has been a Study Director of the Dutch Parliamentary Election Study. He has recently published (with Kees Niemoller) Electoral Change in the Netherlands (1983) and (with E. A. van Zoonen) Time Series Analysis for the Social Sciences (1983).

Nancy Zingale is Associate Professor in the Department of Political Science at the College of St. Thomas, Minnesota. Her publications include Political Behaviour of the American Electorate (with William H. Flanigan) and, most recently, Partisan Realignment and Analyzing Electoral History (both with Jerome M. Clubb and William H. Flanigan).

PREFACE

In March 1980 we organised a small workshop
under the auspices of the European Consortium for
Political Research (ECPR) to identify themes and
problems of research in electoral behaviour that
were common to large numbers of Western democracies,
especially in Europe. One of the topics to which
discussion persistently returned was the apparent
growth of electoral volatility in many - but not all
- democracies and its impact on countries' party
systems. A variety of questions presented
themselves within this broad theme. What does that
rarely defined term 'volatility' actually amount to?
How should it be measured? What factors have led to
its growth? Is it an international phenomenon
reflecting social and political forces common to all
the advanced industrial democracies? Or is it
restricted to a few countries only, such as Britain
and the United States, and if so why these in
particular? What is the link between volatility and
changes in the party system - between partisan
dealignment and partisan realignment? To answer
these and allied questions a follow-up workshop on
'Electoral Volatility in Western Democracies' was
organised for the ECPR Joint Sessions at the
University of Lancaster in March 1981. A series of
papers were commissioned, each devoted to electoral
volatility and changes in the party system in a
specific country. This book is based on most of the
papers presented.
    Inevitably it proved impossible to cover all
the major advanced democracies in the workshop or,
susbequently, the book. Shortage of space precluded
coverage of every one of the smaller democracies,
such as Iceland and Luxembourg, on which valuable
papers by, respectively, Olafur Hardarson and Derek
Hearl, were presented at the Lancaster workshop.
(These are available from the ECPR Central Services
office at the University of Essex.) New or
interrupted democracies, such as Spain, Portugal,

Greece and Turkey were excluded because a free and
competitive party system has not existed for long
enough in these countries for one to come to
sensible conclusions about long-term trends. Other
omissions, such as Norway, Finland and Sweden,
reflect our inability to find a willing contributor.
But we were fortunate to obtain papers on Italy by
Percy Allum and Renato Mannheimer and on Austria by
Christian Haerpfer, which were not presented at the
workshop.

The purpose of this volume, however, is not to
provide a comprehensive coverage of Western
democracies but to focus on a sufficient variety of
examples - large and small, multi-party and two-
party, economically successful and economically
declining - to place the study of electoral
volatility and party system change in comparative
perspective. To that end we have tried to ensure
that each chapter follows a similar structure and
contains the same core of information. We recognised
that limits to the availability of suitable data and
the special features of each country would make it
impossible for contributors to conform to an
identical format down to the last detail.
Nonetheless, we believed it to be practical for
chapters at least to run along parallel lines. We
wanted the book to bring out the distinctive
characteristics of each country; but we also wanted
to avoid a mere assortment of unconnected single-
country studies. Authors were therefore invited to
organise their chapters into the following sections:

1. Introduction: a brief description of the
country's party system, electoral system and
chronology of party control of government.

2. Volatility Since 1945: an account of trends
and fluctuations in both net and gross
volatility since World War II.

3. Sociological Explanations of Volatility and
Stability: an analysis of the impact of changes
in the social structure - class mobility, the
spread of higher education, secularisation etc.
- and of changes in the relationship between
social and political cleavages.

4. Ideological Explanation of Volatility and
Stability: an analysis of the impact of changes
in the electorate's position on, and degree of
concern about, major issues; and the changing

relationship between issue and party cleavages.
Authors were invited to pay special attention
to the impact of new issues – ecological,
feminist, 'post-material', linguistic etc. –
which have cut across established partisan
divisions.

5. Governmental and Party System Performance as
an Explanation: an analysis of the relationship
between electoral volatility and the perceived
success or failure of successive governments,
and of the party system, in dealing with the
country's major problems, especially the
economy.

6. Electoral Volatility and Partisan Stability:
a concluding section on whether the country's
electoral volatility represents short-term
fluctuation within a stable party system or
part of a longer-term trend towards a new
party system.

All chapters conform at least roughly to this format
and sub-headings are identical, or very similar,
from one chapter to another. Readers can therefore
make comparisons between equivalent sub-sections of
chapters.

We wish to record our gratitude to the European
Consortium for Political Research for hosting the
two workshops which inspired this book and to the
Economic and Social Research Council (then the
Social Science Research Council) which gave
financial support to the second workshop at
Lancaster University.

Our debt to our wives is even greater than
normal. We are grateful not only for their patience
while the book was compiled, but more specifically
for the English translation of Gerard Grunberg's
chapter on France by Jill Crewe and for the typing
of most of the chapters by Barbara Denver. We are
grateful to Fiona Knowles Lote for checking the
typescript for errors; her eagle eye never faltered.
The Department of Politics of the University of
Lancaster allowed David Denver to monopolise their
word processing equipment for long periods and their
tolerance is appreciated. Finally, Peter Sowden of
Croom Helm was most helpful with advice and
encouragement.

Ivor Crewe
David Denver

Chapter 1

INTRODUCTION: ELECTORAL CHANGE IN WESTERN DEMOCRACIES: A FRAMEWORK FOR ANALYSIS

Ivor Crewe

As little as a decade ago a volume of research essays on recent electoral change in Western democracies would probably not have been attempted. For in the early 1970s the watchwords were continuity, stability and resilience; not, as they are now, change, volatility and erosion. Summarising their monumental study of the historical development of party systems since the franchise extensions in the nineteenth century, Lipset and Rokkan (1967, p. 50) concluded with two sentences that mesmerised political scientists for a decade:

> ... the party systems of the 1960s reflect, with few but significant exceptions, the cleavage structures of the 1920s ... the party alternatives, and in remarkably many cases the party organisations, are older than the majorities of the national electorates.

This impression that voting alignments and the social divisions they reflected had been frozen into shape by the events of half a century ago was confirmed shortly after by Rose and Urwin (1970). In a statistically more systematic study of trends in party support since 1945, they concluded:

> Whatever index of change is used - a measure of trends or any of several measures of fluctuations - the picture is the same: the electoral strength of most parties in Western nations since the war has changed very little from election to election, from decade to decade, or within the lifespan of a generation... the first priority of social scientists concerned with the development of parties and party systems since 1945 is to

explain the absence of change in a far from
static period in political history. (p. 295)

Scholars did not have to look far for
explanations. The two dominant approaches to the
study of voting behaviour both focussed on sources
of stability rather than change. The first was a
'social structural' paradigm, well represented in
the separate work of both Lipset and Rokkan. It
assumed that party systems and the voting alignments
on which they were based were refractions of the
country's social structure. Most electors voted not
as the autonomous individuals beloved of liberal
theorists but as members of a social group, or, more
accurately, an organised community based on their
class or religion but occasionally based on
language, race, national origin or region. These
communities supported an overlapping network of
institutions, including but by no means confined to
political parties, which inculcated loyalty to the
community - and its party. Elections were an
occasion on which political parties mobilised their
pre-organised, deeply-rooted support; the vote was
an opportunity to re-affirm one's communal
loyalties. Social structures change but glacially;
parties and their allied trade unions, churches and
other associations have ample time to adapt to these
gradual changes; hence it was hardly surprising that
elections registered continuity rather than change
in party systems and their mass base.
    The 'social structural' paradigm was
particularly apt for much of Continental Europe,
where organised communities often pre-dated the mass
franchise and where proportional representation
encouraged the separate party representation of
distinct religious and economic groups. The second
paradigm, anchored in the concept of party
identification, was developed in the United States.
Here organised mass parties pre-dated the class and
religious communities of modern America and were
encouraged by the simple-plurality, presidential
electoral system to aggregate interests and groups
into a broad coalition rather than represent them
exclusively. The party identification 'model' (Crewe
1976, pp.40-41) assumes that most electors acquire
an enduring allegiance (an 'identification') to a
major, established party; that this identification
not only determines their vote but colours their
general perception of the world of party politics;
and that it is therefore self-reinforcing and self-
strengthening over time. It persists long after the

event or issue which originally provoked it has disappeared from the scene; indeed it tends to be bequeathed from one generation to the next. Thus party identification in the electorate gives the party system ballast, sustaining it against sudden gusts of public opinion or the storms of political crisis. Any one election will register a modest amount of change, perhaps enough to supplant the party in office, but the change reflects the strictly short-term forces released by the campaign. Over the long-term, party support reflects the distribution of party identification; single election results are short-lived and self-cancelling deviations from a stable 'normal vote'.

These two approaches were complementary, not contradictory. The emphasis on social structure did not deny the existence of party identification but regarded it as the inevitable concomitant – and merely one particular facet – of a wider communal loyalty. Similarly, the authors of the party identification model did not discount the importance of social structure; they recognised that class, religious and other group loyalties were frequently the origin and sustainer of a party identification. Common to both approaches was an emphasis on those forces, whether structural or psychological, which made for electoral stability.

Over the last decade, however, this picture of rock-like stability was increasingly called into question. Fragmentary yet accumulating evidence suggested that party systems were not as impervious to change, the electorate not as staunchly loyal, as they had been in the earlier post-war period. Particular election results themselves sowed some seeds of doubt. Dominant parties that had governed almost uninterruptedly for a generation were turned out of office in West Germany in 1969 (the Christian Democrats), in Austria in 1970 (the People's Party), in Sweden in 1976 (the Social Democratic Party), in France in 1981 (the Right-wing coalition), in Norway in 1981 (the Labour Party) and in Australia in 1983 (the Liberal-Country party coalition). In other countries election results were at the expense of all the governing parties, as in Denmark in 1973 and in Britain in February and October 1974. Some major parties suffered a slow decline throughout the 1970s, notably the British Labour Party, the French Communist Party, the People's Party in Sweden, the Liberal party in Norway and the various Christian parties in the Netherlands.

There were also examples of minor parties, some

of them new, making substantial advances. The
regional-linguistic parties of Belgium, which had
first emerged as a political force in 1965 and 1968,
established themselves as part of the party system
in successive elections in the 1970s. The resurgence
of Liberal support in Britain in 1974 was checked in
1979 only to revive again, in an alliance with the
newly founded Social Democratic Party, in 1983. The
Scottish National Party broke through (in Scotland)
in 1974, and although they have lost support in the
two subsequent elections, retain a permanent
foothold in Scotland's party system. Similarly, the
anti-tax Progress Party, which emerged with such
force in Denmark in 1973, has become a permanent if
slightly fading feature of the party landscape. Most
recently, the ecology movement has entered the party
lists in many Western countries, with varying
degrees of success, including a notable breakthrough
into the Bundestag by the German Greens. Defeats of
once dominant parties, minor party breakthroughs,
the gradual decline of some major parties – all
appeared to reflect a new volatility in the mass
electorate. Even where the shape of the party
system was unchanged the electorate appeared to be
more fickle. Perhaps because of the deep recession
incumbent governments found it increasingly
difficult to get re-elected in the late 1970s. In
Australia, Austria, Canada, France, Greece, the
Irish Republic, Norway, Portugal, Spain, Sweden, the
United States and West Germany the most recent
election (at the time of writing, May 1984) has
turned out the government. And in Finland, Italy and
Japan the most recent election has recorded the
lowest support for the permanent party of government
for generations.

A plethora of explanations and theoretical
insights, often speculative, has accompanied this
scattered evidence of change. Gradual alterations to
the social structure have encouraged political
observers to assume that parties representing
contracting groups would languish, whereas new
parties (or re-furbished old ones) would emerge to
represent rising ones. The widespread, sometimes
accelerating, secularisation of much of Western
Europe has inevitably provoked forecasts of a slow
doom for the explicitly confessional Catholic
parties or fundamentalist Protestant parties; the
steady decline and eventual merging of the three
Christian parties in the Netherlands, and the more
erratic decline of the Christian People's/Social
Party in Belgium are particles of evidence in

favour. Similarly, the continuous population drift from country to town and the gradual replacement of manufacturing industry by the service sector has inevitably raised questions about the future viability of farmers' and peasants' parties on the one hand, and about the eventual partisan loyalties of the burgeoning 'new middle class' on the other.

The most fruitful attempt to draw plausible conclusions from these social and political changes was made by Inglehart in The Silent Revolution (1977; see also the follow-up article of 1981). In the quarter century after World War II, he argued, a combination of unparalleled prosperity, sustained peace on the European Continent, a vast expansion of higher education and increased travel and communication between countries combined to inculcate a new set of 'post-materialist' values in the younger generation - especially its better educated and more prosperous members. Accustomed to physical and economic security, to the absence of war and scarcity, this new generation raised its sights to civic and 'cultural' rights, to the alleviation of alienation as well as of exploitation. 'Post-materialist' values emphasised internationalism and localism at the expense of the nation state; protection of natural resources, 'meaningful' jobs and workplace democracy at the expense of economic growth (whether market-induced or state-planned); sexual freedom as opposed to traditional sexual morality; active participation and direct democracy as distinct from the passive choice of parties at intermittent elections; a preference for small, face-to-face institutions and communities over large, impersonal bureaucracies; and the aggressive promotion of the rights of women and of sexual and ethnic minorities. Many of the emerging social and political movements of the 1970s, and the new parties they spawned, were led by this younger generation of 'post-materialists'. With common origins in the New Left student protest of the late 1960s, the women's, green and regional-autonomy movements of the late 1970s were all, in different ways, reflections of the growth in 'post-materialist' values. Although more sympathetic to parties of the Left than Right, 'post -materialists' kept their distance from the established Left because of its traditional attachment to economic growth and a strong, centralised state. Thus a new political cleavage, based on cultural rather than economic or religious divisions, on conflicts of values not interests or communities, was slowly spreading across the Western democracies.

The other conceptual foundation of electoral studies, party identification, was also undergoing scrutiny in the 1970s. The accumulating series of national election surveys in the United States and Britain revealed a gradual decline in the incidence and strength of party identification in both electorates (Converse, 1972, 1976; Ladd and Hadley, 1975; Crotty and Jacobson, 1980; Crewe, 1977, 1984). There were many other signs that the electorate's long-term attachment to the established parties was diminishing: a growing number of self-declared Independents and 'split ticket' voters in the United States; a resurgence of support for third parties in Britain; rising rates of vote switching and abstention in both countries. Both countries had experienced a 'partisan dealignment', accompanied by a marked growth of electoral volatility. Fewer and fewer voters were staunch party loyalists; more and more were 'available'. Moreover, this detachment from the major parties was particularly in evidence among younger voters; and in the United States, although possibly not in Britain, this appeared to be a permanent generational change, such that partisanhip in the electorate would continue to weaken as older generations died out (Crewe, 1980).

By the close of the 1970s, therefore, fragments of evidence suggested that the solidity of Western party systems was flaking; but they hardly added up to incontrovertible proof. For every election tremor that hinted at a possible earthquake to come there was another to confirm the permanence of the party landscape. The slow mutations of social structures underlined the _potential_ for party system changes, but their very slowness explained the capacity of many parties to adapt in time. The flourishing survival of Sweden's Centre (formerly Agrarian) party, Ireland's Fianna Fail party, and even Italy's Radicals in the face of an eroding social base was testimony to the resilience and flexibility of long-established parties. Anglo-American partisan dealignment found an echo in a few other countries, notably Canada and Denmark, but there were counter-examples in France and Germany, where the major parties appeared to be strengthening their grip over the electorate's loyalties (Inglehart and Hochstein, 1972; Kaase, 1976). Similarly, it is unclear what long-term significance, if any, to attach to the rash of government defeats at recent elections. The electoral volatility they reflect does not necessarily signify a profound change of party system. It might be short-lived, and even if not, would not entail a fundamental, enduring change of party system; fluctuations around a party's average level of support could increase while the average remained stable. Electoral volatility does not entail partisan dealignment; and partisan dealignment does not entail a change of party system.

Recent attempts to subject this conflicting and patchy evidence to systematic analysis have had to make do with mixed and tentative conclusions. Pedersen (1979, 1983) examined the electoral volatility of post-war European party systems and found no overall, European-wide movement. In general volatility between consecutive elections rose, albeit slightly, between the 1950s and 1960s, and again between the 1960s and 1970s, but this overall trend masked sharp differences between countries and some major exceptions: in France, Germany, Ireland and Italy, for example, volatility declined from one decade to the next. In a more ambitious exercise, Ersson and Lane (1982) did not confine themselves to post-1945 electoral volatility, but monitored trends and fluctuations since 1918 in various aspects of party systems, including their polarisation, fractionalisation, radical as opposed to conservative orientation and representation of social cleavages. They reached similarly untidy conclusions. Every European country had undergone a significant trend or fluctuation in at least one aspect of their party system, but these varied from country to country, revealing no clear pattern. An extension of Rose and Urwin's analysis to the period 1969-1979 for fifteen European countries came closest to discerning a distinct pattern of change in the 1970s, and one which, moreover, corroborated some of the impressionistic speculation described earlier (Maguire, 1983). Although the 'normal' volatility of each party's vote (defined by the standard deviation from the mean) had slightly diminished, the number of parties experiencing significant and cumulative trends in electoral support had risen. More of these trends were losses than gains, and they tended to be incurred by large, old-established parties, in line with the thesis of partisan dealignment, and by agrarian and social democratic parties, in line with well-documented changes in the social structure.

Nonetheless, the overriding picture was still one of relative stability in party systems, and of depths of resilience among individual parties.

Differences with the earlier post-war period, although real, were slender; patterns of change, although discernible, were faint; and general conclusions, although feasible, were qualified by major exceptions. In all three studies, moreover, the dominance of peculiarly national factors over international forces as explanations for developments in a party system was clear. These national factors included economic circumstances and aspects of the social structure but also the distinctive features of the country's representative institutions - its electoral system and, indeed, the forces for persistence and change generated by the existing party system itself. An adequate understanding of patterns of party system change therefore requires a country-by-country analysis, although within a standard comparative framework, of the kind attempted in this book. Some key components of this framework are discussed next.

ELECTORAL VOLATILITY: CONCEPT AND MEASUREMENT

A systematic and standard measurement of electoral volatility is the first requirement. Vogue phrases are usually vague phrases: 'electoral volatility' is simply a fancy phrase for changes in party preferences within an electorate. But it is a multi-layered and multi-dimensional concept. The changes may occur at different levels of the representative system, and take different forms. Changes on one level or dimension are not necessarily matched by changes on other levels or dimensions.

A party's strength can be measured by its share of 1) office; 2) seats; and 3) votes. The relationship between volatility of office and volatility of seats is determined, in the absence of one party enjoying an absolute majority, by the outcome of bargaining over the make-up of coalition or minority governments. That outcome reflects an amalgam of factors other than the parties' mere numerical strength, such that a rapid succession of governments does not necessarily reflect equal turbulence within the electorate: Belgium and Italy are cases in point. The relationship between volatility of votes and volatility of seats is determined by the electoral system. Under a system of pure proportional representation the volatility in vote shares and seat shares will be identical. In the Anglo-American single-member, simple-plurality (SMSP) systems small shifts in a party's share of the vote tend to generate a much larger net turnover of seats. In an evenly-balanced two-party race the relationship between vote and seat volatility is roughly predictable by the 'cube law', now undergoing modification as the 'two-and-a-half' or even 'square' law (see Laakso, 1979; Curtice and Steed, 1982, 1984).

It is at the level of votes that the first important distinction must be made - between net volatility and overall volatility. Net volatility refers to changes in the share of votes obtained by each party, as revealed by election returns at constituency, regional or national level (which can, of course, differ markedly at the same election, as the chapters on Australia, Canada and the United States show).

The measure of net volatility adopted throughout this book is the 'Pedersen Index' (Pedersen, 1979), which was derived from very similar measures adopted by Rose and Urwin (1970) and by Ascher and Tarrow (1975). It is defined as "the net change within the electoral party system resulting from individual vote transfers" and is measured by summing the percentage point change in each party's share of the vote compared with the preceding election and dividing by 2. (Summing the percentage point changes for all the gaining parties, or alternatively for all the losing parties, would give the same score since gains must equal losses.)

The Index's attractive simplicity inevitably brings its own drawbacks. By giving each party equal weight, whatever its size, it counts the same absolute increment or decrement of votes as equally significant; but one might consider the doubling of a minor party's support from 5 to 10 per cent to constitute 'sharper' volatility than a rise from 45 to 50 per cent for a major party. Indeed, the Index begs the question of what constitutes a 'party'. Criteria which emphasise the proportion of seats contested rule out strong regional (and usually regionalist) parties such as the Parti Quebecois and the Scottish Nationalists, yet include the tiny 'fringe' parties that can adopt a national slate of candidates in list electoral systems and, under the purer forms of proportional representation, secure one or two seats. In the latter case it normally makes sense to place some of the tiny parties into a residual 'Other' category, but this reduces the country's overall volatility score, albeit fractionally. A related problem arises from the merging and splitting of parties, and the difficulties this raises for comparison across elections. Should the votes of the two or more components of a party that has split, or will come to be merged, be added together or counted separately for purposes of comparison with the previous, or following, election? The answer matters, because the country's volatility score will almost certainly be substantially higher if the second rather than first course is adopted. The case against adjustments (the second course) is that the schisms and fusion of parties reflect volatile electoral forces; the case for adjustments is that these structural changes stem from decisions made at the party's apex, not from pressure from its electoral base. In practice these problems have been rare: in the one country covered by the book where they have occurred Belgium, the main parties split into Flemish and Walloon sections in the late 1960s and the obvious solution was to count their votes together.

Overall or gross volatility refers to the total amount of individual vote switching, as revealed by large-scale national sample surveys. It is well known that the net change in votes is the product of a much larger amount of overall change; and that vote-switching is often multi-directional: the partisan tide might be running strongly one way but there will be cross-currents and counter-eddies. Moreover, the precise proportion of votes moving from one party to another cannot be measured by the aggregate statistics, especially when, as in a number of countries in the 1970s, the situation is confounded by the entry and advance of minor parties. Although a substantial amount of net volatility must reflect at least an equally large overall change in individual vote preferences, the reverse does not hold: a small, even zero, net volatility could be the product of considerable, but self-cancelling, change in the electorate. There is no logical reason why net and overall volatility should rise and fall in perfect tandem, indeed there is no predictable relation between them, but in practice roughly parallel movement is the usual pattern.

The measurement of overall volatility is also subject to problems. The panel survey is the ideal method but not altogether free from biased estimates. As a result of sample 'mortality' the second and subsequent waves of a panel normally

under-represent the politically less interested –
the section of the electorate most prone to abstain
intermittently and thus add to the volatility in the
system. The absence of panel studies in many
countries, especially the smaller ones, forces the
investigator to rely on the long-term memory of
respondents in a one-off survey. There is now
overwhelming evidence that such recall data are
deeply flawed: in particular, respondents tend to
'project' their current voting preferences onto
their actual past behaviour, thus giving a false
impression of voting consistency, which in turn
leads to under-estimates of the true level of
overall volatility (see Himmelweit et al, 1978; Katz
et al, 1980; Sarlvik and Crewe, 1983, pp. 345-55;
Van Der Eijk and Niemoller, 1979). A further problem
of measurement, which even a perfect panel design
could not solve, arises from the contribution made
to overall volatility by the physical replacement of
the electorate – the entry of the young (and
immigrants) and the departure of emigrants and the
dead; identifying the past vote of this latter
category is, for obvious reasons, acutely difficult.
      It is well understood that net volatility masks
the amount of overall volatility between two
elections. It is less commonly recognised that the
latter in turn fails to capture all forms of change
in party preference. A second distinction worth
making, therefore, is that between inter-election
and intra-election volatility. The first refers to
volatility between two consecutive elections, the
natural time unit to adopt (although not one without
technical disadvantages in countries with variable
election intervals, like Britain and Ireland).
Intra-election volatility refers to changes in party
preferences, at aggregate and individual level,
between a general election and a point preceding the
subsequent one, as indicated by local and regional
elections, by-elections (special elections) or the
regular opinion polls. Much of the early evidence
for the alleged increase in electoral volatility
in Britain was in fact taken from some spectacular
by-election results and opinion poll fluctuations in
the late 1960s, and not from inter-election
volatility. One would expect trends in the two types
of volatility to track each other, although they
need not do so. It is not far-fetched to imagine an
electorate exhibiting high and increasing levels of
intra-election volatility but low and stable levels
of inter-election volatility (Ireland is perhaps an
example). Whether this kind of mid-term protest

voting counts as evidence of electoral volatility, or of a deep-rooted electoral stability, is a moot point.

Gross inter-election volatility will also fail to capture vote-wavering. A consistent voter at two consecutive elections might have seriously contemplated voting for a different party, or might have decided how to vote only late in the campaign. Whether wavering by consistent voters should count as volatility is, admittedly, open to question. An increase in wavering could be taken to show that the forces making for partisan stability were undiminished or, with equal plausibility, were increasingly vulnerable.

If there is a sense in which consistent voting between two elections can mask an intervening fluctuation or faltering of party preferences, so also, in a different sense, inconsistent voting between two elections can mask what turns out to be, over a longer period, relatively stable voting. Volatility between two elections is but one frame in the film. The voter switching between parties might be a permanent convert to the new party; a persistent floater; a temporary protestor against his or her usual party; or a 'homer', returning to the party fold after temporarily straying at the previous election. If a substantial proportion of inter-election volatility consists of 'protestors' and their counterparts, 'homers', the balance of overall movement across three or more elections can result in long-term stability. Substantial overall volatility coupled with negligible net volatility can be even more striking for a series of consecutive elections than it is for a pair. However, if a substantial proportion of volatility turns out to consist of permanent converts, the election marks a major change in the party system: either the balance of support between parties has been jolted into a new pattern, or the social bases of party support have shifted, or both.

There is a final sense of electoral volatility which none of the measures described so far can capture. To describe somebody as volatile is to describe someone who not only changes temperament, perhaps dramatically, but who does so suddenly, unpredictably and on the smallest of pretexts. A volatile person is a sensitive person. A volatile electorate might also be regarded as sensitive, i.e., one which not only (or necessarily) switches votes more than before but does so in response to ever-weakening 'shocks'. For example, the identical increment of unemployment or inflation might produce increasing amounts of vote-switching over time.

Finally, it is worth giving some thought to what constitutes an increase or decrease in electoral volatility. The Pedersen Index measures the amount of net volatility between two elections; panel surveys gauge the magnitude of overall volatility. But <u>direction</u> as well as magnitude is important. We might wish to count a 'straight conversion' between two large parties, on different sides of a major ideological or social cleavage, as more significant than a switch from either major party to abstention or to a minor party, on the grounds that the voter had 'travelled' further. Similarly, at the aggregate level we might wish to place more weight on the net change for the major, established parties than on that for the smaller ones.

Another component of the 'amount' of volatility is its relative uniformity or heterogeneity in the electorate. A volatile electorate might be depicted as one in which there is a strong uni-directional <u>flow</u> in favour of one party at the expense of another (or a number of others). But it might also be depicted as one in which there is a strong multi-directional <u>flux</u>, from which one party might benefit, but only modestly in relation to the amount of gross volatility. At the aggregate level one might wish to distinguish between countries or elections in which constituency or regional changes in net party support were uniform – in magnitude as well as direction – and those cases where they were not. The increasing heterogeneity of constituency 'swings' in the two most recent British elections (Curtice and Steed, 1980, 1984) is one aspect of Britain's increasing electoral volatility, just as the sharply divergent direction of change between the Deep South and the rest of the United States in the 1964 and 1968 presidential elections indicated a realignment of the party system in the South. But a 'realignment of the party system' is as multi-faceted a concept as electoral volatility and equally cries out for definition.

PARTY SYSTEM CHANGE: CONCEPT AND MEASUREMENT

For the purpose of analysing changes in a competitive party system one should again distinguish between three levels – levels which correspond to those adopted in the analysis of electoral volatility: 1) electoral base ; 2) party superstructure; and 3) governmental composition. The electoral base consists of the social and ideological cleavages underlying party choice: a marked change in the foundations, whether in the form of gradual erosion or sudden earthquake, will reveal itself by a correspondingly gentle or sharp rise in electoral volatility. The party superstructure refers to the institutional profile of a party system – the number, relative strength and ideological position of the parties competing for votes. The level of governmental composition distinguishes between 'governing' and 'non-governing' parties – an admittedly imprecise division between those parties whose parliamentary size or pivotal position enable them to participate in office at least intermittently, and those whose ideological position or small parliamentary size, or both, entail a permanent place in opposition.

The form of party system change that has attracted most scholarly attention in recent years is the 'partisan realignment' brought about by a 'critical election' for the President of the United States. (For example, see Burnham, 1970; Sundquist, 1973; Clubb, Flanigan and Zingale, 1980). Elections of this type marked significant and enduring changes at all three levels of the party system. The term 'partisan realignment' has recently degenerated through over-usage to refer to any decisive election result. When first used by V.O. Key (1955), the term signified more than a big win. It meant, first, a switch of party loyalties, not simply party support, and thus one that might last for a generation. It meant, secondly, a marked shift in the two-party balance – either a further consolidation of the governing party's electoral standing, or a long-term reversal of roles between the normal party of government and the normal party of opposition. It meant, thirdly, a change precipitated by more than an appraisal of the administration's record but by a transformation of the social structure, in the parties' broad positions and in the relationship between the two. And it meant, finally, a marked shift not only of voting patterns but in the balance of power among groups and interests and in the intellectual climate surrounding the conduct and discussion of public affairs. A truly realigning election crystallises a structural change in the mass basis of the political order, much as an earthquake is both cause and effect of a geological shift in the landscape.

Genuine partisan realignments of this type are, in fact, just about as rare as major earthquakes. There are only three agreed examples in the United States (1852 and 1856; 1896; and 1932 and 1936) and no replicas in Western Europe. The closest parallels are, perhaps, Sweden in 1932, when the Social Democrats began forty uninterrupted years in office; those Allied countries that had undergone German occupation which, in the first post-war elections, saw their parties of the Left make more or less permanent electoral advances; and France in 1958 when de Gaulle's democratic coup, consolidated by the new constitution, enabled his followers to dominate cabinet and legislature for sixteen years. But none are as cut and dried examples as those of the United States. The special set of social and political conditions which nurtured partisan realignments in the United States - two catch-all parties exclusively competing for the support of an electorate regularly injected with newly enfranchised, or at least newly politicised, immigrant-citizens - are not found in Western Europe, or even the 'frontier' states of Australia and Canada.

Compared with the United States, changes in the institutional profile of most Western party systems have traditionally been much less tidy: shifts of votes have occurred not only, or primarily, between two governing parties, but between major and minor parties, and minor parties have appeared and disappeared with more frequency. Students of European party systems have formulated concepts and measures appropriate for their less symmetrical format and messier history. Mayer's measure of aggregation (Mayer, 1980), Rae's index of party fractionalisation (Rae, 1971, pp. 46-64) or simpler measures of party domination like the proportion of the total vote captured by the two largest parties allow for the monitoring of party system change. An unmistakable trend towards greater fractionalisation as in Belgium since the early 1960s or Britain since the mid 1950s, or towards two-party concentration as in Germany and Austria since the immediate post-war years, constitute clear examples of a change of party system.

The ideological distance and polarisation in a party system is more difficult to measure. The precise ideological range and centre of gravity of a party is always a matter of controversy, partly because of the frequent divergence between the party's rhetoric in opposition and restraint in office. These problems are compounded in attempts to compare the ideological position of parties from one country to another, even when they bear the identical label. Nonetheless, these problems are not so acute as to hide indisputable examples of polarisation, such as in Britain since the 1970s, or of de-polarisation, such as in France between the early 1950s and early 1980s.

The increased fractionalisation of a party system encompasses a variety of patterns. One is a more even spread of support for existing parties as major parties lose votes to minor parties. The slow and uneven revival of the Liberal party in Britain at the expense of both the two major British parties is a case in point. But a more frequent pattern is the breakthrough and at least medium-term survival of new parties. The 1970s and 1980s offer many examples: the Volksunie and various Walloon parties in Belgium in 1965; the Democrats '66 in the Netherlands in 1967; the Progress Party in Denmark in 1973; the Scottish Nationalists in 1974 (but earlier in Scotland's local elections); the Greens in Germany in 1983; the SDP, in alliance with the Liberals in Great Britain in 1983. In no case has the new party become a major party, but in every case it has enjoyed - or seems set to enjoy - more than a short-lived existence. The pattern of government formation has barely been affected, but the institutional profile of the party system has changed, and voting has become more volatile.

ELECTORAL VOLATILITY AND PARTY SYSTEM CHANGE:
THE LINKS

The recent literature on party system change in Western democracies is frequently based on an implicit model which might be represented as follows:

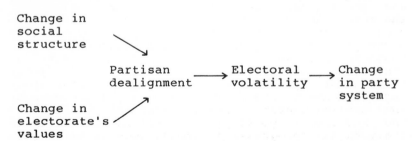

Introduction

Familiarity with the history of different countries' party systems reveals a far from neat and tidy relationship between electoral base and party superstructure. The chapters on individual countries that follow describe instead a bewildering variety of connections, and sometimes the absence of connections altogether.

The failure of changes in the social structure and value-priorities at the electoral base to always produce a partisan dealignment and consequent rise in net electoral volatility has already been discussed. In this book Ireland and Austria provide telling examples of the capacity of old-established parties to deflect or absorb new social and ideological forces. But even if an electorate undergoes some partisan dealignment, the impact on the party superstructure is unpredictable: there is no cut and dried relationship between electoral volatility and party system change, no logical tie between <u>fluctuations</u> and <u>trends</u> in the vote for a party. In a period of partisan dealignment the pool of relatively unattached electors swells: more voters are 'up for grabs'. But this does not necessarily undermine the established party superstructure, let alone transform it in a predictable direction. The main parties might grab voters from each other. If they do it simultaneously, turbulence in the electorate can still produce a stable outcome: overall volatility greatly exceeds net volatility. This situation, following LeDuc's description of Canada (see Chapter 3), might be described as one of <u>stable dealignment</u>. If they take turns, landslide elections will become more frequent, as has happened in United States' presidential elections: one might describe the situation as one of <u>unstable dealignment</u>. In both cases heightened electoral volatility leaves the existing party superstructure intact.

A special sub-category of this phenomenon is the <u>social</u> or <u>ideological</u> realignment. The social and ideological bases of party support change, but the number and strength of existing parties remains much the same. Cases in point include the American South since 1964, where Democratic predominance at Congressional and lower levels has survived, but increasingly on the basis of the black vote rather than, as previously, on the white (and segregationist) vote; the increasingly urban base of the Swedish Center (formerly Agrarian) party; and the successful appeal of the small Radical Party in Italy to new 'progressive' groups such as feminists and environmentalists. The electoral foundations are shifting yet the institutional structure stays solid.

Of course, if an established party grabs and then retains its new supporters, the existing party superstructure survives but the party balance will undergo an enduring change. In a pure or close to pure two-party system such a change amounts to the two-party partisan realignment that has figured so prominently in analyses of the United States. And if one or more minor or new parties scoop the pool a multi-party partisan realignment ensues: the party superstructure fragments as in Belgium in the mid-to-late 1960s and Denmark after 1973. However, the forces eroding the support for established parties have an equal, and usually greater, impact on the new and minor parties: multi-party partisan realignments are therefore acutely vulnerable to a surge and decline of support, as Borre describes for Denmark (Chapter 14) and Crewe for Great Britain (Chapter 5).

The existence of electoral volatility does not guarantee party system change; and its absence does not preclude it. The party superstructure can change despite a stable electoral base. Small fluctuations of support for one or more parties are consistent with slow, cumulative trends in favour of one or at the expense of another. From the early 1950s to the early 1970s volatility in West Germany was low but support for the SPD persistently if modestly rose such that it narrowed and eventually overturned the Christian Democrats' initially large lead. The almost unremitting decline in Labour's vote in Britain since the early 1950s is another case in point, although volatility in Britain has generally been higher than in Germany, especially in the last twenty years. Changes in the party superstructure are as likely to be imperceptible as dramatic: they do not require a critical or watershed election to take place.

These deviant cases notwithstanding, it remains the case that electoral volatility and party system change tend to accompany each other. Nonetheless, one should not infer that it is always the former that produces the latter. For example, studies of the 4th Republic (Converse and Dupeux, 1962) demonstrated a marked stability in the ideological tendance of French electors, despite the kaleidoscopic changes of party organisations, alliances and labels. It was impossible for French electors on the ideological Right or Centre to

18

identify with, or even vote for, the same party from one election to the next because of the rapid entry and exit, mergers and schisms, of different parties. Nonetheless, the French electorate displayed a stable ideological partisanship. Their electoral volatility was a consequence, not the cause, of a change in the party superstructure. A more recent example, perhaps, is the Netherlands, where an almost pure form of proportional representation encourages disaffected party factions to break away and gives the smallest of parties every incentive to contest elections. At every election, therefore, Dutch electors are confronted with an exceptionally large and ever-changing choice of parties (in the form of national party lists); on the other hand, the ideological and social 'range' of their allegiances is no wider than that of other European democracies. Because the ideological and social 'space' of the Dutch electorate is filled by so many parties, the 'distance' between the typical elector and the 'nearest' party is particularly short, which encourages vote-switching and identification with more than one party; but as Van Eijk and Niemoller show in this book the Dutch vote in an ideologically consistent way even when they switch parties, and the ideological distribution of the Netherlands electorate is stable. Again, party system change is the instigator, not the consequence, of electoral volatility.

The impact of the party superstructure, as distinct from the electoral base, on electoral volatility is a reminder of the importance of political institutions as shapers of party systems. Indeed, party superstructures contain the seeds of their own preservation or destruction, some being inherently more stable than others. The institutional profile of the party system - the number of parties, their relative strength, their ideological location and formal links with churches, trade unions and other mobilising institutions - have an independent impact on electoral volatility which rebounds back onto the party system. A well-known example is the damage done by the 'wasted vote' argument in SMSP electoral systems to attempts by third parties to convert sympathy into actual votes: the very structure of a system dominated by two evenly-matched governing parties is a major explanation for its continuation.

The party superstructure is itself the product of electoral laws and party political practices, which vary from one country to the next. Each of

the countries described in this volume contains a
nationally-unique combination of institutions which,
in combination with the electoral base, structures
the party system. Does compulsory voting (as in
Australia, Belgium, and Italy) reduce the amount of
electoral volatility by eliminating the opportunity
for electors to protest against their normal party
without voting for another? Do federal states
(Australia, Canada, West Germany, the United States)
encourage the formation of different party systems
in different component states? Does a directly
elected president, as in the United States, France
and Austria, encourage the formation of two-party
systems? Do national-list systems of proportional
representation, as in Italy, the Netherlands and
Denmark, encourage breakaway parties whereas the
Single Transferable Vote system, as used in Ireland,
allows dissatisfied factions and candidates to stay
within their party, competing against fellow-party
candidates in multi-member constituencies? Answers
to these and earlier questions are attempted in the
chapters that follow and are summarised in the
Conclusion. They turn out to be different for each
country.

REFERENCES

Ascher, W. and Tarrow, S. (1975) 'The Stability of
    Communist Electorates: Evidence from a
    Longitudinal Analysis of French and Italian
    Aggregate Data', American Journal of Political
    Science, 10, 475-499
Burnham, W. D. (1970) Critical Elections and the
    Mainsprings of American Politics, W. W. Norton,
    New York
Budge, I., Crewe, I. M. and Farlie, D., eds. (1976)
    Party Identification and Beyond, John Wiley &
    Sons, London
Clubb, J.M., Flanigan, W.H. and Zingale, N.H. (1980)
    Partisan Realignment: Voters, Parties and
    Government in American History, Sage
    Publications, Beverly Hills and London
Converse, P. E. (1972) 'Change in the American
    Electorate' in Angus Campbell and Philip E.
    Converse, eds., The Human Meaning of Social
    Change, Russell Sage Foundation, New York, 263-
    338
----------(1976) The Dynamics of Party Support, Sage
            Publications, Beverly Hills and London

Converse, P. E. and Dupeux, G. (1962)
'Politicization of the Electorate in France and
the United States', Public Opinion Quarterly,
26, 1-23

Crewe, I. M., Sarlvik, B. and Alt, J. (1977)
' Partisan Dealignment in Britain, 1964-1974',
British Journal of Political Science, 7, 129-90

Crewe, I. M. (1980) 'Prospects of Partisan
Realignment: An Anglo-American Comparison',
Comparative Politics, 12, 379-400

----------(1984) 'The Electorate: Partisan Dealign-
ment Ten Years On', in Hugh Berrington, ed.,
Change in British Politics, Frank Cass,
London, 183-215

Crotty, W. J. and Jacobson, G. C. (1980) American
Parties in Decline, Little, Brown, Boston and
Toronto

Curtice, J. and Steed, M.(1980) 'The Analysis of the
Voting', Appendix 2 in David Butler and Dennis
Kavanagh,The British General Election of 1979,
Macmillan, London, 390-431

----------(1982) 'Electoral Choice and the Production of Government: The Changing Operation of
the Electoral System in the United Kingdom
since 1955', British Journal of Political
Science, 12, 249-98

----------(1984a) 'Analysis', Appendix 2 in David
Butler and Dennis Kavanagh,The British General
Election of 1983, Macmillan, London, 333-73

----------(1984b) 'The End of the Cube Law', paper
presented at the Workshop on 'Comparing Electoral Systems ' held at the Joint Sessions of the
European Consortium for Political Research,
Salzburg.

Eijk, C. van der, and Niemoller, B. (1979) 'Recall
Accuracy and its Determinants', Acta Politica,
14, 289-342

Ersson, S. and Lane, J-E. (1982) 'Democratic Party
Systems in Europe: Dimensions, Change and
Stability', Scandinavian Political Studies, 5
(New Series), 67-96

Himmelweit, H. T., Jaeger, M. and Stockdale, J.
(1978) 'Memory for Past Vote: Implications of
a Study of Bias in Recall', British Journal of
Political Science, 8, 365-76

Inglehart, R. (1977) The Silent Revolution: Changing
Values and Political Styles Among Western
Publics, Princeton University Press, Princeton,
New Jersey

----------(1981)'Post-Materialism in an Environment
    of Insecurity',The American Political Science
    Review, 75, 880-900
Katz,   R.S., Niemi, R.G and Newman, D. (1980)
    'Reconstructing Past Partisanship in Britain',
    British Journal of Political Science, 10,505-15
Key, V.O. (1955) 'A Theory of Critical Elections',
    Journal of Politics, 17, 3-18
Laakso,M. (1979) 'Should a Two-and-a-Half Law
    Replace the Cube Law in British Elections?',
    British Journal of Political Science, 9, 355-62
Ladd,   E.C.   with   Hadley,   C.D.   (1975)
    Transformations of the American Party
    System, W. W. Norton, New York
Lipset, S. M. and Rokkan, S. (1967) 'Cleavage
    Structures, Party Systems and Voter Alignment:
    An Introduction' in Seymour Lipset and Stein
    Rokkan, eds., Party System and Voter
    Alignments, Free Press, New York, pp.1-64
Maguire, M. (1983) 'Is There Still Persistence?
    Electoral Change in Western Europe, 1948-1978'
    in Hans Daalder and Peter Mair, eds.,
    Western European Party Systems: Continuity and
    Change, Sage Publications, Beverly Hills and
    London
Mayer, L. (1980) 'A Note on the Aggregation of Party
    Systems' in Peter H. Merkl, ed., Western
    European Party Systems, New York, 515-20
Pedersen, M. N. (1979) 'The Dynamics of European
    Party Systems: Changing Patterns of Electoral
    Volatility', European Journal of Political
    Research, 7, 1-27
----------(1983) 'Changing Patterns of Electoral
    Volatility in European Party Systems, 1948 -
    1977: Explorations in Explanation' in Hans
    Daalder and Peter Mair, eds., Western European
    Party Systems: Continuity and Change, Sage Pub-
    lications, Beverly Hills and London
Rae, D. Jr., (1967) The Political Consequences of
    Electoral Laws, Yale University Press, New
    Haven, Connecticut
Rose, R. and Urwin, D. W. (1970) 'Persistence and
    Change in Western Party Systems since 1945',
    Political Studies, 18, 287-319
Sarlvik, B. and Crewe, I. M. (1983) Decade of
    Dealignment, Cambridge University Press,
    Cambridge
Sundquist, J. L. (1973) Dynamics of the Party
    System, The Brookings Institution, Washington,
    D.C.

Chapter 2

UNITED STATES

William H. Flanigan
Nancy H. Zingale

Traditionally, analysis of American voting behaviour has emphasised stability in partisanship. Individuals were seen as acquiring a party affiliation early in life, usually through familial inheritance, and holding that loyalty, probably with increasing strength, throughout their adult lives. (See Campbell, Converse, Miller and Stokes, 1960, for the major statement of this position.) The high level of partisanship in the electorate has been viewed as providing stability to the system, lessening the attractiveness of ´flash´ parties and the appeals of extremist candidates outside the traditional parties (Converse, 1969). Electoral outcomes could be analysed as short-term deviations around a stable baseline of partisanship, the normal vote of an electorate, measured by the proportions of various kinds of partisans and their propensity to turn out to vote and to be loyal to their party (Converse, 1966a).

In this conceptual context, the increase in electoral volatility in the United States in the past two decades suggests that partisanship is eroding in two ways. First, the loyalties of partisans to their parties may be weakening such that they more easily defect to another party´s candidates, thus making party identification, or the normal vote, a less accurate predictor of vote choice and electoral outcomes. Second, the incidence of partisanship itself is declining, with greater numbers of voters remaining independent or apolitical and former partisans abandoning their partisanship for independence. This erosion of partisanship has led to speculation that the party system in the United States is ripe for realignment, a pool of voters or potential voters having been created who are available for conversion to one or the other of the major parties, or perhaps a third party. Somewhat more extreme speculation suggests that the current dealignment presages a period of continued instability in electoral behaviour and consequent inability of the parties to govern effectively (Burnham, 1975).

In this chapter, we shall examine the evidence of increased volatility in the American system, explore its characteristics, and consider its likely impact on the future of American political parties. But first we shall offer some brief discussion of the major features of the American party system.

CHARACTERISTICS OF THE AMERICAN PARTY SYSTEM

Since the Civil War in the 1860s, the political system of the United States has featured competition between two major parties, the Republicans and Democrats, with only minor and short-lived intrusions by third parties and independent candidates. During this period, electoral volatility has usually meant departures from loyalty to either the Democratic or Republican parties. Other parties, where and when they existed, have seldom gained representation in government. This has led most political analysts to characterise the American system as one of the most stable two-party systems, and, of course, in terms of party competition, such a characterisation is correct. It does, however, cover up a substantial amount of long-term change in the regional and social support for these two major parties, as well as considerable change in the policy positions of the parties themselves.

In Stein Rokkan's terminology (Lipset and Rokkan, 1967, pp.1-64), the American party system was 'frozen' during the trauma of the Civil War. Immediately prior to that time, reasonably stable competition between Whigs and Democrats had dissolved in the turmoil over the question of slavery. Both parties factionalised along regional lines; splinter groups and wholly new single-issue parties appeared. One such new party, the Republican Party, replaced the Whigs as the second major competitor in the system and came to power as a minority party in a four-way contest in 1860. The Republican Party then achieved a long-term dominance through the combination of war, secession and military occupation of the defeated South. The party system emerged from the Reconstruction period in a

close competitive balance nationally, but with a
regional cleavage - the South strongly Democratic
and the North with an edge in favour of the
Republicans. Since that time, no other party has
seriously threatened to replace either of these
parties in national politics.

Notwithstanding this freezing of the party
system, the bases of support and the competitive
position of the parties have changed considerably
since then. In the realignment of the 1890s, the
Republican Party reasserted its electoral dominance
nationwide, gaining additional strength in the
North, while the southern base of the Democrats was
augmented by support in the agrarian West. More
dramatically, the New Deal realignment of the 1930s
gave majority status to the Democratic Party. At
the same time, a social class cleavage became more
pronounced, with working-class voters
disproportionately supporting the Democratic Party
and middle-class voters supporting the Republican,
at least in the North. The South remained solidly
Democratic for a while longer. Thus the social
class cleavage modified but did not supplant the
regional cleavage that was the legacy of the Civil
War. Nor was the social class cleavage entirely a
product of the 1930s. The Democratic Party had an
edge in winning the support of the southern and
eastern European immigrants of the first decades of
the twentieth century, an advantage that was
increased by the attraction to Catholic and urban
voters of the Al Smith candidacy for the presidency
on the Democratic ticket in 1928.

In large part, the electoral volatility of the
past two decades represents the erosion of the
realignment forged in the 1930s. Table 2.1 presents
the distribution of party identification at ten year
intervals from 1952 to 1982.(1) The table documents
the relative stability of partisanship over this
time period, together with a gradual decline in
strong partisans and an increase in independents
since the 1950s. The modest decline in
identification with both parties, it should be
noted, has not led to an increase in support for
some third party.

Although the longevity of the Republican and
Democratic parties is clearly rooted in the
traumatic memories of Civil War, their protection
from incursions by additional parties is
considerably aided by the single-member plurality
electoral system, which is used for voting for
legislative bodies everywhere in the United States.

Small parties have virtually no hope of gaining representation in the legislature and new or independent political movements have had no hope of being anything but small, given the traditional party loyalties of a substantial portion of the electorate. Furthermore, lasting factional disputes exist throughout both major parties and, by reflecting quite dissimilar perspectives within a party, may function as something of a substitute for third parties.

Table 2.1: Party Identification in the United States, 1952-1982

	1952 %	1962 %	1972 %	1982 %
Strong Democrats	22	23	15	20
Weak Democrats	25	23	26	24
Independents	22	21	35	30
Weak Republicans	14	16	13	14
Strong Republicans	13	12	10	10
Apolitical/Don't Know	4	5	2	2
Total	100	100	100	100
Number of cases	1799	1297	2705	1418

Source: Survey Research Center/Center for Political Studies.

The Electoral College system for electing the president is in some respects an even greater detriment to the fortunes of third parties. Essentially it is a winner- take- all system with weighted voting: all the electoral votes of a state (equal to the number of representatives that the state has in the two houses of Congress) go to the winner of a plurality of popular votes in that state. Thus, a small party has no chance to win any electoral votes and thereby affect the outcome unless it is regionally concentrated. On the other hand, if a third party is regionally based and strong enough to carry a few states, as was for example the George Wallace candidacy in 1968, its potential for disrupting the choice of president, if not winning the election, is very great. To be elected, a presidential candidate must win a majority of the electoral votes; if no candidate receives a majority in the Electoral College, the election goes to the House of Representatives where each state, regardless of size, has one vote. The prospect of actually using this bizarre, unpredictable and, since 1824, untested procedure is alarming enough that it can itself become a political issue used against third party candidacies.

A single-member plurality system may always deter small parties and tend to push in the direction of a two-party system, but in a federal system like the United States, it does not, and indeed has not, guaranteed that the same two parties will face each other in every constituency. Occasionally, a new party has displaced either the Democrats or the Republicans at the state level, and in other circumstances a minor party has retained considerable importance in a given state by influencing the ideological position of one or both of the major parties. Usually, however, such parties fall victim to the realities of two-party politics in the Congress and their own inability to be a force in presidential politics. At the same time, one can argue that the two major parties vary widely from state to state, in many cases sharing little more than a common name. Thus, while the electoral system may impede the proliferation of small parties, it does not require much organisational coherence of either of the major parties beyond agreement on a common presidential nominee.

The staying power of the Republican and Democratic parties depends to a considerable degree on their capacity to shift positions on issues and to encompass factions, and sometimes third parties, with different views. This ability to adjust means that the major parties conceal changes in the party system by moving with the political tides rather than declining in strength while new parties arise. At the same time, these ´umbrella´ parties may conceal a great deal of meaningful political change on the part of the voter. Voters can shift positions on issues or ideology and never leave the party.

One might say that the electoral system in the United States tends to dampen electoral volatility by discouraging flash parties. In contrast, two other features of the American constitutional structure – the separation of powers and federalism – work to increase it. In most of the other political systems discussed in this volume volatility is a product of changing patterns of voting over time. Either individuals switch parties

from one election to the next or the movement of
voters into and out of the electorate creates
fluctuation in the aggregate results. While this is
obviously also the case in the United States, the
American voter has additional opportunities to
behave erratically. In major elections American
voters typically face choices in a dozen or so
races. Voters may vote for one party for Congress
and the other for the presidency and split their
tickets in myriad ways for state and local offices.
As we shall see, some of the most persuasive
evidence for the recent volatile behaviour of the
American electorate comes from these intra-election
patterns.

TRENDS IN ELECTORAL VOLATILITY SINCE WORLD WAR II

Our conceptualisation of volatility involves
two related notions: fluctuating change and
unpredictability. Both ideas seem to be important
to the common meaning of volatility. Some
´back-and-forth´ element in the change seems
necessary. A steady trend in one direction or a
change from one stable state to another would not
satisfy our sense of what is volatile. There can,
of course, be fluctuations that are quite
predictable - the fluctuations in turnout from
presidential to off year elections in the United
States, for example. We would not want to call
these changes volatility, so the element of
unpredictability is also essential. If predictor
variables such as party identification which have,
in the past, adequately accounted for behaviour
cease to predict as before, we would say that voting
behaviour has become more volatile.
Corresponding to these two elements, we shall
rely on two types of indicator to measure electoral
volatility. On the one hand, we shall use such
evidence of fluctuating or divergent behaviour as
aggregate partisan swing from election to election,
individual vote switching between elections and
individual split-ticket voting. On the other hand,
we will make assessments of the departure from a
stable baseline of behaviour, in this case, party
identification.
The widespread impression that the United
States´ electorate has become increasingly volatile
in the post-war years is largely created by
observing voting patterns in presidential elections.
And, indeed, voting for president has been volatile

Table 2.2: Voting for President and Congress and
Indicators of Electoral Volatility, United
States, 1948-1982

	Presidential voting		Pedersen index	Congressional voting		Pedersen index
	Dem.	Rep.		Dem.	Rep.	
	1	2	3	4	5	6
	%	%	%	%	%	
1948	49.6	45.1	4.6	51.9	45.5	8.0
1950				49.0	49.0	3.5
1952	44.4	55.1	10.0	49.7	49.4	0.7
1954				52.5	47.0	2.8
1956	42.0	57.4	2.4	51.1	48.7	1.7
1958				56.2	43.4	5.3
1960	49.7	49.5	7.9	54.7	44.8	1.5
1962				52.5	47.2	2.4
1964	61.1	38.5	11.4	57.2	42.3	4.9
1966				50.9	48.3	6.3
1968	42.7	43.4	18.4	50.0	48.2	1.0
1970				53.4	45.1	3.4
1972	37.5	60.7	17.3	51.7	46.4	1.7
1974				57.6	40.6	5.9
1976	50.1	48.0	12.7	56.3	42.0	1.4
1978				53.5	45.0	3.0
1980	41.1	50.1	9.0	50.4	47.9	3.1
1982				55.5	43.8	5.1

Note: The Pedersen index is calculated using percentages of the total vote.

with no party holding the presidency for longer than
eight years consecutively since 1952 and with some
rather remarkable swings in party fortunes occurring
from election to election. Yet we find a sharp
contrast when we look at voting for the U.S. House
of Representatives which has been quite stable,
producing Democratic majorities in every year since
1952.(2) This dual pattern of volatility in
presidential voting and stability in congressional
results is shown in columns 1 through 6 in Table
2.2. These columns display the percentage of the
vote for both parties plus Pedersen's Index of
volatility in voting for both kinds of races since
1948.(3)
    These results from aggregate data represent net
volatility only, since compensating movements on the
part of voters will cancel out. Not many sets of
panel data exist for the United States, but the CPS

Table 2.2 (contd.)

	Different parties for President	Pres–Cong ticket-splitting	State–local ticket-splitting	Inds.	Defections Pres.	Cong.
	7	8	9	10	11	12
	%	%	%	%	%	%
1948	--	--	--	--	--	--
1950	--	--	--	--	--	--
1952	29	12	23	22	15	13
1954	--	--	--	22	--	--
1956	38	15	25	24	16	9
1958	38	--	13	19	--	--
1960	42	14	25	23	14	11
1962	41	--	39	23	--	--
1964	39	15	40	22	16	15
1966	49	--	50	28	--	--
1968	43	26	48	29	23	18
1970	48	--	52	31	--	--
1972	54	30	61	35	27	18
1974	57	--	60	36	--	--
1976	53	25	--	36	17	21
1978	--	--	--	38	--	--
1980	57	30	59	35	21	23
1982	--	--	56	30	--	--

Notes: Column 7 displays the percentage of the electorate reporting they have voted for presidential candidates from different parties in past elections. Column 8 displays the percentage of all voters reporting that they voted for candidates from different parties for president and Congress in the current election. Column 9 displays the percentage of all voters reporting that they split their tickets in state and local elections in the current election. Column 10 shows the percentage of people answering ´Independent´ to the party identification question. Columns 11 and 12 show the percentage of ´strong´ and ´weak´ partisans defecting from their party in voting for president or Congress. In column 10 all Wallace voters in 1968 are counted as ticket-splitters. Omitting Wallace yields 18%. Similarly Anderson voters in 1980 count as ticket-splitters. Omitting Anderson yields 28%.

Sources: Inter-university Consortium for Political and Social Research; Survey Research Center/Center for Political Studies.

panel study for 1972-74-76 verifies this conclusion
that presidential voting is somewhat more volatile
than congressional. In the presidential elections of
1972 and 1976, 28 per cent of those voting in both
elections voted for candidates from different
parties, whereas in the two pairs of congressional
elections, 1972-74 and 1974-76, the figures were 21
per cent and 26 per cent respectively.

Another indicator of electoral volatility is
offered by reports of voting for presidential
candidates for different parties over the years.
The percentages reporting having voted for different
parties for president, displayed in column 7 of
Table 2.2, steadily increased in the period from
1952 to 1980, reflecting the increased volatility in
presidential voting.

Individual data on voting for president and
Congress provide direct evidence on ticket-splitting
for these two offices. The total percentage who
voted for one party for the presidency and another
party for Congress is shown in the eighth column of
Table 2.2. Two periods with distinct patterns of
ticket-splitting emerge, one period from 1952 to
1964 when about 15 per cent of all voters supported
different parties in voting for president and
Congress and the second period from 1968 to 1980
with about twice as much ticket-splitting. In both
1968 and 1980 some increase in the percentage of
ticket-splitters is attributable to the supporters
of third party candidates for president, almost all
of whom voted for Democratic or Republican
congressional candidates.

As we have mentioned above, American voters
have many opportunities to split their tickets
because state and local offices are typically on the
ballot at every national election. The data
presented in column 9 of Table 2.2 indicate that
they have been taking advantage of this opportunity
with increasing frequency over the last two decades.
By the late 1960s more than half of all voters
reported voting for different parties for state and
local offices, a doubling of the rate in the early
1960s. As far as we can tell, no special partisan
bias is involved in these ticket-splitting patterns
although any general deterioration of party loyalty
has a proportionately greater effect on the more
numerous Democrats than on the Republicans.

The proportion of the various kinds of
partisans who reported splitting their tickets for
state and local office over the years since 1952 are
shown in Table 2.3. Each category of partisans has

approximately doubled in the proportion of
ticket-splitters over these thirty years, even
though independents, of course, have a higher rate
of ticket-splitting than strong partisans.

Table 2.3: Ticket-splitting for State and Local
Offices, United States, 1952-80

	Democrats		Independents			Republicans	
	Strong	Weak	Dem.	Ind.	Rep.	Weak	Strong
	%	%	%	%	%	%	%
1952	14	31	44	45	35	28	15
1956	16	28	42	57	44	31	17
1960	13	26	44	35	49	32	21
1964	20	47	63	47	67	56	29
1968	28	57	68	76	57	51	26
1972	35	63	72	73	70	60	40
1980	38	61	77	79	72	66	39

Note: The question was not asked in 1976.
Source: Survey Research Center/Center for Political
Studies.

        Loyalty to the established parties is a
powerful force for stability in voting behaviour.
As these loyalties weaken or disappear, voting
behaviour becomes less predictable. Thus an
important indicator of volatility, as well as a
partial explanation for its increase, is the
impressive rise in the proportion of Independents in
the American electorate; after 1964 the percentage
of self-identified Independents and others without a
partisan identification rose from 22 per cent to a
high of 38 per cent in 1978, although the percentage
has declined somewhat since then. By the same
token, those who call themselves partisan have
become more likely to ignore the appeals of their
party in the voting booth. We can examine this by
assessing the extent of departure from a baseline of
normal party loyalties. Almost all analysis of the
American electorate utilises party identification
for such purposes, or the closely related construct,
the normal vote, developed by Converse (1966a).
Figure 2.1 shows the trend in the normal vote from
1952 to 1982. The normal vote has been stable over
this period of time, reflecting the absence of a
realignment since the 1930s. The calculation of the
normal vote does, however, disguise the increasing
proportions of independents in the electorate and
essentially reflects the fairly stable ratio of
Democrats to Republicans. The actual votes for

president and Congress plotted around the normal vote estimate in Figure 2.1 illustrate again the greater volatility of presidential voting.

An even simpler view of defections from party loyalty is presented in columns 11 and 12 of Table 2.2 where the percentages of votes for president and Congress that cross party lines are shown. The national data indicate an overall increase in defections from 1952 to 1980 in both races.

These data on defection from party loyalty offer a distorted view of electoral volatility in two respects. First, in landslide presidential elections, defections generally affect the followers of only one party. Thus changes in the number of defections from election to election may simply reflect whether the larger or smaller party was advantaged in those years, rather than changes in the amount of volatile behaviour. Second, in congressional voting, defection rates are rather strongly associated with incumbency. They therefore affect the followers of both parties but in a reasonably steady pattern from year to year. In this case the behaviour is quite regular and predictable, though not predictable on the basis of party identification.

Another aspect of electoral behaviour, not always thought of as being associated with volatility, is turnout. Periods of low turnout are usually treated as having the potential for introducing instability into the electoral system. Rapid, massive mobilisation resulting in sharply increased turnout would presumably be the destabilising, volatility-producing factor. This is really one element of the familiar analysis presented by Angus Campbell (1960) as ´surge and decline´. The hypothesis of interest here is that the extra voters mobilised by a high stimulus election are more susceptible to short-term forces and accentuate the fluctuations in support for the parties between presidential and mid-term elections.

While there is no doubt that a growing body of non-voters creates symbolic problems for the political system and suggests an increasing potential for an unsettling impact on future elections, the discussions of low turnout in the United States over the last decade have been overdrawn. First, the decline in turnout from the high in the early 1960s to the present is less than ten per cent. Some of the decline can be attributed to increasingly large numbers of older citizens who vote at lower rates and the addition to the

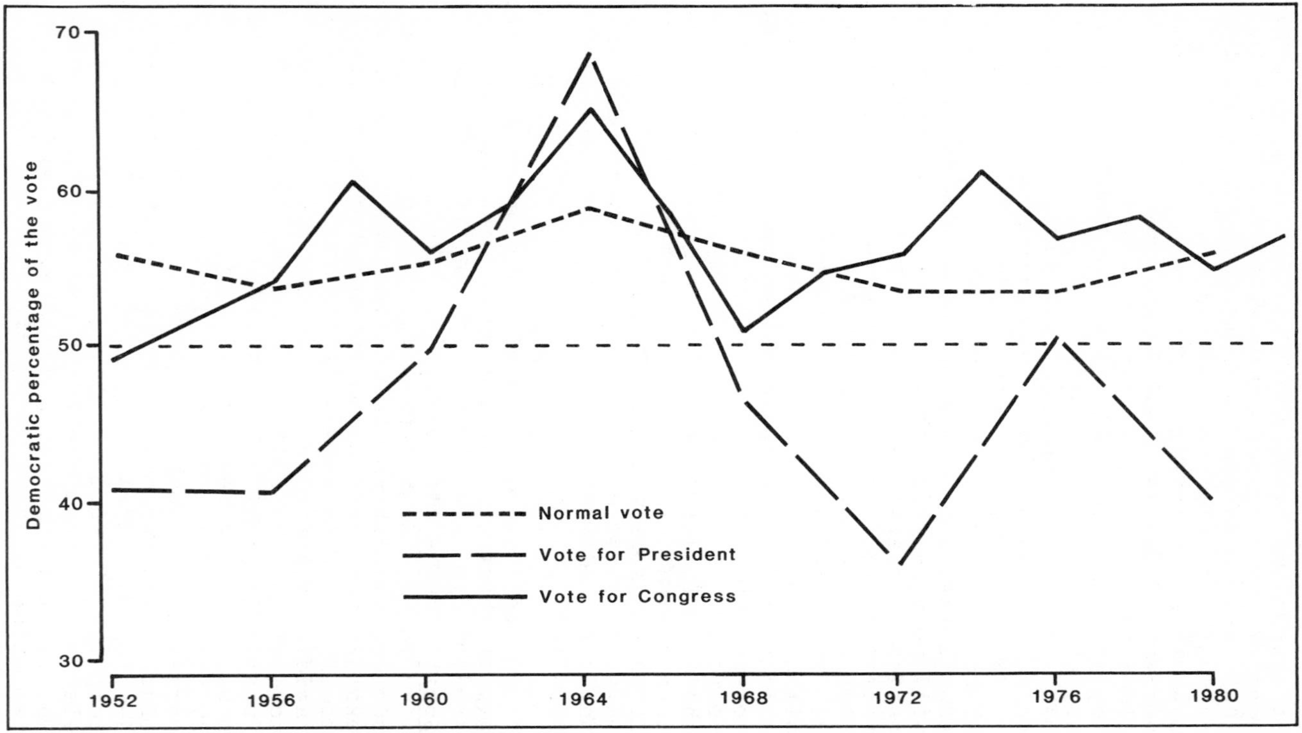

Figure 2.1: Democratic Normal Vote, Vote for President and for Congress, 1952-82

torate of the eighteen to twenty-year-olds who vote at very low rates. Cohort analysis, not presented here, of those individuals eligible to vote in both 1960 and 1980 reveals no change in their level of turnout. Most of the aggregate decline in turnout over these years results from the steady increase of non-voting young people and the disappearance of older people who voted at higher rates. Thus, the key to the decline in the overall turnout rate is not change in individuals´ behaviour through time but rather in the lower and lower initial levels of turnout of each cohort of incoming voters.

Furthermore, most non-voters in a given election have voted previously if they were old enough, and a majority of non-voters in one election will vote within the next four years. In the national elections between 1972 and 1976, the only recent period for which there are panel data, one in five of those eligible to vote did not vote in any of the three elections and about one-third voted in all of them. The remainder, almost half of the electorate, participated irregularly. Another way to summarise the quality of increased non-voting is to note that among citizens who do not care who wins the election and are not interested in the campaign, turnout was lower in the 1970s than in the 1960s. It is arguable which condition should be considered more volatile - having larger numbers of uninterested, less concerned citizens in the voting population or outside it.

EXPLANATIONS

Social Change and Volatility

Three sets of social changes in American society suggest themselves as possible candidates to explain the increase in electoral volatility over the last two decades: (1) the politicisation of the racial cleavage as a result of the civil rights movement of the 1960s; (2) the development of a ´post-industrial´ class structure, i.e., a growth in public sector and service occupations filled mainly by the middle class (Inglehart, 1977) and a corresponding embourgeoisement of the working class (Butler and Stokes, 1969, pp.101-15); and (3) the development of a political ´generation gap´, by the temporal distance of the younger members of the electorate from the Great Depression, the issues of which still form the basic dividing line between the two major political parties.

In our analysis of the volatility of social groups we have opted for two steps: first, to examine shifts in underlying partisanship, and then, to examine departures from partisanship over the years. There are, then, two types of change examined: group shifts in party identification (as incorporated in the calculation of the normal vote) plus the group difference between actual vote and expected vote.

The social changes associated with the civil rights movement show the clearest connection with political change. There is considerable evidence that the Goldwater-Johnson contest of 1964 redefined the positions of the parties on the racial issue in the minds of many white voters, primarily but by no means exclusively, in the South, and in the minds of blacks. In the case of white southerners and some working-class northern whites this has meant greater willingness to defect from traditional Democratic loyalties as the Democratic Party became more closely associated with the interests of racial minorities. This behaviour has contributed substantially to the pattern of increased electoral volatility. The other major change, however, has probably decreased the amount of volatility - since 1964 blacks have become overwhelmingly loyal to the Democratic party and highly unlikely to defect from it in voting. On the other hand, they have been willing to abstain from voting in some elections and this, in turn, may contribute to volatility.

The dramatic change in partisan loyalty that has occurred in the South has taken two forms. The first is a shift in partisanship itself, with some white southerners beginning to identify with the Republican Party and much larger numbers identifying themselves as independents. A fair amount of discussion has centred around whether the increased Republicanism results fron the conversion of former Democrats or from the in-migration of Republicans from the North (Converse, 1966b; Beck, 1977; Campbell, 1977), but in either case the normal vote of the southern electorate has declined from 72 per cent Democratic in 1952 to 61 per cent in 1982. The increased independence of southern voters is correctly viewed as increasing the unpredictability of voting and perhaps representing a greater susceptibility to third party candidates such as George Wallace.

The second form of partisan change is the high rates of defection from party loyalty among the remaining partisans. As Table 2.4 shows, white

southern voters have been breaking ranks in
presidential elections since the 1950s. Defections
were at their highest, over 40 per cent, in the
elections of 1968 and 1972. By this one standard
the South would appear considerably more volatile
than the non-South, although overall we might
conclude that white southern voters are responding
to rather stable conservative ideological
preferences that are reflected best in Republican
votes for president. There has as well been a
steady increase in defections from party in
congressional voting. This perhaps reflects the
organisational resurgence of the Republican Party in
many parts of the South, giving conservative-minded
Democratic supporters more conservative candidates
to vote for in congressional elections. These
trends have been accompanied by increasing turnout
in the South to the point that it is now not
noticeably lower than in the rest of the country.

Table 2.4: Defections from Party Identification in
Presidential and Congressional Voting for
Blacks and Northern and Southern Whites,
United States, 1952-1980

	Presidential defections			Congressional defections		
	Whites		Blacks	Whites		Blacks
	North	South		North	South	
	%	%	%	%	%	%
1952	15	30	14	15	8	6
1956	14	26	16	10	8	4
1960	9	26	16	12	12	7
1964	16	19	10	15	16	9
1968	19	41	4	19	15	16
1972	22	44	10	19	19	8
1976	17	21	7	23	25	3
1980	25	20	6	24	29	5

Source: Survey Research Center/Center for Political
Studies

At the same time that Democratic loyalty was
declining among southern whites, blacks have
increased their partisan loyalty to the Democratic
Party and made their vote one of the most stable of
any analytic category. As can be seen from Table
2.4, blacks have been consistently less likely than
whites to defect from their party in voting for
president or Congress. Blacks have, if anything,

become less volatile in making vote choices. Blacks
have become more Democratic through the mobilisation
of individuals who did not perceive themselves as
participants in the electoral system two or three
decades ago and by the conversion or death of the
small number of black Republicans from an earlier
era. The only real uncertainty in the vote of
blacks is how many will turn out to vote. They
consistently deviate from their already
pro-Democratic normal vote in a Democratic direction
since black independents vote overwhelmingly
Democratic rather than dividing evenly.

A number of analysts have attributed the
increased tendency of middle-class people,
particularly the younger middle class, to vote
Democratic to a restructuring of the social classes
in the post-industrial age (Nie, Verba and Petrocik,
1976; Ladd and Hadley, 1975). Since the new middle
class is more likely to be salaried, rather than
self-employed, and increasingly likely to be
dependent on government or non-profit organisations
for employment, their economic self-interest makes
them view the Democratic Party more favourably than
did their entrepreneurial predecessors. A counter
movement among white working class and union members
to desert the Democratic Party is presumed to result
from their growing affluence and an identification
of their economic self-interest with the policies of
traditional middle-class Republicanism.

There is some evidence to support these
hypotheses. In the North, the relationship between
social class and party identification is declining.
In the South, in contrast, the relationship has
increased rather dramatically, a result of the
increasing Republicanism or independence of the
white middle class, while blacks, largely working
class, remain solidly Democratic. The South is now
much like the North in its degree of class
polarisation. It is clear that the convergence in
the partisanship of the social classes in the North
has much to do with current volatility in voting
patterns. The relationship between social class and
vote choice has not declined significantly. In
1972, the index of class voting fell to near zero, a
result of McGovern´s lack of appeal to the working
class; however, in the presidential election of
1976, it bounced back to one of its highest levels
since World War II. In any event, there has never
been much of a class cleavage in American politics,
so an erosion in class voting is not likely to
result in dramatic changes.

During the late 1960s and early 1970s much was made of the so-called generation gap between the young and those on the other side of thirty. In fact, there was always as much division within the younger generation as between it and older people on such issues as the war in Vietnam and civil rights. But in one respect young people are distinct from their elders and that is in their propensity to be less partisan. It has always been true that the young are most likely to be independent or apolitical, but this difference has become accentuated in the past two decades. More young people identify themselves as independents and they stay independent longer than in the past. In 1952, 28 per cent of those under thirty were independent; by 1980 the proportion was 45 per cent. Young people who have become partisans, however, are only slightly more likely to defect from party ties than older voters.

Paul Beck (1974), in developing an explanation for the cyclical pattern to partisan realignment in the United States, also offers an interpretation of the increased level of political independence among young people since the 1960s. He argues that the transmission of partisan loyalties from parents to children will become less successful with the lengthening of time since the last realignment (in this case, the 1930s). In other words, the generation that experienced a realignment and developed political loyalties from it will have very strong partisanship and will transmit these loyalties with a high rate of success to their children. The next generation, because they did not experience the realignment personally, will be less successful in transmitting feelings of partisanship to their children. Thus, as time passes, greater and greater proportions of the incoming young voters will view themselves as independents.

The independence of young people means that they contribute substantially to electoral volatility. On the other hand, their very low rate of electoral turnout undoubtedly dampens this effect. Should young people be mobilised, of course, their lack of party ties would make them a particularly volatile element in the electorate. Indeed, they constitute a pool of available voters and potential voters, that, if mobilised in favour of one party, could produce a major realignment of the party system.

Population changes have also been mentioned as possible contributors to current electoral

volatility. The contribution of the changing
composition of the population to overall volatility,
however, is not significant in comparison with other
factors. And, indeed, it is difficult to imagine
what kinds of short-run population change could
substantially alter electoral behaviour (Norpoth and
Rusk, 1982).

Ideology, Issues and Volatility

It is reasonable to suppose that a fundamental
cause of electoral volatility, especially as it
produces defections from underlying partisan
loyalty, is the cross-cutting impact of issues and
ideology. More particularly, as issues arise which
do not coincide with the old partisan cleavage and
the issues associated with it, we expect these new
issues to foster conditions that increase partisan
defections. In the post-New Deal era, this implies
that issues on matters of foreign policy like
Vietnam or on race relations or on cultural
questions like abortion will have some potential for
weakening the party loyalties established in the
1930s.

Not all of the evidence from the past several
decades on issues and ideology supports this
expectation. In the mid-1960s the party cleavage
became more strongly aligned with certain issues and
probably the liberal-conservative dimension as well
(Pomper, 1975). The issues that followed this
strengthened relationship with party identification
could generally be classified as more recent
versions of the old New Deal issue alignment.
Generally it is supposed that the presidential
campaign of 1964 was the main cause of this shift
and to a considerable degree that campaign hearkened
back to the issues and cleavages of the earlier era.
And most of this symbolic clash was cast in terms
of traditional liberalism and conservatism.

At the same time, there is evidence that, since
1964, racial attitudes have become an increasingly
important dimension underlying both party
identification and vote choice (Stimson and
Carmines, 1982), a fact which should not surprise us
given the changes in southern voting patterns
already noted. The 1972 presidential election also
seemed to indicate that a new cluster of issues,
unrelated to the economic dimension of the New Deal
party system, was structuring vote choice. Apparent
polarisation of attitudes about race, law and order,
the military and the counter-culture life style -

attitudes that were highly related to vote for
president in that year, but not to party
identification - led Miller and Levitin (1976) to
suggest that a realignment was underway. Perhaps
because of the crushing defeat of McGovern in 1972,
these issues have not figured largely in later
presidential campaigns and what looked like the
start of a new and enduring alignment of the party
system, in retrospect appears to have been an
example of short-term deviating change. Thus, while
these issues may help to explain the volatility of
voters in one election, they alone do not account
for the continuing pattern of volatility over the
subsequent decade.

The New Deal issues such as support for
government guarantees of jobs or governmental med-
ical care programmes remain the most strongly
related to party identification and vote choice in
congressional elections and most presidential
elections, indicating that the ideological and issue
structure underlying the party system remains
intact, although in weakened form. New issues such
as the rights of criminal. defendants, abortion,
women's rights and environmental concerns are more
weakly related to both party identification and vote
choice. However, the crucial question is: do
departures from party loyalty turn out to be
associated with these new and potentially disruptive
issues?

In general, the answer to this question appears
to be 'no'. This is not to suggest that in any
election there are no voters who defect to another
party's candidate because of some cross-cutting
issue. There are doubtless many such voters.
Opposition to the war was strongly related to a vote
for McGovern in 1972; Reagan's celebrated 'gender
gap' suggests the importance of women's issues for
some segment of the 1980 electorate. What does seem
clear, however, is that defections from party on the
basis of these issues were small compared with the
massive defections resulting from the negative
assessments of McGovern's personal qualities in 1972
and Carter's performance as president in 1980. The
failure of issues to be disruptive of party
loyalties is not to say that issues are unimportant
influences on vote choice. The increasingly large
number of independents are at times strongly
influenced by issues in voting but these same issues
do not contribute to electoral volatility in the
form of party defections.

We should add a caveat to this conclusion that

41

cross-cutting issues make rather minor contributions to electoral volatility. One much-discussed form of issue voting that might be assumed to contribute substantially to defections from party loyalty and split-ticket voting is so-called ´single issue´ voting, whereby individuals determine their vote choices solely on the basis of the candidates´ stands on one issue such as abortion. Such voters, to the extent that they exist, are difficult to detect through traditional survey analysis. Such votes are likely to be cast in election races other than the presidential race, races in which national survey analysts seldom inquire about the issue basis for the vote. Moreover, in presidential races, and in many races down the ticket also, the presence of single issue groups is more likely to be felt in organisational and financial support than in the number of pure single issue votes cast. Such groups may increase substantially the ability of candidates to run without party support and without conforming to their party´s stand on issues. They thus may contribute to the general deterioration of the parties´ ability to provide coherent platforms (never strong in the United States anyway) and to organise and discipline their elected office-holders for purposes of governing. If the parties seem not to be able to put their programmes into effect, the voter may opt for political independence or to vote for ´the man, not the party´. In this indirect way, such issue concerns may have a powerful impact on the continued electoral volatility of the American voter.

Governmental Performance and Electoral Volatility

Given the non-ideological character of the American parties, it is not surprising that the defections from party loyalty that form a substantial part of the current electoral volatility are virtually unrelated to ideology. No broad scale realignment based on a restructuring of political attitudes is discernible at the present time. The lack of connection between issues and vote choice is often taken as implied criticism of the American voter as non issue-oriented, ignorant and uninterested in public affairs. Such a portrait is probably exaggerated. While voters in the United States are quite likely to vote for candidates with whom they disagree on a range of issues, they are also quite capable of making judgements about the ability or inability of public officials to solve public problems.

Such judgements can take two forms. As Fiorina (1981) puts it, voters may retrospectively assess the performances of parties and candidates in carrying out their campaign promises, rather than calculating the benefits they might derive from promises of future benefits. To a considerable extent, this serves to explain the widespread defections from party in the presidential election of 1980. Democrats who voted for Reagan overwhelmingly disapproved of President Carter's handling of the economy and his handling of the hostage crisis in Iran. Far more than a 'Reagan revolution' in public attitudes (although it may have produced one in policy outputs), 1980 was a rejection of Carter. The election of 1968 can also be interpreted as a rejection of a Democratic administration which could not win (or would not get out of) the war in Vietnam, even though the sitting President had already bowed to public sentiment and did not seek re-election. Although the election returns in 1976 very closely followed party lines, if there was an issue that contributed to President Ford's defeat, it was the public judgement that he was wrong to pardon former President Nixon for Watergate-related offences.

Voters in the United States also make judgements on the leadership qualities of candidates. Twice in the past two decades - in 1964 and in 1972 - landslide victories coupled with massive defections from party loyalty were associated with the widespread view that the losing candidates, Goldwater and McGovern respectively, were unfit to serve as president.

It is important to note that this sort of evaluation of the performance of public officials is concentrated on the president. Presidents are the focus of media attention; they inevitably must contend with, and indeed often foster, the notion that they are 'in charge' and, consequently, they bear the brunt of criticism, fairly or unfairly, when things go wrong. Governors are in a similar situation in state government. In contrast, members of Congress seem to escape such scrutiny, for the most part. Fenno (1975) observes that voters everywhere condemn the Congress but love their Congressman, and attributes the former to recognition that Congress collectively is not solving, and probably is contributing to, national problems, and the latter to the positive evaluations of the constituency services members perform. Thus incumbent Congressmen are re-elected because they answer their mail and bring home pork-barrel projects while presidents are thrown out of office for being unable to control inflation, unemployment, foreign leaders or the Congress. The result is the volatility in presidential voting and considerable stability in congressional voting that has already been noted.

Voters in parliamentary systems do not have the dubious luxury enjoyed by Americans of being able simultaneously to reward the legislature with re-election while turning the executive out of office. The stability in congressional voting, combined with fluctuation in presidential voting, thus leads to a special kind of unpredictability in American politics - divided control of government wherein Congress can prevent the president from carrying out his desired policies or, less frequently, the president can stalemate Congress. (Indeed, the separation of powers and the organisational disarray of the American parties allows the same to happen when the presidency and Congress are controlled by the same party.) One might argue that these checks and balances in American government make it next to impossible for political leaders to come to grips with major policy problems before they reach crisis proportions. In this way, successive administrations may appear incompetent to govern and be rejected by the voters, leading to a rather long-term pattern of electoral volatility.

CONCLUSION: THE DEALIGNMENT OF THE AMERICAN PARTY SYSTEM

Most analysts would agree that the American party system has been in a period of dealignment for at least the last two decades. (See, for example, Burnham, 1970; Ladd and Hadley, 1977; Clubb, Flanigan and Zingale, 1980; Nie, Verba and Petrocik, 1976; Beck, 1977; Norpoth and Rusk, 1982.) Much of the evidence for dealignment is exactly the same as we have presented to demonstrate the increasing volatility of the American electorate: a rise in the proportion of independents in the electorate; a decline in the number of strong partisans; increases in split-ticket voting and in defections from partisanship; greater deviations from the normal vote; fluctuations from year to year in the partisan division of the vote; in short, all the indicators of a decline in the attachment of the voters to the existing political parties.

This consensus is fairly recent and does not extend to questions about the probable future of the party system. For several years after the onset of the symptoms of dealignment, the decay of partisanship was most often seen as evidence of imminent realignment. The massive reversal of the geographical location of support for Democratic and Republican presidential candidates in 1964 suggested to some a more regionally-based realignment to the advantage of the Democrats (Burnham, 1968; Pomper, 1968 ch.5). To others, Republican victories in 1968 and 1972 signalled a realignment in favour of the Republican Party (Phillips, 1969). And political pundits on election night 1980 were quick to announce a Reagan realignment-in-the-making.

When the period of disaggregation and electoral volatility continued longer than in previous realignment cycles, some analysts concluded that the lengthy dealignment had rendered the system incapable of realignment (Burnham, 1975). The involvement of the mass media and special interest groups in enabling candidates to run for office without party support was seen as a sign of the parties' organisational demise, making it doubtful that they could ever again command the loyalty of significant portions of the electorate (Ladd and Hadley, 1975). In this view, the New Deal party system will eventually be replaced, if it has not already been, by a 'no party' system, even though the Democratic and Republican labels might survive.

Elsewhere we have argued for a somewhat different view (Clubb, Flanigan and Zingale, 1980). The dealignment period, it seems to us, should be seen as creating the conditions for a realignment, not as an incipient realignment. The detachment from party ties that occurs during a dealignment and is manifested in the electoral volatility of such a period creates a pool of available voters and potential voters who might convert or adopt a partisan identification if one of the parties acted in such a way as to win their allegiance. We would argue that, because of this, the shape of the next realignment is not predictable from studying the electorate. As we have seen in preceding sections, no widespread change in the ideological structuring of political attitudes nor in the underlying social cleavages of the society has occurred. Even the behaviour of southern whites can best be described as a disengagement from Democratic loyalties rather than an adoption of Republican ones, perhaps because the national Republican Party, as distinct from some of its candidates and elected officials, has not publicly endorsed a turning back of the clock on civil rights. The only exception to this conclusion of the lack of basic change in the electorate is in the behaviour of blacks, who rather clearly realigned in favour of the Democratic Party in the 1960s. And there is no doubt that they did so because of the relatively aggressive pro-civil rights and anti-poverty positions of the Johnson administration and of other important Democratic leaders.

The electorate reacts, it rarely anticipates. If the parties do not keep their policy promises, voters choose candidates on the basis of their personal characteristics rather than their party label. If the parties fail to provide coherent positions on issues of current importance, young voters remain independent rather than adopting a party identification of no relevance to their concerns. For the last two decades, the electorate has been responding to repeated failures to govern well by throwing the incumbent administration out of office and electing the opposition party. The missing ingredient in the current dealignment is an administration that can successfully handle, or at least be perceived as successfully handling, the major policy problems confronting the nation. Should an administration be able to do that, we see nothing in the behaviour of the electorate that would preclude a significant portion of those currently disengaged from the political parties - the independents and ticket-splitting, defecting partisans - from adopting the partisanship of the administration´s party. In this light, the ´failure´ of the electorate to realign over the past twenty years might better be viewed as a series of botched opportunities on the part of successive administrations.

And what of the future? If we continue this line of reasoning, it is clear that the Reagan administration has an opportunity to capture the loyalty of the large pool of available voters and potential voters who could fuel a significant realignment of the party system. While the Reagan victory in 1980 ought properly to be viewed as a judgement on Jimmy Carter rather than an endorsement of Reagan´s political or economic philosophy, Reagan seized the opportunity presented by his landslide victory to present and force adoption of a

comprehensive restructuring of economic and social
policies. If these policies, perhaps aided by a
fortuitous economic boom, appear successful, we can
easily imagine a long-term gain in Republican party
identifiers. But should the bottom drop out of the
economic recovery or should American troops become
mired in Central America as they did in Vietnam, we
would expect a continuation of the current
dealignment, even if Reagan´s personal charm along
with Democratic ineptitude might win him another
term of office.

FOOTNOTES

1. These and all other data in this chapter
were provided through the Inter-university
Consortium for Political and Social Research. The
survey data were collected by the Survey Research
Center and the Center for Political Studies at the
University of Michigan.
2. Voting patterns for the U.S. Senate are more
difficult to analyse in these terms because the same
set of seats are not up for election every two
years. Thus change in the vote results from year to
year do not necessarily represent changes in voter
sympathies but more probably reflect differences in
the constituencies being contested.
3. Since the data in Table 2.2 are national
results, they might conceal highly volatile but
compensating behaviour by individual states.
Therefore, it would be prudent to look also at the
average value of the index calculated for states.
An examination of these patterns (in data not shown
here) reveals about the same level of volatility in
the state averages as found in the nation as a
whole. Thus we can safely assume that the
system-wide data are not masking more volatile
patterns at the state level.

REFERENCES

Beck, P.A.(1974) ´A Socialization Theory of Partisan
    Realignment´ in R. Niemi et al., The Politics
    of Future Citizens, Jessey-Bass, San Francisco,
    pp.199-219
--------- (1977) ´Partisan Dealignment in the
    Postwar South´, American Political Science
    Review, 71, 477-96

Burnham, W.D. (1968) 'American Voting Behavior and the 1964 Election', Midwest Journal of Political Science, 12, 1-40
---------- (1970) Critical Elections and the Mainsprings of American Politics, W.W. Norton and Co., New York
---------- (1975) 'American Politics in the 1970s: Beyond Party?' in W.N. Chambers and W.D. Burnham (eds.), The American Party Systems, Oxford University Press, New York, pp.308-57
Butler, D. and D. Stokes (1969) Political Change in Britain, St. Martin's Press, New York
Campbell, A. (1960) 'Surge and Decline: A Study in Electoral Change', Public Opinion Quarterly, 24, 397-418
Campbell, A., P.E. Converse, W.E. Miller and D.E. Stokes (1960) The American Voter, John Wiley & Sons, New York
Campbell, B.A. (1977) 'Patterns of Change in the Partisan Loyalties of Native Southerners: 1952-1972' Journal of Politics, 39, 730-61
Clubb, J.M., W.H.Flanigan and N.H. Zingale (1980) Partisan Realignment: Voters, Parties and Government in American History, Sage Publications, Beverly Hills, California
Converse, P.E.(1966a) 'The Concept of a Normal Vote in A. Campbell et al.(eds.), Elections and the Political Order, John Wiley & Sons, New York, pp.9-39
---------- (1966b) 'On the Possibility of Major Political Realignment in the South' in A. Campbell et al.(eds.), Elections and the Political Order, John Wiley & Sons, New York, pp.212-42
---------- (1969) 'Of Time and Partisan Stability', Comparative Political Studies, 2, 139-171
Fenno, R. (1975) 'If, as Ralph Nader Says, Congress is "the Broken Branch", How Come We Love Our Congressmen So Much?' in N.J. Ornstein (ed.), Congress in Change, Praeger Publishers, New York
Fiorina, M. (1981) Retrospective Voting in American National Elections, Yale University Press, New Haven, Conn.
Inglehart, R. (1977) The Silent Revolution, Princeton University Press, Princeton, N.J.
Ladd, E. and C.D. Hadley (1975) Transformations of the American System, W.W. Norton & Co.,New York
Nie, N.H., S. Verba and J.R. Petrocik (1976) The Changing American Voter, Harvard Unversity Press, Cambridge, Massachusetts

Norpoth, H. and J. Rusk (1982) 'Partisan Dealignment
    in the American Electorate: Itemizing the
    Deductions since 1964', American Political
    Science Review, 76, 522-37
Phillips, K.H. (1969) The Emerging Republican
    Majority, Arlington House, New York
Pomper, G. (1968) Elections in America, Dodd, Mead,
    New York
---------- (1975) Voters' Choice, Dodd, Mead, New
    York
Stimson, J. and E. Carmines (1982) 'Racial Issues
    and the Structure of Mass Belief Systems',
    Journal of Politics, 44, 2-20

Chapter 3

CANADA

Lawrence LeDuc

INTRODUCTION
    The Canadian party system, at least at the
federal level, presents an outward appearance of
dominance by a single party and of substantial
stability over time. As the largest party in a
three or four party system, the Liberal party
commands a wide lead over its nearest rival, the
Progressive-Conservatives, and the main 'third'
party in the system, the New Democratic Party (NDP).
Other minor parties such as the Social Credit party
have emerged from time to time to play a minor (and
sometimes disruptive) role in Canadian federal
politics, but they have rarely threatened the
position of the governing Liberals. Since 1921, the
Liberal party has lost only five federal elections
and has spent a mere twelve of the past sixty years
in opposition, the longest such period being the six
year span of Conservative government under John
Diefenbaker from 1957 to 1963. The most recent
(1980) federal election would seem to confirm these
long-standing historical patterns, with the Liberal
party under Pierre Trudeau being returned to power
decisively only nine months after a defeat at the
hands of Joe Clark's Conservatives in the 1979
election.
    The strong position of the Liberal party in the
Canadian federal party system is not due to any
ability to overwhelm their opponents at the polls.
Only rarely does the Liberal share of the vote in a
federal election approach the 50 per cent mark and
the party has frequently found itself presiding over
a government commanding only a minority of the seats
in Parliament (the 1963, 1965 and 1972 elections are
recent examples). Historically, the Liberals have
been able to combine solid support in Quebec with
pockets of strength in urban Ontario and in the
Atlantic provinces. The party has generally done

50

well among French speaking Canadians, Roman
Catholics and younger voters. The Conservatives, at
least since the time of Diefenbaker, have been
particularly strong in Western Canada and have also
traditionally won support in the rural areas and
small towns of Ontario and the Atlantic provinces.
The Conservatives' lack of electoral strength in
Quebec has been one of the party's most serious and
persistent weaknesses. The left-wing NDP has
emphasised its ties with organised labour in
national campaigns in recent years, and indeed does
well in certain urban constituencies in industrial
Ontario. But, reorganised from the remnants of a
farm-labour party in 1961, it continues to win most
of its seats in historic areas of socialist strength
in the West and has been vulnerable to sharp,
short-term fluctuations in its parliamentary
representation. These general tendencies in sources
of party support should not be overstated. Social
and structural variables are generally poor
predictors of individual voting behaviour in Canada,
and traditional factors such as occupation and
social class are particularly weak.(1)
    The Liberals' persistent electoral strength is
reflected in the patterns of party identification
(Figure 3.1). Forty-five per cent of all Canadians
in the most recent national election study
identified with the Liberal party, compared with 28
per cent who considered themselves Progressive -
Conservatives. Thirteen per cent of the 1980
national sample were New Democrats, but a mere one
per cent identified with the rapidly declining
Social Credit Party. It is thus accurate to
characterise Canada at the present time as basically
a three party system in which the Liberal party
holds a strong advantage. With the exception of the
decline of Social Credit from a level of about five
per cent, the figures shown in Figure 3.1 are not
significantly different from the levels of party
strength which have been found since regular
national surveys began in Canada in 1965. Most
Canadians who identify with a party tend to report
an identification that is at least 'fairly strong'.
Only about one in five are 'weak' identifiers and
about ten per cent of the Canadian electorate
considers itself independent of party ties. These
proportions of weak identifiers or non-identifiers
have likewise not shown any increase in recent years
over previously established levels, a pattern which
runs counter to the dealignment trends found in some
other countries.

Figure 3.1: Direction and Intensity of Party Identification in Canada, 1980 National Sample

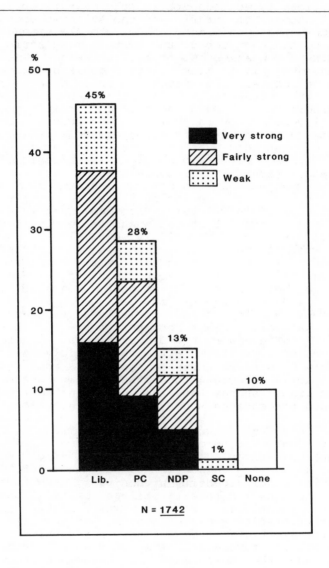

Table 3.1: Distribution of Popular Vote in Federal
        Elections, Canada 1945-80

	1945	1949	1953	1957	1958	1962	1963	1965
	%	%	%	%	%	%	%	%
Liberal	41	49	49	41	34	37	41	40
Prog.-Con.	27	30	31	39	54	37	33	32
NDP/CCF	16	13	11	11	9	14	14	18
Social Credit	4	4	5	7	2	12	12	8
Other	12	4	4	2	1	x	x	2
% Turnout	76	74	67	74	79	79	79	75
Pedersen Index		10.9	2.8	9.2	14.7	16.7	4.8	5.5

Table 3.1 (cont.)

	1968	1972	1974	1979	1980	Mean	S.D.
	%	%	%	%	%		
Liberal	46	39	43	40	44	42	4.4
Prog.-Con.	31	35	35	36	33	34	4.4
NDP/CCF	17	18	15	18	20	15	3.3
Social Credit	4	8	5	5	2	6	3.3
Other	2	1	1	1	1	2	3.2
% Turnout	76	77	71	76	69	75	3.5
Pedersen Index	5.4	7.1	5.2	3.6	6.4		

Notes: x = less than one per cent. S.D.= standard
deviation. Pedersen index scores are calculated
from exact shares of the vote and not from the
rounded percentages shown in the Table.

TRENDS IN ELECTORAL VOLATILITY

        The seemingly dominant position of the Liberal
party in Canadian federal politics is due not to
party   identification   alone but rather to the
relative stability of the system. In the last seven
federal elections, the Liberal percentage of the
vote has fluctuated across a range of only seven per
cent and the percentage of the main opposition
Progressive - Conservatives has varied within an
even narrower five per cent range. Also, as is seen
in Table 3.1, the Pedersen index shows only a modest

amount of electoral volatility in Canada since 1963.
A good deal of volatility is accounted for by the
minor parties, both in earlier periods and in recent
years, and the Conservative landslide under John
Diefenbaker in 1958, which accounts for the higher
values of the index in 1958 and 1962, has not since
been repeated. By measures of aggregate volatility,
Canada would tend to rank among the world´s most
electorally stable countries.

Two explanations might be advanced to account
for this apparent stability of the Canadian federal
party system. The first of these might be that
Canadians hold strong and enduring party ties,
firmly anchored in key reference groups which change
only slowly over time and which are major
determinants of voting behaviour i.e. a system of
strong and enduring partisan alignment. While few
Canadian scholars have actually held this view of
the party system, much has been written about the
persistence of regional, religious, ethnic and
linguistic factors in Canadian politics.
Nevertheless, a view of the Canadian party system as
one of stable and enduring alignment based on strong
and stable party identification at the individual
level is difficult to sustain in the light of
established empirical evidence (see Clarke et
al.,1979, chs.5,10). Not the least of the factors
which undermine this hypothesis is the much greater
level of electoral volatility which is found when
the unit of reference is the province or single
constituency rather than the nation as a whole. In
1979, for example, the decline in the Liberal share
of the vote was ten percentage points in British
Columbia compared with three percentage points for
the nation as a whole, and the NDP in the same
election increased its vote in Newfoundland by a
phenomenal 22 points. Such variation is even more
commonplace at constituency level.

A more compelling explanation of the aggregate
stability of the Canadian political system may be
developed from a closer examination of partisanship
at the individual level. Aggregate stability does
not necessarily imply individual stability. In
Canada, the weak, unstable and inconsistent ties to
political parties which are held by many voters
create an electorate in which the potential for
large electoral swings is actually very high (Clarke
et al., 1979, pp.365-80). The predominant electoral
pattern, however, is one of relative stability
because short-term forces can only rarely be
combined across the country in such a way as to

uniformly favour any single party. There have on occasion been circumstances when the impact of short-term forces in the system has been fully demonstrated, as in the elections of 1958 or 1979. But the normal pattern might be termed one of ´stable dealignment´, in which the potential for change is high but the actual aggregate fluctuations from one federal election to another is surprisingly low.(2)

This view of the Canadian political system as one which is substantially dealigned but nevertheless relatively stable is consistent not only with much of the survey-based evidence which has been collected in recent years but also with the pattern of the 1979 and 1980 election outcomes (Table 3.2). In the Conservative victory of 1979, a net gain of only one per cent in the Conservative vote produced an increase of 41 parliamentary seats, many of which were subsequently lost in the 1980 contest. The Conservative vote in 1979 increased in only six of the ten provinces, and the Liberals actually improved both their vote and their parliamentary representation in the province of Quebec even while losing the election. These differing provincial and regional trends illustrate not only the fact that individual level change is invariably greater than aggregate change in most elections, but also that the major short-term forces that produce electoral change in Canada rarely operate in a single direction across the entire country.

To a considerable extent, the influence of short-term forces on the fortunes of the three main political parties in Canada and the resulting high level of electoral volatility is shown in the fluctuation of the Gallup Poll over the 1974-1980 period (Figure 3.2). Following their majority victory in the 1974 election, the Liberals maintained a substantial lead in all polls until late in 1975 when their advantage began to slip, at first slowly and then much more rapidly following a change in the Conservative leadership. The Progressive - Conservatives held a comfortable lead in the poll until the victory of the separatist Parti Quebecois in the Quebec provincial election of 1976. After this the attention of the country turned sharply towards the ´national unity´ issue. Mr. Trudeau and the Liberals regained a wide lead in the polls, which held until mid-1978 when Liberal fortunes began to decline once again. Shaken by a poll in April 1978 which showed them level with the

Table 3.2: Election Results by Province, 1980, 1979
       and 1974

		LIBERAL			PROG.-CON.		
		1980	1979	1974	1980	1979	1974
Newfoundland	Vote (%)	47	38	47	36	31	44
	Seats	5	4	4	2	2	3
Prince Edward	Vote (%)	47	40	46	46	53	49
Island	Seats	2	0	1	2	4	3
Nova Scotia	Vote (%)	40	36	41	39	45	47
	Seats	5	2	2	6	8	8
New Brunswick	Vote (%)	50	45	47	33	40	33
	Seats	7	6	6	3	4	3
Quebec (a)	Vote (%)	68	62	54	13	13	21
	Seats	73	67	60	1	2	3
Ontario	Vote (%)	42	37	45	36	42	35
	Seats	52	32	55	38	57	25
Manitoba	Vote (%)	28	24	27	38	44	48
	Seats	2	2	2	5	7	9
Saskatchewan	Vote (%)	24	20	31	39	42	36
	Seats	0	0	3	7	10	8
Alberta	Vote (%)	21	21	25	66	67	61
	Seats	0	0	0	21	21	19
British Columbia	Vote (%)	22	23	33	41	45	42
	Seats	0	1	8	16	20	12
Yukon/N.W.T.	Vote (%)	37	33	28	32	37	39
	Seats	0	0	0	2	2	1
CANADA	Vote (%)	44	40	43	33	36	35
	Seats	146	114	141	103	136	95

Note: (a) excludes Frontenac by-election in 1980.

Conservatives, the governing Liberals cancelled
plans for a Spring election and instead began to
plan for a possible Fall contest. By Fall, however,
the Government's political position had worsened
even further and they opted instead to hold by-

Table 3.2 (cont.)

		NDP			ALL OTHER		
		1980	1979	1974	1980	1979	1974
Newfoundland	Vote (%)	17	31	9	x	x	x
	Seats	0	1	0	0	0	0
Prince Edward Island	Vote (%)	7	7	5	x	x	x
	Seats	0	0	0	0	0	0
Nova Scotia	Vote (%)	21	19	11	x	x	x
	Seats	0	1	1	0	0	0
New Brunswick	Vote (%)	16	15	9	1	x	11
	Seats	0	0	0	0	0	1
Quebec (a)	Vote (%)	9	5	7	10	20	18
	Seats	0	0	0	0	6	11
Ontario	Vote (%)	22	21	19	x	1	1
	Seats	5	6	8	0	0	0
Manitoba	Vote (%)	34	33	24	x	x	1
	Seats	7	5	2	0	0	0
Saskatchewan	Vote (%)	36	37	32	1	1	1
	Seats	7	4	2	0	0	0
Alberta	Vote (%)	10	10	9	3	3	5
	Seats	0	0	0	0	0	0
British Columbia	Vote (%)	35	32	23	2	1	2
	Seats	12	8	2	0	0	0
Yukon/N.W.T.	Vote (%)	31	29	33	x	1	x
	Seats	1	1	1	0	0	0
CANADA	Vote (%)	20	18	15	3	6	6
	Seats	32	26	16	0	6	12

elections for 16 vacant parliamentary seats, twelve
of which were won by the Tories. This debacle
effectively ended any prospect of an election before
the expiry of the Liberals´ mandate in mid-1979 and
the Government simply hung on until the election
called in May 1979. Through the winter, the two
major parties ran nearly even in most polls and

Figure 3.2: Fluctuations in Party Support 1974-80 (Gallup)

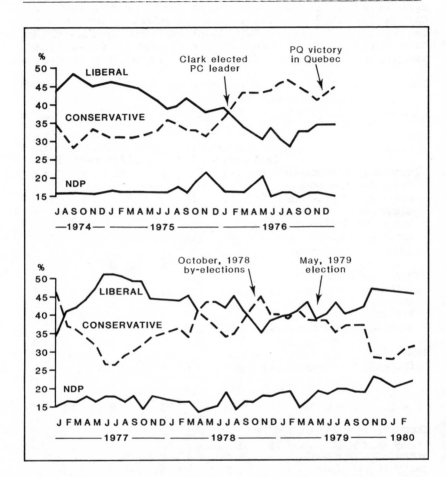

the Conservatives did not begin their sharp decline in popularity until after their assumption of power and the first meeting of Parliament in October 1979.

Although it might be expected that levels of vote switching would be higher in elections such as 1979 or 1980 which saw changes of government than in those which did not (such as 1974), data from national surveys conducted after each of these three elections suggest that this is not necessarily the case.(3) The percentage of voters switching between the 1974 and 1979 elections was only five per cent

higher than was found between 1972 and 1974 (Table
3.3), and the percentage switching in 1980 was
actually slightly lower than in 1974. It is thus
apparent that levels of individual volatility in
Canada in 1979 did not exceed boundaries that might
be considered ´normal´ in Canadian electoral politics even though the outcome of the 1979 election
was sharply deviant. What differs primarily among

Table 3.3: Individual Level Changes in Three Federal
Elections, 1974-80

	As % of total electorate (a)			As % of voters in two elections only		
	1974	1979	1980	1974	1979	1980
´Permanent´ Electorate	%	%	%	%	%	%
Voted for the same party as in previous election	60	55	68	78	73	79
Voted for different parties (1972-74, 1974-79 or 1979-80)	17	20	18	22	27	21
Transient Voters						
Previous non-voters re-entering electorate	5	7	5			
Previous voters leaving electorate	13	6	9			
New Voters						
Entering electorate	5	12	x			
(N)	(2060)	(2276)	(1576)	(1586)	(1691)	(1353)

Summary: 1974-79-80(b)

	%		
Voted for the same party in all three elections	44	Voted for a different party in at least one election	32
Did not vote in one or more election	21	New voters	13

Notes: (a) Excluding non-voters in both waves of all
election pairs and new voters not voting.
(b) 1979-80 panel (N=1525). Excludes non-voters in
all three elections and new voters not voting in at
least one election. Percentages do not total 100
because categories are not mutually exclusive.
x = less than 1% (not sampled in 1980).

these three elections is the concentration of switching in 1979 toward the Conservatives, rather than the mixed pattern of 1974 which produced no clear advantage for one party, or the aggregation of small effects in 1980 which favoured the Liberals (see Clarke et al., 1979, chs.11,12; LeDuc, 1983a; Clarke et al., 1984, chs.7,8).

Taking the three elections together, it can be seen that 32 percent of the sample voted for a different party in at least one election, while 44 per cent supported the same party in all three contests. This represents a level of individual volatility slightly greater than is found in a comparable calculation for Britain or the United States over a similar period of time for which panel data are available.(4) Thus, in spite of its seemingly more stable aggregate electoral patterns, Canada exhibits levels of volatility at the individual level as high or higher than those found in countries where patterns of volatility in elections are more readily apparent.

EXPLANATIONS

Social and demographic factors

The explanation for this relatively high level of individual volatility is rooted in part in the weakness of long-term forces as determinants of the vote in Canada. Although some of the regional patterns which are often clearly evident in Canadian elections are to some degree associated with the major ethnic and linguistic divisions of the country, such factors are generally rather poor predictors of individual voting choice. In an AID analysis by Rose (1974, pp.13-20) only 15 per cent of the variance in voting behaviour in the 1965 federal election could be explained by 'social structure' variables such as occupation, religion, or region, placing Canada eleventh among 15 countries studied. A multiple regression analysis of 1980 survey data using a larger number of variables yields generally similar results (Table 3.4). No more than 16 per cent of the variance in the vote for any of the three parties can be explained by the seven variables included in this analysis (region, religion, social class, language/ethnicity, age, sex, and community size).(5) While the patterns displayed are the familiar ones in which region, religion and language/ethnicity are the strongest correlates, it is clear that in Canada socioeconomic or social cleavage models of voting behaviour remain unsatisfactory in their ability to explain either individual voting choice or the outcomes of particular elections.

Table 3.4: Multiple Regression Analysis of Canadian Voting Behaviour, 1980 Federal Election

	DEPENDENT VARIABLE					
	Liberal Vote		P.C. Vote		NDP Vote	
	r	BETA	r	BETA	r	BETA
REGION						
Atlantic provinces	.01	-.04	.00	.05	-.04	.03
Ontario	-.02	-.12*	.07	.12*	.06	.12*
Western provinces	-.24*	-.26*	.21*	.22*	.09*	.14*
RELIGION						
Catholic	.27*	.17*	-.32*	-.21*	-.06*	.00
Other Non-Prot	-.05	.02	.05	-.04	-.03	-.05
None	-.07*	.00	-.02	-.09*	.05	.00
SOCIAL CLASS						
Subjective:						
working class	.01	.02	-.08*	-.07*	.08*	.08*
Objective						
Blishen SES	-.03	.00	.11*	.07*	.02	.01
Union member	.00	-.01	-.12*	-.08*	.12*	.11*
LANGUAGE/ETHNICITY						
French	.24*	.01	-.28*	-.01	-.11	-.03
Non-French						
Non-English	-.01	.03	.00	.03	.06*	.04
AGE (years)	-.03	.00	.11*	.06	-.06*	-.05*
SEX (F)	.06*	.05*	-.08*	-.08*	.00	.00
COMMUNITY SIZE	.02	.01	-.06*	-.06*	.08*	.08*
R^2 =	.11		.16		.06	

Note: * = significant at .01.

Partisanship

Although the Liberal party retains a significant advantage over its competitors in the number of Canadians who identify with it, this has not, as noted earlier, led to inevitable Liberal successes at the polls. The fact that fewer than one third of Canadians consider themselves "very strong" party identifiers (Table 3.5) and the tendency of party identification in Canada to travel with vote and to be relatively unstable over time (Clarke, et al., 1979; LeDuc, 1981) invite some caution in assumptions that might be made on the basis of party identification alone. However, only a small proportion of the Canadian electorate consider themselves true 'independents' or non-partisans, and, unlike the case of the United States, this proportion has not been increasing in recent years.

Partisanship in Canada is further complicated by the existence of provincial partisan ties which are as strong as those at the federal level for many individuals and which, in the case of provinces such as British Columbia or Quebec, are keyed to distinctive provincial party systems. Even in provinces where similar party systems exist however, such as Ontario or Nova Scotia, identification with provincial parties is distinctive, and may act to weaken or destabilise the tie to a federal party. This is a phenomenon which we have referred to as 'split identification', and it appears to be of much greater importance in understanding the nature of partisanship in Canada than is the case in other federal systems such as the United States or Australia (Jenson, et al., 1975; Clarke, et al., 1979).

The effect which party identification in Canada exerts on voting behaviour depends on three specific characteristics of partisanship - intensity, stability, and consistency across levels - each of which contributes independently toward the likelihood of changes in voting choice from one election to the next (Clarke, et al., 1979, pp.151-61). Employing an index which takes into account all three of these attributes, it may be seen (Table 3.5) that slightly more than a third of the Canadian electorate holds a party identification that is at least 'fairly strong', has been stable over time, and is consistent at least with respect to direction of identification across the two levels of the political system. About the same proportion varies on one of these attributes from a model of strong, stable, consistent partisanship and the balance varies on more than one. These percentages are not significantly different across the three surveys but they illustrate the relative unreliability of long term partisan ties as predictors of voting choice for much of the Canadian electorate.

The panel data available for the period 1974-1980 confirm the characteristics of partisanship in Canada persistently shown in the cross section surveys , particularly with respect to its relative instability over time. Thirty-one per cent of the 1974-79 panel were found to have changed party identification, while 22 per cent did so over the much shorter 1979-80 period (Table 3.5). Over the entire six year period, 39 per cent of the panel changed their identification with a federal party at least once. These relatively high levels of partisan instability constitute further evidence of the weakness of long-term forces in Canadian electoral politics and the corresponding importance of various short-term factors in explaining patterns of electoral change.

Table 3.5: Characteristics of Party Identification in Canada - 1974, 1979 and 1980

	1974 %	1979 %	1980 %
Intensity			
Very strong	28	27	31
Fairly strong	40	43	42
Weak	20	19	17
Ind./No identification	12	11	10
Stability			
% recall ´ever´ having identified with another party	36	32	37
% of panel reporting identification different from previous wave	--	31	22
Consistency			
% with fully consistent federal & provincial identification	48	46	46
% with different federal & provincial intensity only	22	21	20
% with different federal & provincial identification	30	33	34
Summary			
Number of deviations from strong*,stable,consistent partisanship			
0	37	38	36
1	35	35	37
2	21	22	21
3	7	5	6
(N)	(2343)	(2514)	(1747)

Notes: * From at least ´fairly strong´ partisanship. Variations on consistency are tabulated for direction only.

Issues and Ideology

Evidence regarding the weakness of long-term forces in Canadian elections is also found in political party images, as measured by open-ended questions in the three national surveys.(6) As Table 3.6 shows, the largest component of images which Canadians held of the federal political parties in 1979 was made up of issue and policy related items (51 per cent), closely followed by those dealing with 'performance' or 'style' (50 per cent). Similar patterns are shown in the data collected in 1974 and 1980. In general, the categories of images which recur with the greatest frequency are those which change most readily over relatively short periods of time in response to changes in party programmes or leadership. Ideological or group-related images, an important psychological source of the stability of party systems in many countries, are distinctly weaker elements in the structure of political party images in Canada.

Table 3.6: Content of Federal Party Images, 1974, 1979 and 1980 National Samples

	1974 %		1979 %		1980 %	
Policy/Issue	61	(1.3)	51	(1.1)	60	(1.2)
Style/Performance	47	(0.8)	50	(1.0)	60	(1.2)
Leadership/Leader	38	(0.7)	37	(0.6)	51	(1.0)
General/Party	35	(0.5)	42	(0.6)	40	(0.6)
Area/Group	28	(0.4)	27	(0.4)	31	(0.5)
Ideology	14	(0.2)	15	(0.2)	18	(0.2)
(N)	(2445)		(2670)		(928)	

Notes: The figures show the percentage of the sample associating a party with the image dimensions listed. Percentages do not total 100 because of multiple responses. Mean numbers of images are shown in parenthesis. The figures for 1980 are based on a random half sample of all respondents.

Issues in Canada tend to fluctuate sharply from one election to another. Across the three elections considered here, there were substantial variations in the degree of importance ascribed by voters to economic issues such as 'national unity' or the threat of Quebec independence.(7) More specific issues appear and disappear abruptly in each of the last three elections as illustrated by the campaign emphasis placed on the issue of wage and price controls in 1974, the tax treatment of mortgage interest in 1979 or an 18 cent tax which had been placed on petrol in 1980. This is in keeping with the nature of political parties´ images mentioned above, in that voters´ perceptions of the parties are greatly affected by the particular issues and policies of the day, which themselves tend to exhibit considerable volatility from one election to another.

Electoral Replacement and Generational Change

The physical replacement of one group of voters by another, either over time or in a single election, does not provide a powerful explanation of the volatility of the Canadian electorate, although it has contributed substantially to the composition of that electorate. Approximately 2.3 million new voters came of voting age between the 1974 and 1979 elections, comprising 15 per cent of the total eligible electorate in 1979. Additionally, about one voter in five did not vote in at least one of the three elections covered by the panel (Table 3.3). Since most non-voters in Canada return to the active electorate in a subsequent election, these are best thought of as ´transient´ voters who periodically move into and out of the electorate, rather than merely as non-participants in the electoral process (Clarke, et al., 1979, ch.10). In the 1979 election, approximately equal numbers of transient voters are found entering and leaving the active electorate, while in 1980 nearly twice as many voters left the electorate as returned to it (Table 3.3). Clearly, either type of replacement has the potential to effect electoral change. The infusion of a large contingent of new voters will do so if these differ in any substantial way from those already in the electorate. Changes in turnout may also account for variations in election outcomes if the voters leaving the electorate and/or those entering it, differ in their behaviour from established patterns.

New voters account at least partly for the Liberal margin of victory in the 1974 election as this group has voted more heavily Liberal than any other cohort (Clarke, et. al., 1979, pp. 380-93). However, there is little evidence that the youngest cohort of voters has the potential to effect permanent changes in the behaviour of the Canadian electorate. Indeed, the partisan leanings of this cohort are as weak and unstable as are those of the electorate more generally (LeDuc, 1983b). Thus, while tending toward the Liberals in recent elections, the youngest cohort of voters cannot be counted on to provide similar support for this party in future elections. Patterns of generational replacement are more suggestive of a continuation of the pattern of ´stable dealignment´ in Canadian elections than of either a hardening or softening of partisan attitudes.

A similar argument may be made regarding the entry and exit of transient voters. These contribute to electoral volatility in Canada in that their movement from one election to another represents an important source of potential electoral instability. But it represents a kind of ´permanent´ instability, in that such movements occur in much the same way in every election. Thus, although the decline in turnout hurt the Conservatives slightly in the 1980 election, there is no long-term trend toward lower turnout in Canada (Table 3.1). We would therefore expect that the movement of a small complement of transient voters into and out of the electorate will always account for a certain proportion of the volatility in a given election, but it does not represent, at least at present, a source of increasing volatility.

Over the 1974-80 panel (Table 3.3) it may be seen that electoral replacement and electoral conversion have been approximately equal sources of aggregate volatility in Canada, each representing approximately one-third of the total electorate (32 per cent switching parties at least once and 34 per cent being either transient or new voters). Somewhat less than half (44 per cent) of the Canadian electorate of 1979-80 consisted of people who were in the active electorate in 1974 and who on both occasions supported the same party as they had in that election. Given that this six-year interval represents a period only slightly greater than that between a normal pair of elections, this might be seen as an impressive level of total change to have taken place over a relatively short time. However, none of the phenomena which comprise this change are in any sense atypical of either the demographic trends or the pattern of individual behaviour which have characterised the Canadian electorate in recent years. Given the persistence of these patterns, it is reasonable to expect that a 1984 or 1985 election will see a comparable aggregate level of change and a similar balance of conversion and replacement forces accounting for that change. Only as declining birth rates may begin to slowly affect the composition of the electorate will the effects of generational replacement slowly begin to decrease, but it is more likely that the effects of transient voting and of switching as established behaviour patterns of Canadian voters will continue indefinitely into the future.

Electoral Volatility and Partisan Change

The relatively high levels of individual electoral volatility in Canada do not in themselves imply equally high levels of instability in party identification. We have already established, however, that a majority of Canadians are ´flexible´ partisans - having either weak party ties, differing federal and provincial partisan identities or a tendency to have changed party identification in the past (Table 3.5). There is every reason, then, to expect that party identification in such a system will exhibit a greater tendency toward instability than would be the case in a system where more powerful long-term factors supported a pattern of stronger and more enduring partisan loyalties.

Across the three-wave panel, 41 per cent are found to have changed their party identification, either by switching from one party to another or by moving to or from a position of non-identification, while an equal proportion are stable on both party identification and vote. This represents a higher total level of partisanship than is found in either the United States or Britain, but not quite so high as in certain countries such as the Netherlands in which party identification has been found to be highly unstable (see LeDuc, 1981, 1983; Thomassen, 1976). As is seen in Table 3.7, most of those changing party identification over the 1974-80 period exhibit a tendency for party identification to travel with vote. Only eleven per cent of the total sample consists of persons who have changed their vote one or more times across the last three elections without any disruption of party identification.

This is not to argue, however, that party identification in Canada is eroding or weakening over time. There is no net increase between 1974 and 1980 in the proportion of Canadians reporting weak or inconsistent partisanship or abandoning a party identification altogether. Rather a party

Table 3.7: Party Identification and Voting Behaviour
in Three Elections, 1974-79-80

	Maintained same identification in all three waves	Changed party identification at least once	Moved to or from non-identification
	%	%	%
Voted for same party in three elections	41	3	7
Switched at least once	11	16	9
Did not vote at least once	13	6	6
Total	59	23	22

Notes: N = 791. Percentages are of all respondents,
that is 1974-79-80 panel respondents only, excluding
three -time non-voters. Rows and columns do not
total and do not total 100 because not all
categories are mutually exclusive. The third column
includes 2% of the sample who reported
non-identification in all three waves.

identification which is weak, unstable or
inconsistent for a large number of voters has
essentially remained so throughout this period.
Although the net shift of both voting choice and
changes in party identification operated heavily in
favour of the Conservatives in 1979, the Tories were
able to retain very little of this new-found support
subsequently. Were it otherwise, the outcome of the
1980 election, occurring only nine months after the
Conservative victory of May 1979, would almost
certainly have been different.
　　　　Neither do the data support the contention
that the 1979 Conservative upset was a simple
deviation from an otherwise firmly Liberal long-term
pattern. While it is true that party identification
in Canada continues to favour the Liberals, among
younger as well as older age cohorts, party
identification is not in itself a powerful enough
force to ensure continued Liberal victories at the
polls.(8) Too many voters are weak identifiers or
move too easily to temporary independence or to an
alternative identification. Party identification in
Canada is heavily affected by many of the same
short-term forces that account for electoral

volatility. And, as we have argued elsewhere (Clarke et al., 1979, 1984), these are more powerful factors than are many of the longer-term forces that might support a pattern of more stable and enduring partisan alignment. This is due in large part to the weakness of many of the persistent social and demographic cleavages, coupled with the existence of quite independent provincial party ties which compete for the allegiance of voters.

ELECTORAL VOLATILITY AND THE PARTY SYSTEM

There is little evidence at present of genuine dealigning or realigning trends in Canada. Realignment would imply the replacement of one stable, long-term pattern of alignment by another. But, as has been argued here, long-term forces (at least at the individual level) are relatively weak in Canada and there is no evidence to date that a new, stronger set of such forces is emerging. Indeed, Canadians continue to define much of their political world in terms of highly changeable, short-term forces such as policy or issue factors, style and performance, or leadership. A realignment would require a strengthening of at least some of the longer-term forces which affect voting in Canada as well as a strengthening of individual party ties. Neither of these appears probable at the federal level in the near future.

Neither is the pattern of dealignment which exists in Canada part of an ongoing, dynamic process which could lead to the abandonment or further weakening of party ties. The proportion of flexible partisans remains more or less constant over time but nevertheless accounts for nearly two-thirds of the total electorate. The interpretation of Canadian politics that best fits the data reported here is that of a political system which is already substantially dealigned but nevertheless undergoing relatively little fundamental change. This condition of dealignment is stable in the sense that it is not being significantly altered by electoral trends such as the Conservative victory of 1979 or by patterns of long-term replacement in the electorate. The short-term effects evident in virtually every Canadian election leave little lasting imprint on the partisan make-up of the electorate. Neither has generational change contributed to any longer-term process of dealignment or realignment because the younger cohorts entering the electorate share many of the partisan attributes of older voters. Parental transmission of partisanship has long been observed to be relatively weak in Canada (Clarke et al.,1979, pp.365-72; Irvine, 1974; Jenson, 1975). Thus, although more than 40 per cent of all those currently eligible to vote in Canada have attained voting age since the accession of Mr. Trudeau as Prime Minister in 1968, there is no evidence of fundamental change which might be attributable to patterns of socialisation of new voters or to the replacement of one generation by another.

The interpretation of volatility in the Canadian political process presented here rests heavily on a demonstration of the relevance of short-term forces such as issues, leaders and government style and performance in Canadian electoral behaviour, the weakness of long-term correlates of voting choice such as religion, ethnicity or social class, and the particular characteristics of partisan attachment held by many Canadians. In any given election there is likely to be sufficient volatility in the vote to produce at least the potential for a victory by the opposition as well as significant disruption of seemingly established patterns of behaviour. That large-scale electoral upsets do not occur more frequently in Canada is due primarily to the difficulty which any party finds in effectively harnessing the many short-term forces at work at a given time in a large and diverse country with many distinctive regional and sub-national trends operative in its politics. However, on those occasions when short-term forces operate more or less in one direction across the country, as in 1958 or 1979, the extent of electoral change which can occur is striking indeed. The Liberals, as the largest national party, often benefit from the cross-cutting nature of short-term effects in Canadian elections, but they are by no means assured of victory in any federal election. The Canadian party system, therefore, although it sometimes presents an appearance of aggregate stability, remains in fact a highly volatile one.

FOOTNOTES

1. For a general discussion of sociodemographic factors in Canadian politics, see Schwartz (1974a, 1974b) and Clarke et al. (1974, pp.93-131). The persistence of religion as a factor

in Canadian politics is particularly interesting, as is the weakness of social class. On the former point, see Irvine (1974) and Meisel (1975, ch.6). Alford (1963) characterised Canada as 'pure, non-class politics' in his comparison of the importance of occupational factors in voting in the Anglo-American democracies. Although the strength of social class in Canadian politics remains a point of contention (Wilson, 1968; Chi, 1973), class related variables have generally been weak predictors of behaviour in Canada, at least at the national level (Clarke et al., 1979). Religion continues to exhibit some strength, but it is often confounded with linguistic and regional variables.

2. A similar position is taken by Irvine and Gold (1980) in a comparison of the determinants of partisanship in Canada and Australia. They cite Burnham's example of Weimar Germany in describing Canada as a party system which is simultaneously weak and stable (Burnham, 1973, p.15).

3. These studies were directed by Harold Clarke, Jane Jenson, Lawrence LeDuc, and Jon Pammett, and funded by the Social Sciences and Humanities Research Council of Canada. Field work was conducted by Canadian Facts Ltd., of Toronto. The 1974 National Election Study was a single wave post-election survey of the eligible Canadian electorate, consisting of extensive personal interviews with a national sample of 2562 respondents. In 1979, 1338 of these respondents were re-interviewed to create a 1974-79 panel, and two new cross-section samples of the electorate were also interviewed in a major post-election survey. Following the February 1980 federal election precipitated by the parliamentary defeat of the Clark Government, all respondents to both the 1974-79 panel and the 1979 cross-section surveys were contacted by telephone. Successful re-interviews were obtained with 1747 respondents, of which 857 were also members of the 1974-79 panel. A fourth wave of interviewing was carried out in Quebec only following the May 1980 Referendum.

4. Using the 1974-1979 British panel and the 1972-1976 panel version of the U.S. election studies, it was found that 28 per cent of the sample in both countries reported a different voting choice in at least one of three elections. U.S. estimates are for Congressional vote in the 1972, 1974, and 1976 elections, while the British figure covers February and October 1974 and 1979. Abstention is of course substantially higher in the United States

than in the other two countries. A more detailed
discussion of these cross-national comparisons may
be found in LeDuc (1981) and LeDuc, et al.(1984).
The data from these studies was made available to
the author by the SSRC Data Archive (University of
Essex) and the Inter-University Consortium for
Political and Social Research, neither of which
bears any responsibility for these estimates of
volatility.

5. Similar results are obtained in analyses of
data from other Canadian election surveys, with
different multivariate techniques, or with other
versions of the variables shown in Table
3.4.(Clarke, et al., 1979, ch.4).

6. Questions employed were as follows: "Is
there anything in particular that you like about the
federal Liberal party?----------Anything
else?---------- Is there anything in particular that
you dislike about the Liberals?----------Anything
else?----------" etc. The sequence was repeated for
all parties (federal and provincial), and up to
three like and dislike mentions for each party were
coded for each respondent. Multiple responses to
these questions were categorised according to type
as shown in Table 3.6. For a more detailed
discussion of these data, see Clarke, et al., (1979,
ch.6.).

7. Some examples drawn from the 1974-79 data
illustrate this point. While 57 per cent of the
national sample specifically mentioned inflation as
one of the two most important issues in the 1974
election, only 18 per cent of the 1979 sample took
the same position. Similarly, 37 per cent of the
1979 sample mentioned various confederation issues
as most important, while only 5 per cent of the 1974
sample had cited issues in this category. A more
extensive discussion of the volatility of issues in
Canada, with comparisons to similar phenomena in
other countries, may be found in Hildebrandt, et
al., (1983).

8. A more extended treatment of the nature and
source of the instability of party identification in
Canada may be found in LeDuc, et al.(1984). An
argument that the strength and stabilility of party
identification may be somewhat understated in
´textbook´ theories of Canadian politics is made by
Sniderman, et al. (1974). A critique of their
position may be found in Jenson (1975).

REFERENCES

Alford, R. (1963) Party and Society, Rand McNally, Chicago

Burnham, W.D. (1973) 'Political Immunization and Political Confessionalism: the United States and Weimar Germany', Journal of Interdisciplinary History, III, 3-25

Chi, N.H. (1973) 'Class Voting in Canadian Politics', Carleton Occasional Papers Series, No. 1.

Clarke, H., J. Jenson, L. LeDuc, and J. Pammett (1979) Political Choice in Canada, McGraw-Hill Ryerson, Toronto

---------- (1984) Absent Mandate: The Politics of Discontent in Canada, Gage, Toronto

Dalton, R., S. Flanagan and P. Beck (eds.) (1983) Electoral Change in Industrial Democracies, Princeton University Press, Princeton

Hildebrandt, K., H. Clarke, L. LeDuc and J. Pammett (1983) 'Issue Volatility and Partisan Linkages in a Period of Economic Decline in Canada, Great Britain, the United States, and the Federal Republic of Germany', paper presented to the annual meeting of the Canadian Political Science Association, Vancouver

Irvine, W. and H. Gold (1980) 'Do Frozen Cleavages Ever Go Stale?', British Journal of Political Science, X, 213-25

Jenson, J. (1975) 'Party Loyalty in Canada: the Question of Party Identification', Canadian Journal of Political Science, VIII, 543-53

Jenson, J., H. Clarke, L. LeDuc and J. Pammett (1975) 'Patterns of Partisanship in Canada: Split Identification and Cross-Time Variation', paper presented to the annual meeting of the American Political Science Association, San Francisco

LeDuc, L. (1983a) 'Is There Life After Dealignment?', paper presented at the Workshop on Electoral Behaviour, European Consortium for Political Research Joint Sessions, Freiburg, West Germany

--------- (1983b) 'Canada: the Politics of Stable Dealignment' in R. Dalton et al., Electoral Change in Industrial Democracies

--------- (1981) 'The Dynamic Properties of Party Identification: a Four Nation Comparison', European Journal of Political Research, IX, 257-68

LeDuc, L. , H. Clarke, J. Jenson and J. Pammett (1984) 'Partisan Instability in Canada: Evidence from a New Panel Study', American Political Science Review, (forthcoming)

Meisel, J. (1975) Working Papers in Canadian Politics, McGill-Queen's Press, Montreal

Rose, R. (ed.) (1974) Electoral Behaviour: A Comparative Handbook, Free Press, New York

Schwartz, M. (1974a) 'Canadian Voting Behaviour' in R. Rose, Electoral Behaviour: A Comparative Handbook, pp.543-617

---------- (1974b) Politics and Territory, McGill-Queen's Press, Montreal

Sniderman, P., H.D. Forbes and I. Melzer (1974) 'Party Loyalty and Electoral Volatility', Canadian Journal of Political Science, VII, 268-88

Thomassen, J. (1976) 'Party Identification as a Cross National Concept: Its Meaning in the Netherlands' in I. Budge, et al., Party Identification and Beyond, Wiley, London

Wilson, J. (1968) 'Politics and Social Class: the Case of Waterloo South', Canadian Journal of Political Science, I, 288-309

Chapter 4

AUSTRALIA

Don Aitkin

Volatile people are changeable, fickle people, unpredictable in their behaviour. Volatile electors are relatively unpredictable at election times: they may vote for the party they supported last time (having undergone one or many changes of heart in the interim), vote for another established party, vote for a minor party or a non-party candidate, or abstain from voting altogether. An electorate containing a significant proportion of such citizens may, after a point, be described as a volatile electorate. Volatile people, electors, electorates and times are to be contrasted with the non-volatile: the predictable, reliable, cool, relatively unchanging.

These broad definitions imply that in making sense of 'electoral volatility' we need to compare across polities and over time. That task has been attempted for post-war European democracies by Mogens Pedersen (Pedersen, 1979), and his 'index of volatility' will be employed to estimate the extent of volatility in the Australian party system, both at the state and federal levels, since the late 1940s. But first, some scene-setting.

INTRODUCTION: THE AUSTRALIAN PARTY SYSTEM

Although commonly labelled 'a young country', Australia possesses a well-established national party system that has retained its principal characteristics for a long time (Aitkin, 1982; Jaensch, 1983). The nation's major political force, the Australian Labor Party, emerged in 1891, a decade before the federation of the Australian colonies in 1901. The essentials of parliamentary government through a bi-cameral legislature, the secret ballot and manhood suffrage were all

75

established in the 1850s; women received the vote at the turn of the century. The distinctive elements of the Australian electoral system are not quite so ancient, although venerable enough: compulsory enrolment (1911), 'preferential voting' or the alternative vote (1919), and compulsory voting (1925).

Although political parties of the modern kind first appeared in Australia in the 1880s, the modern national party system can be said to date from 1910, when a Labor Party, affiliated with trade unions and pragmatically Left in character, faced a Liberal Party which was essentially a coalition of the political representatives of the urban and rural middle classes. These two parties won all the seats save one, and 95 per cent of the vote, at the national elections of that year. In 1919 the Liberal Party split, most of its rural elements joining together in a Country Party, which drew support also from former rural adherents of Labor. In 1923 the two non-Labor parties arranged a formal coalition in government, and this alliance has endured almost unbroken to the present, though it is informal when the parties are in opposition.

Since 1910 the Liberal Party has reformed organisationally three times, long periods in office being followed by defeat, depression and disunity, most dramatically in 1943, when the disintegration of the United Australian Party (as the principal non-Labor party was then known) produced not only a variety of warring factions but the largest number of independent candidates to offer themselves for a federal election. The Labor Party has suffered three agonising splits, the first in 1916, over the question of conscription for military service, the second in 1931, over the correct response to the great Depression, and the third in 1955, over the question of domestic Communism. The first two splits provided the non-Labor parties with some notable leaders (W.M. Hughes and J.A. Lyons) and the bonus of some easy electoral victories. The third split produced a small splinter party, the Democratic Labor Party (DLP), which flourished from 1955 to 1974 mostly because the proportional representation system used to elect Senators gave it a few parliamentary members who sometimes held the balance of power in Australia's powerful second chamber. The Country Party, the principal (but by no means the sole) representative of Australia's farming districts, kept hold of its seats and

Table 4.1: Party Shares of the Formal First Preference Vote, Elections for the House of
Representatives, 1910-1983

Year	Lab. %	Lib. %	Country %	Minor %	Others %	Net Volatility
1910	50	45	--	--	5	7.6
1913	48	49	--	--	3	2.7
1914	51	47	--	--	2	2.1
1917	44	54(a)	--	--	2	6.9
1919	42	45	9	--	4	9.9
1922	42	40	13	--	5	11.5
1925	45	42	11	--	2	10.7
1928	45	39	12	--	4	2.8
1929	49	34	11	--	6	5.1
1931	38(b)	42(c)	12	--	8	16.7
1934	41	37	13	--	9	7.4
1937	43	34	16	--	7	4.9
1940	48(d)	30	14	--	8	8.4
1943	50	21(e)	12	--	17	25.9
1946	50	33(f)	11	--	4	15.2
1949	46	39	11	--	4	11.2
1951	48	40	10	--	2	2.4
1954	50	39	8	--	3	2.9
1955	45	40	8	5(g)	2	6.2
1958	43	37	9	9	2	5.4
1961	48	34	8	9	1	5.2
1963	45	37	9	7	2	7.9
1966	40	40	10	7	3	5.4
1969	47	35	8	6	4	7.8
1972	50	32	9	5	4	4.3
1974	49	35	10	1	5	4.9
1975	43	42	11	1	3	9.3
1977	40	38	10	9(h)	3	9.0
1980	45	37	9	7	2	5.9
1983	49	34	9	5	3	4.8

Notes: (a) Nat, (b) two groups, (c) UAP, (d) three
groups, (e) various groups, (f) Liberal, (g)
Democratic Labor, (h) Australian Democratic.
Sources: Hughes and Graham (1968); Hughes (1977) and
supplements; unofficial reports published by the
Australian Electoral Officer.

support, suffered no splits, and changed little. In 1977 a dissident Liberal and former Minister, D.L. Chipp, formed a new party of the ´soft centre´, the Australian Democratic Party (ADP). In a time of some disenchantment with the established parties the Democrats secured nearly ten per cent of the vote after only six months´ existence, and gained representation in the Senate. Three years later, while its Senate representation increased, the new party saw its share of the House of Representatives´ vote fall to seven per cent. It had not, any more than the DLP before, affected the control of the House of Representatives and in 1983 its House vote declined again even though it now controlled the balance of power in the Senate.

The parties´ shares of the vote have changed very little over the twentieth century. The Labor Party generally secured between 40 per cent and 50 per cent of the vote, the Country Party ten per cent (plus or minus one), and minor groups and independent candidates three or four per cent; the Liberal Party gained the balance. Neither the ADP nor the DLP has managed to reach double figures in lower house elections or to elect lower house MPs, and, despite its present representation in the Senate, the ADP does not look to be a permanent fixture in the party system.

Table 4.1 sets out the shares of the vote won by each party from 1910 to 1983. The broad similarity of each party´s share of the vote over time suggests it is stability rather than volatility that is characteristic of Australian party politics. The Australian party system has exhibited long periods of calm and short periods of turbulence, party splitting and reorganisation. Since the system has been dominated by two major parties, the crises of one party tend to have a powerful effect on the life of the other - if only to guarantee it a further term in office. The crisis times for a party have occurred in 1916-17, 1930-1, 1943-4, 1954-5 and 1977. If these crises illustrate volatility, then it is clear that volatility is not a new phenomenon in Australia.

The six states and two territories that constitute the Commonwealth of Australia (1) possess party systems that underwent similar processes of adjustment during the century. In 1983 they present great similarity and the differences are easily explicable. The Country Party (now renamed the National Party) tended to be strongest in Queensland (where it is the major partner in the coalition),

New South Wales and Victoria; in the other states it now barely exists where it exists at all. The Labor Party is electorally strong at every level and currently forms the Government in New South Wales, Victoria, South Australia, Western Australia, and in Canberra. Labor has in fact been more successful at the state level than in federal politics, where it has held office in only one quarter of the years since the century began. In New South Wales, by way of contrast, it held office continuously from 1941 to 1965, and has held it again since 1976. Long continuous runs of Labor in office have been known in the other states, Victoria excepted. In Canberra Labor´s last sustained period in government was from 1941 to 1949. Thereafter it has held office only from 1972 to 1975 and since March 1983.

TRENDS IN ELECTORAL VOLATILITY

´True´ or ´gross´ volatility would be represented by the proportion of all electors who behaved differently in adjoining pairs of elections, either by voting for different parties, or by voting in one election and abstaining in the other. Electors who vote in only one election through the timing of coming-of-age, naturalisation, emigration, or death, contribute to the volatility of the system but are not to be regarded as volatile themselves – at least with respect to that pair of elections. Panel survey data provide the best estimates of true volatility; less reliable estimates come from survey data in which respondents recall the direction of their vote in pairs of elections. We shall consider some examples shortly.

Net volatility can be defined, following Pedersen (1979, p.4), as "the cumulated gains for all winning parties in the party system" or as the average of all party gains and all party losses.(2) Net volatility is a much less satisfactory measure than gross volatility since it need bear no relation to it in a given case. Apparent stability from one election to another could conceal the movement of equal numbers of partisans between two parties. Given a large enough set of elections, however, we should expect some trends in volatility to show up, notwithstanding the possibility of masking. Pairs of elections results do not, after all, tend to resemble each other exactly, and although net volatility will always be smaller then gross volatility, we would expect the same trends to appear over the long haul.

Volatility at the Federal and State Levels

Let us begin with net volatility, first at the
level of the Commonwealth. Following Pedersen
again, one should begin with the 1949 election,
since the rebuilding of the major non-Labor party
after the collapse of the 1943-44 period had not
proceeded a long way by the time of the 1946
elections. By 1949, however, that process was
virtually complete, and the two-and-a-half party
system of the 1920s and 1930s was evident again.The
mean net volatility score for the 14 elections from
1949 to 1983 is 5.8, and the standard deviation is
2.1.(3) This is a good deal less than the European
mean of 8.1 calculated by Pedersen for 13 countries

Table 4.2: Net Volatility at the State Level,
1949-1983

	Federal elections		State elections	
	Mean	SD	Mean	SD
New South Wales	5.4	2.4	6.3	3.8
Victoria	6.5	4.4	7.8	6.2
Queensland	5.5	2.9	7.9	5.6
South Australia	7.1	4.8	6.2	4.3
Western Australia	7.8	3.4	7.8	2.3
Tasmania	4.9	2.8	6.6	3.3
Mean (unweighted)	6.2		7.1	
Commonwealth	5.8	2.1		

Notes:SD = standard deviation.
This conventional arrangement of the Australian
states is in order of diminishing population size.
New South Wales and the rather smaller Victoria hold
62 per cent of the Australian population.

over the period 1948 to 1977, and the dispersion
around the mean is also very low, lower indeed
(although not by much) than any European country.
Australia falls into the group characterised by
Pedersen (1979, p.7) as having 'a relatively stable
distribution of party strength'; it then included
Switzerland, Austria, Sweden and the United Kingdom,
and in terms of mean volatility and standard

deviation Australia most resembled Sweden.

The states serve as arenas both for the contesting of federal elections and for state political battles. Although state party systems strongly resemble each other and the national party system they are not identical, and a comparison of state volatilities is therefore of interest (Table 4.2). Essentially the picture is one of similarity, with net volatility being rather less at federal elections than at state elections. What is true of the nation as a whole is true also of its parts: in each case the means and standard deviations are the result of a mixture over time of calm and turbulence. Some states, like Queensland and Victoria, have been notably turbulent in state politics although Queensland also produced a pair of election results close to identical.(4) The Commonwealth´s low mean net volatility score and its low standard deviation are in part the results of states moving in opposite directions (e.g. Tasmania´s going against Labor in 1983 when the other states showed swings to Labor).

Trends in Volatility over Time

Table 4.1 suggests that over the whole of the present century volatility was actually less pronounced in the postwar period than before it; and indeed for the 16 elections from 1910 to 1949 the mean net volatility score was 8.8 and the standard deviation 6.1 - evidence of some very dissimilar election results. But are there trends in the postwar period that point towards increased volatility? The evidence is set out in Table 4.3, which once again follows Pedersen (1979, Table 1). The period means suggest that in federal politics volatility increased from the 1950s to the 1960s, and increased a little again from the 1960s to the 1970s. In state politics, however, volatility declined in the 1960s but grew again to the level of the 1950s in the 1970s. Close inspection points to four modes present in the three time-periods:

		No. of Cases
(1)	increasing volatility throughout	2
(2)	increased volatility, then stability	5
(3)	stability, then volatility	2
(4)	similar levels of volatility in periods I and III, with lower levels in period II	4

Table 4.3: The Volatility of the Australian Party
System, 1949-1980

	1949-59	1960-69	1970-79	N of elect. periods
Federal elections				
Commonwealth	4.2	6.6	6.7	13
New South Wales	3.0	6.7	6.4	
Victoria	7.3	4.6	7.8	
Queensland	3.5	6.4	6.5	
South Australia	4.5	7.9	7.1	
Western Australia	6.5	7.4	8.6	
Tasmania	3.6	3.9	6.7	
Period Mean	(4.7)	(6.2)	(7.1)	
State elections				
New South Wales	8.5	2.8	7.9	11
Victoria	13.4	3.6	6.2	11
Queensland	10.2	5.4	8.1	12
South Australia	3.4	5.6	8.8	12
Western Australia	7.5	6.7	9.8	11
Tasmania	4.4	7.2	7.0	9
Period Mean	(7.9)	(5.2)	(8.0)	
N of election periods	52	46	59	

Pedersen uses his evidence to advance some
plausible hypotheses about European party systems.
The Australian data do not so lend themselves,
unless to denying the proposition that the
Australian party system is growing more volatile (
the Commonwealth falls into mode 2). If we are to
account for the volatility that exists we will need
to advance particular explanations about particular
cases, and that is attempted below. It is time to
turn from the rather arid statistics of net
volatility and consider the unfortunately limited
survey data that enable us to measure gross
volatility.

Table 4.4 offers the only example of Australian
national panel data concerning electors´ votes in
two adjoining elections. The main diagonal displays
those electors who voted for the same party or
refrained from voting on both occasions (5); it

contains just 76 per cent of the sample. The off-diagonal cells contain the volatile, two-thirds of whom moved between voting for the governing coalition and voting for the Labor opposition.

Table 4.4: Gross Volatility in Australian Federal Elections 1966-69

	1969					
1966	Lib-CP %	Labor %	DLP %	Other %	NV %	Total %
Lib-CP	40	12	2	1	1	57
Labor	4	33	1	1	*	39
DLP	1	*	2	*		3
Other		*		*		*
NV	1	*			*	1
Total	45	46	5	2	2	100 (N=1296)

Notes: NV = Did not vote; * = less than 0.5 per cent. The Liberal and Country parties in coalition formed the government and did not campaign against each other in the great majority of seats. The table includes only those who were eligible to vote in both elections and remembered how they had voted. Report of 1966 vote was obtained in 1967 and that of 1969 in 1969. Rounding within cells means that cell frequencies do not always sum to marginal frequencies.
Source: Australian Survey Project, 1966-69 panel; data obtained from Australian Consortium for Social and Political Research and originally collected by Don Aitkin and Michael Kahan.

The table nicely displays the ´masking effect´: the marginal frequencies produce a ´net´ volatility measure of twelve per cent, while the cells of the table provide a gross volatility just twice as great - 24 per cent. Had the movements between the Labor party and the coalition been even, at eight per cent, and had all other cells remained the same, net volatility would have been eight per cent although gross volatility would not have altered.
A few moments with pencil and paper will show how the relationship between net and gross volatility is affected both by the proportion of electors found on the main diagonal and by the flow of electors off the diagonal. Where all movement is one way - parties either gain or lose but not both -

then net and gross volatility will be identical. In the case where all movement is equally matched - parties lose exactly as many voters as they gain - net volatility will be zero and gross volatility can range between 0 and 100 per cent. In practice, partisan loyalty is likely to keep gross volatility well below 50 per cent in any established party system. The necessity for mass parties to have a policy for everything means that at any time they tend to attract new supporters and to lose old ones: net volatility is therefore likely to be low.

Table 4.5: Gross Volatility in Australian Federal Elections, 1975-77

	1977					
1975	Lib-NCP %	Labor %	ADP %	Other %	NV %	Total %
Lib-NCP	47	2	1		*	51
Labor	2	42	1	*	*	46
Australia	*	*	*			1
Other	*	*	*	1		1
NV	*	1		*	*	1
Total	50	45	3	1	1	100 (N=1672)

Notes: The table refers to House of Representatives vote. NV = did not vote; * = less than 0.5 per cent. The Australia Party was a very small party formed in the late 1960s as a Liberal breakaway over Australian policy on the war in Vietnam; it was absorbed by the Australian Democrats (ADP) in 1977. These figures under-represent the Democrats' share of the vote in 1977, which was nine per cent; one cause is that the sub-sample is necessarily of voters aged at least 22 in 1979, and the Democrats polled well among new voters. Recall of a Democrat vote in 1977 was nonetheless notably deficient, and reminiscent of British Liberal voting (see Aitkin, 1982, pp.342-6).
Source: Macquarie University National Political Attitudes Survey, 1979; data made available by the Australian Consortium for Social and Political Research and originally collected by Don Aitkin.

Table 4.5 allows a second estimate of this relationship, from the 1970s. In this case the two observations are drawn from the same interview: respondents in 1979 were recalling their 1977 and

1975 votes. Some allowance must therefore be made
for errors of memory and wishful thinking, and the
sample is not representative of the youngest voters.
Nevertheless, our interest lies in the relationships
within the table: gross volatility is nine per cent,
net volatility two per cent.(6) In comparison with
Table 4.4, there is a very much more even flow of
electors around the party system: the result is to
make net volatility decline almost to vanishing
point - yet one voter in eleven moved.

The survey data sets allow two further
estimates of gross volatility, this time for two
elections plus a hypothetical election held
´tomorrow´. They are not properly comparable, since
in the 1960s the hypothetical election lay between
the two actual elections, while in the 1970s it
followed them. A proper response to all
hypothetical questions is ´I don´t know´ and eight
per cent in 1967 and seven per cent in 1979 gave
that reply when asked how they would vote
´tomorrow´. Such uncertainty pushes volatility up,
since such electors can hardly be disregarded.
Gross volatility measured for 1966-1967-1969 was 32
per cent (that is, 68 per cent would have voted the
same way on each occasion); for the period
1975-1977-1979 gross volatility was 23 per cent. We
may be confident that a ´proper´ cycle of elections,
1966-1969-1972 or 1975-1977-1980, for example, would
have produced rather lower gross volatility measures
than these, since there is ample evidence to show
that many uncertain voters return to their customary
party when they actually have to cast a vote. But
more than that we cannot say, and it is time to
ponder on what the evidence, aggregate and survey,
suggests.

The data so far considered point to two broad
categories of departure from stability in the
Australian party system. The first is a large
transfer of voters between the major parties, to the
substantial benefit of one of them. Table 4.1
suggests that this occurred in 1949, 1961, 1966,
1966 and 1975. Each of these elections is memorable
for large changes in parliamentary numbers which
resulted from them. The second category is the
incursion into the system of a new party, which can
cost both major parties some support and disturbs
for a time the established order in the
constituencies. Such elections occurred in 1955 and
1977 (and earlier, of course, in 1919). After its
establishment in 1955 the Democratic Labor Party was
essentially a stable element in the system, an

anti-Labor auxiliary whose raison d´etre collapsed with the election of a Labor government in 1972. At the next election its electoral support had largely departed, to swell the ranks of the Liberal and Country parties, so far as we can tell. The Australian Democrats have had a much briefer existence since their own establishment in 1977, but they too have, for the moment, become a relatively stable element in the system.

The impact of the DLP at the state level was greatest in Victoria and Queensland. In Victoria the DLP was able to win as much as 17 per cent of the vote in the state as a whole, while in Queensland the new party was produced by the factional destruction of a Labor government that had been continuously in office since 1932 (the Country-Liberal coalition that came to power in 1957 is still there, 26 years later). In other states the impact of the DLP was less pronounced (see Table 4.3). The impact of the Australian Democrats, some 20 years later, was more evenly experienced across Australia: the party´s ´heartland´, if such exists, is Australian suburbia, not the state of Victoria, the home of its leader, Senator Chipp.

If we now look at the incidence of volatility in the last 30 years as a consequence of ´transfer´ and/or ´incursion´ effects, we can present a general account for the Commonwealth along the following lines. At the end of the 1940s the reformation of the Liberal Party combined with a growing distaste for a relatively long-lived Labor government produced substantial transfers from Labor to the Liberal and Country Parties. A Labor recovery in the 1950s was ended by internal dissension in the ALP, which produced a new party, the DLP. The system quickly absorbed the new party, and in the 1960s volatility was caused mostly by transfers - to the Labor Party in 1961 and 1969, and against it in 1966. The first half of the 1970s was comparatively stable, but then another transfer in 1975 and the incursion of another new party in 1977 pushed up the level of volatility for the decade.

The 1980s have begun, like the 1970s, rather quietly. At the state level we need to produce separate accounts, each with a substantially special character, even though party fortunes at the federal level would be woven in. None of these accounts, however, would portray an Australia or a state in which the volatility of the party system was growing. And to some extent this is counter-intuitive. A number of phenomena suggest that Australians ought to be more volatile than they once were, whatever the statistics say.

WHY ELECTORAL VOLATILITY SHOULD HAVE INCREASED (BUT DIDN'T)

Changes of Government

The last ten years or so have seen a notable increase in the number of changes of government. Victoria apart (and then mostly for the period from the mid-1940s to the mid-1950s), Australians have been used to long runs in office by the dominant party or party group. Outside Victoria there were only four changes in government across six states in the 1940s and only three in the 1950s. Counting Victoria, there were four changes in seven states in the 1960s, eight in the 1970s and five (to the middle of 1983) in the 1980s. Political commentators and party activists have been prone to talk of a new volatility in the Australian electorate since the early 1970s and it is changes in government to which they point. Changes in government can, of course, occur without massive changes within the electorate. But clearly there is something to explain.

The Enfranchisement of the Young

The notion that adulthood and therefore citizenship begins at 21 is a respectably old one. Throughout the 1960s, sparked by examples abroad and by political conflict at home (those conscripted for military service during the war in Vietnam were aged 18), a movement to reduce the voting age to 18 gathered force. New South Wales and Western Australia made the move in 1970, South Australia did so in the following year and the Commonwealth and the remaining states save Tasmania followed suit in 1973.

Since the young have a less habituated attachment to their party than those older, the sudden addition to the electorate of hundreds of thousands of young voters ought to have contributed to the volatility of the system. It is, unfortunately, difficult either to prove or disprove this plausible notion. As it happens the volatility index in 1974 was 4.9, rather less than the Commonwealth mean of 5.8. And although volatility in the later 1970s was high, with substantial transfers in 1975 and strong incursion effects in

Table 4.6:   Changes   in   the   Party   Composition   of
             Australian Governments, 1949-1983

	Commonwealth (UAP-CP,1934)	New South Wales (UAP-CP,1932)	Victoria (Country,1935)
1940-49	1941 Lab 1941 L-CP	1941 Lab	1943 Lab 1945 CP-UAP 1945 Lib 1947 Lab 1947 L-CP 1948 Lib
1950-59			1950 Country 1952 Elect. Reform 1952 Country 1952 Lab 1955 Cain Lab 1955 Lib
1960-69		1965 L-CP	
1970-79	1972 Lab 1975 L-CP	1976 Lab	
1980-	1983 Lab		1982 Lab

	Queensland (Lab,1932)	South Australia (Lib,1933)	Western Australia (Lab,1933)	Tasmania (Lab,1934)
1940-49			1947 L-CP	
1950-59	1957 CP-Lib		1953 Lab 1959 L-CP	
1960-69		1965 Lab 1968 Lib		1969 L-CP
1970-79		1970 Lab 1979 Lib	1971 Lab 1974 L-CP	1972 Lab
1980-		1982 Lab	1983 Lab	1982 Lib

Note: The party/ies in office in 1940, and the date
they began their period in office, are given in
brackets.   In the 1930s and early 1940s the Liberal
Party was known as the United Australia Party (UAP).
For coalitions the major party is shown first.

1977, the politics of the period affected the whole electorate, and not especially the young. Survey evidence from 1979 does not suggest that young voters were more likely than those older to support different parties in 1975 and 1977. Their contribution to total volatility in the 1970s is unlikely to have been dramatic.(7) There is no other pair of elections for which we have comparable information.

Increased Awareness of Politics

In the 1980s the Australian electorate is considerably more aware of political affairs than was the case in the 1960s. Part of the cause is the marked increase in the proportions completing high school and going on to university or other tertiary institutions, compared to the 1960s; part is the heightened interest in politics now displayed by women (Aitkin, 1982, ch.18). Should not an interest in politics lead citizens to think for themselves, and to resist the claims of party when the party in question has not been performing well? This is another plausible conjecture. Unfortunately, survey evidence suggests that the causal arrows are more firmly pointed elsewhere. High levels of interest in politics accompany high levels of partisan loyalty: the deeply involved tend to be the ones most aware.(8) And in 1979 levels of party identification were if anything higher than they had been in the 1960s: there is no evidence in Australia of the kind of ´partisan dealignment´ portrayed in different ways for the United States (Nie, Verba and Petrocik, 1979) and the United Kingdom (Crewe, Sarlvik and Alt, 1977).

As for the influence of women, the evidence does not show that women are notably more volatile than men.(9) It is likely that the changing status of women - more than half of the Australian electorate - will be an essential part of any explanation of the nature of Australian politics in the 1970s and 1980s, since the declining political conservatism of women in the 1970s was instrumental in Labor´s victory in 1983. But so far there is little evidence to show that it is women who are responsible for volatility.

The weakening of the class-party link

For several generations it was assumed that Australian politics was simply the struggle between

classes carried out at another level, that the Labor
party was (as its name suggested) the party of the
workers, the Liberal party the party of the bosses,
and so on. The first comprehensive survey analysis
dispelled the most simplistic of these notions,
since Australia was shown to have a relatively weak
class basis to its party system (Aitkin and Kahan,
1974; Rose, 1974; Aitkin, 1977). More recent work
by Kemp (1978) and Aitkin (1982) has made clear that
the link betwween class and party has been weakening
since the second world war at least, and continues
to weaken. Alford´s index of class voting, around 35
to 40 in the 1950s (Alford, 1964, pp.183-88), was
down to 22 in 1979 (Aitkin, 1982, p.319).

If the link between class and party has become
so weak, surely the party system is in some danger
of falling apart? Is not the volatility we see
about us evidence of that decline? So at least some
have argued. But a counter argument can be offered.
First, it is clear from Table 4.1 that in Australia
there was greater net volatility before the second
world war when class polarisation was presumably
also greater. Second, it is now clear also that in
forming party loyalty parental models are more
powerful than ´class´, and that parental models have
become more powerful as class factors have lost
their importance (Aitkin, 1982, ch.20).

Hard Times
    Post-war Australia enjoyed, until the
mid-1970s, the most sustained economic growth in the
nation´s history. It was also a most stable period
in terms of changes of government. In common with
the rest of the world, Australian economic history
since the OPEC oil-price increases of 1973 has been
one of low growth, increased unemployment (ten per
cent, compared with the one per cent or less that
was the rule for most of the postwar period) and
continued inflation. It has also been a period of
rejection of governments. The notion that hard
times galvanise voters into turning out governments
that have failed to stop the rot is another
respectably ancient one. It has some impressive
Australian supporting evidence: out of all
Australian governments that went to the people
between 1930 and 1933, the onset of the depression,
only one was re-elected.

    Recent evidence is less compelling. The 1979
respondents were united in seeing the economy as the
central political problem of their time, and were

much more critical of the institutions of government, the public service, the political parties, and the leading politicians than had been true of their counterparts in the 1960s. Yet this manifest discontent had been contained within the party system - despite the fact that both sides of politics had been in office during the hard times and neither had seemed notably competent in ending them. Indeed, the Fraser coalition government, which held office from 1975 to 1983, proved to be Australia's third most long-lived government. And although rejection of governments has increased, the great increase has occurred in 1982 and 1983, a decade after the hard times began.

Four of these five phenomena offer <u>prima facie</u> a plausible explanation of why Australians might be less set in their partisan ways than they once were. Unfortunately, the trend that they help to explain does not itself exist. That governments lead more precarious lives than they once did cannot be denied, but the weight of evidence, not to mention a sensitivity to ecological fallacies, should prevent us arguing that precarious governments have volatile voters to blame for their situation.

What seems to have happened at the level of the party system is that with the demise of the DLP the Labor and non-Labor parties moved to a position much closer to parity. In the DLP era the combined electoral weight of the Liberal, Country and Democratic Labor Parties was nearly always more than 50 per cent, and often a good deal more. The gap between the two sides was of the order of five to ten per cent, and as much as 17 per cent in 1966. In the 1970s and 1980s that gap has narrowed, the more so because the Australian Democrat preferences tend to be evenly divided. In consequence, a change in the structure of the party system has occurred, and that has had the effect of making relatively small transfers bring about changes in government, something that larger transfers could not produce in the 1960s.

CONCLUSION: ELECTORAL VOLATILITY AND THE ELECTORAL SYSTEM

If there were any electoral volatility in Australia in the 1970s it was of a cyclical and therefore familiar kind, the accompaniment of a time of turbulence in the party system that followed a long period of calm. Party identification seemed as potent as ever, and the irruption of a new party did not do more than temporarily challenge the dominance of the three established players in the party game. Comparative data and analysis are needed before we can decide whether the conditions for volatility apparently found elsewhere have been absent in Australia, or whether, although present, they have been offset by other local circumstances. Nonetheless, it seems worthwhile finally to consider some of the likely effects of the electoral system in containing any tendency toward electoral volatility.(10)

Compulsory Voting

Australians have been used to compulsory voting for more than half a century, and it is clear that (notwithstanding the legend about Australians being contemptuous of authority) they strongly approve of it. They see elections as central to democracy, and, given that an explicit mandate theory is prominent in Australian political rhetoric, a ´proper´ election result is one which follows an election in which everyone, or nearly everyone, votes. Deliberate abstention seems to disadvantage the more unpopular of the party groups. Attendance at the polls followed by deliberately invalid voting - blank or defaced ballots - may run at about a half of one per cent on average.(11)

A widespread preparedness to vote makes abstention a non-alternative when the voter is out of love with his or her party. One consequence is presumably to make it harder for the voter to depart from a party identification once it has been formed. Another, almost contradictory, is to make one´s traditional political enemy a possibility for support, once the decision to depart has been made. A third, assisted by preferential voting, is to make minor parties, if appropriate in the circumstances, a temporary compromise.

Very high levels of turnout ought, on the face of it, to depress electoral volatility, but comparative evidence is suggestive rather than compelling. Of the countries Pedersen found to have stable distributions of party strength over time ,(i.e. to have relatively low volatility), Austria and Sweden have notably high average turnout (94 per cent and 85 per cent respectively). Another one, Switzerland, does not, while Denmark and the Netherlands, two countries with high volatility, also have high turnout (Crewe, 1981). New Zealand, a comparison closer to home, is very like Australia : high turnout (90 per cent) and low volatility - a mean score of 6.0, for the period 1945 to 1981. We need, it is clear, a set of close inspections.

Preferential voting

What is universally called 'preferential voting' in Australia is a special case of STV, where the number of members is one, and the quota therefore 50 per cent + 1. First adopted for the general election of 1919 it is even older than compulsory voting, although by no means as popular; perhaps half the electorate at any time would prefer the simple-majority system. This appears to be for two reasons. First, at least two-thirds of the electorate are committed partisans, who feel that the possibility of ordering preferences on the ballot paper is of little importance. Second, it seems generally to be believed that a result in which candidate B defeats candidate A after the distribution of preferences, when candidate A had possessed the greater plurality of primary votes (i.e. 'first preferences'), is more unfair than candidate A's winning, even though more voters preferred other candidates. Perhaps the electorate would be even unhappier after a return to the old system, something threatened from time to time by the ALP. 'Optional preferences', already introduced in New South Wales, are a likely modification of the current federal electoral system. Opinion about the likely consequences is divided.

Preferential voting does allow a protest vote : the voter votes 1 for a minor party or independent candidate, but 2 for his usual party. The risk is that if sufficient others do the same, the usual party may poll so poorly that its own candidate finds his votes, rather than those of the minor party, being distributed to others. The other risk is that disgruntled partisans will vote 1 for the minor party and 2 for the enemy, perhaps believing that by doing so they are not 'really' voting for the other side.

Both scenarios occur, but neither so powerfully nor so often that preferential voting can be seen as a major political variable in itself. Douglas Rae is right to say (1967, p.108) that the Australian 'majority system' behaves as though simple-majority voting were in force. But preferential voting becomes more important when considered alongside the fact that the Senate is elected through a system of proportional representation.

PR and the Senate

The founding fathers of Australia's Constitution wanted a second chamber that would be functional and therefore powerful - or at least, such a chamber was seen to be an indispensable condition if the smaller colonies were to become members of the federation. For the Senate was to be a State's House, in which each state had equal representation, on the pattern of the United States. Simple-majority and then preferential systems proved unsatisfactory in Senate elections, as they tended to reward overwhelmingly the winning party (thus Labor had 33 of the 36 members of the chamber after two good general election results in 1943 and 1946) (12) and proportional representation was introduced for the election of 1949.

This was arguably a more profound change than either compulsory voting or preferential voting. First, PR meant that subsequent governments would be likely to find themselves either in a small majority or in a small minority in the Senate. Second, PR allowed small parties without regional strongholds to win parliamentary representation in the Senate, and thus gain the kind of respectability and authority that comes from having won election somewhere. Third, for both these reasons, it made the Senate more important. Fourth, for all these reasons, it gave the Senate a different character, and probably widened the meaning of the vote: it can no longer be doubted that Australians are beginnning to develop a kind of bi-cameral awareness, in which party identificatiion serves to structure the vote for the lower House and determine which party should govern, while other considerations apply more strongly for elections to the Senate. Certainly the major parties are less well supported in Senate elections, and the cause cannot simply be the pattern of candidature at lower House elections. (13)

The contribution of electoral laws to politcal stability and volatility requires a lengthy discussion it cannot receive here.(14) But for our purposes it is at least possible that the electoral rules operating in the 1970s operated to reduce electoral volatility. We might set out a tentative explanation like this:

    -Since citizens continued to feel that they
    ought to vote, they were forced (as had been

true for 50 years) to find their salvation within the system.

-The failure of the Labor government to prevent the economic decline of the mid-1970s caused an entirely predictable swing to the Liberal-National Country Party opposition in 1975.

-The failure of the L-NCP government in turn to stop the decline produced a centre-party grouping - the Australian Democrats - which secured much of the protest vote in 1977. (15)

-Continuing hard times improved the chances of the Labor party in opposition, which did well in the 1980 elections, but mostly at the expense of the Democrats. In the Senate elections, however, the Democrats established themselves as a popular force, securing enough places to share (with a single Independent Senator) the balance of power.

-Labor won office again in 1983, partly because economic conditions worsened in 1982 and partly because slow changes in the political behaviour of women and the foreign-born had reached sufficient momentum. It seems unlikely that there was greater volatility in 1983 among voters than at previous elections.

-There was nothing unprecedented in any of this.

FOOTNOTES

* I am grateful to Clive Dean for providing some New Zealand data, and to Colin Hughes and Don Rawson for commenting on an earlier draft.

1. The territories are the Northern Territory (population in 1983: 131,400) and the Australian Capital Territory (population in 1983: 233,200), the location of the national capital, Canberra. Each territory possesses a single-chamber Legislative Assembly, and each has a measure of self-government, further advanced in the Northern Territory. Each territory is also represented in the national Parliament, the ACT having two MPs and two Senators, the Northern Territory one MP and two Senators. The territories will not be further referred to in this paper.

2. The average is to be preferred, I think, unless there are in fact no independent or ungrouped candidates. Independent and tiny-group candidates poll between 1 and 3 per cent of the vote, and ought

not to be treated collectively as a single entity.

3. To construct these measures I have followed the definitions of party used by Hughes and Graham (1968) and Hughes (1976), the authorities in this matter: in practice, any group that polled at least 0.1 per cent of the total. At the federal level that definition provides the three major parties, which have contested every election, the Communist Party of Australia, which contested every election from 1949 to 1972, the DLP, every election from 1955 to 1983 and 16 other ´parties´ which polled at least 0.1 per cent at least once at the national level. Of these latter parties only the Australian Democrats have made any impression on Australian politics.

4. In 1963 and 1966 (1966 percentages second): Labor - 44 (44), Liberal - 24 (26), Country - 20 (19), Queensland Labor - 7 (6), all others - 5 (5). There are several examples of election results that were identical or nearly identical in terms of party shares of the vote.

5. Although voting is ´compulsory´, there is a small proportion who decline to vote, and there are some who forget to do so or are prevented by illness or circumstances from attending the polls. It is attendance which is, strictly speaking, compulsory; another tiny proportion of voters lodges blank or (less commonly) defaced or deliberately invalid ballots. These activities are not without partisan effects (Aitkin, 1977, p.205).

6. Net volatility obtained from the aggregate results for the 1975-1977 pair of elections was nine per cent. The difference between the two estimates of net volatility flows partly from faulty recall (a much larger proportion should have recalled casting a Democrat vote), and partly from the simplified matrix tables used in these analyses of survey data, which leave out those who could not recall how they voted in either of the elections, compress those voting for minor parties and independent candidates into an ´Other´ group and place Liberal and (National) Country party voters together. All these operations can be defended but they do have the effect of increasing the apparent stability of the system and dimishing the measured volatility.

7. Gross volatility among those aged 18 to 25 (the oldest of whom would have been 21 in 1975) ran at 14 per cent, compared with 18 per cent for both those aged 26 to 30 and those aged 31 to 40. Thereafter it fell, to 10 per cent for those in their forties, 11 per cent for those in their

fifties and 8 per cent for those aged 61 and older.
If those aged 18 are not much more likely than those
aged 21 to display volatile behaviour, as might
plausibly be argued, then the effect of
enfranchising the 18-year-olds would have occurred
only once, in any case.

8.   In 1979 43 per cent of those claiming a
'very strong' level of partisanship also claimed to
have 'a good deal' of interest in politics. For
'fairly strong' and 'not very strong' partisans the
proportion was 23 per cent: for those who were not
partisan at all it was 19 per cent. The same
gradient obtained in 1967.

9.   For the 1975-1977 pair of elections the
difference was 2.5 per cent in favour of men (i.e.
men were less volatile). On the other hand, 58 per
cent of men and 62 per cent of women claimed to have
voted for the same party at federal elections.

10.   The most accessible accounts of the
Australian electoral system are contained in Joan
Rydon's chapter 'The Electoral System' in any of the
Mayer and Nelson Australian Politics readers (the
Fifth Reader (1980) is current), and in Aitkin and
Jinks (1982).

11.   Unintentionally invalid ('informal') votes
are cast when electors fail to record a full and
ordinal set of preferences on the ballot paper.
Informal voting in lower house elections is usually
not greater than two or three per cent, but has
reached ten per cent in Senate elections when
electors have been asked to formulate a preference
ordering among more than 70 candidates.

12.   House and Senate elections commonly occur
together, although only half the Senators will be
seeking election (Senators have six-year terms, MPs
three-year terms). But elections for the two Houses
can get out of step since different sets of rules
govern each.

13.   In 1980, for example, the scoreboard in
the two elections was as follows (figures in
percentages):

	Labor	Liberal	NCP	ADP	Other
House	45.1	37.4	8.9	6.6	2.0
Senate	42.2	43.5		9.3	5.0

The non-Labor parties have traditionally run joint
Senate teams, especially in NSW, Victoria and
Queensland; in 1980 the partners could not agree on
a joint team in Queensland and two separate teams

were offered.

14. The persistence of such high levels of partisan loyalty while the social structure in which the party system operates is undergoing steady change is an intriguing puzzle whose explanation must centre around the relative independence of political institutions and behaviour from social structure. In perhaps the most obvious example, the Labor party has survived the decline in the numerical importance of the working class, mostly by securing new supporters among the middle class and among women. The role of electoral laws in this context is considered in the final chapter of Aitkin (1982), especially pp. 347-54.

15. Its founders argue that the ADP represents a new force in Australian politics uniting those who are tired of confrontation, polarised politics and so on. This claim is not new, as an earlier Australia Party (1966-1975) also advanced it. The Australia Party gained its share of publicity but failed to gain votes (it could not secure the election of a Senator even in the favourable circumstances of a double dissolution election in 1974, when all the Senate places were vacant and the quota dropped to 0.1 per cent). The ADP is clearly more successful than the AP, as its votes indicate; but there is no evidence yet that 'the centre' in Australian politics requires a new party.

REFERENCES

Aitkin, D. (1977) Stability and Change in Australian Politics, ANU Press, Canberra
----------(1982) 2nd edition, ANU Press, Canberra
Aitkin, D. and M. Kahan (1974) 'Class Politics in the New World' in R. Rose (ed.), Electoral Behaviour: a Comparative Handbook, Free Press, New York
Alford, R. R. (1964) Party and Society: The Anglo-American Democracies, John Murray, London
Butler, D., H.R. Penniman, and A. Ranney (eds.) (1981), Democracy at the Polls: A Comparative Study of Competitive National Elections, AEI, Washington
Crewe, I. (1981) 'Electoral Participation' in D. Butler et al. (eds.), Democracy at the Polls: A Comparative Study of Competitive National Elections, AEI, Washington

Crewe, I., B. Sarlvick, and J. Alt (1977), 'Partisan Dealignment in Britain', British Journal of Political Science, 7, 129-90

Hughes, C.A. (1977) A Handbook of Australian Government and Politics 1965-1974, ANU Press, Canberra

Hughes, C.A. and B.D. Graham, (1968) A Handbook of Australian Government and Politics 1864-1964, ANU Press, Canberra

Jaensch, D. (1983) The Australian Party System, George Allen and Unwin, Sydney

Kemp, D. (1978) Society and Electoral Behaviour in Australia, University of Queensland Press, Brisbane

Mayer, H. and H. Nelson (eds.) (1980) Australian Politics - A Fifth Reader, Longmans Cheshire, Melbourne

Nie, N.H., S. Verba, and J.R. Petrocik (1979) The Changing American Voter, 2nd edition, Harvard University Press, Cambridge

Pedersen, M. (1979) 'The Dynamics of European Party Systems: Changing Patterns of Electoral Volatility', European Journal of Political Research, 7, 1-26

Rae, D.W. (1967) The Political Consequences of Electoral Laws, Yale University Press, New Haven

Rydon, J. (1980) 'The Electoral System' in H. Mayer and H. Nelson (eds.), (1980), Australian Politics - A Fifth Reader, Longmans Cheshire, Melbourne

Chapter 5

GREAT BRITAIN

Ivor Crewe

INTRODUCTION : THE BRITISH PARTY SYSTEM

It has become almost a cliche that in recent years Britain has undergone a ´partisan dealignment´ characterised by increasing ´electoral volatility´ (among other things). Electoral patterns and party politics in the quarter century after World War II are typically depicted as a neat and tidy binary structure of two classes, two ideologies and two parties bound together and reinforced by the single-member, simple plurality electoral system. This dovetailing of class, ideological and party allegiances formed the framework for an exceptionally stable, evenly-balanced and nationally uniform two-party dominance over the electorate and within Parliament. A degree of democratic responsiveness and accountability was injected into this structure by the benignly exaggerative properties of the electoral system. On the one hand, small parties were badly underrepresented in Parliament, especially if their vote (like the Liberal Party´s) was geographically dispersed rather than locally concentrated. This usually ensured that directly accountable single-party governments could form, confronted by almost single-party opposition. On the other hand, small shifts in the vote for the Conservative and Labour parties were translated into a much larger turnover of seats, thus ensuring that a clear change in the electoral mood would produce a change of government.

A very different picture has been drawn of the post-1970 party system and its electoral base, by myself as well as others (Butler and Stokes, 1975, pp. 206-8; Berrington, 1979; Crewe et al, 1977; Sarlvik and Crewe, 1983; Crewe, 1984a). In this recent era of partisan dealignment, party preferences have been subject to much more

100

short-term change both at and between elections. The change has been geographically uneven and increasingly at the expense of both major parties, especially Labour. Minor parties - the Nationalists in Wales and Scotland, the Liberals and latterly the Social Democratic Party (SDP) - have made modest but apparently lasting breakthroughs. There is accumulating evidence of an ever-loosening fit between class membership, issue positions and party choice, and of issues, including the outgoing government's record, taking over from more enduring factors as the main influence on the vote, especially vote-switching. But these sketches of the pre- and post-1970 periods are so brief as to verge on caricature. The contrasts are not always so clear cut. The purpose of this chapter is, therefore, to shade in the details.(1)

TRENDS IN ELECTORAL VOLATILITY

1945-1970 : A Period of Two-Party Stability

In the eight general elections from 1945 to 1970 voting in Britain displayed three main, inter-connected features (see Tables 5.1-5.3). The first was an almost rock-like stability to the major parties' equal share of the vote, such that elections were decided by tiny fluctuations of Conservative and Labour support. From 1950 to 1970 both parties' share of the vote fell within the narrow six-point range of 43 per cent to 49 per cent, and the average swing (2) between them was only 2.5 per cent. Pedersen's index of volatility averaged a modest 4.6 (see Table 5.1). These slender net changes were magnified by the electoral system into a substantial turnover of seats such as to produce changes of government from one party to the other in 1951 (to the Conservatives), 1964 (back to Labour) and 1970 (back again to the Conservatives). The Liberal share of the vote varied more, but partly as a result of marked changes in the number of candidates it put forward at different elections. As Table 5.1 shows, the average constituency vote share of Liberal candidates fluctuated within a range almost as narrow as that of the major parties.

The second feature of the period 1945-70 was that the ripples of change in vote shares were remarkably uniform, in magnitude as well as direction, across the whole of Britain. In every election but one (1959) at least three-quarters of

Table 5.1: The Parties' Share of Votes and Seats, General Elections 1945-83

	Con	Lab	Lib	Per Lib Cand.	Other	Con+ Lab	Con+Lab Share of Seats
1945	39.4	49.0	9.3	18.6 (306)	2.3	88.4	95.3
1950	43.0	46.8	9.3	12.0 (475)	1.9	89.8	98.0
1951	47.8	48.3	2.6	14.6 (109)	1.3	96.1	99.0
1955	49.3	47.3	2.8	15.4 (110)	0.6	96.6	99.0
1959	48.8	44.6	6.0	17.0 (216)	0.6	93.4	98.9
1964	42.9	44.8	11.5	19.3 (365)	0.8	87.7	98.5
1966	41.4	48.9	8.6	17.0 (311)	1.1	90.3	98.1
1970	46.2	43.9	7.6	14.2 (332)	2.3	90.1	98.7
Feb 1974	38.8	38.0	19.8	23.8 (518)	3.4	76.8	96.0
Oct 1974	36.7	40.3	18.8	19.2 (619)	4.2	77.0	95.7
1979	44.9	37.8	14.1	15.3 (576)	3.2	82.7	97.4
1983	43.4	28.2	25.9	25.9 (633)	2.5	71.6	93.2
Mean	43.6	43.2	11.4	16.8 (381)	2.0	86.7	97.3
Range	36.7-49.3	28.2-49.0	2.6-25.9	12.0-25.9	0.6-4.2	71.6-96.6	93.2-99.0

The column header spans "Share of Total Vote Obtained by:".

Note: Northern Ireland is excluded from this and all other tables.

Table 5.1 (contd.)

	Swing	Pedersen Index		Swing	Pedersen Index
1950	+2.9	3.9	1970	+4.9	6.0
1951	+1.7	6.8	Feb 1974	-0.8	13.3
1955	+1.3	1.7	Oct 1974	-2.2	3.1
1959	+1.1	3.2	1979	+5.4	8.2
1964	-3.1	5.9	1983	+4.1	11.8
1966	-2.8	4.4			
			Mean	2.7	6.2
			Range	0.8-5.4	1.7-13.3

the constituency swings were within 2 per cent of the national median and only a handful of seats bucked the national trend (except, again, for 1959).

To know the swing in Cornwall was to know, within a percentage or two, the swing in the Highlands; to know the results of the first three constituencies to declare on election night, was to know not only which party had won - but by how many seats.

The third feature of the period was that, partly as a result of the first two, the Conservative and Labour parties enjoyed seemingly impregnable dominance over the electorate, and thus over the House of Commons. From 1945 to 1970 the two parties won, on average, 92 per cent of the vote and, because of the electoral system, 98 per cent of the seats. The result was a stable two party system which produced alternating single-party governments. A better example of non-volatility would be difficult to find.

In the 1960s, however, faint stirrings under the calm could be detected. First, intra-election volatility increased (see Table 5.2). The governing party suffered more defeats at by-elections, not only at the hands of the Opposition, but of the Liberals, and the Scottish and Welsh Nationalists won their first post-war seats this way. The mean fall in the governing party's vote share at by-elections, compared with the same constituencies at the preceding general election, rose from two per cent in the 1950-51 and 1955-59 governments, to nine per cent in 1955-59, 14 per cent in 1960-64, and 17 per cent in 1966-70. The oscillations of the opinion polls became sharper, again largely at the expense of the governing party. The trend was cyclical rather than unremitting, but was clear enough. In the three governments of the 1950s the average annual fluctuation was eleven, nine and 14 per cent respectively; in the three governments of the 1960s, eleven, 18 and 19 per cent.

The second movement beneath the surface was the steady erosion of the share of the electorate won by the two main parties combined (see Table 5.3). This increased from 1945 (66.7 per cent) to 1951 (80.3 per cent), but thereafter declined steadily to 64.8 per cent in 1970. The decline in Labour's share of the electorate was particularly noticeable. Thus, although the two main parties' duopoly of votes, seats and office looked impregnable it was based on slowly eroding foundations. The two big party icebergs were beginning to melt a little.

1974-1983 : A Period of Partisan Dealignment

In the four most recent general elections

Table 5.2: Indicators of Volatility of Support between the Conservative and Labour Parties in General Elections, By-elections, and Opinion Polls, 1945–83

Year	National Swing(a)	Mean fall in support for government party in by-elections(d)	Range(c) in Monthly Opinion polls
1945–50	+2.9	4.5	n.a.
1950) 1951)(b)	+1.7	2.0	8.0)10.5 13.0)
1952) 1953) 1954) 1955)	+1.3	1.9	11.0) 6.0) 9.0) 8.5 8.0)
1956) 1957) 1958) 1959)	+1.1	8.8	8.0) 18.0) 16.0)13.6 12.5)
1960) 1961) 1962) 1963) 1964)	-3.1	13.5	9.5) 12.0) 11.5)11.0 9.5) 12.5)
1965) 1966)(b)	-2.8	1.8	18.0) 18.0)18.0
1967) 1968) 1969) 1970)	+4.9	16.8	27.0) 19.0) 17.5)18.9 12.0)
1971) 1972) 1973)	-0.8(f)	13.1	20.5) 10.5)15.3 15.0)
1974(Feb)) 1974(Oct))	-2.2	0.5(e)	23.0) 23.0)23.0
1975) 1976) 1977) 1978) 1979)	+5.4	9.5	21.5) 31.0) 21.5)25.7 16.5) 28.0)

(continued)

Year	National Swing	Mean fall in support for government party in by-elections	Range in Monthly Opinion polls
1980)			13.0)
1981)			36.0)
1982)	+4.1	11.4(g)	31.5)25.4
1983)			21.0)

Notes: (a) Swing is defined as the average of the Conservative percentage gain and the Labour percentage loss in Great Britain.
(b) In the 1950-51 and 1964-66 parliaments Labour was in office but with only a tiny majority. Both periods continued to experience the electoral trends of the previous few years.
(c) Range is measured by the difference between the highest and lowest support for the Conservatives in any one month plus the difference between the highest and lowest support for Labour in any one month. The figures are calculated from Webb and Whybrow (1981, Appendix E).
(d) Calculations for by-elections between 1970 and February 1974 exclude the Speaker's seat, Southampton Itchen, and those cases (N=12) where there was a non-trivial redistribution of constituency boundaries since the previous general election such that meaningful swing figures could not be calculated.
(e) There was only one by-election between February and October 1974.
(f) This is a misleading figure since there was a substantial fall in the vote shares obtained by both the Conservatives (-7.4%) and Labour (-5.9%).
(g) If the three by-elections held during the Falklands War are excluded, the fall is 13.7%.

(February and October 1974, 1979 and 1983) the British electorate appears to have edged away from the patterns of voting that characterised the 1945-70 period. The February 1974 election recorded the largest amount of net volatility since the long-delayed, immediate post-war election of 1945, a volatility at the expense of both main parties. The emerging re-patterning of party support was confirmed by the closely-following election of October 1974. The 1979 election produced the largest national swing between the two main parties - 5.2 per cent from Labour to Conservative - since 1945. And in the most recent election (1983) the total amount of net volatility (23.6) approached the

record set in the unusual circumstances of February
1974 (26.6). This increase in volatility is neatly
summarised by the Pedersen index, which doubled from
a 4.6 average in 1945 to 1970 to a 9.1 average in
the four elections of 1974 to 1983. Intra-election
volatility has also increased. Oscillations in the
regular opinion polls have become sharper, creating
fresh post-war records in 1976, 1979 and 1981 (see
Table 5.2). The 1979-1983 Parliament offers some
good examples. In the space of eighteen months, for
instance, each of the three parties - the
Conservatives, Labour and the newly-formed
Liberal/SDP Alliance - at some stage held a
double-digit lead in the monthly Gallup polls yet
saw their support fluctuate by over 20 percentage

Table 5.3: The Major Parties' Share of the
Electorate, General Elections 1945-83

Percent of total electorate
obtained by:

	Con	Lab	Con+Lab
1945	29.7	37.0	66.7
1950	36.2	39.3	75.5
1951	39.5	40.8	80.3
1955	37.9	36.4	74.3
1959	38.5	35.3	73.8
1964	33.1	34.6	67.7
1966	31.5	37.2	68.7
1970	33.2	31.6	64.8
Feb 1974	30.7	30.0	60.7
Oct 1974	26.8	29.3	56.1
1979	34.2	28.7	62.9
1983	31.6	20.6	52.2
Mean	33.6	33.4	67.0
Range	26.8- 39.5	28.7- 40.8	56.1- 80.3

Notes: These figures are based on the registered
electorate in Great Britain which includes people
who have died, emigrated or moved out of the
constituency by the time an election takes place.
Adjustment for the age of the register at the time
of an election would raise the figures (by 4% on
average) but not alter the direction or magnitude of
the trend over the period.

points. At first sight the fall in the governing
party's share of the vote at by-elections appears to
be less marked in the period after 1970 than in the
1960s. However, when adjustment is made for the
lower general election base against which
by-election support is compared, the fall turns out
to be more serious, not less.(3) Wavering has also
increased. The proportion of respondents who
'seriously thought of voting for another party
during the campaign' averaged 22 per cent in the
three elections of 1964, 1966 and 1970, stayed the
same in the two 1974 elections but rose to 31 per
cent in 1979. The proportions of respondents who
left the decision on how to vote until the campaign
averaged 14 per cent in 1964-70, jumped to 22 per
cent in the two 1974 elections, and again to 28 per
cent in 1979. Unfortunately, comparable data for
1983 do not exist.

    This electoral instability has been accompanied
by a geographical unevenness unknown since the
1920s. In the two 1974 elections the party system
in Scotland was transformed by the advance of the
Scottish Nationalists (on which see David Denver's
chapter). In addition, the party landscape in rural
and suburban England, especially in the South,
looked substantially different because of the
emergence of the Liberals as major challengers to
the Conservatives. In the 1979 election there were
even more marked discrepancies between the regions
(especially between Scotland, the North and the
South), but also within regions between the major
cities and their rural and small town hinterlands.
The standard deviation of constituency swings was
the highest since the war (Curtice and Steed, 1980,
pp.394-95); and the number of different local
factors that appear to have acted as a brake or
accelerator on national swing was greater than in
any post-war election. These geographical patterns
re-emerged in 1983. The more middle class,
suburban, rural and Southern a constituency the
bigger the drop in the Labour vote and the higher
the level of Alliance support. As a result the 1983
election left two two-party systems 'on the ground'.
Throughout the South (except for inner London), as
well as in the suburbs and the countryside in
Britain generally, the Alliance was the main, if not
always very threatening, challenger to the
Conservatives, with Labour trailing in third -
frequently a very poor third - place. In industrial
and urban Britain outside the South, however, the
real contest continued to be between the

107

Conservative and Labour parties, with the Alliance occupying a clear third place.

Of more importance, the February 1974 election cracked the Conservative and Labour parties' post-war grip on the electorate. The Conservative share of the vote slumped to its lowest level since 1906; eight months later it fell further still. Labour's vote share in February 1974 also ebbed to its lowest level since 1931. The major parties have not managed to re-establish their earlier dominance within the electorate in the decade that has since elapsed. Although the Conservative vote recovered in 1979, and only slipped a little in 1983, it did not revert to its pre-1970 levels. Its recent landslide victory was based on its third lowest share of the electorate this century. For Labour these four elections mark its worst performance since the early 1920s, when it was replacing the Liberal Party as the principal opposition to the Conservatives in the wake of the 1918 extension of the franchise to almost all adult men and women.(4) Its 28.2 per cent vote in 1983 in fact constituted the worst vote per Labour candidate since the party was founded in 1900.

These changes are reflected in the downward trend of the two-party proportion of the vote. In 1945-70 it averaged 92 per cent; in the two 1974 elections it fell to 77 per cent and in 1983 it dropped further to 72 per cent. The two-party share of the electorate has descended down a parallel path, dropping from 71 per cent between 1945-70 to 61 per cent in February 1974, 56 per cent eight months later and to 52 per cent in 1983. By the last election, therefore, the supposedly major parties could only persuade half the registered electorate to vote for them. The portion of the vote and of the electorate captured by the Liberals has correspondingly increased in fits and starts; in 1983 the Liberal-SDP vote was the Centre's best performance for half a century. Thus the 1974 elections do appear to mark a break in the post-war pattern of party support and net volatility, albeit not a dramatic one. The Conservative and Labour icebergs went on melting - and melting faster.

Overall Volatility Since 1945

Following the now classic analysis of Butler and Stokes (1975, pp. 247-275) I shall divide overall electoral volatility into the following four components:

1. Direct switching between the Conservative and Labour parties.

2. The circulation of Liberals and other minor party supporters, i.e. the two-way traffic between each major party and the Liberals, or another minor party (e.g. the Scottish Nationalists or Plaid Cymru). Note that this component will incorporate some involuntary volatility as a result of variations in the number and location of minor party candidates from one election to another. A Liberal voter at one election without a Liberal candidate to vote for at the next has no choice but to switch votes.

3. The circulation of non-voters i.e. changes from voting to non-voting (the net impact of abstention) or vice versa (the net impact of turnout). Non-voting includes abstention for technical and virtually involuntary reasons (e.g. sickness, absence abroad) but not ineligibility to vote at one or other election.

4. The physical replacement of the electorate: the electorate is subject to constant renewal (through coming of age and immigration) and depletion (through deaths and emigration). An elector who votes at one election but is ineligible to do so at the prior or subsequent election is by definition a ´volatile´ voter. The contribution of the physical replacement of the electorate to gross volatility will obviously depend on the length of time between two elections: the longer the interval the larger the proportion of electors who leave or enter the electorate in the intervening period. These four categories exhaust the components of volatility with the exception of switches between different minor parties - a negligible proportion of the British (although not Scottish or Welsh) electorate.

The availability of panel data on each of the six pairs of elections from 1959 to 1979 (there is no 1979-83 panel) makes it possible to reach some tentative conclusions about the nature of short-term overall volatility over this twenty year period. We turn first to questions of magnitude. What is the general level of gross volatility? Has the electorate gradually become more fickle, as the developments in the 1970s might suggest? And if so,

Table 5.4: Rates of Individual Constancy and Change Between Each Pair of Elections, 1959-79

	1959-64	1964-66	1966-70	1970-Feb 1974	(1970-Oct 1974)	Feb 1974-Oct 1974	Oct 1974-1979
	%	%	%	%	%	%	%
Remained constant by twice:							
Voting for major party							
Conservative	26)	26)	24)	23)	(21))	22)	21)
	)51	)55	)47	)43	)(41)	)45	)42
Labour	25)	29)	23)	20)	(20))	23)	21)
Voting for Liberal or minor party	2	4	3	4	(4)	10	7
Abstaining	11	15	16	11	(13)	14	13
Total Constant	64	74	66	58	(58)	69	62
Changed by moving between:							
Conservative and Labour	5	3	5	5	(3)	1	4
Conservative or Labour and Liberal or Nationalist	7	4	4	8	(7)	8	9
Voting and Abstention*	24	19	25	29	(32)	22	25

Notes: * Also includes a very small number of switchers between minor parties e.g. Liberal and Nationalist. Data for 1979-83 cannot be provided as there was no 1979-83 panel study.
Sources: for 1959-64, Butler and Stokes 1964 cross-section sample; 1964-66, Butler and Stokes 1964-66 panel sample; 1966-1970, Butler and Stokes 1966-70 panel sample; 1970-Feb 1974, British Election Study 1970-Feb 1974 panel sample; 1970-Oct 1974, BES October 1974 cross-section sample; Feb-Oct 1974, BES Feb-Oct 1974 panel sample; Oct 1974-1979, BES Oct 1974-1979 panel sample.

what form has the growth in this volatility taken?
Answers are provided by Table 5.4 which presents the
rates of individual constancy and change for each
pair of consecutive elections between 1959 and 1979.
Change resulting from the physical replacement of
the electorate is excluded since its magnitude is a
function of the length of time between elections,
not of changes in individual preference.

As expected, the figures reveal that the
overall amount of vote-switching in the electorate
is far greater - by a factor of nine or ten - than
the net volatility between the two main parties. It
ranges from 26 per cent to 42 per cent. Just under
half the electorate entitled to vote at both
elections were consistent supporters of either major
party; only one in twenty was a consistent Liberal
or Nationalist; between 11 and 16 per cent
consecutively abstained. Thus little more than half
the electorate provide the parties with consistent
support over a pair of elections; over three or more
elections, the proportion will be less.

It is noticeable that the figures reveal the
same broad pattern over the entire twenty year
period, barely reflecting the marked changes in
party fortunes in the 1970s. There is only the
slenderest increase in overall volatility. The
proportion switching votes rose from 36 per cent in
1959-1964 and 34 per cent in 1966-1970 to 42 per
cent in 1970-February 1974 and 38 per cent in
1974-1979. Not surprisingly, the level of vote
switching was lower in the short gap between the two
1974 elections (31 per cent), although the gentle
growth of electoral inconstancy is reflected in the
fact that it exceeded the level for the previous
short Parliament of 1964-1966 (26 per cent).

However, the little erosion of voting stability
that has occurred has taken the form that might be
expected from developments in the 1970s - a gentle
ebbing of constant support for the two main parties.
The level drops from 51 per cent in 1959-1964, to
47 per cent in 1966-1970, and down again to 43 per
cent in 1970-February 1974 and 42 per cent in
1974-1979: a persistent if modest trend. A
comparison between 1964-1966 and February-October
1974 is again instructive: although there were
fewer, and so presumably more committed, major party
supporters in February 1974 than 1964, and although
the interval between the two 1974 elections was
exceptionally short, consistent Labour and
Conservative voting was less in evidence on the
second occasion (45 per cent) than the first (55 per

cent). A corresponding slight increase in regular
Liberal and minor party voting has occurred. If
proper account is taken of the varying intervals
between pairs of elections, the short-term overall
volatility figures for 1959-1979 constitute clear
although unspectacular evidence of a declining
public commitment to the two governing parties.

If, as Table 5.4 suggests, British electors
have become less willing to cast a regular vote, to
what pattern of volatility are they turning? The
figures establish that direct switching between the
major parties has not increased. This purest form
of volatility continues to be the exception: there
is still very little crossing of the major partisan
divide. The table also reveals that despite the
trebling of the Liberal vote between 1970 and 1974,
and its continuation eight months later, there was
only a small increase in the velocity of Liberal
circulation; in fact it was no greater than during
the earlier Liberal resurgence between 1959 and
1964. The form of electoral volatility which
continues to account for the large part of all
electoral instability is movement to and from
abstention: at both the beginning and end of the
twenty year period it accounted for one elector in
four and two changers in three. The volatility of
the British electorate would thus appear to rest
less upon its changing choice of party than upon its
choice of whether to vote at all.

From questions of magnitude we turn to the
question of partisan advantage, by exploring the
contribution of different components of electoral
change to the fluctuating fortunes of the two major
parties over the last twenty years. Do some
components of change regularly help one major party
rather than the other, whatever the overall
direction of change? Or do all components feed into
the general stream of change, albeit in different
degrees, thus producing an overall vote _flow_ rather
than overall vote _flux_? Or do both patterns
co-exist, with some components always helping the
same party, and others always conforming to the
overall trend? We can begin to answer such
questions by inspecting Table 5.5 which presents the
magnitude and direction of the components of major
party change for each pair of consecutive elections
between 1959 and 1979. For this purpose the four
components of volatility listed earlier are refined
into six: (1) direct switching (2) circulation of
Liberals (3) circulation of minor party supporters
(4) differential turnout (5) differential abstention

112

Table 5.5: Components of Major Party Change for each Pair of Successive Elections, 1959-79

Component of major party change	1959-64	1964-66	1966-70	1970-Feb74	Feb74-Oct74	Oct74-1979
Straight conversion	-0.6	-3.2	+4.8	0.0	0.0	+3.4
Circulation of Libs						
Defection to Libs	-1.5)	+0.3)	+0.4)	+0.7)	-1.1)	+0.5)
Recruitment from Libs	+0.3)-1.2	+0.5)+0.8	+0.8)+1.2	+0.2)+0.9	-0.4)-1.5	+2.0)+2.5
Other Circulation	n.a.	n.a.	n.a.	+0.4	-0.3	-0.1
Differential turnout	-1.6)	-0.9)	0.0)	-0.2)	-1.1)	+2.5)
Differential abstention	+0.8)-0.8	-0.7)-1.6	+2.8)+2.8	+0.5)+0.3	+0.2)-0.9	+0.5)+3.0
Replacement of the Electorate						
New Electors	-0.6)	-0.4)	-2.4)	-2.1)	-0.3)	-1.0)
Electors died/emigrated	-1.1)-1.7	0.0)-0.4	+0.1)-2.3	-0.2)-2.3	0.0)-0.3	-0.4)-1.4
	-4.3	-4.4	+6.5	-0.7	-3.0	+7.4

Notes: n.a. = not ascertained; + = change in favour of Conservatives, - = change in favour of Labour.

Sources: As for Table 5.4.

and (6) the physical replacement of the electorate. In addition the components are defined only in relation to support for the Conservative and Labour parties, since the aim is to explore the contribution of each component to the fluctuating fortunes of the two main parties. With no more than six pairs of elections, and a swing to the Conservatives at only two of them, the data are far from ideal. Moreover, the variations of time between elections affect the proportions entering and departing from the electorate and therefore the amount of major party change attributable to such turnover. Nevertheless, a number of patterns over the twenty year period do emerge.

A glance down each column reveals, first, that in none of the elections did every component of change benefit the same party. The net change in the percentage lead of one major party over the other was always less than the overall change that contributed to it. The higher-swinging elections (1964, 1966, 1970 and 1979) were marked by relatively more uniformity in the direction taken by the different components of change, but not one escaped counter-trends. There was always <u>flux</u> as well as <u>flow</u>. In Labour's comfortable victory year of 1966, for example, the Conservatives managed to benefit slightly from the circulation of Liberal votes; at its decisive defeat at the following election Labour still gained substantially from the replacement of the electorate. In every election, therefore, runaway victories and humiliating defeats have been partially forestalled by the existence of small electoral movements against the overall trend.

Not only did one or two components of change always flow against the general current; no components conformed to the net major party change in all six elections. It proves impossible to say, at least for the period under discussion, that whichever party benefitted from one component of change would win the election - or even be the party on the upswing. Of all the components of change differential turnout came closest to moving in tandem with the general trend, the only exception being 1970 when its net impact was nil. This probably reflects the susceptibility of intermittent, uncommitted voters to immediate partisan forces rather than the two parties' relative ability to mobilise non-voters. It is possible, however, to pick out a number of components of change which appear to help one party rather than the other. First, there was an almost continuous trickle of Liberals defecting to the Conservatives' advantage, suggesting, perhaps, a permanent movement to the Right among electors as they mature. In addition, differential abstention – non-voting by previous voters – worked against Labour at every election except 1966 (when Labour had its best election in the two decades). The element of electoral change most conspicuous for its partisan bias, however, was the physical replenishment of the electorate. At every election the increment of new electors preferred Labour to the Conservatives, usually by a substantial margin, such as to save it from yet deeper humiliation in 1970 and 1979 and to hoist it into office in the close-run elections of 1964 and February 1974.(5)

A CASE STUDY : THE SOFTNESS OF THE LIBERAL VOTE

For our final exploration of short-term electoral volatility we turn from the telescope to the microscope, in order to illuminate an important feature of electoral volatility (and the party system) in Britain: the 'softness' of the Liberal, and latterly the combined Liberal and SDP, vote.(6) (For simplicity's sake, the 1983 Liberal-SDP Alliance vote will usually be referred to as the 'Liberal' vote in this section).

Between 1945 and 1970 the Liberal share of the vote, especially the vote share per Liberal candidate, stayed fairly constant. Butler and Stokes (1969, Ch.14) showed how this was the outcome of exceptional volatility, not stability, at the individual level. Through an unequal exchange rate between the Liberal party and the two major parties, the Liberal vote kept in 'balance': at each election the Liberals would lose a substantial proportion of its prior voters, but replace them with smaller proportions of prior Conservative or Labour voters. The process could be compared with a continuously running bath with the plug out: the Liberal votes lost through the plug hole were constantly replenished by new votes from the Conservative and Labour taps, the precise water level depending on the balance of in-flow and out-flow. Thus, compared with the two major parties the Liberal vote consisted of a small core and a large periphery.

The five elections from 1970 to 1983 provide an ideal case study for further exploration of this phenomenon: they cover a period in which the Liberal vote first advanced, then retreated and finally, in alliance with the SDP re-advanced to new heights;

there was less variation in the number of Liberal (or Alliance) candidates and two elections were held very close together. The rise and fall of the aggregate Liberal vote is summarised in Table 5.6.

Table 5.6: The Liberal Vote 1970-83

	1970	Feb 1974	Oct 1974	1979	1983
Total Lib. Vote (000s)	2,117	6,060	5,347	4,305	7,781
% of total vote (Great Britain)	7.6	19.8	18.8	14.1	25.8
Vote share per candidate	14.2	23.8	19.2	15.3	25.8

Note: For 1983 Liberal and SDP votes are combined and the votes of three Independent Liberals who stood against official (SDP) Alliance are excluded.

It trebled between 1970 and February 1974, was approximately the same eight months later, fell back in 1979 without returning to its 1970 level, and then nearly doubled in 1983, rising beyond its previous post-war peak of February 1974. Only a small part of this trend can be attributed to the lower number of Liberal candidates in 1970 than later, as the trend in the vote share per Liberal candidate shows. We can therefore investigate the extent to which, if at all, the Liberal vote ´firmed up´ in 1974 and after. As support for the two main parties declined in the 1970s, did ´core´ Liberal support grow?

Table 5.7 sets out, for each of the six pairs of elections between 1959 and 1979 the <u>retention</u> and <u>recruitment</u> rates of each of the three parties. The table shows that the two major parties have much higher retention rates that the Liberal party. The rates fluctuate a little according to whether the party was on the up or down swing, but on average both major parties could count on keeping three-quarters of their vote from any one election to the next; the Liberals, by contrast, could not count on keeping as much as half. The recruitment rates of the three parties follow the opposite pattern. They too fluctuate according to the partisan climate at each election. But, on average, only one out of four Conservative or Labour voters is a recruit, compared with one out of two Liberal voters. Thus the Conservative and Labour vote is

116

Table 5.7: Vote Retention and Recruitment Rates for each Pair of Elections 1959-79

	1959–64	1964–66	1966–70	1970 Feb 74	Feb 1974–Oct 74	Oct 1974–1979	Average 1959–79
Conservative retention rate	68	78	80	70	73	81	75
Labour retention rate	72	85	63	63	76	72	72
Liberal retention rate	44	45	38	64	52	41	47
Conservative recruitment rate	21	19	30	28	18	41	26
Labour recruitment rate	26	22	22	31	22	25	25
Liberal recruitment rate	77	40	53	78	41	46	57

Notes: Retention rate is defined as the proportion of those voting for a party at the first election who were eligible to vote at the second and who stayed with the same party. The recruitment rate is the proportion of a party's voters at one election who voted differently or abstained at the previous election. In both cases only those eligible to vote at both elections are included.
Sources: As Table 5.4.

117

fairly firm, with only a moderate proportion being
newly won or lost at any one election. The two
blocks of votes still look like icebergs even if
they melt and re-freeze more than the net figures
suggest. The Liberal vote is much softer, with
large proportions newly won or lost at each
election.

These features of the three parties´ support,
moreover, have not changed over the last twenty
years. The Liberal retention rate was not higher at
the end of the period than at the beginning.
Indeed, the elections of the 1970s only serve to
re-emphasise the lability of the Liberal vote. For
example, even between 1970 and February 1974, when
the Liberal vote trebled and both major parties lost
votes heavily, the Liberals´ retention rate was no
higher than that of the other two parties. And in
1979, when the party´s fortunes had slipped
unusually low, after two elections at which they
were exceptionally high, almost half its vote (46
per cent) consisted of fresh recruits.

Most illuminating of all, however, is the
massive discontinuity of Liberal voting between
February and October 1974. A more striking instance
of the disparity between net and gross electoral
change would be hard to find. Aggregate Liberal
support over the eight months gave every indication
of stability, slipping a mere one per cent. But as
Table 5.7 shows, the Liberal party was abandoned by
almost half (48 per cent) of its February 1974
supporters - about three million voters - a mere
eight months later, yet attracted over two million
new voters within the same brief interval. Although
less than one voter in five was a Liberal at either
election, one in three (32 per cent) cast a Liberal
vote at least once. No other party (not even other
minor parties like the Nationalists) is subject to
so much displacement; even non-voters show more
consistency. The Liberal party is distinguished for
the rapidity with which it can simultaneously win
and lose large segments of the electorate.

Finally, we can explore the longer-term impact
of the Liberal surge in 1974. How many of the
Liberal recruits to the major parties stayed Liberal
five years later when its fortunes were low? In
fact, most of the Liberal party´s 1974 recruits had
deserted it by 1979. For every ten who moved to the
Liberals in either February 1974 or in October 1974,
seven had moved away again by 1979. Of those who
switched to the Liberal party in February 1974, and
stayed with it in October 1974, over half had left

by 1979. Indeed, even amongst the ´core´ of thrice-voting Liberals the attrition rate in 1979 was 30 per cent - higher than amongst their Conservative and Labour counterparts (nine and 21 per cent respectively). Thus the Liberal party´s rise in popularity in 1974 did produce some enduring gains over the rest of the decade; nonetheless electoral progress for the Liberals took the slow and frustrating form of three steps forward, two steps back.

The lack of 1979-83 panel data unfortunately precludes precise comparisons with the 1983 election. Nonetheless, the ´impure´ evidence of recall data suggests that the pattern of retention and recruitment for previous elections did not change significantly. For example, the Alliance´s retention rate in the 1983 election was 72 per cent, compared with 77 per cent for the Conservatives and 63 per cent for Labour. Now at first glance this might appear significantly higher than in the 1960s and 1970s. It does exceed that recorded at any earlier election for the Liberals and, for the first time, surpasses that of a major party. But in the circumstances of the 1983 election it is less impressive: the Alliance´s vote rose steeply after the Liberals´ unexceptional 1979 performance; there had been two years of intense media coverage of the SDP breakaway, its partnership with the Liberals and the Alliance´s surge in the opinion polls and by-election victories; there was even speculation about a possible Alliance government. Yet more than a quarter (28%) of 1979 Liberal voters could not bring themselves to continue voting for their party, or its SDP partner, despite its being on the upswing, a mere four years later.(7)

Table 5.8: Direction and Strength of Party Identification, 1979 and 1983

Strength of party identi-fication	Direction of Party Identification					
	Conservative		Liberal		Labour	
	1979	1983	1979	1983	1979	1983
	%	%	%	%	%	%
Very strong	23	37	23	16	27	35
Fairly strong	53	44	48	55	50	41
Not very strong	24	19	39	29	23	25
N of cases	719	1562	208	587	681	1342

Sources: BES 1979 election survey; BBC TV/Gallup election survey, 8-9 June,1983.

The pattern of volatility in the Liberal vote described above suggests two large, hard-packed voting blocs with a smaller, looser cluster of Liberal support in between. This picture is reinforced by the relationship between party identification and vote. Three features of this relationship are worth noting. First, compared with their major party counterparts, Liberal identifiers are much weaker in their partisanship (Table 5.8). In both 1979 and 1983 Liberal (and SDP) identifiers were only half as likely as Conservative or Labour identifiers to describe themselves as 'very strong' identifiers. As a result, secondly, they are more likely at elections to vote for another party. Almost a third did in 1979 (30%), compared with five and 13 per cent of Conservative and Labour identifiers respectively. Even in the Liberals' boom election year of 1983, when every constituency was contested by the Liberal party or its SDP partner, the vote defection rate was 16 per cent among Liberal and SDP identifiers compared with ten per cent among Conservatives (but 24 per cent among Labour identifiers). Thus Liberal identifiers do not resemble a hard-core minority resistant to the pull of the big parties – even when the political climate is favourable.

Thirdly, a similar observation can be made of Liberal <u>voters</u>. In 1979 almost 40 per cent of Liberal voters, and in 1983 as many as half did not identify with the Alliance parties, which suggests that they were new and potentially short-lived recruits, whereas the non-identifying proportion of Conservative and Labour voters never exceeded 20 per cent at either election. Thus of the 12 per cent of voters in 1979 (and the 14 per cent in 1983) whose party identification and vote did not coincide, three quarters (two thirds in 1983) are solely accounted for by Liberals – the 'soft Centre'.

The large defection rate among Liberal and SDP identifiers is conventionally attributed to the electoral system. By severely under-representing the Alliance parties in Parliament, and thus artificially sustaining its small-minority status, it allegedly discourages potential supporters from 'wasting' their vote on its behalf. Unable to convert votes into seats, the Liberal party (and SDP) are unable to convert sympathy into votes. This argument is consistently supported by the survey evidence.(8) However, it is also arguable that it is precisely the party's innocuous status that allows it to attract so large a proportion of its vote from Conservative and Labour identifiers. Because the Liberal party is not seen as a likely government, or government partner, it is regarded as a safe haven of protest.

Table 5.9: Party Identification and 'Negative Partisanship', 1979

Direction and Strength of Party Identification	% of each row category of voters who are 'very strongly against':		
	Conservative Party	Liberal Party	Labour Party
Conservatives			
Very strong	--	10	76
Fairly strong	--	8	47
Not very strong	--	4	26
All	--	8	49
Liberals			
Very strong	39	--	27
Fairly strong	15	--	26
Not very strong	5	--	18
All	14	--	23
Labour			
Very strong	69	13	--
Fairly strong	38	6	--
Not very strong	14	4	--
All	41	7	--

This possibility is prompted by the configuration of the strength of positive identification with, and strength of negative identification against, all three parties (see Table 5.9). It shows (for 1979), as one would expect, that strength of attachment to one major party is associated with strength of hostility towards the other major party. The Liberal party, however, is subject to a different pattern of relationships, being both the object and source of much weaker negative feelings. Liberal identifiers, however strong their attachments, are less likely to be 'strongly against' either of the two main parties (in 1979 a mere two per cent were strongly against both); in turn the Liberal party is less likely to be strongly rejected by Conservative or Labour identifiers. Towards the end of the paper we shall see that this pattern is repeated in terms of party supporters' policy positions. It is not surprising, therefore, that the Liberal party and more recently, the Liberal-SDP Alliance, should be such a busy terminus - for both arrivals and departures - on the main party line.

EXPLANATIONS FOR ELECTORAL VOLATILITY IN BRITAIN

Psychological Sources of Electoral Volatility

A large part of the overall volatility between any two elections arises from the response of electors to short-term factors - the issues, events and personalities of the election campaign. Judgement of the out-going government's record is especially important. James Alt (1978, Ch.7) shows, for example, that much of the two-party swing at any one election can be accounted for by the electorate's judgement of the economic record of the party in office, partially discounted by its judgement of the future economic performance of both parties. A detailed analysis of the contribution of these and other short-term factors at each election cannot be undertaken here. But anyway, explanations of this sort leave important questions unanswered. In particular, they cannot explain why the swing in British elections, although higher in the 1970s and 1980s than in the 1960s or 1950s, remains relatively low, given the incontrovertible failure of successive governments to halt Britain's economic and international decline. If short-term factors are so crucial, why have post-war elections not resulted in consecutive landslides and/or sustained major breakthroughs for the Liberals and Nationalists?

The answer, of course, is that deeply held attachments to the two main parties do still exist. They sustain the loyalties of most Conservative and Labour supporters in times of doubt or disillusion, and thus protect each party from the full electoral consequences of a spell of unpopular government. They underpin the stability of the party system by breaking the amplitude of swing, and by resisting the blandishments of 'flash' parties. But did the 1970s witness a diminishing of such attachments? And if so, what is the connection, if any, between this decline and the moderate growth of volatility in the 1970s?

Simplifying radically, three sources of enduring party attachments can be distinguished: psychological, social and ideological. 'Psychological' sources refer to the attachments induced by family upbringing and neighbourhood tradition, reinforced by processes of selective perception over the elector's lifetime. 'Social'

sources refer to the attachments engendered by an
elector´s sense of belonging (or not belonging) to a
social group whose interests are seen as represented
by the party. And ´ideological´ sources refer to
the attachments produced by an affinity between the
elector´s opinions and values on the one hand and
the party´s policies and objectives on the other.
Each of these shall be examined in turn.

This section on psychological sources of
enduring party attachments will refer to trends in
the incidence and intensity of identification with
the two major parties, as measured by the standard
party identification questions.(9) This familiar
variable has proved an excellent surrogate for many
aspects of partisan behaviour, in particular
electoral constancy and its shadow, volatility.
(See Sarlvik and Crewe, 1983, pp. 295-300 and Crewe,
1980).

Table 5.10 displays the level and strength of
Conservative and Labour party identification from
1964 to 1983 and reveals a marked loosening in the
electorate´s psychological bonds to the two parties.
In 1964 two thirds of the electorate (66 per cent)
were ´fairly´ or ´very´ strong Conservative or
Labour identifiers - committed partisans, in other
words - whereas two decades later the proportion had
dropped to well under half (45 per cent). There are
technical reasons for believing that the real
decline may have been steeper still.(10)

This general picture of attenuating ties to the
two parties needs to be qualified in various ways.
First, the willingness of respondents to give
themselves some kind of party identification, weak
or strong, major or minor, has lessened only
slightly and remains remarkably widespread (86 per
cent in 1983). Much smaller proportions of the
electorate volunteer, or, after pressing yield a
class or religious identification. Positive
repudiation of the party alternatives, or
indifference between them, has not grown to
significant levels; instead the evidence suggests a
mature party system familiar to and accepted by the
mass electorate. Secondly, the proportion
identifying with the two main parties has fallen,
but not by much, from 81-82 per cent in the 1960s to
a still high 70 per cent in 1983. Indeed,
identification with the minor parties, despite their
eruptions of support at elections, barely changed
over the twenty years. The drop in the incidence of
major party identification from 1964 to 1983 (one
per cent) was therefore less than the fall in the

Table 5.10: The Incidence and Strength of Party Identification, 1964-83

	1964	1966	1970	Feb+Oct 1974	1979	1983
% with a party identification	93	91	90	90	90	86
% identify with Con	38	35	40	35	38	38
% identify with Lab	43	46	42	40	38	32
	81	81	82	75	76	70
Strength of Identification						
All Electors	%	%	%	%	%	%
Very Strong	44	44	42	26	22	26
Fairly Strong	38	38	37	50	46	38
Not very Strong	11	9	11	14	23	22
No identification	7	9	10	10	10	14
Mean Strength*	2.19	2.17	2.11	1.92	1.81	1.76
Con identifiers only	%	%	%	%	%	%
Very Strong	48	49	50	29	23	34
Fairly Strong	41	39	40	50	53	43
Not very Strong	11	12	10	21	24	23
Lab identifiers only	%	%	%	%	%	%
Very Strong	45	50	47	37	27	32
Fairly Strong	43	41	40	44	50	39
Not very Strong	12	9	13	19	23	29

Note: * Mean partisan strength is based on scoring 'very strong'= 3, 'fairly strong'= 2, 'not very strong'= 1 and no identification = 0.
Sources: 1964, 1966, 1970: Butler and Stokes' election surveys (cross-sectional samples); Feb. 1974, Oct 1974, 1979: BES (cross-sectional samples); 1983: BBC TV/ Gallup election survey.

major party share of the vote (-15 per cent) or of the electorate (-16 per cent). The figures are testimony to the glacially slow rate at which a major party in Britain is finally abandoned by the electorate. In the era of partisan dealignment between ten and 20 per cent more electors continue to think of themselves as Conservative or Labour than actually vote for them; many more neglect or defy their party loyalties than abandon them. The two parties retain a sizeable base from which to recover temporary losses of support, and prophecies of collapse are clearly premature.

However, what has markedly declined over the past two decades is the <u>strength</u> of psychological ties to the parties. Scoring 'very strong' identifiers 3, the 'fairly strong' 2, 'not very strong' 1 and those without a party identification zero, the electorate's mean partisan strength has fallen at each election, from 2.19 in 1964 to 1.76 in 1983. The proportion of 'very strong' Conservative and Labour identifiers has almost halved, from 40 per cent in 1960s to 23 per cent in 1983; the proportion of 'not very strong' Conservative and Labour identifiers has almost doubled, from nine to 17 per cent. Only one elector in five can now be described as a truly committed, unswerving Conservative or Labour loyalist.

This loosening of ties has occurred, moreover, at a uniform rate within both parties, and irrespective of sex, social class and, more important, age. The patterns within age categories and age cohorts ('generations') are worth closer attention, however, because they provide some clues about the partisan strength of the electorate in the future. Table 5.11 sets out the mean partisan strength of identical, overlapping, eight-year age categories for each election from 1964 to 1979 (the two 1974 elections are combined). Two main patterns emerge. One is the long-known tendency for partisanship, at any one time, to be stronger among the old than the young (see the columns); this is true for all the elections covered here. The other, as already mentioned, is the evenness of the rate of partisan weakening within the same age <u>category</u> (as opposed to cohort) across the 1964-79 period (see the rows). Thus at each election (except 1979) the electorate has been injected with a batch of young, first-time electors whose partisanship has been successively weaker:

1964	1966	1970	Feb/Oct 1974	1979	1983
1.97	1.95	1.82	1.72	1.77	1.58

This does <u>not</u> mean that the overall weakening of partisanship can be pinned onto the younger generation alone, since similar (or slightly higher) rates of weakening have occurred amongst those in their thirties, forties, fifties and sixties. But

Table 5.11: Mean Partisan Strength Scores of Eight-Year Overlapping Age-Cohorts, 1964-79

Age Group	First entered Electorate In	1964	1966	1970	Feb & Oct 1974 (average)	1979	Age-Cohort Differences 1964-79	Age-group Differences 1964-79
18-25	1958-64 (20-27)	1.97 (1.97)	1.95	1.82	1.72	1.77		-.20
22-29	1954-61 (24-31)	1.96 (1.97)	1.95	1.86	1.73	1.81	+.09	-.15
26-33	1950-57 (28-35)	1.97 (1.98)	1.94	1.90	1.77	1.83	+.01	-.14
30-37	1946-53 (32-39)	2.03 (2.04)	1.96	1.97	1.83	1.83	-.12	-.20
34-41	1942-49 (36-43)	2.10 (2.13)	2.17	2.06	1.87	1.88	-.09	-.22
38-45	1938-45 (40-47)	2.18 (2.21)	2.18	2.16	1.88	1.94	-.03	-.24
42-49	1934-42	2.22	2.24	2.23	1.90	1.97	-.01	-.25

(continued)

Table 5.11 (contd)

Age Group	First entered Electorate In	1964	1966	1970	Feb & Oct 1974 (average)	1979	Age-Cohort Differences 1964-79	Age-group Differences 1964-79
46-53	(44-51)	2.21	2.23	2.25	1.96	1.99	-.05	-.22
	1930-37	(2.22)						
50-57	(48-55)	2.23	2.24	2.28	2.01	2.02	-.11	-.21
	1926-33	(2.21)						
54-61	(52-59)	2.28	2.27	2.32	2.02	2.06	-.15	-.22
	1922-29	(2.24)						
55-65	(55-63)	2.35	2.29	2.38	2.07	2.09	-.13	-.26
	1918-22	(2.32)						
	(60-67)	(2.37)						
62-69		2.36	2.32	2.44	2.14	2.11	-.10	-.25
66-73		2.35	2.37	2.48	2.18	2.12	-.12	-.23
70-77		2.38	2.41	2.44	2.17	2.20	-.12	-.18
74-81		2.42	2.44	2.43	2.18	2.29	-.08	-.13
ALL		2.19	2.17	2.11	1.92	1.81		

Notes: The entries in each column are smoothed from raw data by setting each cell entry equal to the average of itself and its two nearest neighbours, except for entries on the ends of columns, which represent the average of self and single nearest neighbour. The overlap of age-groups is for the purpose of reducing sampling error resulting from small numbers. (All numbers were never less than 100 except for the 74-81 age group). The figures in parentheses should be used for 1964 if the reader wishes to follow the progress of an age cohort. All respondents includes those aged 82 and above.

it does mean an increased probability (although no certainty) that the electorate´s overall partisanship will <u>continue</u> to weaken. The partisan weakening that arises from the dying out of staunchly loyal older generations is now less likely to be balanced by the stiffening of attachments amongst younger generations. This is partly because the more recent cohorts of new electors have slightly more catching up to do; but mainly because the normal process of partisan consolidation as electors mature through their thirties and forties has been retarded in the last fifteen years by countervailing forces. This can be clearly seen by comparing the difference in partisan strength between two age-groups who are sixteen years apart in the same year of 1964 with the difference in partisan strength of the same age cohort over the (almost-sixteen year) period of 1964-79. For example, in 1964 the partisanship amongst those aged 36-43 was 0.16 stronger than amongst those aged 20-27. If both the overall partisan strength and the size of the electorate is to remain constant over the future, <u>ceteris paribus</u>, we would therefore expect those aged 20-27 in 1964 to have strengthened their partisanship by 0.16 by the time they reached the age of 36-43 in 1979. But instead the partisanship of this cohort <u>weakened</u> over this period, by 0.9. Parallel comparisons for those aged from 24-31 to 40-47 and from 28-35 to 44-51 reveal a similar pattern of retardation.

Analysis of this kind, however, only registers the fact of partisan weakening; it does not explain it. As the concept of party identification is rooted in a more general approach to electoral behaviour which stresses the importance of parental socialisation, changes in the pattern of such socialisation might account for the trends. The growth of social and residential mobility, the earlier leaving of the parental home (both physically and spiritually), the rise of non-partisan television as a source of young people´s values and knowledge, and the rapid growth of single-parent and second-parent families are all plausible grounds for attributing the weakening of partisanship to a loosening of the partisan tie between parents and children. However, if this were the true explanation we should expect to find a sharper fall in partisan strength over the period 1964-79 amongst young age-categories than amongst the middle aged and elderly. But as the age-category/age-cohort analysis shows (see Table

5.11) this is simply not the case. We shall, therefore, search for explanations elsewhere.

Sociological Sources of Electoral Volatility

Outside Northern Ireland, social class (if broadly defined to include housing tenure) remains the single most important social basis of enduring party attachments. A sociological account of British electoral behaviour would assume that if most electors were class conscious, and automatically regarded the Conservative and Labour parties as the natural representatives of, respectively, middle and working class interests, they would regularly vote for their class party. Conversely, if the incidence and strength of class allegiance declined, or perceptions of the link between class and party diminished, one could expect a growth in electoral volatility.

This is a tempting explanation of the gradual growth of volatility in the 1970s. The alignment between class and party has indeed weakened over the last two decades (see Table 5.12). Class voting, as measured by Alford's index, ·has halved, dropping from a score of 42 in 1964 to a score of 21 in 1983. The Alford index of class and party identification, perhaps a preferable measure because less subject to short-term fluctuation, has also fallen gradually, from 39 in 1964 to 22 in 1983. A more readily understandable statistic is the proportion voting for, or identifying with, the ´natural´ class party i.e. non-manual Conservative + manual Labour as a proportion of all voters or electors. The trend in these two figures clearly brings out the degree of class dealignment over the past two decades. In 1964 natural class party voting accounted for 63 per cent of all voters, natural class party identification for 58 per cent of all electors. In 1983 the figures were 47 and 45 per cent respectively. In other words, by 1983 social class could ´correctly´ predict the vote or identification of less than half the British electorate.(11)

This class dealignment has occured because both sides of the class divide have moved away from their ´natural´ party, almost entirely to the benefit of non-class parties like the Liberals and the Nationalists This has been particularly marked at the top and bottom of the class ladder. For example, over the period 1964-1983 the proportion identifying with the Conservatives fell 14 percentage points among both ´managers and off-

Table 5.12: Indices of the Class-Party Alignment, 1964-83

	1964	1966	1970	Feb/ Oct 1974	1979	1983	Change 1964-83
Alford class index of Lab voting	42	43	33	34	27	21	-21
Alford class index of Lab party iden- tification	39	36	29	31	27	22	-17
Non-manual Con voters + manual Lab voters as % of all voters	63	66	60	55	55	47	-16
Non-manual Con identifiers+man- ual Lab ident- ifiers as % of all electors	58	57	54	51	50	45	-13

Note: The Alford index is the % of manual workers who vote/identify with Labour minus the % of non-manual workers who do so. A respondent's manual or non-manual status is measured by the occupation of the head of household. Non-voters are excluded from the index of voting but non-identifiers are incorporated into the index of party identification. Sources: As Table 5.10.

icials' and 'employers and the self-employed' while Labour identification actually rose, by one and two per cent respectively. Conversely, Conservative identification fell by only one per cent over the same period among 'skilled manual workers' and 'semi- and unskilled workers' whereas the proportion with a Labour identification plummeted by, respectively, 11 and 13 per cent. The net 'swing' in party identification was therefore 8.0 per cent to Labour among managers and officials and 7.5 per cent to Labour among the employers and the self-employed but 6.0 per cent to the <u>Conservatives</u> among semi- and unskilled worker and 5.0 per cent to the <u>Conservatives</u> among skilled manual workers.(12)
Class dealignment is a tempting explanation of

electoral volatility for a second reason. Most
changes in the post-war social structure lead one to
expect a diminishing of class consciousness. The
occupational structure has bulged in the middle,
through the expansion of routine white collar work
and the ´new´ professions, and has been squeezed at
the ends through the contraction of unskilled manual
work and the decline of the independent employer or
professional practitioner. Partly as a consequence,
but also because educational opportunities have
expanded, social mobility and marriage across class
lines have increased markedly. Only a small and
diminishing proportion of the electorate conform to
class stereotypes, in the sense of possessing
uniformly working-class or middle-class attributes
(Rose, 1980, p.29). A large and increasing
proportion of the electorate have a mixture of
different class attributes and are thus subject to
partisan cross-pressures: the growing number of
working-class home owners and middle-class trade
unionists are cases in point.(13) Moreover, new
social cleavages are competing with social class for
partisan allegiance, such as nation in Wales and
Scotland, race in parts of urban England, and
perhaps economic sector (public vs. private) in
Britain generally. At the same time, political
changes have probably dimmed the electorate´s view
of the link between class interests and party
representation, notably the embourgeoisement of the
Parliamentary Labour Party (especially Labour
cabinets) and the petit embourgeoisement of
currently powerful factions within the Conservative
party.

 But the difficulty with the purported
connection between the dissolution of class
allegiance and the growth of electoral volatility is
the lack of supporting evidence. To begin with, the
willingness of electors to volunteer a class
identity did not decline in the 1970s. The
proportion of respondents who, in answer to the
question ´Do you ever think of yourself as belonging
to any social class?´ mentioned a class without
further probing or prompting was 48 per cent in
1964, 47 per cent in 1979. Among manual workers the
proportion answering ´working class´ slipped
slightly, from 44 to 39 per cent; among non-manual
workers the proportion answering ´middle class´
showed no discernible trend. As a measure of class
consciousness this is undoubtedly crude, but it is
surely the minimal requirement (even if not a
sufficient one) for evidence of a sense of class

membership. These figures are striking not for the absence of decline, but for their low level in the first place. In the context of the growth of trade union membership throughout this period, the outbreaks of industrial militancy in 1972, 1974 and 1979, the post-1973 recession, and the increasingly 'third generation' composition of the urban working class, these figures do point to a remarkably weak sense of class interest. (For corroborative evidence on other facets of class awareness see Crewe, 1982a, p. 20 and Table 1.8).

Secondly, there is no convincing evidence that the class image of the major parties has in fact become more blurred. Here comment is effectively restricted to the Labour party and its supporters, since the Conservative party does not use explicit class rhetoric (preferring to appeal to a 'national' interest), and its supporters do not explain their party preference by reference to class or group interests. As regards the Labour party a frequent suggestion is that since the 1950s it has slowly abandoned its working class image; it no longer looks or behaves like the party of, or for, workers. But this assertion has always been based on mere impression, not hard evidence; and what evidence exists suggests the opposite. If we consider all the dimensions to the Labour party's electoral appeal – all the different things that electors say they like about the Labour party – positive references to Labour as the party of the 'worker', 'the ordinary working man', and the 'trade unionist' were higher in 1979 than 1964 (see Crewe, 1982a, Table 1.9). It is true that positive appraisal of the Labour party in class terms is restricted to a minority (although no other single factor is favourably mentioned as often); but on these data it is difficult to attribute the weakening of Labour partisanship to the supposed shedding of its class appeal.

Finally, it is worth exploring the possibility that the slow growth of electoral volatility has some connection with the known increase in the proportion of the electorate who have 'mixed' class characteristics and find themselves under cross-class partisan pressure. There does appear to be a connection, but only a tenuous one. Table 5.13 illustrates this unexciting finding by providing data on middle-class trade unionists, working-class house owners, and respondents who have married outside their class. There is a consistent tendency for those in cross-class positions to have a weaker

Table 5.13: The Electoral Volatility of Selected Groups in Cross-Class Locations, 1979

| | Difference between working class house-owners and | | | Difference between middle class trade unionists and | | | Difference between respondents married 'out of class' and | |
	All respondents	Working class renters	Middle class owners	All respondents	Middle class unionists	Working class unionists	All respondents	Those married 'within class'
Mean partisan strength	-0.08	-0.14	-0.04	-0.09	-0.06	-0.09	-0.09	-0.09
% changing vote Oct1974-79	--	-3%	+6%	+1%	+2%	--	-2%	+3%
% decided vote in campaign	+5%	+5%	+7%	+4%	+6%	+1%	+4%	+7%
% thought of voting for different party	+7%	+6%	+6%	+6%	+4%	-4%	+5%	+6%

Notes: Two examples from the table might assist interpretation. The top left-hand cell means that the mean partisan strength of working class house-owners was 0.08 less than that of all respondents; the bottom right-hand cell means that, compared with all respondents, 5% more of those who had married 'out of class' thought of voting for a different party in 1979. 'Working class' = manual workers, 'middle class' = non-manual workers. Head of household's occupation is used except in the case of cross-class marriage where respondent's occupation is taken. Home-owners include those buying their house on a mortgage. 'Changing vote' includes changing to and from non-voting but excludes those ineligible to vote at either election.
Source: BES, 1979 (cross-section).

partisanship, to waver more during the campaigns and to be more volatile, but the difference between them and those in class-consonant positions is fairly slender. Social fluidity had some bearing on the electoral fluidity of the 1970s but can only account for a small part of it.

Ideological Sources of Electoral Volatility

The 'ideological' approach to electoral behaviour assumes that the way people vote - and change their vote - can be explained in terms of the relationship between their own positions and the parties' (perceived) position on major, divisive issues. We would expect volatility., at both the individual and collective level, to arise where there was a divergence between the two; and to grow if the divergence grew. The assumption is that if a party's supporters are overwhelmingly committed to that party's objectives, and to its strategy in obtaining them, their allegiance will be unimpaired by dissatisfaction with any of the party's particular policies, leaders or spells in office. Doubts and disappointments can be more easily swallowed if one believes in what the party stands for.

There are good grounds for believing that this approach will be more fruitful than the sociological approach. Widespread evidence establishes that, at least in recent years, voters' party choices are more closely associated with their issue positions than with their social attributes. For example, Rose (1980, p.48) reports that a set of ten social structural variables explained 21 per cent of the variance in Conservative vs. Labour voting in 1959 but successively less at each subsequent election; by 1979 the identical set of variables explained only 12 per cent.(14) In the 1979 British Election Study an AID analysis based on nine social structural variables explained only 21 per cent of the variance in Conservative vs. non-Conservative voting whereas respondents' evaluations of the parties on three issues alone - prices, unemployment and strikes - were sufficient to explain 48 per cent of the three-party vote (Sarlvik and Crewe, 1983, p. 266). Researchers who have incorporated both social structural and issue-attitudinal variables in the same regression model of party choice all report that the social structural variables are largely 'washed out' in the process (Budge and Farlie, 1977; Himmelweit et al., 1981, Chs. 4, 5 and 8; Whiteley,

1983, 100 - 106).

The most recent detailed exploration of the relation between issue positions and the vote is Decade of Dealignment (Sarlvik and Crewe, 1983). A discriminant analysis based on respondents' positions on a full set of 1979 campaign issues correctly predicted the vote of 90 per cent major party voters and of 69 per cent of the three-party vote. The large majority of errors consisted of the incorrect prediction or non-prediction of the Liberal vote - a pattern that fits in well with the discussion of the high turnover of the Liberal vote earlier in this chapter. The discriminant analysis was also the basis for effective prediction of electoral volatility. Voters' overall issue position was closely associated with whether their vote deviated from their party identification, and whether it had changed from the previous election. Once again, the distinctive features of actual and potential Liberal support were underlined. For example, the overall issue position of voters switching from Conservative to Liberal was virtually identical to those switching in the opposite direction; similarly the overall issue position of those changing from Labour to Liberal was identical to those travelling the other way. This ideological 'middle ground' was occupied by at least 25 per cent of the electorate (and on less restrictive definitions by more) even though the 1979 vote for the 'centre' party, the Liberals, was only half as much.

One further point needs to be made about ideological sources of volatility - its unequal effect on supporters of the two main parties. As even the occasional analyst of surveys in Britain knows, since at least the early 1950s Labour voters have been indifferent and sometimes actively hostile to some aspects of Labour party policy and in favour, sometimes enthusiastically, of certain aspects of Conservative policy; whereas amongst Conservative supporters there is no such policy mis-match. In both 1979 and 1983 a majority of Labour voters - whose ranks were considerably depleted by 1983 - could be found opposing key elements of Labour policy and supporting key elements of Conservative policy. (15) In this respect there has for long been an asymmetry in British politics. Labour wins votes despite its policies, the Conservatives because of theirs.

This asymmetry is displayed in Figure 5.1, which shows the average location of different

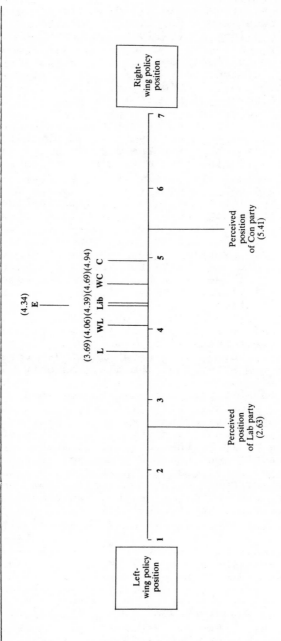

Figure 5.1: Electoral Configuration of Partisan Groups on Eight Position Issues, 1979 General Election

Notes: C = very/fairly strong Conservatives; WC = not very strong Conservatives; Lib = Liberal; WL = not very strong Labour; L = very/fairly strong Labour; E = whole electorate.
Source: British Election Study, 1979 cross-section.

136

partisan groups on the eight 'position' issues (as distinct from 'performance' issues) that dominated the 1979 election, and their relation to the electorate's perception of where the two main parties stood. It shows that Liberal identifiers and weak Labour partisans were 'closer' to the Conservative party's perceived position than to the Labour party's; it also shows that very/fairly strong Labour partisans were much further away from the Labour party than their Conservative counterparts were from the Conservative party. Separate configurations for each of the eight issues in the analysis reveal this pattern in six of the eight cases.(16)

What needs to be explained, however, is not simply the existence of volatility in 1979 but its growth since the 1950s. Accounts of issues as a source of increasing volatility are often couched in terms of the emergence of 'cross-cutting cleavages': new issues arise which divide the electorate along lines that cut across existing voting blocks and thus loosen voters' ties to their usual party. A number of such issues have come to the forefront at particular times in the 1960s and 1970s. First, the question of British membership of the EEC (and, after 1971, of British withdrawal) has divided supporters of both parties since the early 1960s. Most Conservatives were eventually won round to membership by the 1975 Referendum, but Labour supporters (and the Labour Movement) have been badly split, in diverging and fluctuating proportions, from the very beginning. Secondly, from 1962 to 1979 both parties have attempted to impose some form of incomes policy when in office and have turned against it when in Opposition; division and ambivalence over the issue are equally characteristic of their electoral supporters. Thirdly, the 'Nationalist' dimension came to dominate Scotland's politics in the 1970s. The one party which stood unequivocally for 'Scotland First', the Scottish National Party, attracted votes away from both main parties, whose traditional supporters were divided on the issues, like the party leaderships (Miller, 1981). The Conservatives did not settle upon a traditionally Unionist anti-devolution position until the late 1970s, and the Labour party was not fully reconciled to a devolutionist policy until the early 1980s. A fourth cross-cutting issue is black immigration and race relations. The electorate has consistently been overwhelmingly hostile to further black immigration and the issue has erupted with some intensity from time to time (1962-64, 1968-70, 1971-72, 1978-79) (Studlar, 1974). Although both parties, especially when a Labour government faces a Conservative Opposition, officially sanction a restrictive immigration policy, the Conservatives do so with relish and stridency, the Labour party with regret and embarrassment. Labour supporters, a majority of whom favour restrictions on immigration, undoubtedly see the Conservatives as the anti-immigrant party (Fox, 1975; Crewe, 1983, Ch. 6, p. 262-3).

Each of these issues has undoubtedly contributed to volatility at particular elections, notably immigration in 1970 (Studlar, 1978; Miller, 1980), devolution in February and October 1974 (in Scotland) and, possibly, incomes policy in February 1974 and 1979. Their overall impact on the growth of volatility, however, has probably been short-lived and limited. Parties are protected from the full potential impact of cross-cutting issues in various ways. Unless the issue is highly salient it will not determine the eventual voting decision; instead party supporters, especially the strong partisans, will follow the policy lead given by the parliamentary party, even if it chops and changes. This was the case with both EEC membership (Butler, 1979; Sarlvik et al. 1976) and incomes policy. Moreover, fluctuations, divisions and studied ambiguity over the issue on the part of the party leadership can leave the electorate confused about the party's true position. This allows voters to reduce cognitive dissonance by assuming that their party's position coincides with (and the enemy party's diverges from) their own. This too appears to have occurred in the case of incomes policy, the EEC and devolution, especially among Labour supporters in the latter two instances (see Sarlvik and Crewe, 1983, Ch. 10; Miller, 1981, p. 124). Immigration is the one clear-cut issue on which a large proportion of a party's usual supporters found themselves at odds with their party's outlook and priorities.

Trends in attitudes to the established, basic principles and strategies of each party probably offer a more rewarding line to pursue. Comparable data over the post-war period is hard to come by, but the attempt is made in Tables 5.14 and 5.15. These reveal a quite exceptional movement of opinion away from Labour's traditional positions amongst Labour supporters over the last twenty or so years.

Table 5.14: Long-Term Trends in Support for Labour Policies amongst Labour Supporters

% of Labour Identifiers:	1964	1966	1970	1974	1979	Change 1964-79
In favour of nationalising more industries	57	52	39	53	32	-25
Who do not believe that trade unions have 'too much power'	59	45	40	42	36	-23 (1964-74)
In favour of spending more on social services	89	66	60	61	n.a.	-28 (1974-79)
	n.a.	n.a.	n.a.	43	30	-13 (1974-79)
						-41 (1964-79)

% of Labour Voters in Favour of:	1957	1980	Change 1957-80
Restricting dividends and profits	83	63	-20
Cutting down on defence expenditure	76	49	-27
Abolishing the House of Lords	61	48	-13
Giving more aid to backward countries	50	40	+10

Notes: n.a. = not asked; percentage bases exclude 'don't knows'. An alternatively worded question on social services spending was asked in 1974 and subsequently adopted as the sole question on the issue in 1979; comparisons for 1964-74 and for 1974-79 are therefore given separately.

Sources: Comparison of identical questions in Gallup survey, September 1957 and MORI survey, June 1980, cited in Harrop, 1982, p.155. See also sources for Table 5.10.

Table 5.15: Long-Term Trends in Support for Conservative Policies amongst Conservative Supporters

% of Conservative Identifiers:

	1964	1966	1970	1974	1979	Change 1964-79
Against nationalising more industries	96	92	93	94	95	-1
Believing that trade unions have 'too much power'	83	87	88	88	95	+12 (1964-74)
Against spending more on social services	32	56	65	55	n.a.	+13 (1974-79)
	n.a.	n.a.	n.a.	54*	67*	+13 (1974-79) +26 (1964-79)

% of Conservative Voters:

	1957	1980	Change 1957-80
Against restricting dividends and profits	70	71	+1
Against cutting down on defence expenditure	62	80	+18
Against abolishing the House of Lords	81	84	+3
Against giving more aid to backward countries	49	64	+15

Notes: * = % saying cut back social services 'a bit' or 'a lot'. See also notes to Table 5.14.
Sources: See Tables 5.10 and 5.14.

There has been a spectacular decline in support for the 'collectivist trinity' of public ownership, trade union power and social welfare. In 1964 a clear majority of Labour identifiers approved of further nationalisation (57 per cent) and repudiated the idea that trade unions were too powerful (59 per cent); an overwhelming majority wanted more spending on the social services (89 per cent). By 1979 support for each of these three tenets was down to barely a third, and support for all three under a quarter. On electorally less salient issues, like defence spending, the House of Lords, foreign aid and the restriction of dividends and profits, there was also a substantial if less spectacular drift to the Right. What was already an ideological gap between party and supporters in the 1960s had turned into an ideological chasm by 1979.

By contrast the convergence between the policy positions of the Conservative party and its supporters has remained strong and stable throughout the 1960s and the 1970s (see Table 5.15). What change has occurred consists of a moderate movement to the Right. The fit between official party policy and the views of Conservative supporters has, if anything, grown closer. Thus the Conservative party's vulnerability to a loss of support lies exclusively in its record in government (as in February 1974 and 1964) whereas Labour appears to be subject to a longer-term erosion of issue-based support in addition to any loss sustained occasioned by a disappointing period in office. In this connection it is significant that since the war the Conservative party has always recovered its share of the vote after a full Parliament in opposition (as in 1950, 1970 and 1979) whereas Labour's has fallen as much during periods of Opposition (1951-64, 1970-February 1974, 1979-83) as during periods of government. The components of electoral volatility that seem most attributable to ideological sources are Labour losses and Conservative recoveries, the former reflecting ideological distance, the latter ideological closeness between a party and its traditional supporters.

ELECTORAL VOLATILITY AND THE FUTURE OF THE BRITISH PARTY SYSTEM

The main findings reached in this chapter can be summarised as follows. Firstly, net volatility has gradually increased both at and between successive elections since the war. The growth has been somewhat erratic and unspectacular, but one can safely describe the 1970s as more volatile than the 1960s, and the 1960s as more volatile than the 1950s. Secondly, this increase in net volatility has only been partially reflected at the level of overall volatility, where the rise has been very slight. This is because much of the overall volatility consists of multi-directional flux rather than uni-directional flow. Thirdly, the growth in net volatility has occurred less at the expense of one major party to the benefit of the other, and more at the expense of both to the benefit of the minor parties. Fourthly, trends in the psychological, sociological and ideological bases of partisan attachments suggest that the potential for volatility is likely to increase further. Identification with the Conservative and Labour parties has weakened within the electorate overall and, ceteris paribus, will continue doing so for some time. Social structural factors, especially social class, account for a declining proportion of the vote. A sense of class identity has been modest for twenty years. The number of electors in mixed-class situations, which appears to be associated with volatility, will continue to grow in the foreseeable future. The broad ideological position of electors, which is clearly connected with party choice and vote switching, has shifted to the Right over the past two decades, to the inevitable disadvantage of the Labour party.

This dealignment of partisanship has made a realignment of the party system more likely, but neither guarantees its occurrence, nor determines its shape. For reasons spelled out in the Introduction, increased volatility in the electorate can nonetheless produce stable outcomes at the parliamentary level. Moreover, even if it produces instability - in the form of landslide results, breakthroughs by new parties, or the rise and fall of minor parties - the old system will not necessarily be replaced by a new one of any permanence. However, in the light of recent elections, especially 1983, three possible realignments have some claim to plausibility: a realignment towards the Right; a realignment away from the Left (which is not the same thing); and a realignment towards the Centre. This chapter concludes by briefly examining the case for each.

A realignment of the Right is given credence not simply by the landslide proportions of the

Conservative victory in 1983 (144 seats), but by the circumstances in which it was obtained. The clear rightwards shift between 1979 and 1983 in the political and social climate; the revival of intellectual interest in right-wing thought; the catalytic effect of the Falklands War; above all, the fact that the Conservatives were re-elected in the midst of a deep recession can all be woven together into an argument for this view. Yet the Conservatives' massive majority owed almost everything to the electoral system, almost nothing to the nature of its support. There is no hard evidence to show that the line dividing the Conservative from the non-Conservative portion of the electorate has shifted. By historical standards the Conservative vote in 1983 was low, not high (and less than in 1979); identification with the party has not grown; much of its 1983 support was negatively motivated; even Mrs Thatcher's much vaunted popularity was not, by past standards, exceptional and is anyway an inevitably short-term phenomenon. The Conservatives' runaway triumph was a historical moment, not a historical juncture.

Predictions of a realignment away from the Left are even more tempting, but still premature. It is true that the line dividing the Labour from non-Labour portion of the electorate has gradually shifted over the past thirty years. Labour's share of the electorate has fallen almost uninterruptedly from 41 in 1951 to 21 per cent in 1983 - one of the very few examples in Western Europe of a long-term, substantial decline in a major party's vote (Maguire, 1983). It is also true that the electoral arithmetic of a full Labour recovery by the next election is formidable. To win a durable, outright majority (20+) in 1987/88 Labour will have to gain every one of the 127 Conservative seats in which it was runner up in 1983 on the basis of an 11.5 per cent swing - more than double that obtained by either major party at any one election since 1945. Nonetheless, nothing about a trend, even a 30-year one, guarantees its continuation and there is no iron law against two-digit swings: the electorate is increasingly volatile. Labour's 'natural' level of support is undoubtedly higher than its 1983 vote, which was reduced to its low ebb by an unprecedented combination of short-term mishaps. This is suggested by the higher proportion of Labour identifiers (32 per cent) than Labour voters (28 per cent) and confirmed by the immediate, sharp and enduring rise of Labour support in the opinion polls when Neil Kinnock replaced Michael Foot as party leader.(17) The Labour party was badly down in 1983, but far from out.

The third possibility, a realignment of the Centre, has already taken place to a modest degree. Since the mid 1950s, cycles of Liberal surge and decline have moved along an upward spiral: each successive Liberal peak has reached higher, lasted longer and subsided less than its predecessor. This pattern recurred in the 1983 election and has continued since.(18) It has enabled the Liberal-SDP Alliance to attain the status of a large minor party. However, despite the SDP´s formation, and the Centre´s exceptionally good vote in 1983, the Alliance has failed to establish itself as a truly major party, let alone the second party, in the eyes of the electorate. In structure and motivation SDP support closely resembles what has been reported about the Liberal vote in the past (Crewe, 1982b; Curtice, 1983). For both parties electoral support appears to be as shallow as it is wide. Identification with either of the Alliance parties combined was barely greater in 1983 (16 per cent) than with the Liberal party alone in 1974 (14 per cent). By and large Alliance voters are Conservative and (especially in 1983) Labour renegades, not committed partisans. The two parties have failed to mobilise a distinctive social base; and they are not yet the beneficiary of any major new issue conflict or social cleavage which cuts across existing partisan divisions. Instead of creating a new social and ideological constituency, the SDP seems to have attracted, at least temporarily, part of the large, volatile, potential Liberal vote which has existed in Britain for many years.

The least reckless prognosis, perhaps, is that the two major party icebergs will continue to melt. From time to time one or other will lose a substantial chunk. More and more loose ice will float about in the electoral sea. Some will re-attach itself to the big icebergs; the rest will form a soft-packed third iceberg precariously floating alongside, but dwarfed by, its bigger rivals.

FOOTNOTES

1. Some passages in this chapter, especially the section on overall volatility since 1945 are closely based on Sarlvik and Crewe (1983, ch. 2).

Parts of the section on explanations for electoral volatility are revisions of Crewe (1984a).
2. Defined throughout this chapter as the average of the percentage point rise in the Conservative share of the vote and the percentage point loss in the Labour share of the vote.
3. In the 1959-64 Parliament the average percentage point fall at by-elections in the Conservative share of the vote was 13.5 from a 1959 vote of 48.8%; its by-election ´base´ was therefore 35.3%. In the 1970-74 Parliament the average fall of 13.1 from a 46.2% vote in 1970 produced a lower by-election base of 33.1. The Conservative by-election base in 1979-83 was virtually the same (33.5) but would have been lower except for the three by-elections held during the Falklands War. Labour´s by-election base was 32.1 in 1966-70 but 30.8 in 1974-79.
4. In 1918 the franchise was extended to all men of 21 and over and to all women of 28 and over. The voting age for women was lowered to 21 in 1928.
5. However, in 1983, for the first time since the war, new electors clearly preferred the Conservatives to Labour. According to the BBC TV/Gallup survey on the eve-and-day of the election, the three-party division of the vote among new electors was Conservative 41%, Lib/SDP 30%, Labour 29%. The physical replacement of the electorate between 1979 and 1983 undoubtedly hurt the Labour party.
6. The Social Democratic Party (SDP) was formed in March 1981 after a breakaway from the Labour party two months earlier by 12 MPs and prominent members outside Parliament who included many former cabinet ministers. It agreed to form an electoral alliance with the Liberal party whereby the two parties would fight on a common manifesto, integrate their national campaign organisations and, crucially, not put up rival candidates in the same constituency. After protracted and sometimes acrimonious negotiations throughout 1982 the two parties agreed on a share-out of all but three seats.
7. This number of defectors was perhaps swelled by the fact that under the terms of the Alliance Liberal supporters had no Liberal (as distinct from SDP) candidate to vote for in 1983.
8. For example, the 1983 BBC TV/Gallup election survey found that 16% of its respondents had at some time ´seriously considered´ voting for the Alliance only to decide against by polling day.

Of these 58% gave purely strategic reasons: 31% said
that it was obvious the Alliance could not win; the
others said they were afraid that an Alliance vote
would let Labour (18%) or the Conservatives (9%) in.
See Crewe, 1983a, p. 60.
 9.   The questions are: "Generally speaking do
you usually think of yourself as Conservative,
Labour, Liberal or what?", followed by "And how
strongly (Conservative, Labour, Liberal etc,) you
generally feel?".   Respondents answering ´none´ or
´don´t know´ to the first question were asked "Do
you generally think of yourself as a little closer
to one of the parties than the others?", and if they
mentioned a party in reply were counted as ´not very
strong´ identifiers.
 10.   Self-declared strength of party
identification tends to be higher in surveys
conducted close to general elections than in
mid-term (see Butler and Stokes, 1975, p. 470). The
interviewing for the election surveys in 1964, 1966,
1970, 1974 and 1979 was done a few weeks after the
general election, whereas that for the 1983 election
was done on the eve and day of polling.
 11.   On the other hand, it remained a very good
predictor of the major party that an elector would
not vote for.
 12.   These figures are derived from Heath et
al. (1984, Table 9) to whom I am indebted for
permission to quote their data. The seven-class
schema adopted by Heath et al. are not the seven
´social grades´ used by Butler and Stokes (1975) and
Sarlvik and Crewe (1983), the most important
difference being the creation of a separate class of
´employers and self-employed´ which cuts across the
manual/non-manual division.
 13.   In the mid-1950s only a fifth of all
manual workers owned their own homes; now over half
(51 per cent) do. By 1980 the expansion of the
public sector and the rise in the number of
professionally qualified employees has led to a 44%
rate of trade union membership among non-manual
workers. (See Central Statistical Office, 1982, pp.
115, 152.) As regards social mobility, the
proportion of manual working fathers whose sons held
non-manual jobs was 21 per cent in the late 1940s
but 31% by the early 1970s and almost certainly more
by the 1980s. Already in 1972 barely a third (34%)
of all households consisted of husband, father and
father-in-law all in manual jobs; the figure for
consistently non-manual households was 13%. The
remainder - over half of all two-generational

families - were socially mixed. These figures are taken from Heath (1981, pp 54, 63, 86 and 240).

14. These variables were occupation, union membership, housing, car ownership, telephones, education, age, sex, nationality and religion.

15. In 1979, for example, overwhelming majorities of Labour voters were in favour of the Conservative proposals, all opposed by the Labour party, to ban secondary picketing (96%), hold a free vote in the House of Commons on the death penalty (88%) and sell more council houses to tenants (69%). On the other hand, further nationalisation was opposed by 67% to 33%; and more spending on social services by 71% to 29% (after excluding 'don't knows'). In 1983 a majority of Labour voters opposed the scrapping of Polaris and supported stricter laws on trade union activities. (See Crewe, 1981, 294-5; Sarlvik and Crewe, 1983, 190-1 and Crewe 1984b.)

16. The issues were all ones on which the respondents were first asked to choose between two 'positions' and then say how strongly he or she supported that position. The eight issues covered unemployment policy (reliance on state or market); the legal reform of trade union activities; incomes policy vs. free collective bargaining; nationalisation vs. de-nationalisation; cut back vs. extend social services; ending of immigration vs. more aid to urban areas as solution to race relations; cut taxes vs. maintain public services, and co-operation vs. non-co-operation in the EEC. Each issue was converted into a seven-point scale, from left (low score) to right (high score). To appreciate some of the limits to this approach, however, see Crewe and Sarlvik, 1979, p. 249 and fn. 9.

17. Neil Kinnock was elected leader in early October 1983. In the period July to September 1983, under Michael Foot's leadership, Labour support in the monthly Gallup polls averaged 26%. In October 1983 it shot up to 35.5% since when it has fluctuated between 33.5 and 38.5%.

18. Since October 1983, when Neil Kinnock's election as Labour leader restored Labour's position as second party, support for the Alliance has averaged 21% in the monthly Gallup polls. Average support for the Liberals in the Gallup polls for the first nine months after earlier Conservative election victories was 14 per cent in 1979-80, 8 per cent in 1970-71 and 9 per cent in 1959-60. See Webb & Whybrow, 1981, Appendix E.

REFERENCES

Alt, J.E. (1978) The Politics of Economic Decline, Macmillan, London
Berrington, H. (1979) 'Towards a Multi-Party Britain?', West European Politics, 2, 29-52
Budge, I. and Farlie, D. (1977) Voting and Party Competition, John Wiley, London
Butler, D. (1979) 'Public Opinion and Community Membership', Political Quarterly, 50, 151-56
Butler, D. and Stokes, D. (1969) Political Change in Britain (1st edition), Macmillan, London
---------- (1975) Political Change in Britain (2nd edition), Macmillan, London
Central Statistical Office (1982) Social Trends 13 (1983 edition), HMSO, London
Crewe, I. (1980) 'Negative Partisanship: Some Preliminary Ideas Using British Data', paper prepared for the Planning Session on Problems in Comparative Survey Reseach in Political Behaviour, Joint Sessions of the European Consortium for Political Research, Florence, mimeo
---------- (1981) 'Why the Conservatives Won', in H. Penniman, (ed.), Britain at the Polls, 1979, American Enterprise Institute for Public Policy Research, Washington, D.C., 263-305
---------- (1982a) 'The Labour Party and the Electorate', in D. Kavanagh (ed.), The Politics of the Labour Party, George Allen and Unwin, London, 9-49
---------- (1982b) 'Is Britain's Two-Party System Really About to Crumble?', Electoral Studies, 1, 275-313
---------- (1983a) 'Why Labour Lost the British Election', Public Opinion, Washington D.C., 6, 7-9, 56-60
---------- (1983b) 'Representation and the Ethnic Minorities in Britain' in N. Glazer and K. Young, (eds.), Ethnic Pluralism and Public Policy, Heinemann Educational Books, 258-84
---------- (1984a) 'The Electorate: Partisan Dealignment Ten Years On', in H. Berrington, (ed.), Change in British Politics, Frank Cass, London, 183-215
---------- (1984b), 'How to Win a Landslide Without Really Trying: Why the Conservatives Won in 1983', in H. Penniman and A. Ranney, (eds.), Britain at the Polls, 1983, Duke University Press, Durham, North Carolina

Crewe, I. and Sarlvik, B. (1979) 'Popular Attitudes and the Conservative Party' in Z. Layton-Henry (ed.), Conservative Party Politics, Macmillan, London, 244-75

Crewe, I., Sarlvik, B. and Alt, J. (1977) 'Partisan Dealignment in Britain, 1964-1974', British Journal of Political Science, 7, 129-90

Curtice, J. and Steed, M. (1980) 'Appendix 2: An Analysis of the Voting, in D. Butler and D. Kavanagh, The British General Election of 1979, Macmillan, London, 390-431

Curtice, J. (1983) 'Liberal Voters and the Alliance: Realignment or Protest?', in V. Bogdanor (ed.), Liberal Party Politics, Clarendon Press, Oxford, 99-122

Fox, A. (1975) 'Attitudes to Immigration: A Comparison of Data from the 1970 and 1974 General Election Surveys', New Community, 4, 1-12

Harrop, M. (1982) 'Labour-voting Conservatives: A Survey of Policy Differences between the Labour Party and Labour Voters', in R. Worcester and M. Harrop, (eds.), Political Communications: The General Election Campaign of 1979, George Allen & Unwin, London 152-62

Heath, A. (1981) Social Mobility, Fontana, London

Heath, A.F., Jowell, R.M. and Curtice, J.K. (1984) 'Class Dealignment Revisited', paper presented to the Annual Conference of the Political Studies Association, Southampton, mimeo

Himmelweit, H.T., Biberian, M.J. and Stockdale, J. (1978) 'Memory for Past Vote: Implications of a Study of Bias in Recall', British Journal of Political Science, 8, 365-75

Himmelweit, H.T., Humphreys, P., Jaeger, M. and Katz, M. (1981) How Voters Decide, Academic Press, London

Maguire, M. (1983) 'Is There Still Persistence? Electoral Change in Western Europe', in H. Daalder and P. Mair (eds.), Western European Party Systems, Sage, Beverly Hills, 67-94

Miller, W. (1980) 'What was the Profit in following the Crowd? The Effectiveness of Party Strategies on Immigration and Devolution', British Journal of Political Science 10, 15-38

---------- (1982) The End of British Politics?, Clarendon Press, Oxford

Rose, R. (1980) 'Class Does not Equal Party: The Decline of a Model British Voting', Centre for the Study of Public Policy Paper, No. 74, University of Strathclyde, Glasgow

Sarlvik, B. and Crewe, I. (1983) <u>Decade of Dealignment: The Conservative Victory of 1979 and Electoral Trends in the 1970s</u>, Cambridge University Press, Cambridge

Sarlvik, B., Crewe, I., Alt, J. and Fox, A. (1976) ´Britain´s Membership of the EEC: A Profile of Electoral Opinions in the Spring of 1974 - With a Postscript on the Referendum´, <u>European Journal of Political Research</u>, 4, 83-114

Studlar, D. (1974) ´British Public Opinion, Colour Issues, and Enoch Powell: a Longitudinal Analysis´, <u>British Journal of Political Science</u>, 4, 371-82

---------- (1978) ´Policy Voting in Britain: The Coloured Immigration Issue in the 1964, 1966 and 1970 General Elections´, <u>American Political Science Review</u>, 72, 46-64

Webb, N. and Whybrow, R. (1981) <u>The Gallup Report</u>, Sphere Books, London

Whiteley, P. (1983) <u>The Labour Party in Crisis</u>, Methuen, London

Chapter 6

SCOTLAND

David Denver

INTRODUCTION

It may seem odd, at first sight, that electoral
volatility in Scotland should be considered
separately from and in addition to volatility in the
United Kingdom as a whole. Unlike all other
countries covered in this volume Scotland is not a
state. Moreover, textbooks on British politics
written in the 1950s and 1960s tended to stress the
social and political homogeneity of Britain and the
uniformity of electoral behaviour. There are many
features of Scottish society which make it
distinctive from the rest of Britain - for example
Scottish legal, religious and educational
institutions are quite different from those found
elsewhere, there is a specifically Scottish morning
press, a separate Scottish local government system,
Scottish national teams in many sports, and so on -
but these were generally played down in the face of
impressive evidence of British electoral
homogeneity.

Today, however, things are rather different.
The electoral success of the Scottish National Party
(SNP) from the late 1960s onwards pushed the
'Scottish question' on to the agenda of British
politics where it stayed throughout the 1970s.
After years of debate, government plans to set up a
devolved Scottish legislative assembly only just
failed to come to fruition in 1979. The devolution
debate prompted a new interest in Scottish politics
on the part of political scientists and others and a
new emphasis upon the differences, not the
similarities, between Scotland and the rest of
Britain (Rose, 1970). From this perspective there
is an identifiable Scottish political system which,
according to Kellas, is both dependent and
independent within the British system (Kellas, 1973,

151

p.18).

It was not only the emergence of the SNP that distinguished Scottish electoral politics in the 1970s. Scottish election results also increasingly diverged from those in England and Wales in respect of the relative strengths of the Conservative and Labour parties - a trend which continued in the 1983 general election.

Table 6.1 shows the distribution of votes in Scotland at each general election since 1945. The rise (and subsequent decline) of the SNP is clear. Having been founded in 1934 with a policy of independence for Scotland, the SNP remained very much on the political fringe until the late 1960s. Then a series of spectacular by-election results followed by local election successes brought the party to the centre of Scottish politics. Support in general elections increased to 30.4 per cent in October 1974 when the Conservatives were pushed into third place in terms of popular support. Since then there has been some decline but even so, with 11.7 per cent of the votes and two seats won in the 1983 election, the SNP remains an important electoral force in Scotland. Clearly the SNP has no parallel in England (and in Wales the nationalist party, Plaid Cymru, has been much less successful than the SNP) so that the pattern of party competition in Scotland is much more complex than in the rest of the country.

The differences between Scotland and the rest of Britain in terms of support for the three major British parties can be measured in a variety of ways (see Miller, 1982). In Table 6.1, however, two simple indicators are used to show this. The first is the difference between the shares of the vote obtained by the Liberals in England and Wales and the shares obtained by them in Scotland. The Liberals have consistently had poorer results in Scotland but not very markedly so, with the exception of the two elections in 1974. In these elections it appears that in Scotland the SNP benefitted, at least in part, from the movement away from the major parties which produced relatively high levels of Liberal support elsewhere. In 1983, however, the alliance between the Liberals and the SDP (Social Democratic Party) somewhat contrary to expectations, polled almost as well in Scotland as in the rest of the country.

The second indicator of Scotland's electoral divergence is the relative support for the Conservative and Labour parties, shown by the Con-

Table 6.1: Distribution of Votes in Scotland,
General Elections 1945-1983

	1945	1950	1951	1955	1959	1964
	%	%	%	%	%	%
Conservative	41.1	44.8	48.6	50.1	47.2	40.6
Labour	47.6	46.2	47.9	46.7	46.7	48.7
Liberal	5.0	6.6	2.7	1.9	4.1	7.6
SNP	1.2	0.4	0.3	0.5	0.8	2.4
Others	5.1	2.0	0.5	0.8	1.2	0.7
% Lib England & Wales minus % Lib Scotland	4.7	3.0	-0.1	1.0	2.1	4.2
Con lead England & Wales minus Con lead Scotland	-3.4	-2.7	-2.5	-1.6	4.0	6.9

Table 6.1: (contd.)

	1966	1970	Feb. 1974	Oct. 1974	1979	1983
	%	%	%	%	%	%
Conservative	37.7	38.0	32.9	24.7	31.4	28.4
Labour	49.9	44.5	36.6	36.3	41.6	35.1
Liberal	6.8	5.5	8.0	8.3	9.0	24.5
SNP	5.0	11.4	21.9	30.4	17.3	11.7
Others	0.6	0.6	0.6	0.3	0.7	0.3
% Lib England & Wales minus % Lib Scotland	2.0	2.4	13.0	11.6	5.7	1.7
Con lead England & Wales minus Con lead Scotland	5.3	9.6	4.9	9.0	19.1	24.2

Note: The 1983 figure for Liberals refers to the
share of votes obtained by the Liberal/SDP Alliance.

servative lead over Labour in England and Wales
minus the Conservative 'lead' in Scotland. A
negative figure indicates, therefore, a better
performance by the Conservatives in Scotland and a

positive figure indicates a better Labour
performance. In the first four post-war elections
Scotland deviated towards the Conservatives,
although by small and decreasing amounts. From 1959
the deviation is towards Labour. It should be
noted, however, that according to Miller (1981,
p.216) Labour would be expected to have a lead of
about eight percentage points more in Scotland than
in England simply because of the differences in the
class structure of the two nations. It was,
therefore, only in the 1970s that Scotland exhibited
a very marked propensity to be more strongly Labour
than England and Wales. But in the elections of
1979 and 1983 the gap between the two became
enormous. The divergence between Scotland and the
rest of the country is now so great that talk of the
uniformity of British electoral behaviour is clearly
outdated. In terms both of the number of seriously
competing parties and of patterns of party support
Scotland is a distinctive unit within the British
system.

TRENDS IN ELECTORAL VOLATILITY

In the introductory chapter a distinction was
made between ´net´ and ´gross´ volatility. The
former refers to the net change in the outcomes of
successive elections, the net change in the parties´
shares of the votes cast. This could be summarised
in various ways but, as in other chapters, the measure used here is the ´Pedersen index´ of volatility.
Table 6.2 shows the scores obtained when this
index is computed for successive pairs of general
election results in Scotland. Since, a priori,
greater stability would be expected over shorter
time periods the three elections which were called
soon after a previous one are listed separately.
Clearly electoral instability in Scotland has
steadily increased throughout the post-war period.
Change from 1945 to 1950 was affected by the unusual
circumstances of the 1945 election. After that, the
volatility index for elections with a four to five
year intervening gap more than doubled between the
1950s and 1960s and then roughly doubled again in
the 1970s before climbing to a peak in the most
recent election. The pattern in elections held
shortly after a previous one is less clear cut but
even so the index score for the election of October
1974 (8.8), which took place just eight months after
the previous one, is significantly larger than any

other score in the 1950s or 1960s.

Table 6.2: Pedersen Index of Volatility, Scotland

Elections	Index	Elections	Index
1945-50	5.3	1950-51	5.5
1951-55	2.0	1964-66	3.8
1955-59	2.9	Feb74-Oct74	8.8
1959-64	7.1		
1966-70	6.7		
1970-Feb74	13.0		
Oct74-79	13.1		
1979-83	15.5		

The trend in net volatility is clearly related to the changing pattern of party competition. Thus in the 1950s the two traditional British parties dominated elections and volatility was low. The elections of 1964, 1966 and 1970 witnessed a growing but still relatively minor challenge by the SNP and volatility generally increased. In 1974 and 1979 the SNP polled extremely well and the volatility index shows high scores. In 1983 the SNP still obtained significant support but a fourth electoral force, the SDP/Liberal Alliance, appeared on the scene and the volatility index reached a new high.

There is something of a chicken and egg problem here. Electoral success on the part of third and fourth parties clearly boosts the volatility index score. Can it be said, then, that new parties in a sense create volatility? Or is it that there is an underlying volatility in a looser sense - an increased predisposition to change on the part of electors - which is a precondition of the electoral success of minor parties? I will return to these questions below.

Although the main concern here is with volatility in national elections, such elections in Britain can be viewed as infrequently appearing tips of icebergs. A fuller understanding of electoral trends requires consideration of movements in opinion between elections. Three main indicators of this are commonly used in Britain - parliamentary by-elections, local elections and public opinion polls.

There are severe problems in using parliamentary by-elections for the purposes of this paper, however. Their results are crucially affected by the point in the life-cycle of governments at which they occur; the personalities of candidates, local issues and the efficiency of party organisation all appear to be more influential than in general elections; many more 'other' candidates contest them than is normal in general elections. For these reasons by-elections are not reliable guides to trends in volatility.

Local elections are far more reliable. They are held at fixed intervals (in Scotland annually until 1973 and then, when the local government system was completely revised, in 1974, 1977, 1978 and every two years thereafter). Moreover, local election results, especially in urban areas, reflect the electorate's attitudes towards the national parties, national issues and national personalities rather than being the products of local concerns (Waller, 1980) As such, local election results are widely interpreted as good indicators of electoral opinion.

Table 6.3: Volatility in Local Elections, 1954-1982

Year	Index	Year	Index	Year	Index	Year	Index
1954	3.0	1960	0.6	1966	3.3	1972	5.1
1955	5.6	1961	3.1	1967	13.0	1973	4.3
1956	3.6	1962	5.4	1968	17.3	1974	6.6
1957	2.1	1963	2.4	1969	8.9	1977	12.5
1958	5.0	1964	4.0	1970	15.4	1978	8.9
1959	2.3	1965	9.1	1971	9.7	1980	11.0
						1982	12.4

Note: These calculations are based on the results of local elections in the four major cities in Scotland (Glasgow, Edinburgh, Aberdeen and Dundee). Together these contain about one third of the total Scottish electorate. For each set of elections the votes obtained by the parties in the four cities were aggregrated and the index calculated in the normal way.

Sources: Bochel and Denver (1975 et seq.); Glasgow Herald, Scotsman (Edinburgh), Press and Journal (Aberdeen), Courier (Dundee).

Table 6.3 describes trends in volatility at this level in Scotland since 1954, again using the Pedersen index. As in general elections, volatility was relatively low and fairly stable in the 1950s and early 1960s. In the late 1960s, however, volatility increased sharply and since then it has generally remained at a higher level than before.

As with general elections, the pattern of volatility is related to the rises and falls of minor parties. It was in the late 1960s that the SNP first made an electoral breakthrough, winning a parliamentary by-election in spectacular fashion and making many gains in local elections. Similarly, the high volatility figure for 1982 reflects the success of the Alliance in its first widespread challenge at local level in Scotland. The link between SNP performance and local electoral volatility is illustrated by the fact that over the 25 elections shown in Table 6.3 there is a correlation of 0.85 between the volatility index and the change in the percentage of votes gained by the SNP.

Opinion polls provide an even more regular means of monitoring public opinion. A number of companies now publish regular monthly polls describing current voting intentions. But the regular British-wide polls do not normally have enough Scottish respondents to make separate analysis of them valid. Some authors have sought to overcome this by aggregating a series of polls, thus increasing the number of respondents (Rose, 1980). There are now, however, two regular Scottish polls. A monthly poll by System Three Scotland is published in the Glasgow Herald while the Scotsman has a quarterly poll carried out by MORI (Market & Opinion Research International). Although both of these are valuable, the possibilities for the analysis of trends are limited since the System Three poll dates from 1974 and MORI began regular polling in Scotland only in 1980. By these dates, as has been seen, electoral volatility in Scotland had already reached high levels.

Nonetheless, polls are useful indicators of volatility between elections. 'Volatility' is, of course, being used here in a wider sense in that it does not refer to behaviour in succesive elections (indeed it does not refer to behaviour at all but to stated vote intentions). Poll results can, however, be taken as indicative of the electorate's predisposition to change and of the extent of wavering among voters.

Table 6.4 shows the range of the share of vote intentions received by each party in System Three's monthly poll for two separate inter-election periods. The range is not an altogether satisfactory measure of dispersion and it gives little guidance as to the extent of fluctuation in party support. But it does have the advantage of being simple to calculate and easy to understand.

Table 6.4: Range of Vote Intentions in Scotland 1974-1983

| | 1974-79 | | | 1979-83 | | |
	High	Low	Range	High	Low	Range
Con	39	16	23	31	14	17
Lab	52	24	38	59	38	21
Lib/ Alliance	11	2	9	27	6	21
SNP	36	17	19	22	11	11

Source: System Three Scotland Ltd.

In both periods there were very substantial variations in vote intentions. In the first period, when a Labour government was in office, Labour support was particularly variable ranging from less than one quarter to more than one half of the vote. Variability in Conservative, Labour and SNP support appears to have reduced during Mrs Thatcher's first term in office but the formation of the SDP and the Alliance with the Liberals introduced a new source of volatility. The fact that vote intentions can vary so considerably within the lifetime of a government implies that in inter-election periods very large numbers of electors are predisposed to change their voting behaviour.

Thus far, I have been describing and analysing 'net' volatility in Scotland. This needs to be distinguished from 'gross' volatility. Measures of 'net' volatility are unaffected by self-cancelling change, that is they cannot take account of switching between parties which is matched by switching in the opposite direction. The term 'gross' volatility refers to all changes in behaviour at successive elections and as such has three components, viz.(i) switching between major parties; (ii) switching between major and minor parties or minor parties only; (iii) switching between voting and non-voting.

Clearly the only way to analyse volatility thus defined is by means of surveys of electors. Moreover, given the well-known problem of inaccurate recall of voting behaviour by survey respondents, panel surveys are preferable to a series of cross-section samples (although even with panels inaccuracies still exist, especially in the over-reporting of voter turnout).

There have been only two academic surveys of

voting behaviour covering the whole of Scotland. The first was carried out after the election of October 1974 under the direction of Dr William Miller of the University of Strathclyde. Before this study there had been some survey studies of Scottish electoral behaviour but these were very localised (see, for example, Budge and Urwin, 1966). In addition, the national samples used by Butler and Stokes and the British Election Study surveys from the 1960s onwards contained too few Scottish respondents to allow worthwhile separate analysis.

The 1974 Scottish election study was, then, a major breakthrough for students of Scottish electoral politics and it was followed by a second survey in 1979. In this survey a panel of October 1974 respondents were reinterviewed together with new respondents who were added to 'top up' the sample and thereby achieve a representative cross-section for 1979. Unfortunately this series of surveys was not continued in 1983.

Given that we are concerned to analyse trends in electoral volatilty, the absence of time-series data is a severe handicap. (It is largely a consequence of the fact that mainstream academics, like pollsters and governments, began to take a serious interest in Scottish politics only after the dramatic rise of the SNP). Nonetheless the data presented in Table 6.5, which derive from the two Scottish surveys, are full of interest. The base in each case is the number of respondents who were eligible to vote at the elections concerned and electors are described as 'volatile' when their reported behaviour at successive elections fell outside the main diagonal in the conventional matrix format used to describe vote turnover.

When it is remembered that there is a tendency for survey respondents to recall past voting behaviour inaccurately in such a way as to make it consistent with their current preferences (Crewe and Sarlvik, 1983, pp.345-56) the data suggest very high levels of volatility. More than a quarter of Scottish electors altered their electoral behaviour between 1970 and February 1974 and between the latter election and the one that followed a mere eight months later. Using similar recall data the proportion of volatile electors between 1974 and 1979 rose to 30 per cent although the panel data suggest that the real figure was even higher at 36.5 per cent. When three elections are taken into account the proportion of electors classified as volatile rises to around two-fifths. Given the

image of the British voter portrayed by voting
studies up to the 1970s as displaying rock-like
fidelity to his party, these figures for gross
volatility may fairly be described as staggering.

Table 6.5:   Gross Volatility in Successive Elections

	Total Volatile	Major Party Switchers	Major-Minor Switchers	Change involving Non-voting
	%	%	%	%
1970-Feb74 (N=1032)	28.5	2.5	13.5	12.5
Feb74-Oct74 (N=1116)	26.0	1.0	13.0	12.0
Oct74-1979 (a) (N=340)	36.5	3.5	20.0	13.0
(b) (N=666)	30.0	4.0	15.5	10.5
1970-Feb74-Oct74 (N=1023)	43.0	2.0	21.0	20.0
Feb74-Oct74-1979 (a) (N=340)	44.0	3.0	23.0	18.0
(b) (N=638)	37.5	4.0	21.0	11.0

Note: Two sets of figures are given where the 1979
election is analysed. Those marked (a) are based on
the 1974-79 panel of respondents and refer to 1974
vote as reported in 1974. Those marked (b) are
taken from the entire 1979 sample and refer to 1974
vote as recalled in 1979.
Source: Scottish Election Study.

Table 6.5 also shows the contribution of the
three components of electoral volatility to the
overall figure. It is immediately apparent that
switching between the Conservative and Labour
parties remains rare. Far more important are
changes involving non-voting at one election and
switching between major and minor parties.
(Overwhelmingly the figures in the third column of
the table reflect major-minor movements, and in
particular movements to and from the SNP, rather
than minor-minor ones).
        It is, of course, a moot point whether

non-voting should count as volatile behaviour since
it may be caused by technical factors or illness or
some other accidental reason and the non-voter at
one election may have voted for the same party at
all preceding elections and continue to do so in
future elections. If all respondents who, in three
elections, voted twice for the same party and did
not vote once are considered as constant rather than
volatile then the overall volatility figure for the
first three elections of the 1970s is reduced to 31
per cent and for the second three to 36 per cent -
still substantial slices of the electorate.

No such qualification needs to be made to the
figures for party switching. The survey data
confirm the aggregate data analysis by showing that
the emergence of the SNP was a major contributory
factor to, or consequence of, increased levels of
volatility in Scotland. It may be, of course, that
much of the vote switching involving the SNP was
purely tactical and that such switchers maintained
their traditional party commitment. Widespread
tactical voting was a new phenomenon of the 1970s
and this in itself bespeaks a new willingness on the
part of electors to forsake traditional voting
patterns even if their object in doing so was to
defeat their least preferred party.

As noted above, there was no academic survey of
voting behaviour in the 1983 election. Some
indication of the level of volatility can, however,
be given by analysing opinion poll data. These data
refer, of course, to vote intentions and not to
recalled vote and thus they do not allow for
estimates to be made of volatility arising from
non-voting. In the absence of a post-election
survey, however, the poll data are worth
considering. Combining the results of the two
Scottish campaign polls conducted by MORI shows that
22 per cent of electors intended to switch parties
in 1983 as compared with their 1979 vote. This is a
larger proportion of switchers than was recorded at
any of the preceding three elections using recall
data. As before, switching between the major
parties remained low (3.5 per cent) and switching
between major and minor parties high (18.5 per
cent). But in 1983 it was the Liberal/SDP Alliance,
rather than the SNP, which mainly acted as the
destabilising influence.

Clearly opinion poll data must be treated with
caution when used to measure volatility. But the
MORI polls in question somewhat underestimated
Alliance support in Scotland, which suggests that

the rate of party switching in the election itself
may have been even higher than the figure derived
from the polls. This in turn suggests that gross
volatility, like net volatility as measured by the
Pedersen index, reached a new peak in Scotland in
1983.

EXPLANATIONS

     It seems clear that explanations for increased
electoral volatility in Scotland are inevitably
bound up with explanations of the success of the SNP
from the late 1960s onward and of the SDP/Liberal
Alliance in 1983. As we have seen, switching
between the traditional parties remained relatively
low and it seems likely that change involving
non-voting is fairly constant. It was the emergence
of third and fourth parties which gave rise to high
levels of electoral volatility. Such parties have
existed before, however, without very much success
so that what requires explanation is why electors in
the 1970s and 1980s were willing to desert
traditional loyalties when they had not done so
before.
     Underlying any explanation is the fact that
during the 1960s and 1970s Scotland experienced very
rapid social change. Drucker and Brown describe the
changes in this period as constituting ´the
modernisation of Scotland´ (1980, ch.3). Three
indicators of change are shown in Table 6.6. The
first is the decline in traditional industries. The
Scottish industrial heartland was historically
based on these industries and they sustained
numerous working class communities. But employment
in them declined very sharply - by more than a third
- after 1961. To some extent traditional employment
was replaced by new manufacturing industries - car
manufacturing, instrument and electrical engineering
and so on - but more importantly there was an
explosive growth of the service sector. Between
1961 and 1978 employment in insurance, banking and
professional and scientific services increased from
256,000 to 429,000. According to Drucker and Brown,
´the coincidence of the run-down of heavy
industries, the expansion of new industries and a
shift to the service sector created new social
patterns in Scotland. At one and the same time the
traditional backbone of the Labour movement - the
skilled worker - was being broken and the stage was
set for the development of a larger self-conscious

162

Table 6.6: The Modernisation of Scotland

(a) Employment in Selected Industries (thousands)

	1961	1971	1978
Coal mining	80.4	34.3	39.3
Metal manufacture	63.1	48.2	36.8
Heavy engineering	103.2	92.5	82.6
Shipbuilding	63.4	40.9	40.7
Textiles	98.3	74.4	55.3

(b) Forms of marriage

	1961 %	1971 %	1981 %
Church of Scotland	54.9	45.9	40.1
Roman Catholic	16.9	16.3	14.5
Civil	18.4	30.7	39.1

(c) % Public Sector of New Dwellings Completed

1961-65 %	1966-70 %	1971-75 %	1976-1980 %
76.2	80.2	65.4	49.6

Note: Under (b) columns do not total 100 because other forms of marriage are not shown.
Sources: (a) General Register Office, Edinburgh, Census 1961, Vol. 6, Part II, Table 1; Census 1971, Economic Activity Tables, Table 2; Scottish Abstract of Statistics, 1983. (b) Appropriate volumes of the Annual Report of the Registrar General for Scotland. (c) Scottish Abstract of Statistics, 1971-1983.

middle class´ (1980,p.37).
     The second part of the Table shows that along with these changes came religious changes. There was increasing secularisation as evidenced by the increasing proportion of marriages which were civil ceremonies. Between 1951 and 1961 the proportion of civil marriages increased only slowly from 16.5 per cent to 18.4 per cent. Thereafter, however, this proportion increased very rapidly as marriages in the two major religious denominations decreased.
     Changes in patterns of housing have been slower to take effect. Between the censuses of 1961 and 1971 the proportion of households in Scotland who were owner-occupiers increased slightly from 25.2 per cent to 29.4 per cent. By 1981 this had risen to 34.7 per cent. In contrast, the proportion of

households living in public rented housing hardly changed in the 1970s, increasing from 53.6 per cent in 1971 to 54.6 per cent in 1981. This trend towards private sector housing is clearly demonstrated by the data for house building. From a peak of 80 per cent in the late 1960s the public sector's share of dwellings completed fell to less than half in the late 1970s.

It would be surprising if these and other social changes did not have a destabilising effect on political behaviour, although the connection between the two is difficult to prove empirically. What can be said is that the 1970s saw a weakening in the relationship between class and party support. This can be demonstrated in a variety of ways but, as before, analysis is hampered by the absence of comparable time-series data. Table 6.7, therefore, uses various sources and various measures of the class-party tie, as explained in the notes to the table.

The opinion poll data show a marked drop in the class voting index in the 1970s, indicating a substantial loosening of the class-party link. The figures in the third row are perhaps easier to understand; they show that while in the 1960s almost two thirds of voters supported their 'natural' class party this was true of less than half of them by 1983. Again it should be borne in mind that the 1983 MORI polls, upon which the figures are based, underestimated Alliance support.

The data from the Scottish Election Study show a similar pattern to October 1974, with only just over two-fifths of voters supporting their 'natural' party in that election. In 1979, however, as support for the SNP declined, the class-party relationship was to some extent reasserted. From the evidence available, however, one can be confident that the strength of the relationship was still reduced as compared with the situation before 1970. Given the inroads made by the Alliance in 1983 and the continuing electoral presence of the SNP, we would anticipate a decline in the class voting index and this is confirmed by data from the B.B.C./Gallup election survey. By 1983 the link between class and party in Scotland was as weak as it had ever been.

Richard Rose argues that housing tenure has replaced occupation as the best single predictor of party choice in Britain (Rose, 1980). It might be hypothesised that this would be particularly true in Scotland where public sector housing is much more

Table 6.7: The Changing Relationship Between Class
and Party

_____

(a) Opinion Polls

	1963-66	1970	1974	1979	1983
Alford Index (i)	51	39	n/a	32	33
Alford Index (ii)	33	18	n/a	20	21
% Non-Manual Con or Manual Lab	64	--	--	--	48

(b) Scottish Election Study/Gallup

	1970	Feb. 1974	Oct. 1974	1979	1983
Alford Index (i)	39	35	36	42	33
Alford Index (ii)	24	22	21	25	16
Alford Index (iii)	29	24	25	33	24
% Non-Manual Con or Manual Lab	57	49	43	52	44

_____

Notes: The base in all cases is the number of
respondents who voted (or specified a vote
intention). The Alford Index is defined as the
percentage of manual workers voting Labour minus the
percentage of non-manual workers doing so. The
nature of the data makes it impossible to use the
conventional ABC1/C2DE occupational division
consistently except in the case of the Scottish
Election Study data in row (iii). The other rows
define non-manual workers as the AB group (i) and as
the C2 group alone (ii). The measure of the %
non-manual Conservative or manual Labour uses the
conventional division.
Sources: Butler and Stokes (1974, p.127); Rose
(1974, p.516; 1980, p.42); MORI; Scottish Election
Study; Gallup/B.B.C. Election Survey 1983.

prevalent than elsewhere in Britain and constitutes
the major battlefield of local politics. As with
occupational status, however, the relationship
between housing tenure and Conservative or Labour
voting declined in the 1970s. According to the
Scottish Election Study figures, in 1970 65 per cent
of council tenants voted Labour and 60 per cent of
owner occupiers voted Conservative. By 1983,
according to MORI, 53 per cent of tenants intended
to vote Labour and 48 per cent of owner occupiers
intended to vote Conservative. Throughout the
1970s, to paraphrase Ivor Crewe, knowing an
elector´s housing tenure was only a little better

than tossing a coin in predicting which way he or she would vote.

As the connection between social structural variables and Conservative or Labour support declined in strength, it was not replaced by new correlations between the social structure and third-party support. Indeed, the striking feature of SNP and Alliance support is the extent to which it is not skewed by social factors. This is illustrated in Table 6.8 which shows the social profiles of the parties' support in 1983. The contrast between Alliance and SNP support on the one hand and Conservative and Labour support on the other is clear. Support for the former parties comes much more proportionately from different social groups. This is particularly true of occupation and housing.

Table 6.8: Social Profiles of Parties' Support, 1983

		Con %	Lab %	All %	SNP %	Total %
(a)	Sex					
	Male	45	50	47	57	48
	Female	55	50	53	43	52
(b)	Age					
	18-24	14	16	16	18	16
	25-34	17	21	21	24	20
	35-44	33	32	30	32	32
	55+	36	31	33	26	33
(c)	Occupation					
	AB	20	5	15	11	11
	C1	28	14	23	18	21
	C2	26	31	30	37	30
	DE	50	32	32	34	38
(d)	Housing Tenure					
	Owner Occupier	53	19	37	32	36
	Council Tenant	33	73	53	56	56
	Other	14	8	10	11	9

Note: All= Alliance.
Source: Aggregated MORI polls for the Scotsman.

The weakening relationship between social structure and party choice in Scotland is largely a function of increased support for the SNP and, in 1983, the Alliance. In itself this does not explain volatility but is, rather, a consequence of electors´ increased willingness to desert their traditional allegiances and vote for the SNP or the Alliance. It is this which needs to be explained in order to account for increased volatility.

A good deal has been written on the ups and downs of SNP support but the emphasis and explanations offered have varied depending upon the point in the cycle at which authors were writing. Early explanations, following the apparently poor showing by the SNP in the 1970 general election, saw SNP voting as ´protest´ voting which left traditional party identifications unaltered (see McLean,1970; Bochel and Denver, 1972). On the other hand, people writing at the height of the second surge in the SNP´s popularity tended to assume that high levels of support would be an enduring feature of Scottish politics (Brand,1978). As James Kellas commented after the 1979 election, ´The rise and fall and rise and fall...of the SNP awaits analysis´ (Kellas, 1980).

The most convincing analysis of SNP support to date is that given by Miller (Miller et al., 1977; Miller, 1981). He rejects any simple view that SNP voting was a direct product of a demand for Scottish self-government. He argues that in the 1960s and early 1970s British-wide factors loosened Scottish electors´ attachment to the major parties, just as in the rest of the country. In Scotland, however, there was a pre-existing but unactivated issue cleavage on the question of devolution. The SNP were able to capitalise on this and benefit from disaffection with the major parties. After the election of February 1974 SNP support became self-sustaining since the devolution issue was firmly on the agenda - indeed it was at the forefront of political debate in Scotland. A number of factors - the issue of North Sea oil, distrust in government and the youthfulness of SNP support - interacted and combined to prevent a return to the old two-party system.

Clearly the initial loosening of traditional party attachments is crucial to this explanation. There is no doubt that the 1970s witnessed a sharp decline in electors´ commitment to the Conservative and Labour parties (Crewe and Sarlvik, 1983). A variety of reasons has been put forward to explain this - the growth of a more sophisticated electorate, rapid social change, disjunctions between electors´ policy preferences and party stances, increased television coverage of politics and so on. Whatever the reasons, this process created a large pool of only weakly-aligned voters who were, therefore, more easily detachable from traditional voting patterns.

Table 6.9 shows the extent of Labour and Conservative party identification in Scotland. Despite the very small numbers involved, the data from the Butler and Stokes 1966-1970 panel are included in order to illustrate the extent of change. The proportion identifying with the two parties fell from around 77 per cent in 1966 to 66 per cent in 1974 but recovered to 72 per cent in 1979. More significantly, the proportion who identified 'very strongly' declined very sharply from 1966 to 1974 and then declined again, despite the increase in identification, to a mere 14 per cent in 1979.

Table 6.9: Conservative and Labour Party Identification 1966-1979

	1966	1974	1979
% Identifying Con	34	29	33
% Identifying Lab	43	37	39
Total	77	66	72
% Very Strong Con	15	7	6
% Very Strong Lab	18	12	8
Total	33	19	14
(N)	(90)	(1175)	(729)

Note: The base in each case is all respondents.
Sources: Butler and Stokes 1966-1970 panel; Scottish Election Study.

The decline in strong major-party identification has not been offset by strong identification with the other parties. SNP and Liberal voters are less likely to identify with their parties than are Conservative and Labour supporters and in 1979 only 25 per cent of those who identified with the SNP and eight per cent of those who identified with the Liberals described themselves as 'very strong' identifiers. One effect of this is that SNP and Liberal voting is relatively unstable and liable to vary dramatically from one election to the next. Having introduced higher volatility into Scottish elections, as it were, these parties remain a destabilising influence because of their failure to generate strong party identification among electors.

The decline of party identification provided, then, a pool of potential defectors from the major parties and the issue of devolution channelled these to the SNP for most of the 1970s. In 1979, however, the devolution question was removed from the political agenda, at least temporarily. The years of debate culminated in a referendum in Scotland in March 1979 on the Labour government's proposals to set up a Scottish legislative assembly. The result of the referendum was a narrow majority in favour of the proposals but the percentage voting 'Yes' fell far short of that required to implement devolution and the proposals were dropped (see Bochel, Denver and Macartney, 1981).

The general election which followed in May 1979 is described by Miller as a 'British election'. The devolution issue appeared dead and the election campaign 'marked a return to British politics' (Miller, 1981, pp.254-57). This was reflected in a sharp fall in SNP support and, as has been seen, increases in the class-party index and in major-party identification. But as we have also seen, identification with the major parties was weaker than ever and there was always the possibility that this potential for volatility could be converted into actuality.

This is what happened in 1983. On this occasion, however, with the devolution issue apparently forgotten, (it was mentioned by only four per cent of MORI'S Scottish respondents as an important issue) it was the SDP/Liberal Alliance which scooped up the votes. No factors peculiar to Scotland are needed to account for this. People in Scotland were attracted to the Alliance, or repelled by the other parties for the same reasons as people elsewhere - the perceived extremism of the major parties, especially the Labour party, the personalities of party leaders, a general desire for change - and the Alliance's share of votes in Scotland was within two per cent of its share in England and Wales.

In terms of net volatility, and almost certainly of gross volatility as well, the 1983 election marked a new peak. It remains to be seen whether the rest of the 1980s will see a continuation of the electoral turmoil which manifestly characterised Scottish politics in the 1970s.

ELECTORAL VOLATILITY AND THE PARTY SYSTEM

After the 1983 election the party system in Scotland was highly fractionalised. Table 6.10 shows the scores on Rae´s indices of fractionalisation (Rae, 1971) for Scotland and England and Wales in 1966 and 1983. In terms both of popular support and of seats won, the party system in Scotland has become significantly more fractionalised than in England and Wales. By 1983, five different parties held seats in Scotland - 41 Labour, 21 Conservative, 5 Liberal, 3 SDP and 2 SNP. Whether the minor parties can make further inroads depends upon three main factors.

Table 6.10: The Fractionalisation of the Party System

	England and Wales		Scotland	
	1966	1983	1966	1983
Votes	.580	.652	.601	.722
Seats	.497	.462	.495	.578

Note: Rae´s index of fractionalisation is computed by summing the squares of each party´s proportion of seats or votes and subtracting the sum from 1. The larger the resulting score, the greater the fractionalisation of the system (see Rae, 1971, pp.53-8).

Firstly there is the electoral system. The minor parties were severely penalised by the workings of the system in 1983. With 36 per cent of the votes between them they won only 14 per cent of the seats. Clearly any alteration in the electoral system towards more proportionality would increase the fragmentation of the party system. It must be said, however, that any such change seems unlikely in the foreseeable future and the electoral system will remain an important stumbling block to the emergence of an even more complex party system. Secondly, the fortunes of the minor parties are crucially dependent upon the performance and activities of the main parties. Much minor party support is negative in that it springs from dislike of, or disaffection from, the major parties so that if the latter can project an image of competence, unity and moderation then support may well flow back to them. On the other hand, the Conservative government will probably become unpopular (as all governments do) and there are doubts as to whether Labour can cast off the image of a divided party committed to extreme and unpopular policies. In this situation minor party prospects would be bright. Finally, and more specific to Scotland, it could be that the devolution question will be reactivated. Devolutionists have been quick to point out that in the last two elections Scotland has returned a majority of Labour MPs but found itself governed by the Conservatives. In addition, the pro-devolution parties in Scotland - Labour, the Alliance, and the SNP - together easily outpolled the Conservatives. The issue, then, remains simmering. If it boils up, then the likely beneficiaries will be the SNP since Labour, although officially committed to devolution, in fact remains divided on the issue at grass-roots level in Scotland.

The future of the party system in Scotland is, then, difficult to predict. The reason for this is the continuing volatility of the electorate. Support for the Liberals, SDP and SNP is fragile. These parties do not have a solid core of electoral support that can be utterly relied upon and people who vote for them in one election are liable to drift elsewhere in the next. But commitment to the major parties is also weak and their supporters are detachable.

Political tides have always ebbed and flowed. In Scotland nowadays the problem is not just that the ebbs and flows are more rapid than ever but also that it is difficult to predict which of the four parties will be carried in or carried off by the tide.

NOTE

I am grateful to Hugh Bochel and Terence Karran for help in acquiring data from the Scottish Election Study and to William Miller, University of Strathclyde, for comments on an earlier draft.

REFERENCES

Bochel, J.M and D.T. Denver (1972) ´The Decline of the SNP - An Alternative View´, Political Studies, XX, 311-16
---------- (1975 et seq.) Scottish Local Election Results, Election Studies, Dundee

Bochel,J.M., D.T. Denver, and A. Macartney (eds.) (1981) The Referendum Experience, Aberdeen University Press, Aberdeen

Brand, J. (1978) The National Movement in Scotland, Routledge and Kegan Paul, London

Budge, I. and D.W. Urwin (1966) Scottish Political Behaviour, Longmans, London

Butler, D. and D. Stokes (1974) Political Change in Britain, 2nd ed., Macmillan, London

Crewe, I. and B. Sarlvik (1983) Decade of Dealignment, Cambridge University Press, Cambridge

Drucker, H. and G. Brown (1980) The Politics of Nationalism and Devolution, Longmans, London

Kellas, J.G. (1973) The Scottish Political System, Cambridge University Press, Cambridge

---------- (1980) 'Political Science and Scottish Politics', British Journal of Political Science, 10, 365-79

Mc Lean, I. (1970) 'The Rise and Fall of the Scottish National Party', Political Studies, XVIII, 357-72

Miller, W.L. (1982) 'Variations in Electoral Behaviour in the U.K.' in P. Madgwick and R. Rose (eds.), The Territorial Dimension in United Kingdom Politics, Macmillan, London

---------- (1981) The End of British Politics, Clarendon Press, Oxford

Miller, W.L., I. Crewe, B. Sarlvik, and J. Alt (1977) 'The Connection Between SNP Voting and the Demand for Scottish Self-Government', European Journal of Political Research, 5, 83-102

Rae, D.W. (1971) The Political Consequences of Electoral Laws, revised ed., Yale University Press, New Haven

Rose, R. (1970) 'The United Kingdom as a Multi-National State', University of Strathclyde, Survey Research Centre, Occasional Paper No.6

-------- (1980) 'Class Does Not Equal Party', University of Strathclyde, Centre for the Study of Public Policy, Occasional Paper No.44

-------- (1974) 'Britain: Simple Abstractions and Complex Realities' in R. Rose (ed.), Electoral Behaviour, Free Press, London and New York

Waller, R. (1980) 'The 1979 Local and General Elections in England and Wales: Is there a Local - National Differential', Political Studies, XXVIII, 443-50

Chapter 7

IRELAND

M.A. Marsh

INTRODUCTION

A political system which undergoes three elections within eighteen months, each of them producing a change in party control of government, might be presumed to have a volatile electorate. Yet close analysis of the Republic of Ireland indicates an electoral pattern of considerable stability, although there are underlying trends which raise the possibility that more dramatic electoral shifts may be seen in the near future. Whilst governments have alternated with increasing frequency in recent years the degree of electoral change necessary to bring this about has been quite small; more of the characteristics of a two party system, both electoral and governmental, have developed as the opposition to the once predominant Fianna Fail party has grown more cohesive. Although at present there is little volatility to be explained, many of the factors that might produce considerable levels of volatility are present. This raises interesting questions about the conditions under which volatility takes place and poses questions about the nature and future of Irish politics.

A stable core to Irish politics has been provided by three parties: Fianna Fail, Fine Gael (formerly Cumann na nGaedheal) and the Labour Party (see Table 7.1). The two largest, Fianna Fail and Fine Gael have their origins in divisions within the Irish nationalist movement over the terms of independence from Britain set in the Treaty of 1922. This gave only dominion status to an Irish Free State with Britain keeping a military and governmental presence in that state as well as retaining six counties of Ireland within the United Kingdom as ´Northern Ireland´. Pro- and anti-Treaty

Table 7.1: First Preference Votes in Dail Elections, 1948-82

	1948 %	1951 %	1954 %	1957 %	1961 %	1965 %
Fianna Fail	41.9	46.3	43.4	48.3	43.8	47.7
Fine Gael	19.8	25.7	32.0	26.6	32.0	34.1
Labour	8.7	11.4	12.1	9.1	11.6	15.4
Clann na Talmhan	5.3	2.9	3.1	2.4	1.5	--
Clann na Poblachta	13.2	4.1	3.8	1.7	1.2	0.7
National Labour	2.6	--	--	--	--	--
Sinn Fein	--	--	--	5.3	3.0	--
National Progressive Democrats	--	--	--	--.	1.0	--
Others	8.5	9.6	5.7	6.6	5.9	2.1

Table 7.1 (contd)

	1969 %	1973 %	1977 %	1981 %	Feb. 1982 %	Nov. 1982 %
Fianna Fail	45.7	46.2	50.6	45.3	47.3	45.2
Fine Gael	34.1	35.1	30.5	36.5	37.3	39.2
Labour	17.0	13.7	11.6	9.9	9.0	9.4
Prov. Sinn Fein	--	--	--	--	1.0	--
The Workers Party	--	1.1	1.7	1.7	2.2	3.3
H-Block Protest	--	--	--	2.5	--	--
Others	3.2	3.9	5.6	4.1	3.2	2.9

Note: The Workers Party contested as Sinn Fein in 1973 and as Sinn Fein - The Workers Party in 1977, 1981 and Feb. 1982.
Sources: O'Leary (1979) and Official Results.

forces opposed each other in the Civil War of 1922-23. The victorious pro-Treaty forces afterwards formed Cumann na nGaedheal, which became Fine Gael in 1933. The defeated group, keeping the name Sinn Fein, stayed out of parliament until 1927 when a minority faction formed Fianna Fail and took their seats in the Dail (Irish Chamber of Deputies).

The Labour Party was founded before independence. It tried to stand aside during the Civil War but has never succeeded in imposing its mildly socialist view of political reality on an electorate which has always placed it behind the two nationalist parties in its affections.

The nationalist cleavage remains significant

within the party system. Although most of the original disputes became irrelevant within 20 years as many provisions of the Treaty ceased to have effect, the separate existence of Northern Ireland gave the issue relevance and that issue continues to colour Irish political debate on a wide range of subjects. All Irish parties claim to want Irish Unity - over that there is no division - but different parties have enunciated softer and harder lines over the means to that end and over Irish-British relations in general. Fianna Fail have taken a harder line, Fine Gael (and Labour) a softer one. Other cleavages have been identified, in particular an economic, left-right cleavage and a cultural cleavage seen variously as urban-rural, centre-periphery and secular-clerical (see Mair, 1982, p.9). No party can claim to represent any particular cleavage by itself, nor is any strongly united in its position on the various broad issues involved. Such cleavages divide parties internally as well as one from another. Yet today the Labour Party is broadly left and secular, Fine Gael and Fianna Fail both centrist economically, with Fianna Fail more traditional/clerical on many social issues than Fine Gael. All parties accept the mixed economy, the welfare state, the EEC and the goal of Irish Unity. Differences are those of emphasis but at election time such differences may be as important as any other.

The position of these parties has not been unchallenged and some aspirants have met with considerable, if temporary, success. Agrarian protectionism, nationalism and socialism have provided the ideological basis for minor parties. A farmers' party, Clann na Talmhan, won considerable support in the late 1940s, as did a left-wing nationalist protest party, Clann na Poblachta. Together they significantly fragmented a party system which appeared to be settling down after the first 20 years of independence. Their effect was short-lived, however, and both became negligible forces in the mid-1950s. Recently, The Workers' Party, a group with origins in the anti-parliamentary Official Sinn Fein movement, have mounted a forceful challenge, particularly in Dublin, on a platform whose socialism is more evident than that of the Labour Party's and whose nationalism is subdued. As yet, this party has failed to make the sort of impact in its urban challenge that the earlier parties managed in a more rural Ireland. In 1981 nine candidates stood under an 'H-Block' protest label, as part of the campaign to mobilise support for republican prisoners on hunger strike in Northern Ireland.(1) These candidates won 2.5 per cent of the vote, two seats, and averaged over ten per cent of the vote in constituencies they contested. However, in 1982 when Provisional Sinn Fein ran several candidates, it failed to attract that same level of support in the absence of the hunger strike campaign.(2) The episode suggested the presence of a significant republican vote but also the difficulty of mobilising it.

The nature and style of electoral competition has developed out of the history and ecology of the country but cannot be understood independently of the electoral system within which it takes place. Irish elections are held under the Single Transferable Vote system (STV) in multi-member constituencies. STV gives voters the freedom to state a preference ordering of all candidates. Most electors use that freedom to express their preferences between the candidates offered by at least one party and many give preference orderings covering several parties' candidates.

The consequences for electoral competition of STV are numerous (see O'Leary, 1979). A few are of special importance here. First, the system produces results which are fairly proportional in terms of the match between seats and votes won by a party. This means the electoral threshold for a new party is not so high as under the British system, although it is higher than that in the Netherlands or Denmark. There is some disproportionality however, and this has generally benefitted Fianna Fail and assisted the formation of majority-based governments. Second, and more importantly, the system throws a party's candidates into competition with each other in the electoral arena. Whilst that competition might theoretically take many forms, drawing for instance on the cleavages within the party system, in practice it revolves around fundamentally non-political issues with candidates stressing personal ability and expertise as an intermediary between voters and the administrative apparatus of the state (Bax, 1976; Sacks, 1976; Chubb, 1982). Candidates attract a personal vote and this element may help explain the relatively low degree of constituency-level electoral stability for parties (Gallagher, 1976, pp.68-9). The system also provides an opportunity for voters to switch candidate preferences without switching party preference between elections. Hence, any assessment of volatility which is party centred may underestimate the degree of change which has occurred. There may be a significant shift against incumbent candidates of an unpopular government for instance. A further point concerns the essence of electoral competition. It has been suggested that candidates are more concerned to attract votes from running mates than from opposing parties, that inter-party electoral competition is neglected and that this sustains the existing party system (Carty, 1981). These arguments will be reconsidered later when evidence concerning the degree of political stability has been presented.

Whilst there have been changes in the structure and emphasis of party competition in the electoral arena the pattern of government formation has been more consistent. Essentially it has been a matter of Fianna Fail versus the rest.(3) Fianna Fail have occupied office from 1932-48, 1951-54, 1957-73, 1977-81 and from February 1982 to November 1982. The alternative has been various Fine Gael dominated coalitions: five parties in 1948-51, three in 1954-57 and Fine Gael-Labour coalitions in 1973-77, 1981-February 1982 and from November 1982. Alternation has become the norm over the past five elections with no government returned since 1969.

Governments have at times owed some of their parliamentary strength to the electoral system. Fianna Fail has commonly won a higher proportion of seats than votes. This bonus was reduced in the 1973 and 1980s elections by effective electoral alliances between Fine Gael and Labour and in November 1982 it was the coalition which received the greatest bonus from disproportionality. Changes in government, then, have owed something to effective political organisation as well as to electoral changes.

TRENDS IN ELECTORAL VOLATILITY

Ivor Crewe has elaborated upon the distinction between 'net' and 'gross' volatility in the intro-ductory chapter. On the whole, the trend in net volatility in Ireland has been downwards and it is now well below levels of the late 1940s and 1950s. Surveys provide the opportunity to assess gross volatility, the changes made by individual electors, but this is difficult to establish in Ireland. What evidence there is suggests considerable stability, but there are grounds for suggesting occasional departures from traditional voting patterns and the existence today of a restlessness which may in future be translated into significant electoral change.

The trend in net volatility since 1948, as measured by the Pedersen index, (Pedersen, 1979) is shown on Table 7.2. The data suggest that volatility is declining. At five of the six elections between 1948 and 1965 net volatility was higher than at any of the six subsequent elections and although the index records increasing volatility at the 1973, 1977 and 1981 elections there has been very little change evident in the two elections of 1982. Whether these last two elections broke the trend because they fell so close together remains to be seen.

Table 7.2: Net Volatility 1948-82

	Volatility Index		Volatility Index
1948	13.3	1969	2.7
1951	14.1	1973	3.3
1954	7.1	1977	6.7
1957	11.1	1981	8.5
1961	8.9	Feb.1982	4.3
1965	9.8	Nov.1982	3.4

Source: See Table 7.1.

The fluctuations of the 1940s and 1950s coincided with the success and then decline of the two parties mentioned earlier, Clann na Talmhan and Clann na Poblachta. More recent aspiring parties have been less successful although the Workers' Party vote has shown a slow but steady increase. Since 1969 volatility has been manifested essentially in changes in relative strength between the three main parties. These three parties gained an increasing share of the vote up until the late 1960s winning 97 per cent in 1965 and 1969. Today the figure is a little lower, standing at 94 per cent in both 1982 elections. However, Fine Gael and Fianna Fail between them have continually increased their share which in both 1982 elections stood at 84 per cent, higher than at any time since the 1930s. The party system has become less fragmented. Fianna Fail's vote has remained quite stable but Fine

Gael´s has risen steadily since 1948, increasing at
every election since 1948 with the exception of 1954
and 1977, and Fine Gael is now in a position to
rival Fianna Fail as a party which might govern
alone.
      The reduced extent of electoral change in the
elections of the 1980s is mirrored in the results of
opinion polls. Figure 7.1 shows voting intentions
from November 1974 to June 1983. Fluctuations were
most pronounced in the mid-1970s. Since late 1979
neither Fianna Fail nor Fine Gael-Labour combined
have opened up a gap of more than ten per cent over
its rival, a position contrasting with the 20-30 per
cent Fianna Fail lead in 1976-78. There may be many
changes cancelling one another out. Pedersen´s
index, calculated for sets of polls over time, shows
volatility rising since 1980(4), indicating perhaps
a general restlessness but with no party or group of
parties seeming as attractive as Fianna Fail made
themselves in the mid-1970s.
      Most of the available survey evidence also
points to a fairly stable situation. Surveys which
have included a question on past as well as future
voting intentions give us some indication of gross
change and its direction. Available data from 1969
onwards are reported in Table 7.3. Of those
reporting a preference at two consecutive elections,
over 70 per cent reported one which is stable.(5)
The stability of individual party´s votes is
variable; Fianna Fail´s has varied between 72 per
cent and 91 per cent and Labour´s between 57 per
cent and 89 per cent with Fine Gael´s more
consistent at between 81 per cent and 86 per cent.
A survey just prior to the November 1982 election
suggested that 96 per cent of Fine Gael voters would
stick with the same party, compared with 90 per cent
of Fianna Fail voters (Irish Times, 15 November
1982). Where party switching has been indicated,
this has predominantly been between the three major
parties.
      It is not easy to estimate the degree of
intermittent abstention, as not all surveys
differentiate those who did not vote at the previous
election from those who could not vote, ´don´t
knows´ and non-respondents. Such discrimination is
possible for the 1977-81 period. An Irish Marketing
Survey report indicated that about ten per cent of
the sample claimed 1977 abstention, together with an
intention to vote in 1981 (IMS, 1981a, Table 9).
These voters indicated a disproportionate preference
for the coalition parties. A similar pattern is

Figure 7.1: Voting Intentions in Ireland 1974-82

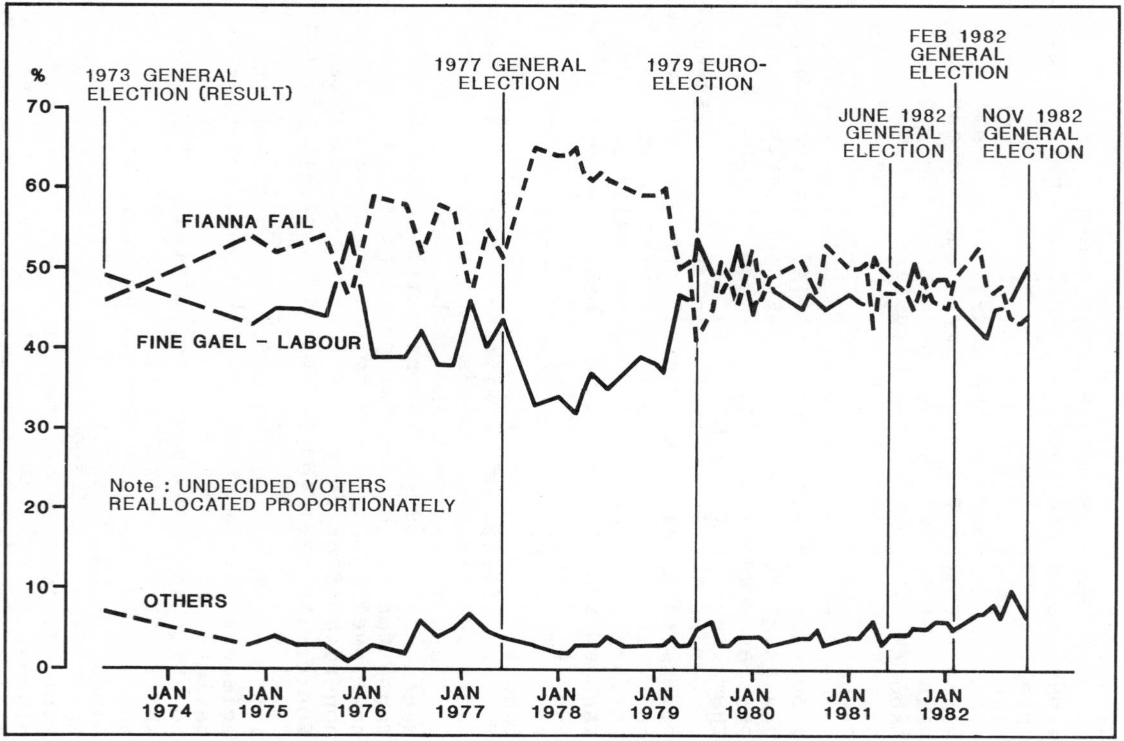

Ireland

Table 7.3: Voting Consistency in Selected Years, 1965-82

	1965-69	1969-73	1977-81	1981-Feb.82
% Party's Voters Staying Loyal at Consecutive Elections	%	%	%	%
Fianna Fail	91	77	72	91
Fine Gael	86	82	85	81
Labour	89	71	64	65
All Parties (incl Others)	90	78	75	84
% Party's Voters Who Remained Loyal from Previous Election and % Who had Changed Party				
Fianna Fail				
- loyal	*	83	74	78
-changers	*	4	5	10
Fine Gael				
- loyal	*	65	49	77
- changers	*	21	30	10
Labour				
- loyal	*	59	48	56
- changers	*	20	23	20

Notes: * = not available. In the second part of the Table the remainder of parties' support came from new voters, previous abstainers, don't knows and non-respondents.
Sources: Carty (1981); IMS (1973, 1981a, 1982a).

evident in February 1982 when non-voters in 1981 gave the coalition a ten per cent lead in contrast to Fianna Fail's three per cent lead amongst those who reported voting in 1981 (IMS, 1982a, Tables 36 and 37). The coalition parties - Fine Gael and Labour - have evidently benefitted more than Fianna Fail from voting inconsistency in recent years. As Table 7.3 indicates, Fianna Fail's vote contains the highest proportion of voters whose preference has remained unchanged from the previous election. Fine Gael's profile has varied with its level of support; its dramatic growth from 1977-81 is reflected in the low contribution loyal voters made to its support in

1981. However, in maintaining its level of support into 1982 it appears to have retained its voters. Fine Gael have recently rivalled Fianna Fail at holding on to its supporters once they have been attracted.

The accuracy of recall evidence is open to doubt. Consistency seems over-reported, as is the reported incidence of voting with turnout figures of over 90 per cent suggested (the real figure being around 75 per cent). Arguably, the complexity of voting under the STV system makes recall particularly questionable although against this could be set the simplicity of the Irish party system. But the similarity of results obtained from separate surveys is striking. For instance, all three polls of Irish Marketing Surveys' 1981 pre-election research produced almost identical results.(6) When compared to results obtained in other countries, the stability of voting preference is marked (Carty, 1981). Certainly there is little in these figures to challenge the picture of stability provided by Pedersen's index.

Further evidence on stability is given by the results of analysis of votes transferred between candidates. Inspection of the lower preferences given by supporters of elected or eliminated candidates can show the extent to which party is an effective constraint on preferences. It has been suggested that 'split-ticket' voting, voting for candidates from different parties, is a sign of volatility in the United States (Huntington, 1975, pp.87-8). Transferring across parties under STV is analogous to this. Gallagher calculated the 'percentage of transfers from each party which went to other candidates of the same party in situations where at least one candidate of the party has been able to receive transfers.' On average, the degree of 'solidarity' measured in this way is highest for Fianna Fail, followed by Fine Gael and Labour (Gallagher, 1978, Table 1). Gallagher's analysis of transfers up to 1977 and evidence from later elections gives no support to any thesis of general decline in party commitment. Labour's 'solidarity' has waned throughout the 1970s from its relatively high levels in the 1960s, but Fine Gael's solidarity has grown and is now comparable to its earlier peak in the 1930s, whilst Fianna Fail's supporters remain apparently as committed as ever. For both these parties, 'solidarity' is over 80 per cent. The growing Fine Gael commitment is perhaps bound up with its increasingly predominant position as the governmental alternative to Fianna Fail, both contributing to and resulting from it. The anti-Fianna Fail alternatives to Fine Gael simply have become less attractive.

In general, then, there is little evidence of volatility in Ireland. Rather, there is considerable stability. Small inter-election changes have been to the long-term benefit of Fine Gael but massive shifts between major parties or the rapid growth of new parties have not occurred in recent times. Some case for there being some potential for more dramatic change could be made by putting together the growing net change through the 1970s, the localised but often dramatically high H-Block vote in 1981 and the continuing instability of the opinion polls. However, the case for stability is more easily made and stability rather than change is what must be explained. What makes the Irish case particularly interesting in this regard is that a good case can be made for expecting volatility. Many factors are present which are thought to provoke electoral upsets but as yet they have not done so.

EXPLANATIONS

Social Change

Irish society has changed markedly since 1948 with several of the changes having implications for electoral affiliations. Irish society has become more urban in residential pattern and economically has moved away from its agrarian, peasant base towards an industrial/service economy, in which the great majority of the workforce are employees (Rottman and O'Connell, 1982). Urbanisation has been consistent over the 1948-83 period with the 40:60 urban-rural ratio which existed in 1948 now reversed. This has been accompanied by an eastward shift in the population, with Dublin and its hinterland now containing about one-third of the population. The decline in numbers working in agriculture has also been a long-term one and has resulted in a dwindling of self-employed workers. Industrial development, for so long retarded, took off in the early 1960s and this gave rise to far more skilled manual and white-collar work. Not only did more of the workforce become employees but the workforce became better educated. Demographic change too is seen in an increasingly young electorate as a high birthrate is no longer combined with high emigration in late adolescence.

Such changes should be set against the prevailing view of Irish parties as having indistinct social profiles. The original division between Fianna Fail and Fine Gael had economic, geographical and cultural underpinnings (Rumpf and Hepburn, 1977; Garvin, 1977; Gallagher, 1976), whilst the Labour Party has strong roots in the trade union movement; but analysis of early surveys in the late 1960s did show that the social structuring of the vote evident elsewhere in liberal democracies was not marked in Ireland. One such analysis typified Irish politics as being ´without social bases´ (Whyte, 1974), although it was clear that Fine Gael drew disproportionately from larger farmers and the middle classes and Labour, as expected, drew disproportionate support from manual workers. In 1948 there were also marked regional disparities in support, with Fianna Fail relatively strong in the more peripheral areas of the country, where Labour´s support was almost non-existent (Garvin, 1977, Table 6). The parochial character of Irish parties, alluded to earlier, is also important here. Whilst social cleavages might not structure voting preferences, the transmission of party preference from generation to generation may still take place. That transmission may be achieved more easily in a stable or slowly changing society. The style of politics itself - the type of candidate and appeals the parties make - has been seen as essentially that of a rural society and not easily adapted to an urban one (see Garvin, 1982, pp.22-3).

The changes in Irish society support expectations of changes in Irish politics. One is the possibility of ´class´ politics becoming dominant. In the wake of the industrial development of the early 1960s the Labour Party argued that the 1970s would be socialist. Whilst that expectation was unfulfilled, the successes of the Workers´ Party in winning a few seats in the elections of the 1980s revives the possibility that as social change creates a larger urban employee workforce so a left-wing party could benefit electorally. Another explanation is that the changes will simply disrupt traditional patterns in no particular direction. Change, bringing ´social mobilisation´, loosens traditional ties and loyalties, leaving people available to form new ones. Whilst class ties are one such possibility, there is no necessity for any new party ties to be formed. Particularly when combined with the higher educational levels attained by more electors, such changes could produce a soph-

Table 7.4: Social Composition of Major Party Vote, 1969-82

	1969 %	1977 %	1981 %	Feb. 1982 %	Nov. 1982 %
Fianna Fail					
Non-manual	32	20	27	25	25
Skilled manual	13	23	25	20	22
Unskilled manual	33	32	29	34	30
Farmers:50+acres	13	9	7	7	8
Farmers:50-acres	9	16	13	14	15
Representativeness	7	10	7	12	9
Fine Gael					
Non-manual	34	31	31	33	35
Skilled manual	12	14	21	22	18
Unskilled manual	19	16	21	22	23
Farmers:50+acres	28	16	15	15	13
Farmers:50-acres	28	16	15	15	13
Representativeness	33	40	21	23	22
Labour					
Non-manual	23	16	26	25	23
Skilled manual	21	28	23	19	25
Unskilled manual	52	53	44	44	45
Farmers:50+acres	2	1	4	4	5
Farmers:50-acres	2	1	3	7	1
Representativeness	51	63	32	27	39
All Respondents					
Non-manual	30	24	28	27	28
Skilled manual	14	21	24	21	21
Unskilled manual	33	29	28	31	30
Farmers:50+acres	15	10	9	10	9
Farmers:50-acres	7	16	11	11	12

Notes: In 1969 the division of farmers is between those having more or less than 30 acres.
Representativeness is calculated by summing the differences between party and whole sample profiles.
Sources: Whyte (1974); IMS (1977, 1981a, 1982b, 1982c).

isticated and significant body of ´floating´ voters. There is no evidence to show that Irish politics is becoming class politics in electoral terms (7): trends in the many surveys over the last

15 years in fact suggest the opposite. Table 7.4 shows the occupational profiles of major party supporters since 1969. A simple index of representativeness, summing the differences between party and population profiles, shows Fine Gael to be now much more heterogeneous occupationally than in the late 1960s. This has been due largely to its increasing support amongst manual workers, both skilled and unskilled, relative to farmers. Labour too is more heterogeneous having lost more support amongst unskilled manual workers than amongst skilled workers, farmers (and farm workers) and the middle classes. It is notable that Fine Gael have attracted this broader support only since 1977 - there is no steady trend. The significance of this will be discussed below.

The evidence relating to trends in volatility has already been discussed and the conclusion was that volatility has not increased. However, it is worth considering whether the volatility that exists can be identified with particular social groups. Generally speaking, volatility, like party support, has no clear social basis. All groups show some fluctuations in their voting behaviour and if some show more than others, differences are not large. Mair has argued that the Dublin region is the most volatile with net volatility there being higher on average since 1948 than other areas (Mair, 1981). Calculating Pedersen's index for four regions over the 1948-82 period shows Dublin with the highest mean score (9.0), followed by the Border counties (7.0), the East and Midlands (6.9) and finally the Western periphery (5.8).(8) Median figures show a similar pattern. Garvin's contention that volatility early in the period was rural whilst modern volatility is urban (Garvin, 1982) is not entirely borne out by these figures since Dublin volatility is higher than others' for both halves of the 1948-82 period, although the magnitude of the differences is greater since 1965.

An examination of fluctuations in pre-election opinion polls suggests that the most volatile social group is manual workers. Table 7.5 shows the net shifts between Fianna Fail and the Coalition parties over recent elections by occupational grouping. Manual workers are most volatile, with the direction of their shift, unlike that of non-manual workers, being to the eventual winner. Interestingly, there is no sign that the growing group of skilled workers is more volatile than the declining group of unskilled workers. This variability of net shifts has been seen to be consistent with the notion of a rational electorate, swayed by appeals to particular interests (Sinnott, 1982). A similar analysis by age shows the least swing in the 55+ group, with rather more in the under 34 and 35-54 groups. It is interesting here that the youngest group is not more volatile than the middle-aged one. Too much should not be read into these figures. Alternative surveys, taken at much the same time give intra-occupational swings of different sizes (9) and the overall net swing suggested by the surveys is not always consistent - again in size - with the election result. Even so, it seems fair to conclude that volatility is not the preserve of any particular group and that the variations in recent election results cannot be seen simply in terms of fluctuations in the preferences of one particular social group. Nor are there obvious signs of volatility rising with occupational trends.

Table 7.5: Net Shifts Between Fianna Fail and Coalition Party Voting in Successive Elections, 1969-82, by Occupation Grouping

	Swing to Fianna Fail			
	1969-77	1977-81	1981-Feb.82	Feb.82-Nov.82
	%	%	%	%
Non-manual workers	-3	-2	18	0
Skilled manual	+23	-8	0	-3
Unskilled manual	+14	-10	+16	-19
Farmers:50+acres	+6	-17	-8	-1
Farmers:50-acres	-17	+16	0	+11
All	+7	-6	+14	-11
(Swing in election result)	(+14)	(-9)	(+2)	(-5)

Notes: No data are available for 1973. In 1969 the division between farmers is between those having more or less than 30 acres.
Sources: As Table 7.4

Ideological Change
    It is arguable that there has been a fundamental change in the salience of certain political issues and outlooks since the Irish party system was founded and that volatility would

increase as a consequence. The Treaty which gave
rise to the original division in the nationalist
movement was of little real significance by 1948.
Economic issues have always been important but
increased governmental intervention and the
willingness of parties to claim competence in, and
by implication, responsibility for economic
management, may make such issues of greater
political significance. Social changes mentioned
earlier have helped raise new issues, in particular
those of morality: divorce, contraception and
abortion. How have these affected electoral
behaviour?

Whilst the Treaty formed the basis of
organisational differences in the Irish nationalist
movement, the attitudinal differences expanded
beyond the provisions of the Treaty which, excepting
the position of Northern Ireland, were of merely
historical interest within a few decades. The
continued separate existence of Northern Ireland
gives nationalists cause to see the nationalist
revolution as unfinished. Parties - all confessedly
nationalist - differ over the attitude towards this
situation. Fine Gael's line has traditionally been
'softer'. Its founding fathers were those who
accepted the original treaty and who made little
effort to change its provisions in the 1920s. Fine
Gael has been less hostile to Britain, more
conciliatory towards different communities in
Northern Ireland, less ideological in their
expression of the essence of the Irish nation.
Fianna Fail took the decisive steps to weaken the
Treaty provisions, maintained neutrality in World
War II and more generally have claimed to embody the
Gaelic cultural underpinnings of Irish Nationalism.
It was a Fianna Fail government and party that was
divided over the 'Arms Crisis' of 1969 when a
cabinet minister was tried and acquitted on a charge
of supplying arms to Northern Catholics. These
divisions persist (see Garvin, 1981). Whilst for
much of the 1970s bi-partisanship was the norm on
'Northern' issues, conflict has been much more open
since the late 1970s and the issue has been raised
in recent election campaigns.

Yet the electorate seems little influenced by
all this. Polls from the 1970s onwards have
suggested that Northern Ireland is not seen as a
particularly important issue by many people. At the
most recent election only six per cent thought
Northern Ireland the 'most important' issue in the
election and although 59 per cent considered the

issue 'important' this figure compares poorly with the 90 per cent recorded on various economic issues (Irish Times, 15 November 1982). One recent poll showed that most people continue to support the goal of Irish unity but few think it will be realised in the short-term (Irish Times, 26 June 1983). Other dimensions of nationalism are no more salient. The revival of the Irish language receives little political attention today and although 'Irish neutrality' has recently been a topic of some debate in the context of European defence plans, this debate has apparently not had a major effect on the electorate's order of priorities.

Economic issues usually top that list with those such as jobs, prices and taxation most marked in pre-election polls. Furthermore, one analysis indicates that 'not only did voters say economic management was the issue, they followed through and indicated an intention to vote in accordance with this priority.' (Sinnott 1978, p 59; cf. Sinnott 1982) (emphasis in original). Obviously, economic issues are not new (See O'Leary, 1979, p.42; Murphy, 1979, p.4; Gallagher, 1981, pp.272-3), but since the 1960s, when Irish governments assumed a more positive economic role, they have perhaps been credited with economic responsibilities greater than their predecessors (see King, 1975 p.288). At the November 1982 election, one poll showed that only 17 to 18 per cent thought there was 'not much anyone can do' about inflation and unemployment, the two most salient issues (IMS, 1982c, Table 11). Parties have differed in the emphasis given to particular problems and there have been changes in their positions. In an analysis of post-1948 manifestos Mair argues that Fine Gael have moved centrally since 1948 and that, although that party has generally occupied the right of the political spectrum on these issues, at certain times, in 1969 and 1973 especially, it has been to the left of Fianna Fail (Mair, 1982). Most recently it has adopted a stronger emphasis on economic austerity than has Fianna Fail but overall differences are slight. Labour remains on the left, giving more emphasis to economic expansion than to fiscal rectitude and difficulties are evident in the relations between the two coalition parties in a time of economic depression.

In addition to issues of nationalism and materialism, Irish political debate has been characterised by some 'new' issues which have arisen in the 1970s. Campaigns for more liberal contraception laws and for the recognition of divorce have highlighted a change in attitudes on moral questions and shown the scope of the Catholic Church's authority to be more limited than in earlier years (see Garvin, 1982 pp.30-32; Chubb, 1982, ch.2). A near majority now favours legal provision for civil divorce; in 1971 only 22 per cent approved such a reform (IMS, 1981b, Chart 2). Contraception has had majority support for longer (Chubb, 1982 p.29) but 'artificial' methods are available technically only on prescription and then only to married couples. Legislation followed a judicial pronouncement that the previously total prohibition was unconstitutional. There are pressures now within the coalition parties, and Labour in particular, for further liberalisation of the law.

Such issues cause considerable difficulty for Irish parties. A liberal/secular dimension cuts through all of them and when such issues arise party unity suffers. In 1974, the then Fine Gael Prime Minister, Liam Cosgrave, voted against his own government's contraception bill and recently Coalition efforts to deal with public demands for a referendum to effect a constitutional prohibition on abortion have been marked by widespread defections on crucial votes in both parties. Fianna Fail, having taken a more clerical, non-liberal position on these various morality issues have succeeded in maintaining a more united public face.

As with nationalist issues, these have not had any clear electoral impact. Prior to the June 1981 election, one per cent thought that family law reform was the most important election issue and only eight per cent thought it important (Irish Times, 25 May 1981). In November 1982 hardly anybody thought abortion was the most important issue (Irish Times, 15 November 1982). Neither issue was mentioned by electors in February 1982 (IMS 1982b). Fine Gael and Labour certainly have tended to line up with the younger, urban voters on these issues (although Fine Gael's credentials in particular have been somewhat tarnished recently by its lack of liberal unity in the referendum episode). As this group seems slightly more volatile, these issues may affect votes. Fine Gael has made significant gains in Dublin and in the younger age groups since 1977 and its more liberal image, rather than any particular policy, may well have assisted this development.(10)

Government and Party System Performance

A third set of explanations for volatility concerns governmental performance. Where the parties are seen to have failed in some important way, dissatisfaction may result in far less commitment to established parties, perhaps giving rise to support for new ones. One problem with this theory is the difficulty of objectively identifying governmental or party failure. Whether an outcome is rated as a success or failure, the magnitude of such success, will depend upon the observer. Survey evidence is available on electoral 'satisfaction' with governments and leaders. This data, though subjective, is the best available measure. Figure 7.2 shows the percentage claiming to be dissatisfied with the government at intervals since 1976. The overall trend is upwards, and although elections seem to arrest and often significantly reverse the trend for a time, it eventually continues upward. The 1977-81 Fianna Fail government enjoyed a long honeymoon period with dissatisfaction not reaching pre-election levels for almost two years. Such periods have been far less blissful in the 1980s and not so prolonged. Dissatisfaction reached pre-election levels within six months of the 1981 election, three months of the February 1982 election and five months after the November 1982 election.

Recent evidence also suggests that distrust of politicians is now widespread. In November 1982 Fine Gael was mistrusted by over 50 per cent Labour by over 60 per cent and Fianna Fail by over 70 per cent of all electors. Even amongst the parties' own supporters, 52 per cent distrusted Fianna Fail, 38 per cent Labour and 32 per cent Fine Gael (IMS, 1982c, Table 16). Fianna Fail's distrust rating had risen since February 1982 in the wake of several government scandals (Joyce and Murtagh, 1983) but the February 1982 figures were broadly similar (IMS, 1982b, Table 13). The significant contrast is with assessments of deputies in 1976 when only about one-third of electors showed clear lack of trust with 36 per cent describing most deputies as 'not sincere', 31 per cent as 'not reliable' and 28 per cent as 'not honest'. Near majorities favoured the opposite verdict (IMS, 1976, Table 30 a/b).

Whilst such distrust has been seen to underlie volatility elsewhere, the disparate nature of the disaffected makes them a difficult target for any mobilisation strategy. Identification of the disaffected here is hindered by the fact that

Ireland

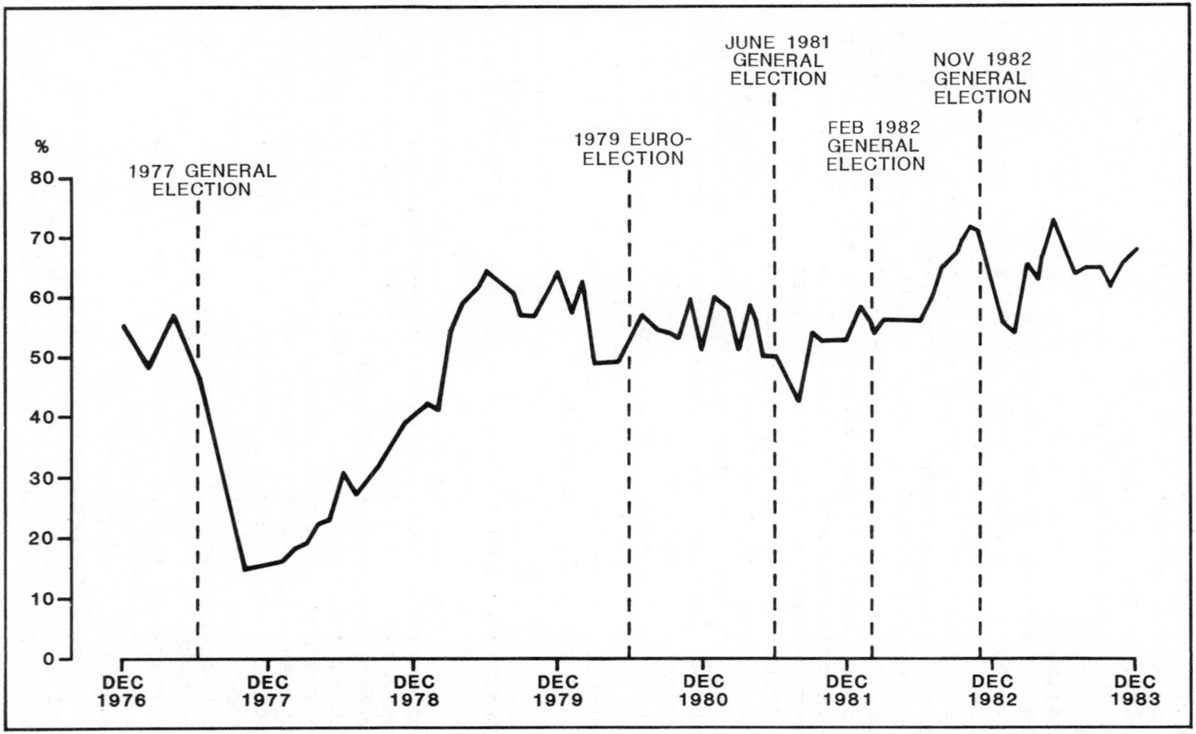

Figure 7.2: Percentage Dissatisfied with the way the Government has been Running the Country

distrust of individual parties is linked to party commitment which itself is not distributed completely evenly across social groups. However, although available data does permit the search for social groups which are disproportionately mistrustful of all three parties, it is not so easy to find them. Small farmers are marginally less trusting than the average voter, although their faith in Fianna Fail mirrors that of the electorate. The middle classes may be a little more trusting of all parties, but not disproportionately so, and those from households whose head is self-employed are disproportionately less trusting - again only marginally. Rural electors are less trusting than urban ones and voters from the western and north-eastern peripheries less trusting than those from other regions. No age group is disproportionately mistrustful. Thus, whilst some groups are particularly disaffected - and these would, on the whole, seem to be from declining areas and social groups - differences are not marked. The most striking aspect of the pattern is precisely the social spread of disaffection which seems - like volatility - to be essentially individual rather than collective. This makes it harder to mobilise. Although individuals may switch parties, this situation makes it less likely that these switches will take the same direction.

ELECTORAL VOLATILITY AND THE PARTY SYSTEM

There are ample grounds for expecting electoral changes in Ireland to be more dramatic than they have been. Social transformation, issue changes and widespread distrust and dissatisfaction have not upset the general post-war pattern of electoral stability. The steady development of a two party system is more pronounced than any pattern of volatility. Before discussing explanations for this lack of fluctuation, it is worth seeing if the general situation has left its mark on popular attachments to parties. Is there any evidence of a decline in support for all parties, even if such decline does not manifest itself in volatile electoral behaviour?

Relatively few attempts have been made to tap party identification in Ireland. Whilst the concept is problematic, the lack of clear social group-party links and the flexibility of the electoral system might be expected to give the concept some of the

value which it has in the American context (see
Budge et al., 1976). Questions similar to those
used by Butler and Stokes (1971) and the Michigan
team (Campbell et al., 1960) provide the data in
Table 7.6, covering the years 1976, 1981 and 1982.

Table 7.6: Party Identification 1976-83

	1976	1981	Nov. 1982
	%	%	%
Fianna Fail	39	42	39
Fine Gael	23	23	32
Labour	14	8	8
Other	1	3	3
None	20	21	14
Refused/Don't Know	3	4	3

Notes: The questions asked were, 'In politics, do
you usually think of yourself as Fianna Fail, Fine
Gael, Labour or what/whatever?'
'Coalition' responses are proportionately divided
between Fine Gael and Labour.
Sources: IMS (1976, 1981a, 1982c).

Two things are evident from these data. First,
the majority of Irish voters have clear party
attachments. Whilst levels of 'no identification'
are about twice those found in Britain in the mid-
1960s, they seem lower than those of several other
European countries.(11) There is no 'dealignment'
in Ireland. Second, there is some sign that the
electorate is more aligned now than in the
mid-1970s. The proportion of Fine Gael identifiers
in 1982 was, for the first time, close to that
party's vote. Fine Gael sympathisers were owning up
to their attachment. Whilst the fact of three
elections in eighteen months may have helped bring
about this new feature of Irish partisan
affiliations, there is no reason why it should not
endure. Fine Gael's gains have come from Labour,
but also from the 'no identification' grouping.
Those without identification tend to be middle
class rather than working class or farmers,
employed rather than unemployed, urban rather than
rural. Alignment is thus more widespread amongst
those groups which seemed - in aggregate - the least
satisfied. Again, this might be thought to weaken
the chances for electoral change.
Thus the Irish case seems to set a puzzle for
students of electoral volatility; grounds for

expecting volatility are much more easily identified than is the phenomenon itself. A few solutions to the puzzle can be indicated here but none are entirely satisfactory. First, it can be argued that the party system is not liable to be disrupted by social change because parties are not tied to social structures in the first place (Gallagher, 1981, p.283). A similar argument may be made with respect to attitudinal change. The main Irish parties, by 1948, had assumed a pragmatic, heterogenous character which could be adapted easily to changing conditions. Particular attitude changes, the growth or decline of particular social groups, posed no fundamental problem. This view has much to commend it. The greater stability of the Fianna Fail vote - the most heterogeneous party over the post-1948 era, is one point in support - and the apparent impact of organisational factors in recent times is another. Fianna Fail´s convincing win in 1977 followed an organisational overhaul with an emphasis on professionalisation (Manning 1978, pp.82-86). The advent of Garret FitzGerald to the Fine Gael leadership following that party´s 1977 defeat saw a similar reappraisal and reformulation. Fianna Fail today is again reviewing its organisation.

This emphasis on party adaptability is not, however, entirely satisfactory. Firstly, the argument overlooks the point made earlier about the parochial nature of Irish politics which itself may be rendered ineffective with social change. Primary socialisation may prove less durable in a more open and mobile society. Secondly, the argument ignores comparative evidence. Heterogenous parties and party systems have experienced considerable volatility elsewhere (Rose and Urwin, 1969; Maguire, 1983). The USA provides one example; Ireland in the 1940s perhaps provides another. Of course such volatility may result from other causes, such as system performance, and parties may prove more or less adaptable by virtue of the skills of their leaders as much as through the constraints of their social base. Thirdly, the argument does not further our understanding of stability. Even if parties can adapt, why should the electoral decision remain stable? In the absence of social or ideological ties, what binds voters to parties?

A second argument has been put forward to meet this problem. It asserts that political competition is primarily intra-party, not inter-party, as a consequence of the STV electoral system. Ties need

not be strong as they come under little strain
(Carty, 1981). Several surveys have asked voters to
say what is the most important criterion in deciding
their vote, giving the options as choosing a prime
minister or ministers, choosing between party
policies and selecting a candidate to look after the
constituency's needs. A significant minority
consistently mentioned the last of these although
this minority may be growing smaller; 46 per cent
gave the parochial answer in 1977, 43 per cent did
so in 1981, 35 per cent in February 1982 and 41 per
cent in November 1982 (Sinnott, 1978,Tables 3-8;
IMS, 1981a, Table 30; IMS, 1982b, Table 12; IMS,
1982c, Table 8). One recent analysis has shown that
the distribution of party preferences between
February 1982 and November 1982 changed less in that
group giving the parochial response than amongst
those claiming to vote on grounds of ministerial
team or party policies (Byrne, (n.d.) p.10). The
same is true if the analysis is extended back to
1981 (although those who vote primarily to choose a
prime minister change least of all). Whilst this
provides some support for the argument on
intra-party competition it is not true that
campaigns are entirely localised. Certainly local
campaigning takes place and its style may indeed
stress local concerns. Intra-party competition is
real and often very sharp but party leaders play a
major, national role in elections. They tour the
country, confront one another on television and it
is usually their images which look down from the
lamp-posts and telegraph poles on potential voters.
    Of course, the electorate's freedom to reject
candidates without rejecting party may reduce
changes of party. Intra-party defeats of incumbents
have increased since 1948, averaging seven in the
1950s, six in the 1960s, nine in the 1970s and ten
over the last two elections. Intra-party volatility
may substitute for inter-party volatility. However,
such behaviour might not result from those
discontents and disturbances previously discussed.
Most authorities see intra-party strife as being
primarily parochial. In addition, it is not always
true that incumbents and challengers represent the
party establishment and its opposition respectively
- the reverse may be the case. Hence it is very
difficult to interpret these figures which may
result as much from the increased attractiveness of
the job, and quality of aspirants for it, as from
the failings of its incumbents.
    A third solution can be to challenge the data.

Has there really been significant social or ideological change? Is the mistrust expressed in the polls anything more than the traditional, characteristic and hardly salient cynicism of the Irish towards their politicians? (See Garvin, 1982 p.30) These arguments are difficult to evaluate in the absence of theoretically defined criteria for significance and salience. Yet the factors for change existing in Ireland do seem comparable to those elsewhere. It is their context and effect which seem to differ. Arguably there is more volatility than has been suggested here. Shifts in the polls and the unevenness of inter-election swings across regional and social subgroups point to more volatility than the Pedersen index describes on national election results. The recall data showing relatively little gross volatility could be unreliable, although the consistency of the results is notable. The heterogeneity of much of the vote switching may make it more likely that switches cancel one another out. Only panel studies can resolve the uncertainty completely. In the absence of such studies, the low net volatility figures, the consistent recall data and the lack of significant new parties must carry weight.

Finally, the solution may be sought in the future. Change has perhaps made the electorate ´available´ to adopt new electoral preferences that will soon be manifested (Mair, 1981). The lack of clear dealignment may not be significant. As Crewe has pointed out, British electoral changes in the 1970s were not foreshadowed by falling levels of party identification (Crewe, 1976). More concrete indicators such as the unrest in the opinion polls and the increasing emphasis given to election campaigns by parties - indicating that they think votes must be won, not relied upon - are grounds for expecting something to happen, or for not being surprised when it does. The next election, due not later than 1987, may resolve our puzzle.

FOOTNOTES

* I would like to thank Basil Chubb, David Denver and Michael Gallagher for comments on an earlier draft of this chapter and Irish Marketing Surveys Ltd. for making data available to me. All are absolved from any responsibility for the contents of the chapter.

1. The term republican in the Irish context refers to (all-Ireland) nationalists.

2. Provisional Sinn Fein is the political wing of the Irish Republican Army, a terrorist, nationalist organisation whose activities are located mostly in Northern Ireland although both see themselves as all-Ireland movements. The term provisional denotes one wing of a divided IRA/Sinn Fein. The former Official Sinn Fein is now The Workers´ Party.

3. Mair (1979) argues that the critical cleavage in Irish politics is between Fianna Fail and its opponents, with Fianna Fail offering single party government against its opponents´ coalitions. This cleavage is the central influence on the behaviour of all parties.

4. The index scores are: 1975, 5.3; 1976, 9.2; 1977, 8.0; 1978, 2.5; 1979, 5.5; 1980, 1.6; 1981, 2.5; 1982, 3.6; 1983 (up to June), 5.0. These are based on averages of polls in three periods of each year (Jan.-April, May-Aug., Sept.-Dec.) since figures are not available for every month.

5. Carty (1981, pp.76-84) also reports a high level of consistency between normal parental vote, own first vote and most recent vote. His data were collected in 1970.

6. Using a complicated technique whereby national inter-party changes are estimated from lower-level aggregate votes, Ryan and McCarthy (1976) produced very similar figures to those of the recall data for the 1969-73 period.

7. Some events outside Dail elections may prove significant. The success of T. J. Maher, a former Irish Farmers´ Association leader, who ran as an Independent in the European Parliament elections in 1979, raised the possibility of a Farmers´ Party being formed, although none has subsequently appeared. Several large trade-union-led demon-strations by direct taxpayers against the Irish tax system, which is seen as inequitable, the taxation of the self-employed (including farmers) being disproportionately low, have also been seen as signs of a basis for class politics. Yet no party has been able to take over this protest which, like so many others, cuts across the largest Irish parties.

8. These regions are defined in Garvin (1977).

9. For instance, data utilised by Sinnott (1978) for the 1977 election which involved aggregating three pre-election polls differs from the 1977 figure utilised here. Such differences,

however, do not alter the conclusions which follow.
10. Surveys show that liberal attitudes are stronger amongst the young and in urban areas, particularly Dublin. See for example IMS (1981b).
11. Butler and Stokes (1971, Appendix) reported that over 90 per cent identified themselves with a party in surveys of 1963, 1964 and 1966. For other European comparisons, see Borre (1977), Kaase (1976), Inglehart and Hochstein (1972), Barnes (1974).

REFERENCES

Barnes, S. (1974) 'Italy: Religion and Class in Electoral Behaviour' in R. Rose (ed.), Electoral Behaviour, Free Press, New York, pp.171-226
Bax, M. (1976) Harpstrings and Confessions, Van Gorcum, Assen
Borre, O. (1977) 'Recent Trends in Danish Voting Behaviour' in K.H. Cerny (ed.), Scandinavia at the Polls, American Enterprise Institute, Washington D.C., pp.3-38
Budge, I. et al. (eds.) (1976) Party Identification and Beyond, Wiley and Sons, London
Butler, D. and D. Stokes (1971) Political Change in Britain, Penguin Books, London
Byrne, D. (n.d.) Ireland at the polls 1982, Irish Marketing Surveys Ltd., Dublin
Campbell, A. et al. (1960) The American Voter, Wiley and Sons, London
Carty, R. K. (1981) Party and Parish Pump, Wilfred Laurier University Press, Waterloo, Ontario
Crewe, I. (1976) 'Party Identification Theory and Political Change in Britain' in I. Budge et al. (1976), pp. 33-62
Chubb, B. (1982) The Government and Politics of Ireland, 2nd ed., Longman, London
Gallagher, M. (1976) Electoral Support for Irish Political Parties 1927-73, Sage, London
---------- (1978) 'Party Solidarity, Exclusivity and Inter-Party Relationships in Ireland 1922-77', Economic and Social Review, 10, 1-22
---------- (1981) 'Societal change and party adaptation in the Republic of Ireland 1960-81', European Journal of Political Research, 9, 269-85
Garvin, T. (1977) 'Nationalist Elites, Irish Voters and Irish Political Development', Economic and Social Review, 8, 161-86

---------- (1982) ´Change and the Political System´ in F Litton (ed.), Unequal Achievment: The Irish Experience 1957-1982, Institute of Public Administration, Dublin, pp. 21-40

Huntington, S. (1975) ´The United States´ in M. Crozier, S. Huntington and J. Watunuki, The Crisis of Democracy, New York University press, New York, pp. 59-118

IMS (1976) RTE ´Survey´ - Politics, September 1976, Irish Marketing Surveys Ltd., Dublin

--- (1977) Political Opinion June, 1977, Irish Marketing Surveys Ltd., Dublin

--- (1981a) Political Opinion Poll, June 7th-8th 1981, Irish Marketing Surveys Ltd., Dublin

--- (1981b) Attitudes to Proposals for Constitutional change, October, 1981, Irish Marketing Surveys Ltd., Dublin

--- (1982a) The Irish Times/IMS Poll February 2nd/3rd 1982, Irish Marketing Surveys Ltd., Dublin

--- (1982b) The Irish Times/IMS Poll, February 13th/14th, 1982, Irish Marketing Surveys Ltd., Dublin

--- (1982c) Irish Independent/IMS Poll, Sunday Independent Poll/IMS Poll November 1982, Irish Marketing Surveys Ltd., Dublin

Inglehart, R. and A. Hochstein (1972) ´Alignment and Dealignment of the Electorate in France and the United States´, Comparative Political Studies, 5, 342-72

Joyce, J. and P. Murtagh (1983) The Boss, Poolbeg Press, Dublin

Kaase, M. (1976) ´Party Identification and Voting Behaviour in the West German Election of 1969´ in I. Budge et al. (1976), pp. 81-102

King, A. (1975) ´Overload: Problems of Governing in the 1970s´, Political Studies, 23, 284-96

Maguire, M. (1983) ´Is There Still Persistence? Electoral Change in Western Europe, 1948-79´ in H. Daalder and P. Mair (eds.), Western European Party Systems, Sage, London, pp.67-94

Mair, P. (1979) ´The Autonomy of the Political: The Development of the Irish Party System´, Comparative Politics, 11, 445-65

-------- (1981) ´Analysis of Results´, in T. Nealon and S. Brennan, (eds.), Nealon´s Guide: 22nd Dail and Seanad Election ´81, Platform Press, Dublin, pp.150-54

-------- (1982) ´Issue Dimensions and Party Strategies in the Irish Republic, 1948-81: The Evidence of Manifestos´, European University Institute Working Paper No. 41, Florence

Manning, M. (1978) ´The Political Parties´ in H.R. Penniman (ed.), Ireland at the Polls: The Dail Election of 1977, American Enterprise Institute, Washington D.C., pp.69-96

Murphy, J. (1979) ´"Put Them Out!", Parties and Elections 1948-69´ in J. Lee (ed.), Ireland 1945-70, Gill and Macmillan, Dublin, pp.1-15

O´Leary, C. (1979) Irish Elections 1918-77, Gill and Macmillan, Dublin

Pedersen, M. (1979) ´The Dynamics of European Party Sytems: Changing Patterns of Electoral Volatility´, European Journal of Political Research, 7, 1-26

Rottman, D. and P. O´Connell (1982) ´The Changing Social Structure´ in F. Litton (ed.), Unequal Achievement: The Irish Experience, 1957-1982, Institute of Public Administration, Dublin, pp.63-88

Rose, R. and D. Urwin (1969) ´Persistence and Change in Western Party Systems since 1945´, Political Studies, 18, 283-319

Rumpf, E. and A. Hepburn (1977) Nationalism and Socialism in Twentieth Century Ireland, Liverpool University Press, Liverpool

Rusk, J.G. and O. Borre (1976) ´The Changing Party Space in Danish Voter Perceptions, 1971-73´, in I. Budge et al. (1976), pp.137-62

Ryan, T. and C. McCarthy (1976) ´Party Loyalty in Referenda and General Elections´, Economic and Social Review, 7, 279-88

Sacks, P. (1976) The Donegal Mafia, Yale University Press, London

Sinnot, R. (1978) ´The Electorate´ in H.R. Penniman (ed.), Ireland at the Polls: The Dail Election of 1977, American Enterprise Institute, Washington D.C., pp.35-67

---------- (1982) ´Electoral Patterns in 1982´, New Exchange, 1 (2), 12-16

Whyte, J. (1974) ´Ireland: Politics Without Social Bases´ in R. Rose (ed.), Electoral Behaviour: A Comparative Handbook, The Free Press, New York, pp.619-52

Chapter 8

FRANCE

Gerard Grunberg

INTRODUCTION

    The French party system since 1945 has been
characterised by four main features: the very large
number of parties, their frequent appearance and
disappearance, constant changes in the systems of
alliances and profound and frequent transformations
in the parties themselves. These features combine
to give the system a high degree of instability.
Three elements of the political system have
sustained this instability. Firstly, under the
Fourth Republic between 1946 and 1958, the
appearance and disappearance of movements opposed to
the regime itself (Gaullism, Poujadism). Next, the
profound change in the voting system in 1958 from
proportional representation to a two-ballot,
majority-voting system. Finally, the constitutional
change in 1962 which introduced the election of the
President of the Republic by universal suffrage (a
two-ballot election in which only the top two
candidates from the first round take part in the
second round). The whole political system, and in
particular the party system, was shattered by this
fundamental change.
    The majoritarian logic inherent in these
institutional changes shattered the systems of
alliances between the parties and brought about the
disappearance of an organised and autonomous Centre.
Since 1974, the party system can be described as a
´bipolar quadrille´. It is dominated by four major
political groupings (tendances), united into two
alliances which oppose each other. A relative
stabilisation of this ´bipolar quadrille´ began in
1978. From 1965, the bipolarisation of political
forces between majority and opposition tended to
mould itself into one of the oldest and durable
cleavages in the French political system, the

division between Left and Right. The impact of this division had weakened under the Fourth Republic because of Communist and Gaullist opposition to the regime. Today it once again structures French political life.

On the Left, two major parties dominate: the Socialist Party (PS), formed in 1905, and the Communist Party (PCF) formed in 1920. The Socialist Party has been thoroughly revived since Francois Mitterrand took control of it in 1971, turning it towards an alliance with the Communist Party. On the Right, there is on the one hand the Gaullist movement, today the RPR (Rassemblement pour la Republique) led by Jacques Chirac, and on the other the liberal tendance. The latter is the melting pot of several traditions: moderate conservative (PR), linked in part from 1958 to the governments of the Fifth Republic and led by Valery Giscard d´Estaing, Christian Democrat (CDS), led by Jean Lecanuet, and Radical. The Radical Party, historically the first major French party, played a crucial role in the Third Republic but is now very much weakened and divided, most of its parliamentarians having joined the Union de la Gauche in 1972. Since 1978 this liberal tendance has been organised into a federation of parties, the Union pour la Democratie Francaise (UDF).

In addition to the four major parties there are several smaller groupings of the far Left and Right, some small Centre-left groups and, since 1974, the ecology movement.

The hostility of the Left to the Fifth republic has become blunted with time. The election of Mitterrand to the Presidency in 1981 in a sense completed this process, since from then on the Left has accepted and used these institutions in a way hardly different from the Right.

From the point of view of the study of volatility, we must add two elements whose effects are very considerable. Firstly, the fact that in this system (where the President is the head of the executive, the National Assembly can overturn the government but the President can dissolve the Assembly) the governmental coalition puts its power in jeopardy at both legislative and presidential elections. Since 1958 there have been seven legislative and four presidential elections. Secondly, there was no alternation of government in France between 1958 and 1981. The latter date marks the first instance of alternation and may equally open a new era in terms of electoral volatility.

The Socialists and Communists had never governed France together and only together. General de Gaulle and his successors, Georges Pompidou and Giscard d´Estaing, had exercised power without interruption since 1958, the Left having been constantly in opposition.

Finally, as regards the social composition of the parties´ support, one can distinguish between the Communist electorate, which remains for the most part working class, the Socialist electorate composed mainly of the working class and white-collar workers, and the electorate of the Right among whom the economically inactive, employers, self-employed workers and senior executives are disproportionately found. The French party system continues to be characterised by strong class alignments.

To sum up, the study of electoral volatility in France must take into account changes in the political system since 1945, consisting of a variety of ruptures in institutions, voting methods, the parties themselves and the system of alliances.

TRENDS IN NET VOLATILITY

The calculation of net volatility in France poses a series of difficult problems, even if it is limited to general elections (see Pedersen, 1979). In particular, whether or not turnout rates are taken into account considerably changes the results obtained. Measuring volatility by means of a single index, such as the Pedersen index, appears to have hardly any meaning. After examining various factors which can contribute to volatility and their heterogeneity, one is led to give up the attempt to make such a calculation. There are a number of reasons for this:

-the very large number of parties and candidates (in 1978, for example, there were about 30 political groupings and an average of nine candidates per constituency) which allows for a variety of categorisations. (Table 8.1 somewhat arbitrarily puts all the groupings into nine categories).
-the institutional ruptures of 1958 and 1962.
-the appearance and disappearance of parties (the RPR in 1951, the Poujadists in 1956, the UNR in 1958, the Centre in 1974, the ecologists in 1974, the Giscardians in 1974).
-the support given to one party by another which agrees not to stand at a particular election, e.g.

Table 8.1: Distribution of the Electorate in Metropolitan France in General Elections (First Ballot), 1945-81

Type	1945 L %	June 1946 L %	Nov. 1946 L %	1951 L %	1956* L %	1958 L %	1962 L %	1965 P %	1967 L %
1.	20.1	18.1	21.9	19.8	17.2	22.9	31.3	15.0	18.9
2.	2.0	1.7	1.4	2.2	2.5	2.4	2.1	0.9	1.8
3.		0.1	0.2			1.0	1.6		1.8
4.	20.3	20.8	21.6	20.1	20.6	14.3	14.5	)	17.9
5.	18.5	16.9	13.7	11.3	12.1	11.7	8.4	27.1)	15.0)
6.	8.6	9.3	8.5	8.0	12.4	5.5	5.1		)
7.	18.9	22.6	19.9	10.0	8.8	8.3	5.4	13.3	11.2
8.	10.3	10.2	12.0	9.3	22.2	19.1	7.9	6.9	3.0
9.									
10.				17.3	3.1	14.7	23.8	36.8	30.5
11.	0.6	0.2	0.3	0.9	0.3				

Notes: For key and explanatory notes see second part of table. * Taking into account the division of the Radicals of the USDR and the Social Republicans (Gaullists) in 1956, the following is the distribution of the votes for the four major tendances: PCF 20.6%, Republican Front (Centre-left) 22.0%, Centre-right (outgoing majority) 26.3%, Extreme Right 10.2% (including Poujadists, UDCA, 9.3%).

the PCF and PSU in 1965 and 1974.
-the diversity of party configurations across the constituencies in legislative elections.
-the diversity of types of elections (presidential, legislative, European) attended by differences in voting methods, political stakes and the role of local factors in the vote.
-the terms of alliances between parties which may or may not decide to put forward a single candidate in each constituency (Socialists and Radicals in 1967 and 1968, Socialists and Radicals of the Left in 1973 and partially in 1978 and 1981).
-the character of alternation, whether recent or not.
-internal change in the parties (UNR in 1958, RPR in 1978, PS in 1973, UDF in 1978).
-extreme variations in turnout (the high turnout of the 1962 and 1981 legislative elections and the low turnout in the 1979 European elections).
-whether the legislative elections take place after

Table 8.1(contd.)

Type	1968 L %	1969 P %	1973 L %	1974 P %	1978 L %	1979 E %	1981 P %	1981 L %
1.	20.0	21.8	18.7	15.1	16.7	38.8	18.4	29.1
2.	1.4	1.0	1.8	0.8	1.7	3.3	1.3	1.0
3.	3.7	3.6	2.8	2.3	2.7	1.8	2.8	1.3
4.	15.7	16.6	17.0	)	16.8	11.9	12.4	11.3
5.	13.0)	3.9	16.5)	36.5)	20.5	13.8	22.7	26.4
6.	)	--	)	--	--	--	--	--
7.	8.2	18.1	10.5)	--	--	--	--	--
8.	1.5	3.6	3.5	4.2	1.0	1.5	1.1	2.1
9.	--	--	--	27.7	19.7	15.9	22.3	13.4
10.	36.5	33.9	29.1	12.2	18.2	9.3	15.8	14.6
11.	--	--	--	1.3	2.4	3.7	3.2	0.8

Notes: The results for the PS for 1978-81 also include left Radicals (MRG).
All percentages are of the registered electorate.
Type of election is given by L = Legislative, P = presidential, E = European.
Key: The rows identified by number are as follows:
1. Abstentions
2. Spoiled ballots
3. Extreme Left and other Left parties
4. Communists (PCF)
5. Socialists (SFIO, PS)
6. Radicals (UDSR, RGR)
7. Reforming Centre Democrats (MRP)
8. Moderates: various Right and extreme Right parties
9. Giscardian majority (UDF)
10 Gaullists (RPF, Social Republicans, UNR, UDR, RPR)
11 Others (including ecologists in 1974, 78, 81)
Appendix to Table 8.1
The tendency of the government after each of the elections listed was as follows:
1945 De Gaulle + tripartism
1946 (both) Tripartism (SFIO-PC-MRP)
1951 Centre-right moderates
1956 Republican Front-SFIO
1958-73 Gaullist
1974-79 Giscardian
1981 P Socialist
1981 L Socialist-Communist

a dissolution or at the normal date (there were
dissolutions in 1955, 1958, 1962, 1968, and 1981).
-the state of the systems of party alliances;
whether or not there is agreement to stand down in
the second ballot, the degree of conflict within
the alliance.
-the time that has elapsed since the last election.
-the partisan affiliation of the President at the
time of the legislative elections.
-changes in the definition of the electorate (e.g.
the lowering of the voting age from 21 to 18 after
the 1974 presidential election).
     For these reasons there is little point in
calculating net volatility scores, even if the
1945-83 period is divided into shorter periods. In
order to understand as well as possible the
movements registered during this period and to
explore the different dimensions of volatility we
will distinguish five periods.(1)

1945-56: Volatility on the Right under the Fourth Republic

     Whereas abstention and the Communist vote
remained stable over the whole of this period and
the Socialist vote declined steadily, the situation
on the Right was characterised by considerable
volatility linked to the instability of the party
system. In 1951 the MRP, the French version of
Christian Democracy located on the Centre-right of
the political spectrum, declined markedly, due to
the emergence of the Gaullist candidates of the RPF.
In 1956 the Gaullist movement was dissolved but a
new anti-parliamentary movement of the Right, the
Poujade movement, performed well. It is difficult
to obtain a precise measure of volatility on the
Right during this period but in any event, the
inability of the MRP and the moderates to represent
the whole of the conservative electorate and to
persuade this electorate to defend the parliamentary
system of the Fourth Republic was clearly revealed.

1958-65: The Triumph of Gaullism - Volatility as an Expression of the Split in One Section of the Electorate Between its Partisan Loyalty and its Support for De Gaulle

     In 1958 all the major parties, except for the
Communists, accepted the new institutions which De
Gaulle wanted. This acceptance limited the success
of the new Gaullist movement (the UNR) in the
November 1958 elections.(2)   Only the PCF lost

support which it did not subsequently succeed in
retrieving. But in 1962 De Gaulle, wishing to
emphasise the presidential character of the regime,
submitted for approval by referendum a fundamental
constitutional change: the election of the President
by universal suffrage. This time all the parties
except the UNR and a small section of the moderates
led by Giscard were opposed. They were decisively
defeated: 46.4 per cent of registered electors voted
for the change, 28.8 per cent against. In the
following month, a section of voters called upon to
elect a new National Assembly (the old one had been
dissolved by De Gaulle) were faced with a serious
dilemma: whether to break with their preferred party
or to renounce their ´Yes´ vote in the referendum.
One group got out of this dilemma by not voting.
The abstention rate was the highest at any
legislative or presidential election over the whole
period. Another group was to vote thereafter for
the party of De Gaulle.

The Centre and the Right who were hostile to
the government were never to recover from this
defeat. At the 1965 presidential election the
turnout was unprecedented: only 15 per cent
abstained. De Gaulle received 36.8 per cent of the
vote in the first ballot. High turnout worked
largely in his favour.

1965-74: Bipolarisation and the Resistance of the Centre

In 1962 the ´third force´ which had enabled the
warring alliance of the Centre under the Fourth
Republic to resist Communist, Gaullist and Poujadist
assaults, appeared to be doomed.

On the Left, a rapprochement between the
Communist Party and the Socialist Party was
developing which was confirmed in 1965 by the
candidature of Mitterrand, who was supported by both
parties. On the Right, the dominance of Gaullism
was firmly established from 1962 onwards. However,
a section of the Centre-right, essentially clustered
around the MRP, attempted to resist this
bipolarisation movement until 1974, hoping to form
an alliance with those electors on the Centre-left
or Centre-right who were hostile to both the
Communists and to Gaullism. But the majoritarian,
two-ballot voting system and the change of strategy
by the other parties in the light of the main
left-right split brought this effort to ruin.

Between 1965 and 1974, however, a certain

volatility in the electorate could be seen between the Centre, the Socialist Party and the presidential majority because of three interlinked factors: the general political situation, the type of election (legislative and presidential) and the configuration of the candidates.

In 1967, the political situation was normal. The legislative elections provided an opportunity for the four major political parties to stand; the democratic Centre put up only 390 candidates in the 470 constituencies. Compared with the 1965 presidential election, the Left gained 7.6 per cent, the democratic Centre lost two per cent and the presidential majority 6.3 per cent. All these movements can probably be explained in part by the volatility of a section of the voters on the Centre-left and Centre-right.

In 1965, part of the Socialist and Radical electorate probably refused to vote for a Left candidate because he was supported by the Communist Party and instead voted for Jean Lecanuet, the Centrist, or even for De Gaulle himself. On the other hand, part of the Centrist electorate may well have voted for De Gaulle in 1965.

In 1967 the former may have reverted to a Socialist or Radical vote, the latter to a Centrist vote. Such an hypothesis is confirmed to a small extent by an opinion poll carried out in 1965 in Boulogne-Billancourt, a constituency on the outskirts of Paris (Michelat, 1969). Of those who had voted for the Centre in 1965 or who intended to vote for the Centre at the next legislative election, only 50 per cent chose the Centre both times. Among those who intended to vote Socialist or Radical at the next legislative election only 59 per cent voted for the Left's candidate in 1965, 13 per cent preferring the Centrist. Thus there seems to have existed a floating vote between the Left and the majority.

At the legislative elections of 1968, after the grave crisis in May, volatility worked to the benefit of the majority. All other parties came out of the events weakened. The rapprochement of the parties of the Left went through a crisis and in the 1969 presidential election following De Gaulle's resignation, and after the negative verdict of the April 1969 referendum, the Centre were in the running once more. There then appeared clear evidence of volatility between the Centre-left and the Centre-right. The split on the Left, Mitterrand's withdrawal and the Socialist candidature of

Gaston Deferre, a supporter of the alliance of the
Centre, opened up a considerable gap for Alain
Poher, the Centre candidate, President of the Senate
and interim President of the Republic.

An opinion poll carried out immediately after
the presidential election showed that 34 per cent of
non-Communist supporters of the Left voted for the
Centre candidate and only 27 per cent for the
Socialist candidate (Lancelot and Weill, 1970).
Paradoxically, this remarkable success for the
Centre was to be the signal for its disappearance.
To make something of his gamble, the Centrist
candidate would also have had to take a considerable
share of the Gaullist vote. In fact, Georges
Pompidou retained the same electoral support as his
predecessor.

In 1973, with the Left once again united and
the Socialist Party won over by Mitterrand, the
Centrist electorate found itself diminished.
Pompidou wanted to draw together the Centre and the
majority. The Centre, meeting a persistent impasse
in the face of the first thrust of the Socialists in
the first round of the 1973 legislative elections,
was to accept a rapprochement with the majority in
the second round. At the May 1974 presidential
election, after the death of Pompidou, Giscard
d´Estaing, representing the moderates who favoured
the Fifth Republic, formed an alliance with the
Centre which would enable him to win the leadership
of a new majority to the detriment of Gaullism.
Thus by 1974 the organised Centre ceased to exist.
On the Left, Mitterrand, again the only candidate of
the Left, considerably improved upon his 1965 vote,
apparently having succeeded in attracting part of
the Centre-left electorate. Giscard d´Estaing
similarly attracted the Centre-right electorate. Of
those who voted for the Centre in 1973, 75 per cent
voted for one of the candidates of the outgoing
majority in 1974 and 17 per cent voted for the
Socialist (Lancelot, 1975). Bipolarisation had
crushed the Centre.

1974-81: The Volatility of the Electorate within the Majority and the Left

From 1974 onwards, the Left and the majority
came into balance. Between 1965 and 1981, the Left
moved in two ways. On the one hand it made
progress, rising from 27.1 per cent in 1965 to 39.9
per cent in 1978. On the other hand, volatility
gradually decreased. Until 1973 there was a

constant difference between the Left's support in legislative and presidential elections. From 1974 onwards this difference disappeared. This stabilisation in the balance of power between Left and Right nevertheless did not put an end to electoral volatility within the Left and the Right.

Table 8.2: Comparison of Left and Right Support (First Ballot), 1965-81

		Non-voters/ Spoilt %	Left %	Centre/ Right %	Difference Centre/Right -Left %
1965	P	15.9	27.1	57.0	+29.9
1967	L	20.7	34.7	44.7	+10.0
1968	L	21.4	32.4	46.2	+13.8
1969	P	22.8	24.1	55.6	+31.5
1973	L	20.5	36.3	43.1	+ 6.8
1974	P	15.9	38.9	44.1	+ 5.2
1978	L	18.4	39.9	38.9	- 1.0
1981	P	19.7	37.9	39.2	+ 1.3

Within the Left, the stability of the Communist vote, which only varied between 14.3 and 17.9 per cent from 1958, suggests that volatility was low between 1958 and 1978. But after the 1978 elections, 23 per cent of Communist voters expressed their intention to vote for Mitterrand and not for Marchais, the probable candidate of the Communist Party in the next presidential election.(3)

On the Right, most of the outgoing 'Pompidou' majority voted for Giscard d'Estaing in 1974 in preference to Chaban-Delmas, the Gaullist candidate. This suggests marked electoral volatility within the majority who stood for the Fifth Republic. At national-constituency elections - the 1974 presidential election and the 1979 Euro-election - the standing of, or direct support for the President (Giscard d'Estaing) bestowed a considerable advantage on the non-Gaullist section of the majority. On the other hand, in the 1978 legislative elections in which the standing and reputation of local candidates played an important role, the local superiority of Chirac's party (the RPR) over Giscard d'Estaing's, counterbalanced the influence of the president.

Finally, there is evidence of the volatility of RPR voters in 1978. After the legislative elections, when asked which candidate they would support if a presidential election were held, the majority chose Giscard d´Estaing rather than the leader of the RPR, Chirac.

A comparison of the 1981 presidential election and the 1978 legislative elections confirms the importance of volatility within the Right and reveals for the first time a strong volatility within the Left, benefitting the Socialist candidate as our 1978 survey foresaw. It must be remembered that these are different types of elections. On the Left, as on the Right, the effective vote for the best-placed candidate within the Left or Right camp probably explains part of the movement recorded between 1978 and 1981. According to a SOFRES opinion poll, almost a fifth of the Communist electorate of 1978 voted for Mitterand even in the first ballot of the 1981 presidential election.

Table 8.3: Comparison of Results of the 1978 Legislative Elections and 1981 Presidential Election (First Ballot: Share of Votes Cast)

		PCF %	PS/MRG %	UDF %	RPR %	Total Left %	Total Right %
1978	L	20.6	24.9	23.2	22.5	49.4	47.0
1981	P	15.3	28.3	27.8	19.6	47.2	48.7

The Socialist victory in the second ballot was made possible by the fact that 16 per cent of Chirac voters switched to Mitterrand (SOFRES poll). This split in the Right caused the defeat of the outgoing president. A page was turned in French electoral history; electoral volatility was to change in nature and breadth.

1981-83: Alternation and Volatility

The second ballot of the 1974 presidential election marked the beginning of an equilibrium between the Right and the Left which lasted until the second round of the 1981 presidential election. During this period there was no alternation and the bipolarisation of political forces deepened. Table 8.4 shows that alternation immediately brought about a strong disequilibrium to the benefit of the Left. What accounted for this sudden and substantial volatility? For some political scientists it was essentially due to the abstention of one part of the

electorate of the Right. Others think that
abstention affected all sections of the electorate,
which would imply that part of the Right-wing voted
Socialist on June 14th 1981.

Table 8.4: Left-Right Difference 1974-81 (Registered
         Voters)

	Left %	Right %	Difference Right-Left %
1974 P 1st ballot	38.8	44.1	+5.3
1974 P 2nd ballot	42.8	43.8	+1.0
1978 L 1st ballot	40.0	38.9	-1.1
1979 E	27.5	26.7	-0.8
1981 P 1st ballot	37.9	39.2	+1.3
1981 P 2nd ballot	43.1	40.2	-2.9
1981 L 1st ballot	39.0	30.0	-9.0

Without entering into this debate here (see
Goguel, 1981, 1982; Jaffre, 1982) and although the
second explanation seems the more likely, there is
little doubt that a substantial part of the Right,
confronted with a situation without precedent since
1958 (the election of a Left-wing president in a
political system where the presidency is the
keystone of all institutions) was discouraged from
voting for its usual candidates and parties.
Moreover, immediately after his election the
President dissolved the National Assembly, in
conformity with common practice since 1962, and
asked the voters to give him a parliamentary
majority, a necessary condition for the proper
working of the system.
      We have hypothesised that the relatively low
levels of volatility in the decade up to 1981 was
due in part to the fact that alternation had not
taken place and that the party system - the ´bipolar
quadrille´ - had more or less established.
      On 23rd June 1981, the Opposition became the
majority at the executive level. For the first time
since 1959, the Left ceased to be identified with
the Opposition. But from January 1982, when there
were four by-elections, the French electoral map
changed considerably. The Left lost these four
elections decisively (see Dupoirier, 1982). In
March 1982 it lost the cantonal elections and in
March 1983 it lost the municipal elections. The
popularity of the President, the Prime Minister and
the Socialist Party crumbled during the first

quarter of 1983. Once it had ceased to be the
Opposition, the Left suffered the effects of
electoral volatility: one section of the electorate
became difficult to mobilise and another was to
swing - or swing back - to the Right (see Parodi,
1982, 1983; Lancelot, 1983; Grunberg and Roy, 1983).

In the 1982 cantonal elections, the difference
in votes cast favoured the Right by 6.3 per cent; in
the 1976 cantonal elections it had favoured the Left
by 4.5 per cent. At the municipal elections in 1983
the same phenomenon occurred; the Left-Right
difference, which at the preceding municipal
elections in 1977 had favoured the Left by 4.5 per
cent, this time favoured the Right by 9.3 per cent.

Could this reversion in the party balance recur
at the next legislative elections scheduled for
1986? Two hypotheses can be offered. The first is
based on the difference between national and local
elections. According to this hypothesis, since the
latter do not put political power directly at risk,
they allow the electorate to record its
dissatisfaction without the aim or consequence of
changing the incumbent government (Parodi, 1983).
This hypothesis is more favourable to the Left and
it does not indicate how the French will vote in
1986. Several arguments can be used in its support:
the Right, when it was in power, lost the 1976 and
1977 local elections but won the legislative
elections in 1978; the majority in office tends to
have more difficulty than the Opposition in
mobilising its supporters in this type of election.
Thus in 1977 13 per cent of those who voted for
Giscard d'Estaing in 1974 said that they had
abstained as against nine per cent of Mitterrand
voters. Parodi suggests that although 14 per cent
of Mitterand voters voted for the Opposition in
1983, 38 per cent of this group described their vote
as a warning to the government, 32 per cent gave it
no political significance and only 23 per cent
agreed that they wanted to show their opposition to
the government (IFOP/RTL survey). He concludes that
many of the Left's deserters could return to the
Left-majority in the near future.

The second hypothesis, less favourable to the
Left, is that this electoral volatility affects
whichever parties are in power and occurs at all
types of election, when economic and social problems
increase dissatisfaction. This makes the
re-election of an outgoing majority, whatever its
political colour, unlikely. Table 8.5 shows that
the Left-Right vote difference did not change

France

between the 1977 municipal elections and the
subsequent legislative elections, which admittedly
were held only one year later. According to the
SOFRES poll, voting intentions in June 1983 for the
legislative elections exactly match the results of
the municipal elections in March.(4) This poll
showed that 43 per cent felt themselves close to the
Opposition and only 41 per cent distant from it.

Table 8.5: Right-Left Differences 1977-83 (% of
           votes cast)

	Left %	Right %	Others %	Difference Right-Left %
1977 M 1st ballot	50.8	46.3	2.9	- 4.5
1978 L 1st ballot	50.6	45.7	3.7	- 4.9
1981 P 1st ballot	48.3	47.5	4.2	- 0.8
1981 P 2nd ballot	53.0	47.0		- 6.0
1981 L 1st ballot	56.9	41.6	1.5	-15.3
1983 M 1st ballot	44.3	53.6	2.1	+ 9.3
Legislative vote intention June '83 (SOFRES)	44	54	2	+10

GROSS VOLATILITY

     As French political scientists have no panel
data at their disposal, it is not possible to follow
the voting patterns of electors over two or several
elections. This is a serious gap in the study of
electoral volatility, all the more so since actual
volatility is probably very substantial.
     According to a study based on an examination of
the official checklists of voters and abstainers
(listes d´emargement) for five elections - the 1979
European elections and the two rounds of the 1981
presidential and legislative elections - abstention
was very high (Subileau and Toinet, 1984). During
this period, marked it is true by heavy abstention
in the European elections and the 1981 legislative
elections, only 43 per cent of registered electors
voted at all five elections and eleven per cent
abstained each time, leaving 46 per cent who
abstained at least once and voted at least once. It
can be presumed, therefore, that individual voting
paths were very varied and that gross volatility was
very high.

EXPLANATIONS FOR ELECTORAL CHANGE 1967-83

Social and Cultural Factors
The period from 1968 to 1981, except for the special case of the 1969 presidential election, saw a continuous reconstruction of the Socialist electorate. The advance of the Left during this period, which was essentially due to the PS, reflected in part a series of social and cultural changes. During the 1970s, both salary and wage earners tended to support the Left in ever-growing numbers. This refers not only to manual workers but also to the salaried and wage earning middle classes - the categories which over the last 30 years have expanded fastest (see Grunberg and Schweisguth, 1981). This movement to the Left by salary and wage earning workers - of which the Socialist Party was the main beneficiary - underlined the class basis of partisan alignments (see Table 8.7). By 1978, in comparison with 1967, the partisan division between salary and wage earners and others had deepened. The former group continued their movement towards a grand realignment on the Left, almost allowing the Left to triumph in 1978.

This change is connected to two different movements. The first concerns white-collar workers. Their shift to the Left was not due to switches from Right to Left but to the fact that those entering this rapidly expanding social class were on the Left from the outset. The second movement concerns manual workers. Here the shift to the Left was a result both of the arrival of new voters who were on the Left to start with and also a shift from Right to Left among a substantial proportion of those who had voted for the Right in 1967 and probably ever since 1958. As has been pointed out, De Gaulle managed to upset the traditional and advantageous relationship between the working class and the Left. The year 1978 marks a provisional stage in the move to the Left of white-collar workers. The Left-Right balance of power was then 50/50. Over the following three years, the balance of power does not seem to have changed markedly.

According to SOFRES-Nouvel Observateur polls, this change also occurred in presidential elections (see Table 8.8).(5) The slide to the Left among supporters of the Right between 1967 and 1981 corresponded, at the ideological level, to two different forms of radicalisation. The first, common to manual workers and the salaried and wage earning middle classes, consisted of an increasingly

Table 8.6: Change in the Social Composition of the French Electorate

	1968 %	1978 %
Farmers,small shopkeepers and self-employed	12.1	8.2
Bourgeoisie	3.2	4.2
Salaried and wage-earning middle classes*	13.3	17.2
Manual workers	18.8	18.6
Sales and service staff	4.8	5.5
Others	2.9	1.8
Non-workers	44.7	44.5

Note: * refers to teachers, salaried and wage-earning health workers, junior administrative executives, technicians and office workers.

Table 8.7: The Left's Share of the Left-Right Vote Among Those in Work in Three Social Groups

	Farmers, small shopkeepers & self-employed		Salaried & wage earning middle classes		Manual workers	
	1967 %	1978 %	1967 %	1978 %	1967 %	1978 %
Aged 18/21 to 39	37	35	56	78	54	82
Aged 40+	35	27	50	59	63	70

Table 8.8: Vote for Mitterrand in the Second Ballot of the 1974 and 1981 Presidential Elections by Occupation

	1974 %	1981 %	Change
Farmers,farmworkers	28	32	+4
Small shopkeepers,self-employed	33	36	+3
Senior executives, liberal proffesions manufacturers, businessmen, middle and junior executives	44	45	+1
Middle class employees	53	62	+9
Manual workers	73	72	-1
Economically inactive, retired	45	45	-
Total	49	52	+3

widespread attachment to the traditional values of the working class movement, symbolised and encouraged by the agreement on a common government programme by the PCF and the PS in 1972. These values include the right to strike, the extension of the nationalised sector and guaranteed work. The second, more specific to the salaried and wage earning middle classes and to a part of the salaried bourgeoisie, concerns what one might call ´cultural liberalism´, a set of anti-authoritarian and hedonistic values embraced particularly by the young. These values are broadly opposed to those of conservative Catholicism which still appreciably shapes the political ideology of the Right. Whereas the traditional values of the Left are very closely linked to a vote for the Left, irrespective of social class, the values of cultural liberalism are particularly linked to a vote for the Left among the salaried and wage earning middle classes (see Table 8.9). (6)

Table 8.9: Left and Right Share of 1978 Vote by Scores on Indices of Left-wing Values and Cultural Liberalism

	White-collar workers		Manual workers	
	Left %	Right %	Left %	Right %
Score on Index of Traditional Left-wing values				
0	14	65	18	61
1	37	42	55	26
2+	76	8	79	10
Cultural Liberalism				
0	32	50	56	33
1	41	44	63	22
2+	66	14	76	9

It thus appears that white-collar workers have placed themselves on the Left in the past few years not only because of their position as white-collar workers but also because of a cultural liberalism which was not adequately catered for by the parties of the Right. The new-style Socialist Party created in 1971 provided a welcome refuge for these white-collar workers.

In 1978, the changers among our sample, numbering 179 respondents, were characterised by a

high proportion of women, of young people and also
of 'affiliated' Catholics, i.e. those who were only
slightly integrated into the Catholic church. Many
of these respondents intended to revert to the Right
in 1981. They seem particularly sensitive to the
cross pressures of conservative Catholic tradition
on the one hand and cultural change on the other.
Their volatility corresponds to this situation and
is not necessarily enduring. This group of people
may, in the long run, settle for the Left, but as
yet there is nothing to support this hypothesis.

<u>After Alternation</u>
     All social categories went through a high
degree of electoral volatility between the
legislative elections of 1978 and June 1983 (voting
intentions), via the 1981 legislative elections.
The fall in the vote for the Left among white-collar
workers - middle and junior executives - between
March 1978 and June 1983 was considerable (-17 per
cent) but hardly more than that found among small
shopkeepers or senior executives. Even if the vote
for the Left fell a little more among the middle
classes than among the other categories, the
differences are not so great as to call into
question the social basis of the Right-Left division
that was established in 1978.(7)
     On the other hand, the IFOP-RTL survey showed
that in the 1983 municipal elections manual workers
abstained in massive numbers (44 per cent of
abstainers as against 29 per cent of voters were
manual workers). We find here, as Parodi puts it 'a
classic demobilisation of the working-class Left in
parallel circumstances to those so well known to
British observers'. Nevertheless, class remains one
of the major structuring variables of the vote in
France together with religiosity, which is still the
strongest determinant. At the 1983 municipal
elections the Left's percentage vote was 13 per cent
among regularly-practising Catholics, 28 per cent
among the irregularly practising, 48 per cent among
non-practising Catholics and 79 per cent among the
non-religious.

<u>Ideological Factors: The Bipolarisation of Political</u>
<u>Forces and the Permanence of Centrist Opinion</u>
     We have seen that in the absence of alternating
movements, the Left, and in particular the PS,
succeeded in catering for and expressing certain

cultural values which were developing during the
1960s and 1970s. We must now stress another
ideological phenomenon, more directly political,
which has been the source of considerable volatility
during the last few years. This is the permanence
of Centrist opinion in a system characterised by
Left-Right bipolarisation and by the disappearance
of autonomous Centrist parties. This leads one to
examine in particular the position of Socialist
supporters on the Left/Right axis and the structure
of Centrist attitudes in relation to the
bipolarisation of the parties.

Our principal hypothesis here is that if the
disappearance of an autonomous political Centre has
strengthened the impact of the Left/Right split on
electoral behaviour in France, there nonetheless
remains a strong element of Centrist opinion among
the electorate, which helps to explain both the
growth of Socialist support between 1973 and 1981
and its decline thereafter. At question here is a
particular form of electoral volatility whose
precise political significance can only be
understood by taking into account the intrinsic
rules of the majority system.

After the 1978 legislative elections, coalition
preferences varied considerably across the
electorate. Only one third of respondents wanted a
Socialist-Communist government, but 28 per cent
wanted a coalition between Socialists and
Giscardians which would exclude both Communists and
Gaullists. Among Socialist voters, this proportion
reached 36 per cent and 38 per cent among Giscardian
voters. In those constituencies where a Communist
(benefitting from the withdrawal of the PS) stood
against a UDF or RPR candidate in the second ballot,
19 per cent of those who had voted Socialist in the
first round switched to the majority. Finally, a
quarter of those who voted Socialist in the first
ballot in 1978 intended, immediately after this
round of the election, to vote for Giscard d'Estaing
in the first round of the next presidential
election: we thus have here a potentially volatile
section of the electorate.

The 1978 survey enables us to characterise with
some precision the small portion of the 1978
electorate which can be considered the most volatile
(see Ysmal, 1981). It consists of 159 respondents
who voted for the Right in 1973 and for the Left in
1978 (see Table 8.10). A much larger proportion of
this group intended to vote for Giscard d'Estaing at
the next presidential election than intended to vote

Table 8.10: Comparison of Stable and Unstable Left
Voters, 1978

	Unstable Voters Right 1973/4 Left 1978 %	Stable Voters Left 1973-74-78 %
Location on Left-Right axis		
Points 1,2,3	35	93
Points 4,5	59	6
Partisanship		
PCF/extreme left	6	42
PS + left Radicals	37	54
UDF or RPR	32	1
Others,refusals,DK	25	3
Reject Communist Party	78	37
Accept Republican Party (Giscardian)	73	36
Want a Socialist/ Giscardian alliance	54	19
Want a Socialist/ Communist alliance	8	52
Would vote at presidential election for		
Giscard d´Estaing	57	9
Mitterrand	19	52

for Mitterrand. **Compared with the stable** voters of
the Left, these voters are characterised by their
position at the centre or on the right of the
Left/Right scale, by their rejection of the PCF and
by their preference for an alliance between
Socialists and the Centrists.

The SOFRES surveys conducted between 1974 and
February 1981 show that voters increasingly over
this period placed Giscard on the Right of the
Left/Right dimension (points 6 and 7 on the SOFRES
scale) (Jaffre, 1982). The figures were 31 per cent
in September 1974, 41 per cent in January 1977, 41
per cent in October 1978, 47 per cent in December
1979 and 50 per cent in February 1981. The shift to
the Right in this image of the President probably
induced a considerable proportion of Centrist-
inclined voters to vote Socialist in 1981. The
post-election SOFRES survey (15-20 May 1981) showed
that among those who voted for Chirac (RPR) in the
first round of the presidential election, eight per

cent considered themselves on the Left or Centre-Left and 41 per cent at the Centre, whereas these proportions were 29 per cent and 49 per cent respectively among those in the group who voted for Mitterrand in the second round. There is no doubt that in 1981 Centrist opinion worked decisively in favour of Mitterrand.

Alternation and the Swing in Centrist Opinion

At the 1983 municipal elections, those who were 'disillusioned with socialism' were characterised by Centrism. Three-quarters of those who voted for Mitterand on 19 May 1981 and for the Opposition in March 1983 were located at the centre of the Left-Right axis (see Parodi, 1983).

It remains to consider the extent to which this Centrism is linked to the electoral volatility of different socio-economic classes. In 1978, senior executives, teachers, junior administrative exec-utives and technicians were the categories which most wanted an alliance of the Centre (between 53 and 56 per cent, as against 36 per cent among all respondents). Recent data on the 'Centrism' of the middle classes or on a possible over-representation of the salaried and wage earning middle classes among the 'Centrists disillusioned with socialism' are not available. Such data would certainly allow us to learn more about the causes of electoral volatility. But for the moment it is not possible to offer rigorous support for the hypothesis, often voiced by sociologists of Marxist persuasion, that the middle classes are ambivalent and lack a true class consciousness, thus wavering more than others in response to their short-term interests and thereby holding the key to each election. Even if every party needs the support of a substantial section of middle-class voters to keep itself in power, this does not mean that the middle classes, and they alone, 'make' the election. In order to say more we would have to inquire further into their potential 'Centrism'. Even though over-represented at the Centre, this would not be sufficient to describe their potential instability as a tendency to 'jump on the bandwagon'.

Governmental Performance

Questioned immediately after the defeat of Giscard d'Estaing on 10 May 1981, 44 per cent of respondents in a SOFRES - Nouvel Observateur poll

explained this result by the failure of the outgoing
president in his fight against unemployment. Other
reasons were linked to the feeling that his
authority had collapsed, to the absence of new
proposals from the outgoing majority and to the
divisions within the majority which were sharpened
by Chirac. An exhausted government incapable of
resolving France´s major problems - that was the
negative image which the French had of their
leaders.

Two years later, the main reasons causing
voters for Mitterrand in 1981 to switch to the Right
in 1983 were: the strengthened role of the unions
(42 per cent), the administration of public funds
(40 per cent), French borrowing from abroad (38 per
cent), the presence of Communist ministers in the
government (34 per cent), arguments over private
schools (35 per cent) and changes in television (34
per cent).(8) Although two of these issues
concerned the government´s economic policy, the
other four reveal a hostility to political change
which was regarded as too abrupt a departure from
the political and social balance.

Was there a misunderstanding in 1981 between
Mitterrand and these voters; did they think that the
Socialists would not carry out major policies that
had been theirs since 1971-2, or had these voters
themselves changed? It is very difficult to answer
these questions. There is no doubt, however, that
if the Socialist party fails to bring this section
of the electorate back into the fold in 1986 its
electoral decline would start to accelerate. It
would face the problem of mobilising both a Left
which would reproach it for not doing enough and a
Centre which would reproach it for doing too much.

At all events, this shows that Mitterrand´s
victory was the result of two slightly different
processes: the culmination of the slow
reconstitution of the Socialist electorate on a
class base (in its broad sense) and the vote in
favour of the only credible opposition to the powers
in office. Once alternation had taken place, the
Left ceased to be the opposition and was reduced to
its own normal strength.

Partisan Alignments and Electoral Volatility

We have seen that electoral volatility in
France can only be studied in the light of frequent
changes in the institutional and party system, at
least until 1981 when alternation opened a new era.

Even the changes corresponding to a long-lasting realignment, such as the reconstruction of a Socialist electorate and the role of the salaried and wage earning middle classes in this reconstruction, are linked to changes in the party system: the rebirth of the PS in 1971 and the disappearance of organised Centrism in 1974.

The role of party identification in the permanence of the vote or in the changes recorded is thus more difficult to discern than in other political systems. The PCF is the only party since the war which has had no great rift. And yet the study of the incidence of party identification, its intensity and significance is a necessary part of an analysis of electoral volatility in France.

At the 1978 legislative elections, in answer to the question ´Would you say that you are very close, quite close, not very close or not close at all to a particular political party?´, 13 per cent said ´very close´, 33 per cent ´quite close´, 21 per cent ´not very close´, 20 per cent ´not close at all´ and four per cent refused to answer. Less than one French voter in two had a strong or fairly strong party identification (46 per cent). Another question asked: ´Here is a list of political parties or movements. Could you tell me which one you feel closest to, or let us say, the least distant from?´. In this case, 84.6 per cent of respondents nominated a party, 9.9 per cent said that they were close to no party and 5.6 per cent refused to answer. We can thus distinguish between the strong and weak identifiers within each party (Table 8.11).

Table 8.11: Intensity of Partisan Support, 1978

Identification:	PCF %	PSU %	PS %	CDS %	PR %	RPR %
Strong	81	57	54	41	46	51
Weak	19	43	46	59	54	48

The Communist Party was the only one whose supporters identified strongly with it. Against that, the Giscardian parties (CDS,PR) had the lowest proportion of close supporters. The lower incidence of strong identification on the Right is traditional, due to the constant changing of the party sub-system on the Right and Centre and to local factors in the vote. This does not mean, as we have seen, that the voters on the Right do not

find their correct bearing on the ideological
compass. But at an election the great fluidity
among supporters of the Right benefits the most
credible candidate or party. The stronger the
identification with a given party, the lower the
volatility (essentially among those on the Right).
Thus after the 1978 elections, presidential voting
intentions among RPR supporters varied markedly
according to the strength of identification with
this party (see Table 8.12).

Table 8.12: Presidential Vote Intention of RPR
Supporters, 1978

Intensity of support for RPR	Chirac %	Giscard d´Estaing %	Others %
Very close	52	47	1
Quite close	47	50	3
Not very close	38	59	3
Not close at all	25	69	6
All RPR supporters	39	57	3

On the Left, Socialist supporters merit special
attention. In 1978 only three-quarters of them were
party identifiers and only half of the identifiers
had strong partisanship. The strength of
partisanship among Socialist supporters is to a
large extent linked to their position on the
Left-Right scale. In 1978, 16 per cent were on the
Left (points 1 or 2), 66 per cent on the Centre-left
(point 3) and 18 per cent on the Centre-right
(points 4 or 5). The closer these supporters were
to the Centre, the weaker their identification: 66
per cent of those on the Left were strong
identifiers as opposed to 57 per cent of those in
the Centre-left and only 30 per cent of those in the
Centre or Centre-right. It is precisely among this
latter group that we find the largest proportion (55
per cent) wanting a PS/UDF alliance (Table 8.13).
Thus there existed in 1978 a substantial proportion
of Socialist supporters, especially among the most
´Centrist´ of them, who wanted an alliance of the
Centre despite the inherent implausibility of such
an idea in the prevailing state of the party system.
It is quite possible that it was among this fringe
of the electorate, part of which was hardly
politicised (le marais) and another part of which

was strongly political, that the PS in 1978, and
even more so in 1981 found the support which gave it
victory. In 1978 the closer Socialist supporters
were to the Centre, the more confidence they had in
Giscard d´Estaing, rejected the Communist Party,
wanted a Centrist government which excluded the PCF
and RPR and intended to vote for the outgoing
president on the first ballot at the next
presidential election. We again see here what we
observed earlier when discussing the permanence of
Centrist opinion in the French electorate.

Table 8.13: Political Attitudes of Socialist
Supporters by Position on the Left-Right
Scale

| | Position on Left-Right Scale | | | |
	Left	Centre-left	Centre/ Centre-right	All
	%	%	%	%
Confidence in:				
Marchais(PCF)	43	28	9	28
Giscard	36	57	70	57
Want a Govt.				
Of the Left	49	23	6	24
Exclusively Soc.	29	30	17	27
Socialist/Centrist	15	36	55	3
Pres. vote intention				
Marchais	4	4	1	3
Mitterrand	86	66	37	64
Giscard	4	17	42	20
Chirac	1	2	4	2

At the 1983 municipal elections, eleven per
cent of Socialist supporters said that they had
voted for the Opposition of the Right (IFOP/RTL
survey). For the moment it is difficult to tell
whether this is evidence of short-term volatility or
the beginning of a partisan dealignment. A
continued weakening of the Left in opinion polls and
at by-elections in the near future may lead the
Socialist party to consider changing the electoral
system and its alliances which, while attempting to
weaken the constraints of majoritarianism, would
change the French political system yet again. Two
questions will be decisive in the near future. Will
the Socialist-Communist alliance, which is already
threatened by division over the economy and

international affairs, survive the coming
legislative elections in 1986? Will the UDF become
a real party, comparable to the PS, the PCF and the
RPR, and will it choose an alliance with the RPR or
make an alliance with the Centrist-left if the
PS-PCF alliance breaks down?

At all events, it will be difficult to achieve
a fundamental change in a political system whose
institutional logic remains majoritarian. That is
why the Right could benefit from the fact that the
PS might find it impossible to extricate itself from
an alliance on the Left which has become more and
more unpopular in the country. But even if the
Right won the next election it would still be very
difficult, if the Left were to decline, to
distinguish between the effects of short-term
volatility which would not jeopardise the long-term
chances of the Left, and the beginning of a
permanent decline similar to the current position of
the British Labour Party.

My feeling is that it will be increasingly
difficult for the PS, now that alternation has taken
place, to remain loyal to the alliance with the PCF
while at the same time retaining the Centrist fringe
of its electorate which it needs to ensure electoral
victories. That is the central issue in the future
political battle. This brings us back to the
question: does the Left's coming to power in 1981
mean that alternation has finally become a normal
phenomenon in French political life, or was this
just an accident which has little chance of
recurring? This is a very difficult question to
answer at present.

FOOTNOTES

1. In this chapter we shall not examine
systematically local elections or the flow of the
vote between first and second ballots.
2. Moreover, Gaullist candidates did not stand
in all constituencies. Where they did stand, their
share of registered voters was 19 per cent.
3. The data for the 1978 elections used in
this chapter are taken from a post-election survey
among 4,500 people. The main results of this survey
were published in Capdeveille et al. (1981).
4. Le Nouvel Observateur, 24 June 1983.
5. This table is taken from Jaffre (1982).
6. 'Cultural Liberalism': by this we mean a
group of values relating to the 'cultural' as

opposed to the economic or social domain. It is
characterised in particular by anti-authoritarianism
and a challenging of traditional morality. We have
constructed an index of cultural liberalism from the
following four items:

	% in sample %
-completely or by and large agree that a girl may take the pill under the age of 18	51
-school should above all educate people to have an alert and critical mind	35
-if I had another nationality I would be just as happy	17
-the courts are too hard on young delinquents	12

Respondents were given a score from 0 to 4,
according to the number of positive responses, and
grouped into three categories - those who scored 0
(35 per cent of the sample), 1 (35 per cent) and 2
or more (32 per cent).

'Traditional values of the Left': here again we have
constructed an index on the basis of the following
items:

	% in sample %
-if the right to strike were abolished it would be a very serious matter	44
-completely in favour of forbidding redundancy where no new job is available	43
-completely or by and large agree with the extension of the public sector	40

As above we have formed three groups: those who
scored 0 (30 per cent of the sample), 1 (30 per
cent) and 2 or more (40 per cent).
   7. This is confirmed by the IFOP/RTL survey.
The scale mentioned is that used by SOFRES and is as
follows: extreme Left 1 2 3 4 5 6 7 extreme Right.
   8. Le Nouvel Observateur, 29 April 1983.

REFERENCES

Capdeveille, J. et al. (1981) France de Gauche, Vote
    a Droite, Presses de la Fondation Nationale des
    Sciences Politiques, Paris
Dupoirier, E. (1982) 'Legislatives partielles: une
    demobilisation des electorats de gauche', Revue
    Politique et Parlementaire, 896
Goguel, F. (1981) Le Monde, 11 November 1981
---------- (1982) Pouvoirs, 23

Grunberg, G. and B. Roy (1983) 'Le choc des elections municipales francais des 13 mars 1983', <u>Tocqueville Review</u>, 1

Grunberg, G. and E. Schweisguth (1981) 'Profession et vote: la poussee de la gauche' in Capdeveille, J. et al., <u>op. cit.</u>

Jaffre, J. (1982) 'France de gauche, vote a gauche', <u>Pouvoirs</u>, 20 (see also <u>Pouvoirs</u>, 24)

Lancelot, A. (1975) 'Opinion polls and the presidential election, May 1974' in H. Penniman (ed.) <u>France at the Polls</u>, American Enterprise Institute, Washington

---------- (1983) 'La gauche a maree basse', <u>Projet</u>, 175

Lancelot, A. and P. Weill (1970) 'Les consultations electorales d'avril-juin 1969', <u>Revue Francaise de Sciences Politiques</u>, 2 April 1970

Michelat, G. (1969) 'Attitudes et comportements politiques dans une agglomeration de la region parisienne' in CEVIPOF, <u>L'election presidentielle de decembre 1965</u>, Presses de la Fondation Nationale des Sciences Politiques, Paris

Parodi, J. L. (1982) 'Une consultation sans obligation ni sanction', <u>Revue Politique et Parlementaire</u>, 897

---------- (1983) 'Dans la logique des elections intermediaire', <u>Revue Politique et Parlementaire</u>, 903

Pedersen, M. (1979) 'The Dynamics of European Party Systems: Changing Patterns of Volatility', <u>European Journal of Political Research</u>, 7

Subileau, F. and M. F. Toinet (1984 'Paris singulier, les enjeux de la participation', forthcoming in a collaborative volume by CEVIPOF

Ysmal, C. (1981) 'Stabilite des electorats et attitudes politiques' in J. Capdeveille et al., <u>op. cit.</u>

Chapter 9

WEST GERMANY

Hans-Dieter Klingemann

INTRODUCTION

There is much talk these days about political change in the Federal Republic of Germany. The Social-Liberal government came to an end on 9 September 1982 and was replaced by the Christian-Liberal coalition formed on 1 October 1982, which was legitimised by the electorate in the election of 6 March 1983. There has arisen a new socio-political movement, the Greens (Die Gruenen). This movement, although quite small, is now not only represented in six out of the eleven West German state parliaments but since the 1983 election in the federal lower house of parliament (Bundestag) as well. For the first time since 1953, when a refugee party entered parliament (Gesamtdeutscher Block/Block der Heimatvertriebenen und Entrechteten, GB/BHE) a fourth party other than the Christian Democratic Union/Christian Social Union (Christlich Demokratische Union/Christlich Soziale Union, CDU/CSU), the Social Democratic Party (Sozialdemokratische Partei, SDP) and the Free Democrats (Frei Demokratische Partei, FDP) managed to overcome the five per cent hurdle set by the electoral law. In addition, the Free Democrats have currently been voted out of five of the eleven state parliaments. Thus, it is no surprise that the theme of change dominates current political debate.

In what one thinks are turbulent times it is tempting to neglect signs of continuity. However, over the past decade differences in election results have not been all that dramatic. Even with the rise of the Greens the share of the valid votes cast for the ´system parties´ (CDU/CSU, SPD and FDP) in federal as well as in state elections has never dropped below the 90 per cent mark. Looked at from this angle the picture is one of stability rather than realigning or dealigning change.

TRENDS IN ELECTORAL VOLATILITY

Net Volatility
     Two elements are important in descriptions of
the format of a party system: the number of parties
competing for the vote and the distribution of the
parties' electoral strength. Pedersen (1983)
concludes that in Western Europe the number of
parties has increased and the distribution of
electoral strength of the parties has changed in
unpredictable ways. New parties have emerged and
there seem to be defections of large portions of the
electorate from older parties to new parties which
are classifiable neither as traditional mass parties
nor as 'catch-all' parties. How does this
conclusion square with the West German experience?
     The seemingly simple task of providing a valid
description of the number of parties competing for
the vote is not without difficulties. Although most
informed observers tend to classify the West German
situation as a two-and-a-half or a three party
system (Blondel 1968; Kaltefleiter 1973; Pappi 1984)
Stoess (1983) reports that about 500 political
groupings have claimed the status of a political
party since 1945. Thus, at least as far as the
choice pattern for the individual voter is
concerned, the common view seems to be oversimple.
Of course, some parties entered only one election
and then faded away. Some parties split, some
merged. And some of these new electoral
arrangements lasted for longer periods of time while
others just pooled their strength for a single
election. Before analysing trends in party support,
however, some characteristics of electoral law have
to be spelled out. As in most other countries,
electoral law is an important intervening variable
which influences the format of the party system.
     In West German federal elections the individual
voter can choose both between candidates who are
elected by a plurality of votes in single member
constituencies and between party lists of candidates
who are nominated at the state level. The
distribution of seats in the Bundestag is calculated
in strict proportional representational terms. From
the total number of seats so calculated, the number
of seats won directly by the candidates in the
constituencies is subtracted. The remaining seats
are allocated to the party lists. In the first

general election in 1949 the voter had only one vote
which served for the election of candidates at both
the constituency level and the state level. Since
1953 citizens have been entitled to two votes: the
first ballot (Erststimme) which is cast in one of
the 248 constituencies, and the second ballot
(Zweitstimme) which is decisive for establishing the
overall distribution of the 496 seats in the
Bundestag. Only those parties which gain at least
five per cent of the second vote or three seats
directly in the constituencies are eligible for
representation in parliament.(1) This constraint
was not originally a German invention but was
included in the first electoral law at the request
of the three Western military governors (Pappi,
1984).

Given these institutional rules, single
individuals (Einzelbewerber), political groupings
(Waehlergemeinschaften) or parties may choose to
compete solely for the plurality of the first ballot
in single member constituencies. They would,
however, by definition not be entitled to any second
votes. In order to obtain second votes a party must
compete at the level of at least one of the West
German states and present a party list of
candidates. Although it is interesting to look at
the choice situation across constituencies (first
ballot), we have chosen to limit this analysis to
the parties´ competition for second votes - the one
exception being the election of 1949 when people had
only one vote.

In federal elections from 1949 to 1983, 47
political parties entered the competition for second
votes (counting the CDU/CSU as one party), 17 on a
nationwide basis. Of the remaining 30 parties, 15
presented candidates in more than one state while
the rest tried their electoral fortunes in only one
state. The pattern has been different from election
to election. Only three parties - the Christian
Democrats, the Social Democrats and the Free
Democrats - competed in all ten federal elections.

In individual elections voters could choose
between seven (1972) and 15 (1976) political
parties. They could also abstain or - for whatever
reason - cast an invalid ballot. The latter options
are real ones for any citizen. It is for this
reason that we have calculated the electoral
strength of the parties based on the total number of
those entitled to vote (see Table 9.1). This
procedure is distinctively different from what is
normally reported by official election statistics

where the distribution of party strength relates to the number of valid votes cast.

It is beyond the scope of this chapter to describe the programmatic profiles of all 47 parties. The interested reader may consult Stoess (1983, 1984) who has compiled the available material in a comprehensive fashion. Although the format of Table 9.1 underlies the calculation of our measures of fractionalisation and volatility, the information must be summarised to outline some general trends in the development of the West German party system.

The political parties may be grouped in many different ways. We have kept the CDU/CSU, the SPD and the FDP separate because of their important role in the postwar development of the Federal Republic. Among the smaller parties we distinguish between a left-wing, mostly anti-capitalist group (13 parties), a group of parties with a more or less strong affinity towards the CDU/CSU (three parties), a group of middle class interest parties (five parties), the right-wing, anti-democratic parties (eleven parties), the refugee parties (two parties), regional parties with separatist overtones (five parties), a curious group of 'European' parties (three parties), and the ecologists (two parties). (See Appendix 2 for a full list of the parties assigned to each category).

Three significant electoral trends are closely tied to the party system's transformation. The first involves the transfer of voting support away from the smaller parties to the advantage of the CDU/CSU and the SPD. The second concerns the decline in the proportion of non-voters and invalid votes. The third pertains to the relation between the three 'system parties', the CDU/CSU, the SPD and the FDP.

The result of the first general election in 1949 displayed many of the characteristics of a 'Weimar'-type situation. About 18 per cent of the total electorate voted for smaller parties, about four per cent for candidates without any party affiliiation (Parteilose) or other local political groupings (Waehlergemeinschaften). Moreover 21.5 per cent of the electorate did not vote and 2.4 per cent of the votes were invalid. This remains up to now by far the highest rate of abstention in any of the federal-level political contests. The only party to the left of the SPD, the Communists (Kommunistische Partei Deutschlands, KPD) gained 4.4 per cent of those entitled to vote. The smaller 'non-left' parties reached almost 16 per cent,

Table 9.1: Results of West German Federal Elections, 1949-83

	1949	1953	1957	1961	1965	1969	1972	1976	1980	1983
	%	%	%	%	%	%	%	%	%	%
'System' parties										
CDU/CSU	23.6	37.5	42.4	38.2	40.3	39.3	40.6	43.7	39.1	43.1
SPD	22.2	23.9	26.8	30.5	33.3	36.4	41.4	38.3	37.6	33.7
FDP	9.1	7.9	6.5	10.8	8.0	4.9	7.6	7.1	9.3	6.1
'Left-wing' parties	4.4	2.8	0.2	1.6	1.1	0.5	0.3	0.3	0.2	0.2
'Clerical' parties and parties close to the CDU/CSU	2.3	0.7	—	—	0.1	*	—	*	—	—
'Middle-class' parties	3.7	2.7	2.9	—	*	*	*	—	—	—
'Right-wing' parties	3.6	1.1	0.9	0.8	1.9	3.7	0.5	0.4	0.2	0.2
'Refugee' parties	—	4.9	3.9	2.3	—	0.1	—	—	—	—
Regional (separatist) parties	3.5	1.5	0.8	0.1	—	0.1	—	*	*	*
'European' parties	—	—	—	—	*	0.1	0.1	*	*	*
'Ecology' parties	—	—	—	—	—	—	—	—	1.3	4.9
Local parties/independent candidates	3.7	—	—	—	—	—	—	—	—	—
Non Voters	21.5	14.2	12.2	12.3	13.2	13.3	8.9	9.3	11.4	10.0
Invalid votes	2.5	2.8	3.3	3.5	2.1	1.4	0.7	0.8	0.8	0.8

Note: * = less than 0.1 per cent.

including the votes cast for independent candidates
and local political groupings. Eleven parties and
three independents were represented in the first
Bundestag.

In 1953, however, support for the smaller
parties declined drastically, as did the proportion
of non-voters. Only two of the small parties, the
newly founded Refugee Party (GB/BHE, 4.9 per cent)
and the German Party (Deutsche Partei, DP, 2.7 per
cent) survived with a still sizeable number of
voters. Up to 1976 there was a further decline in
the small parties. By that time they were down to
0.8 per cent. The right-wing National Democratic
Party (Nationaldemokratische Partei Deutschlands,
NPD) represented the only serious challenge to the
general trend, winning the support of 3.7 per cent
of those entitled to vote in the 1969 election. In
1983, however, the situation changed. The
ecologists (Die Gruenen) attracted 4.9 per cent of
those entitled to vote and gained representation in
the Bundestag. Whether this new development marks a
turning point in the long-term trend remains to be
seen.

The decline of non-voting in the early period,
especially from 1949 to 1953, and the decline of the
number of invalid votes after 1961 indicates the
growing acceptance of democratic elections and the
increasing politicisation of the electorate. This
interpretation is well in line with observations on
the development of political culture in the Federal
Republic (Conradt, 1980) and it squares with figures
reported by Noelle-Neumann and Piel(1983, p.339) who
show that political interest rose from 27 per cent
in 1952 to 57 per cent in 1983.

The third trend important to the transformation
of the West German party system is closely related
to the first two. In 1949 the three ´system
parties´ gained 54.9 per cent of the electorate´s
support. By 1972 their combined proportion had
risen to 89.5 per cent; this subsequently decreased
slightly to 82.9 per cent in 1983. From 1953 the
SPD increased its vote in consecutive elections up
to 1972 when the party gained 41.4 per cent. For
the first and up to now the only time, the SPD in
this election won more votes than the CDU/CSU.
Starting in 1976 the SPD lost popular support and
was back to its 1965 level in 1983 (1965: 33.8 per
cent; 1983: 33.7 per cent). For the CDU/CSU a
somewhat different pattern emerged. This party
dramatically improved its electoral standing in 1953
and 1957. In 1957 the CDU was the first - and to

date the last - political party ever to win an absolute majority of seats in parliament. Since 1972 its electoral strength has fluctuated around the 40 per cent mark. The FPD´s electoral support contrasts sharply with that of the two major parties. Unlike the CDU/CSU and the SPD, the Free Democrats were unable to expand their political base. Their fortunes waxed and waned from one election to the next, mainly depending on their programmatic stance - from national liberalism to progressive liberalism and back again - and their subsequent coalition behaviour. The party scored its biggest electoral success in 1961 (10.8 per cent) and faced the threat of extinction in 1969 (4.9 per cent).

There are a number of factors responsible for the general trend towards concentration and consolidation of the West German party system. Partch (1980 p.87-8) names seven: 1) the five per cent clause of the election law; 2) the 1954 and subsequent income laws which regulated the deduction of political contributions and gave the main parties a financial advantage over the smaller parties; 3) the petition rule for new parties which required at least 200 signatures in each of the 248 constituencies before a party which had not yet been represented in either the Bundestag or any of the state legislatures could put its party list candidates on the ballot; 4) the ´chancellor-effect´ which gave the ruling party high visibility and, if successful, an additional bonus; 5) article 21 of the constitution (Grundgesetz), which stipulates that all political parties have to conform to ´democratic principles´ and which has hung like the sword of Damocles over parties of both the extreme left and right (the Communists (KPD) and the Socialist Reich Party (SRP) were banned as unconstitutional); 6) increasing prosperity following the war which to the public meant that the main political parties were able to translate party policy into government action, thereby increasing their ´competence ratings´, and 7) the parliamentary rule on the formation of ´Fraktionen´ in the Bundestag. This rule requires parties to win at least 25 seats to be able to caucus as a parliamentary party (Fraktion), and this in turn determines a number of important prerogatives such as staff support and committee assignments.

To this list Pappi (1984) adds the licensing policies of the Allied Powers after the war and the differentials in the parties´ coalition potential.

The policies of the Allies meant that only the original four licensed parties were in a position to contest the 1949 election in every state. This Allied decision gave these parties an advantage over the others, with the Communists being the exception. The latter lost their potential for expansion mainly because of the development of a Communist regime in the German Democratic Republic which had no attraction whatsoever for the West German public (Urwin, 1974). As far as coalition power is concerned, the Shapley/Shubik index (Shapley and Shubik, 1954)(2) shows that in the early years no coalition government was possible against the CDU/CSU, which underlines the power of this particular ´system party´ (Pappi, 1984).

All these and other factors led to the establishment of a stable three-party system. Although the FDP, as the smallest party, was several times in danger of not reaching the five per cent threshold, the coalition power index in the period between 1961 and 1982 of each of the three ´system parties´ was exactly one third. Three different two-party coalitions were logically possible and all three did, indeed, occur. From 1961 to 1966 the CDU/CSU and FDP were in coalition; from 1966 to 1969 the two largest parties worked together in the ´Grand Coalition´, and from 1969 to 1982 the SPD and FDP formed the Social-Liberal government. Since 1982 the CDU/CSU and FDP have again formed a bourgeois government. But as Pappi (1984, p.11) notes:

> The entry of the Greens as a fourth party to the Bundestag has changed the power of the parties for the first time in twenty years. The CDU/CSU as the largest party gained power, its (Shapley/Shubik) index going up to 0.5. The SPD and FDP lost power. Their index is now that of the Greens, 0.17.

The index of fractionalisation (Rae, 1967) summarises the process of concentration and consolidation of the West German party system (Table 9.2). The broad choice of party ideologies and interests which was offered to the electorate in each of the federal elections (indicated by the number of parties entering the competition) did not lead to fragmentation. The index of volatility (Pedersen, 1983) shows the highest rate of net change to have occurred between 1949 and 1953. In the late 1960s (1965-69) and in the 1970s (1972-76;

1976-80) these rates proved to be relatively low
(Table 9.2). In general the evidence tends to
support the concentration-consolidation hypothesis.
A decomposition of the index indicates that,
starting in the 1972-1976 period, most of the
observed change can be accounted for by changing
preferences for one of the three ´system parties´,
mainly involving an exchange of votes between the
CDU/CSU and the SPD. In 1983 the Greens enter the
picture. But even so the party system seems to be
stable in many respects. Some find it more
interesting, therefore, to search for the forces of
stability rather than for subtleties of change
(Pappi, 1984).

Table 9.2: Indices of Fractionalisation and
           Volatility in West German Federal
           Elections

Index of Fractionalisation				Index of Volatility			
1949	.833	1969	.692	1953	22.9	1969	6.1
1953	.771	1972	.650	1957	9.5	1972	9.3
1957	.725	1976	.648	1961	12.1	1976	3.8
1961	.732	1980	.684	1965	7.8	1980	5.8
1965	.702	1983	.683			1983	7.7

Note: These calculations are based on the full
election results, counting support for all
individual parties separately, and not on the
summarised version presented in Table 9.1. As noted
in the text, party support is taken as the
percentage of the total electorate and non-voters
are included as a separate category.

Gross Volatility
    Aggregate measures of electoral volatility are
useful for the description of stability and change
in the format of party systems. They do, however,
hide the gross rate of vote changing because the
individual voter may be quite volatile within a
stable aggregate. Long-term panel studies would be
required to estimate the gross rates of change
across subsequent elections. Unfortunately, such
information is in short supply for West Germany.
    The Political Action II study measures party
identification - a variable which is closely related
to the vote in the West Gernam context (Kaase, 1976,

Gluchowski, 1983) - both in 1974 and in 1980.(3) To the best of our knowledge this survey covers the longest period of time that has elapsed between two panel waves for a West German sample. Results support a 'low net-change - high gross-change' assumption. While we would infer six per cent net change from the marginals, the turnover table tells us that the rate of gross change amounts to as much as 45 per cent.

Short-term three-wave panel studies, consisting of two pre-election waves and one post-election

Table 9.3: Stability and Change: Three-Wave Panel Surveys (Two pre- and One post-election), West Germany, 1972-83

Patterns of stability and change	1972	1976	1983
Stability	%	%	%
same party mentioned 3 times	64	63	58
no party mentioned 3 times	3	4	1
'Hard' stability	67	67	59
same party mentioned twice, no party once	9	12	8
a party mentioned once, no party twice	5	4	3
'Soft' stability	14	16	11
Total stability	81	83	70
Change			
different parties mentioned 3 times	1	1	2
'Hard' change	1	1	2
same party mentioned twice, different party once	16	14	25
different parties mentioned twice, no party once	2	2	3
'Soft' change	18	16	28
Total change	19	17	30
N	1222	1196	1016

wave, are available for the 1972, 1976 and 1983
federal elections(4). These data allow us to
estimate the rate of change in individual voting
intentions (first two waves) and reported voting
behaviour (third wave). The period of time covered
ranges from three and four months (1972, 1983) to
six months (1976). Using a ´hard´ criterion for
individual stability (mentioning the same party or
no party three times) the proportion of voters so
defined was 67 per cent in 1972 and 1976 but dropped
to 59 per cent in 1983. This pattern becomes more
pronounced if one ´softens´ the criteria for the
definition of change and stability as described in
Table 9.3. Although individual change between
parties at all three points in time remains an
extremely rare case (´hard´ change) the total amount
of change, including the ´no party mentioned´
category, increases from 17 per cent in 1976 to 30
per cent in 1983. This finding is in line with the
general notion of growing volatility in the
electorates of Western democracies.

As we have pointed out, panel surveys which
would enable one to make a systematic analysis of
individual change across a series of consecutive
federal elections are not available. Thus we have
opted for a second best solution. The data base we
shall explore consists of eight nationwide
cross-section sample surveys, all of which were
conducted shortly before election time and which
were designed to represent the population entitled
to vote.(5) Such surveys are lacking for two
elections: 1949 and 1957. Otherwise all federal
elections are covered. Each survey carries both a
question about the respondent´s vote intention for
the coming election and a question about her or his
voting behaviour in the last federal election. We
are painfully aware of all the pitfalls that the use
of recall questions implies. However, there is no
alternative and our strategy should at least yield a
rough approximation of individual change and
stability between two successive federal elections.

We have distinguished seven different types of
stability and change. The details are presented in
Table 9.4. The 1949-53 pattern exhibits the highest
degree of volatility, mainly due to the sharp
decrease in the proportion of non-voters. As
compared to 1949-53, the 1957-61 situation is
already much more stable. The amount of gross
change falls from 43 per cent to 25 per cent. This
result fits earlier observations made in the context
of the discussion of net change. Due to an increase

Table 9.4: Patterns of Stability and Change: Recall of Voting Behaviour (last election) and Vote Intention (forthcoming election), West Germany, 1949–83

Patterns of stability and change	1949–53 %	1957–61 %	1961–65 %	1965–69 %	1969–72 %	1972–76 %	1976–80 %	1980–83 %
Modes of stability								
Same party	38	60	54	59	64	64	64	69
No party mentioned	17	13	12	13	11	12	12	5
New voters who mentioned no party	2	2	1	1	0	1	2	0
Total stability	57	75	67	73	75	77	78	74
Modes of change								
Party change	8	7	10	11	10	9	9	13
From party to no party	4	6	4	4	2	4	3	3
From no party to party	23	8	14	8	9	5	4	4
New voters who mentioned a party	8	4	5	4	4	5	6	6
Total change	43	25	33	27	25	23	22	26
N	3116	1454	1411	1158	2052	2076	1518	1084

in the proportion of respondents who mentioned a party in answer to the vote intention question, the level of individual volatility reached a third of the electorate between 1961-65. From the period of 1965-69 to 1976-80 there is a slight increase in the overall level of stability, ranging between 73 per cent (1965-69) and 78 per cent (1976-80). The picture changes again in 1980-83 when volatility is on the rise. These figures support what has been said about the general trends of change on the basis of electoral statistics. However, had we calculated the rates of net change using survey data we would have overestimated the rate of net change from 1972-76 to 1980-83. A closer look reveals that this effect is mainly due to the bad prediction of the CDU/CSU vote in this period (1972, 1976, 1980). The ´climate of opinion´ hypothesis (Noelle-Nuemann, 1980) may explain a good part of the phenomenon. Thus, in addition to the problematic status of the recall question and the rather large sampling error of some of the surveys (1969, 1983) our results are biased in some periods of time more than in others. However, although inferences require caution it remains true that better estimates are not available. With all these caveats in mind we can conclude from this analysis that the proportion of gross change between two consecutive federal elections in West Germany fluctuated around the 25 per cent level from the late 1950s to the early 1980s.

These rough indicators of gross change simplify the complex pattern of switching between parties and movement involving non-voting. We are not going to discuss these movements in detail. Instead, we limit our attention to a single aspect. We shall ask how many voters the CDU/CSU, SPD and FDP were able to keep from one election to the next, that is, the extent to which one can predict vote intention from a respondent´s earlier voting behaviour.

For the two main parties results show a relatively high degree of stability (Table 9.5). In general the proportions are well above 80 per cent; they even reach the 90 per cent mark in three out of the 16 cases. The lower stability rates for the CDU/CSU in the 1950s reflect their growing electoral success during this period while the decrease of the SPD´s stability in 1980-1983 signals its declining support.

The pattern observed for the FDP is particularly interesting because it clearly reflects the impact of political events. The high rate of

Table 9.5: Patterns of Stability: Standpatters, West
Germany, 1953-83

	CDU/CSU %	FDP %	SPD %
1949-53	76 (722)	67 (141)	80 (542)
1957-61	79 (622)	83 (65)	90 (340)
1961-65	83 (496)	40 (81)	88 (348)
1965-69	80 (435)	38 (53)	89 (355)
1969-72	86 (602)	62 (90)	86 (857)
1972-76	92 (661)	62 (166)	81 (760)
1976-80	87 (445)	61 (81)	84 (623)
1980-83	92 (420)	33 (73)	79 (412)

Note: Cell entries are the proportion of a party´s
voters at one federal election who voted for the
same party at the next.

change from 1961 to 1965 can be linked to the
party´s supporting another cabinet headed by Konrad
Adenauer of the CDU after the 1961 election, despite
its pledge made during the election campaign not to
do so. Although the FDP entered this coalition with
the understanding that Adenauer would resign in
favour of Ludwig Erhard of the CDU before the
federal election of 1965, this compromise met with
wide criticism and left a long-lasting negative
imprint on the FDP´s image (´Umfallerpartei´). The
further decline of the party from 1965 to 1969,
which is also reflected in a high rate of individual
change, can be interpreted in the light of the FDP´s
changing policy positions and coalition preference.
In October 1966 a tax issue afforded the opportunity
to put an end to the Christian-Liberal coalition led
by Erhard. The FDP assumed the role of an oppostion
party. Kurt-Georg Kiesinger of the CDU became
chancellor and Willy Brandt of the SPD
vice-chancellor of the ´Grand Coalition´. No longer
restricted by governmental responsibilities, a new
´program of Action´ (Aktionsprogramm) was passed by
the FDP at the Hanover convention in 1967, which
called for a change towards a new ´Ostpolitik´ and
the realisation of more democracy in state and
society. The FDP moved to the Left and began to
favour the formation of an alliance with the Social
Democrats at the federal level. This new coalition
preference became most visible when Gustav
Heinemann, the SPD´s candidate for the presidency,
was elected in March 1969 with the help of the Free
Democrats. Shortly before the federal elections of

1969 it was quite clear that the party would indeed try to enter a coalition government led by a Social Democrat. As a consequence of these developments the FDP lost about 40 per cent of its 1965 support in the 1969 contest and 19 of its 49 seats in the Bundestag. The low stability rate in the 1980-83 period may, again, be interpreted in the wider context of the party´s changing coalition behaviour. In September 1982 13 years of Social-Liberal government came to an end and in October 1982 a Christian-Liberal cabinet was formed. Disagreements on enconomic issues were a major cause of the FDP´s move to the Right again. A major portion of the party´s activists as well as its voters did not approve of this reorientation. In addition, style issues contributed to the disaffection with the Liberals. The opinion was widespread in the electorate that the FDP had ´betrayed´ the popular SDP chancellor, Helmut Schmidt. After all, the party had promised to support Schmidt and his policy in the 1980 election campaign and not a few had voted Liberal for just that reason.

Further evidence could be cited to demonstrate the importance of political events as an explanation for electoral volatility in relation to the FDP: for example, split-ticket voting (Kaase 1983) or the overwhelming weight of the issue of coalition formation in the voters´ minds (Klingemann 1980, 1984). As compared to the FDP both the CDU/CSU and the SPD seem to be less affected by political events. The social cleavages in which these parties are rooted are widely regarded as having exerted a strong influence on their rather stable electoral support in federal elections since 1961 (Pappi, 1984).

EXPLANATIONS: THE DECLINING IMPORTANCE OF TRADITIONAL CLEAVAGE ALIGNMENTS

Social class and religion have structured the German party system to a large extent. The Social Democrats have entered an enduring coalition with the working class and the trade unions. The Christian Democrats constantly enjoyed the support of the old middle class and the religious sector of society, especially of devout Catholics. This cleavage system is not symmetric. As far as class conflict is concerned, the status of the new middle class (civil servants and the white-collar workers) remains unclear. And the coalition of Catholics with the CDU/CSU does not imply bitter opposition among Protestants. The CDU/CSU is not like the old Zentrum. It welcomes the support of both Catholics and Protestants. For many Germans the shared Christian heritage seemed to be the only foundation upon which a new Germany could be built in the aftermath of Nazism and World War II. As Pappi (1984, p.18) says: The 'fault line of the religious conflict thus does not run between Catholics and Protestants but between the religiously-oriented and the secularised parts of the population'. But the difference in the CDU/CSU vote between Catholics and Protestants can still be used as a cleavage indicator because religious traditionalists are disproportionately found among Catholics. How stable are these traditional cleavage alignments of the West German populace? Are there any signs that social group politics is on the decline?

These questions have been answered differently by different analysts. Looking at data from 1953 to 1976 Pappi and Terwey (1982, p.193) come to the conclusion that:

> The German polity is characterised by very stable social cleavages... The very phenomenon of the group-anchored character of voting behaviour is an important cause of the continuity of the cleavage system.

Baker et al.(1981, p.193), however, state:

> A long term decline in the determining force of social characteristics as a guide for political behaviour has been found... On the whole German partisanship reflects a social base less and less.

These two statements summarise the opposite positions of the current debate. Both interpretations are possible if one accepts the respective conceptualisations, operational definitions and the statistical techniques used. Conceptually the main difference lies in the authors' treatment of class conflict. Pappi and Terwey contrast the old middle class (the self-employed) and the working class (blue-collar workers). Baker et al. base their conclusions mainly on a comparison between the new middle class and the working class. Operationally, Pappi and Terwey consider a three-party situation (CDU/CSU, FDP, SPD). Statistically, Pappi and Terwey rely on log linear techniques; Baker et al., on the other hand, use a regression model.

With respect to the conceptualisation of the class vote we side with Pappi and Terwey. Certainly it is the old middle class, not the new middle classes which fights the bourgeoisie's battle on election day. Unlike Pappi and Terwey and Baker et al., we do not exclude any respondent from the analysis. In line with the strategy followed in the earlier sections of this chapter we base the proportions on the total number of respondents who qualify as members of the particular social groups under consideration.

We have defined social cleavages as enduring coalitions between population groups and political parties (Stinchcombe, 1975). The difference in party preference between members and non-members of a particular population group can be regarded as an indicator of such a coalition. For the current analysis we have sub-divided the West German electorate into eleven distinct social groups and one residual category. Denomination, church affiliation, social class and trade union membership serve as the criteria for differentiation. (For details, see Appendix 1). As can be seen from Table 9.6, not all of the possible combinations of the variables used have been kept separate – mostly for pragmatic reasons.

As far as the old middle class is concerned, union membership is irrelevant and the small number of cases in most of the surveys does not allow for a further distinction along the dimension of church affiliation. Among Protestants, church affiliation is very low so we did not separate the religious and the secular. Union members of both the new middle class and the working class do not differ very much in their respective voting behaviour. For this reason these groups were also combined.

Because some of the relevant social-structural indicators are not available for 1961, and there is a paucity of data for 1949 and 1957, we limit our interpretation to the 1965-1983 period. Focussing on electoral support for the CDU/CSU and the SPD we can summarise the results shown in Table 9.7 as follows:

1) the Catholic old middle class and the three social groups involving the religious Catholics are dominated by the CDU/CSU at all points in time. With the exception of 1980 the same is true for the Protestant old middle class.

2) The SPD, in contrast, could always count on a

Table 9.6: Typology of Social Groupings, West Germany

	Catholics			Protestants		
	Old middle class	New middle class	Working class	Old middle class	New middle class	Working class
Union Members						
Religious	1	3	3	2	4	4
secular	1	5	5	2	4	4
Religious	1	6	7	2	8	9
Non-Union Members						
Secular	1	10	11	2	8	9

Notes: 1) Social class is defined by occupation of head of household. Old middle class = self-employed excluding farmers; new middle class = white-collar workers (Beamte and Angestellte); working class = blue-collar workers (Arbeiter).
2) Union membership refers to membership of respondent.
3) Denomination refers to denomination of respondent: if contrasted to Catholics Protestants are defined as 'non-Catholics'.
4) 'Religious' = attend church at least once a week; 'secular' = attend church less than once a week (including respondents not belonging to any denomination).

247

Table 9.7: Voting Intention of Selected Social Groupings

	CDU/CSU							SPD						
	'53 %	'65 %	'69 %	'72 %	'76 %	'80 %	'83 %	'53 %	'65 %	'69 %	'72 %	'76 %	'80 %	'83 %
Old middle class Catholics	44	70	61	49	75	57	61	10	7	16	24	11	24	21
Old middle class Protestants	25	45	40	42	45	31	60	13	13	17	32	19	35	17
Religious Catholics/New middle class/Non-union members	63	75	62	62	65	70	81	9	12	13	16	7	12	7
Religious Catholics/Working class/Non-union members	45	65	62	55	67	63	64	14	16	22	32	13	16	24
Religious Catholics/New middle class and working class/ Union members	40	69	71	55	58	46	55	30	17	21	26	33	42	21
Protestants/Working class/ Non-union members	15	29	23	15	20	20	26	38	50	53	66	52	48	60
Protestants/New middle class and working class/Union members	12	15	12	13	16	16	20	60	72	81	73	60	65	71
Secularised Catholics/New middle class and working class/Union members	18	18	27	21	29	30	45	65	61	57	69	53	52	41
Protestants/New middle class/ Non-Union members	31	41	24	26	36	27	40	21	33	40	52	34	44	35
Secularised Catholics/New middle class/Non-union members	42	34	37	31	46	33	53	19	29	35	41	29	34	26
Secularised Catholics/Working class/Non-union members	21	36	34	29	43	22	48	33	51	49	49	35	55	37

majority of the vote among the Protestant, unionised, new middle class as well as the Protestant, non-unionised working class. Up to 1983 a similar pattern could be observed for union members among the secularised new middle class and working-class Catholics.

3) Changing majorities of the two major parties are present in three groups: the non-unionised new middle class both of the Protestant and the secularised Catholic sector and in the non-unionised, secularised Catholic working class.

The results indicate both stability and change. On the one hand, the CDU/CSU and the SPD are still rooted in the traditional cleavage system. The enduring coalitions are clearly visible. The old middle class and the religious Catholics, regardless of class background, support the CDU/CSU. The Protestant working class and the trade unions back the SPD. On the other hand, there are distinct signs of volatility and change among the new middle class and the working class when union membership or church affiliation are lacking. These groups are without voting norms which have grown out of historical experience.

The new middle class shares characteristics of both the old middle class and the working class. Much of the work white-collar workers do is like that of the self-employed; yet they are employees like the working class. Thus, Baker et al. (1981 p. 172) observe:

> Consequently, the new middle class finds itself with a position in the social structure and a life-style that places it between the working class and the old middle class. As a result its loyalties are divided between these other two strata, and its votes are split between the parties of the left and right.

The religiously uninvolved, on the other hand, no longer guided by the authority of the church, look out for new ideas and values which might have a bearing on the organisation of the 'good' polity.

There is much change within groups across time, and between groups. No attempt will be made to discuss these patterns in detail. However, it should be evident from the figures that the gains of the CDU/CSU do not necessarily result in a loss for the SPD and vice versa. For example, the upward trend of the CDU/CSU in most of the groups in 1983

Table 9.8: Patterns of Stability and Change: Means and Standard Deviations for Selected Social Groupings, 1965-83

Social Grouping	CDU/CSU $\bar{x}$	SD	SPD $\bar{x}$	SD	Same Party $\bar{x}$	SD	Party Change $\bar{x}$	SD
Catholic/Old middle class	62.2	8.4	17.2	6.5	64.2	8.1	11.3	6.5
Protestant/Old middle class	43.8	8.6	22.2	8.2	59.8	12.4	13.7	6.3
Religious Catholics/ New middle class/ Non-union members	69.2	7.0	11.2	3.2	69.5	5.4	7.8	3.1
Religious Catholics/ Working class/Non-union members	62.7	3.8	20.5	6.4	69.3	6.5	5.3	3.8
Religious Catholics/New middle class and working class/Union members	59.0	8.6	26.7	8.5	75.2	7.8	8.3	1.8
Secularised Catholics/ New middle class/ Non-union members	39.0	7.9	32.3	4.9	57.7	5.4	10.5	3.1
Secularised Catholics/ working class/Non-union members	35.3	8.5	46.0	7.4	57.7	5.2	11.7	1.9
Secularised Catholics/ New middle class and working class/union members	28.3	8.6	55.5	8.6	67.8	6.7	12.5	3.4
Protestant/New middle class/Non-union members	32.3	6.9	41.0	7.4	58.0	5.5	13.8	1.2
Protestant/Working class/Non-union members	22.2	4.5	54.8	6.2	60.3	8.3	8.2	2.4
Protestant/New middle class and working class/Union members	15.3	2.6	70.3	6.6	74.3	5.3	8.8	2.0

Notes: Same party = recall of previous vote is the same as current vote intention; party change = different parties named for recall of previous vote and current vote intention.

is not always accompanied by a downward trend for the SPD. The decline of the FPD, the rise of the Greens, and the higher proportion of respondents reporting a party preference allow for such partially independent movements among CDU/CSU supporters on the one hand and SPD supporters on the other. A comparison of the standard deviations of the vote for the two major parties, or of the overall figures indicating change and stability between two consecutive elections, are presented for all social groups in Table 9.8 and summarise the empirical evidence.

As indicated by Tables 9.7 and 9.8, volatility is most clearly evident among the non-unionised secular Catholic and Protestant new middle class and among the secularised Catholic working class without union ties. Within these social groups the majority party has changed almost from election to election since 1965. The secular, non-unionised, new middle class moved rather dramatically towards the SPD in the 1965 to 1972 period, but again supported the CDU/CSU in 1983. The same is true for the secular, non-unionised, Catholic working class. This pattern does not point to the emergence of new long-term coalitions between these social groups and the political parties. Rather, it can be explained much more plausibly by political events and the parties' competence to govern. In this sector of society politics is no longer mediated by the old group ties. Politics <u>sui</u> generis seems to be the moving force when it comes to the voters' decision on election day.

Thus results reveal the existence both of social groups which act as stabilising forces and social groups where volatility prevails. To a large extent the future of the party system will depend on the rising or declining weight of the respective groups within the electorate. What are the prospects?

In the past two decades West Germany has developed into a post-industrial society. There has been a change from a goods-producing to a service economy; the majority of the labour force is no longer engaged in agriculture or manufacturing but in services. Over the past twenty years the proportion of the labour force in the tertiary sector rose from 38 per cent to 49 per cent. This change goes hand in hand with a change in the occupational distribution. The expansion of the service economy, with its emphasis on office work, education and government, has brought a shift to white-collar occupations. In 1974, for the first time in German history, white-collar workers outnumbered blue-collar workers. The proportion of

the self-employed dropped from 22.2 per cent in 1961
to 12.0 per cent in 1980. There is also evidence of
continuing secularisation. In 1965 about a third of
the electorate went to church frequently. In 1980
it was about a fifth. Census figures also show that
the proportion of the population which holds formal
membership in a Christian church went down from 96
per cent in 1970 to 86 per cent in 1980. Thus, the
proportion who get no clear clues from their social
environment about which party to vote for, is
rising. While old cleavage structures may be very
stable, the group-anchored character of the voting
behaviour of these strata is becoming less and less
a guarantee for the continuity of stable,
social-group, politics. When Pappi and Terwey
(1982) argue that the new middle class has
developed motivations to vote for the SPD or the FDP
which fit into the old cleavage system one has to
ask where these motivations come from, how stable
they are, and how they will develop in the future?
After all, this situation changed between 1976 and
1983. In a period of increasing individualisation,
with traditional ties diminishing in importance this
will be the decisive question. And it is in this
sense that one should refer to the <u>fragile</u> stability
of the West German party system.

FRAGILE STABILITY AND THE FUTURE OF THE WEST GERMAN
PARTY SYSTEM

No single prediction can be made about the
future of elections and party politics. It is not
only the West German case that shows that the
electorate is moving beyond the boundaries of ´elite
mobilised´ political participation (Barnes, Kaase et
al., 1979). The electorate of today perceives the
differences between its own goals and those of
elites in power much more than in the past. And:
´...elite-challenging action is likely to take place
when one knows how to cope with elites and wants
something different from what the elites want´
(Inglehart and Klingemann, 1979, p.207). It is not
surprising that such activities are mostly supported
by the younger and better educated parts of the new
middle class. These developments are a corollary of
electoral volatility.
In the foregoing sections we have stressed
politics as an important factor for electoral
volatility. Is there any evidence which would
support the view that we are moving from traditional

and stable-group politics towards change-prone issue politics? Dalton and Flanagan (1982, pp.5-6) have argued that as we move towards advanced industrialisation we can observe a transformation from social-group cleavages to issue-group cleavages:

> The increasing levels of urbanisation and occupational and geographic mobility associated with advanced industrialism mitigate against the existence of exclusive social-group networks. The revolutions in education and cognitive mobilisation work against the survival of disciplined, hierarchic clientelistic associations. (Dalton and Flanagan, 1982 pp 5-6).

These arguments are also in line with Allardt's (1968) diagnosis of an educational revolution that is changing political orientations, particularly among the younger age groups. For this group of younger and better educated people, most of whom belong to the secularised new middle class, the cleavage structures of the 1920s are obsolete and do not catch the actual cleavages and conflicts in modern society very adequately. Results of recent analyses of West German voting behaviour tend to support the hypothesis of issue politics. In 1983 an analysis of open-ended questions about the good and bad aspects of the CDU/CSU, the SPD, FDP and the Greens found that more than 90 per cent of the electorate was able to specify both positive and negative political arguments about all four parties. The simple hypothesis was confirmed that voters tended to choose that party for which they could find more positive than negative arguments as compared to the other parties (Klingemann, 1984). With this simple prediction rule, 83 per cent of the vote could be correctly forecast. Thus volatility is not just erratic; current research does not confirm the older notions of the uninterested and uninformed 'floating voter' (Daudt, 1961). Rather, rising volatility should be conceptualised as a development which fits the ideas of Rousseau, Locke, Tocqueville and other political philosophers. There is some reason to believe that we are moving towards a more open, participatory and individualistic style of democracy in West Germany and in other Western nations.

FOOTNOTES

1. Election laws were passed in 1949, 1953 and 1956. Although the basic regulations of the 1956 election law are in effect, there were a number of minor changes in 1956, 1964, 1965, 1968, 1969, 1972, 1974, 1975 and 1979. Details can be found in Schindler (1983, p.16-20). Until 1969 the minimum voting age was 21; in 1972 it was lowered to 18.

2. The Shapley-Shubik index for each party is defined as the proportion of all possible party combinations in which the party concerned is 'pivotal', making the difference between a winning and losing coalition.

3. The Political Action II panel study was carried out in the Netherlands, the United States and West Germany. Klaus R. Allerbeck, University of Frankfurt, Max Kaase, University of Mannheim, and Hans-Dieter Klingemann, Free University of Berlin, were the principal investigators of the West German part of the study.

4. The surveys were supplied by the Zentralarchiv fuer Empirische Sozialforschung, Universitaet zu Koeln. In what follows we cite: year of the study, title of the project, principal investigators, the institute which did the field work, number of cases, time of field work and the Zentralarchiv identification number of the survey(s).

1972 Wahlstudie 1972: Berger, Gibowski, Kaase, Roth, Schleth, Wildenmann: Infratest: N=2052, 23/9-11/10 1972: N=1603, 20/10-6/11 1972: N=1222, 9/12-30/12 1972: ZA-Nr. 0635.

1976 Wahlstudie 1976: Berger, Gibowski, Gruber, Kaase, Klingemann, Roth, Schleth, Schulte: GETAS: N=2076, 19/5-23/6 1976: N=1529, 5/8-18/9 1976: N=1196, 26/10-22/11 1976: ZA-Nr. 0823.

1983 Wahlstudie 1983: Berger, Gibowski, Kaase, Klingemann, Kuchler, Roth, Schleth, Schulte: MARPLAN: N=1622, 12/11-25/11 1982: N=1197, 11/2-24/2 1983: N=1016, 16/3-29/3 1983: ZA-Nr. 1276.

5. These surveys too were supplied by the Zentralarchiv fuer Empirische Sozialforschung, Universitaet zu Koeln. The details are cited as above.

West Germany

1953 Bundesstudie 1953:Reigrotzki: DIVO,IFO: N=3116,
      4/7-30/8 1953: ZA-Nr. 0145.

1961 Koelner Wahlstudie 1961: Baumert, Scheuch,
      Wildenmann: DIVO: N=1454,4/9-18/9 1961: ZA-Nr.
      0056.

1965 Bundestagswahl 1965: Kaase, Wildenmann: DIVO:
      N=1411, 4/9-14/9 1965: ZA-Nr. 0556.

1969 Bundestagswahl 1969: Klingemann, Pappi: DIVO:
      N=1158, 5/9-22/9 1969: ZA-Nr. 0426.

1972 Wahlstudie 1972: Berger, Gibowski, Kaase, Roth,
      Schleth,   Widenmann: INFRATEST: N=2052,
      23/9-11/10 1972: ZA-Nr.0635.

1976 Wahlstudie 1976: Berger, Gibowski, Gruber,
      Kaase, Klingemann, Roth, Schleth, Schulte:
      GETAS: N=2076, 19/5-23/6 1976: ZA-Nr. 0823.

1980 Wahlstudie 1980: Berger, Fuchs, Gibowski,
      Kaase, Klingemann, Roth, Schleth, Schulte:
      MARPLAN: N=1518, 6/9-22/9 1980: ZA-Nr. 1053.

1983 Wahlstudie 1983: Berger, Gibowski, Roth,
      Schleth, Schulte: MARPLAN: N=1084, 22/2-24/2
      1983: ZA-Nr. 1280

REFERENCES

Allardt, E. (1968) 'Past and Emerging Political
      Cleavages' in O. Stammer (ed.) Party
      Organisations and the Politics of the New
      Masses, Free University, Berlin
Baker, K.L., Dalton, R.J., and Hildebrand, K. (1981)
      Germany Transformed. Political Culture and the
      New Politics, Harvard University Press,
      Cambridge, Massachusetts
Barnes, S.H., Kaase, M. et al. (1979) Political
      Action: Mass Participation in Five Western
      Democracies, Sage, Beverly Hills, California
Blondel, J. (1968) 'Party Systems and Patterns of
      Government in Western Democracies', Canadian
      Journal of Political Science, 1, 180-203
Conradt, D.P. (1980) 'Changing German Political
      Culture', in G.A. Almond and S. Verba (eds.),
      The Civic Culture Revisited, Little Brown,
      Boston, pp.212-72

Dalton, R.J. and Flanagan, S. (1982) 'The Changing Content of Ideological Beliefs in Western Europe, the United States and Japan', Paper prepared for delivery at the 1982 Annual Meeting of the American Political Science Association, The Denver Hilton Hotel, Sept. 2-5, 1982

Daudt, H. (1961) Floating Voters and the Floating Vote, Stentfert Kroese, Leiden

Gluchowski, P. (1983) 'Wahlerfahrung und Partei-identifikation. Zur Einbindung von Waehlern in das Parteiensystem der Bundesrepublik', in M. Kaase and H-D. Klingemann (eds.), Wahlen und politisches System, Westdeutscher Verlag, Opladen, pp. 442-77

Inglehart, R. and Klingemann, H-D. (1979) 'Ideological Conceptualization and Value Priorities', in S.H. Barnes, M. Kaase et al., Political Action, Sage, Beverly Hills, California, pp. 203-13

Kaase, M. (1976) 'Party Identification and Voting Behaviour in the West German Election of 1969', in I. Budge, I. Crewe and D. Farlie (eds.), Party Identification and Beyond, Wiley, London, pp. 81-102

--------- (1983) 'The West German Election of 6 March 1983', Electoral Studies, 2, 158-66

Kaltefleiter, W. (1973) Zwischen Konsens und Krise: Eine Analyse der Bundestagswahl 1972, Heymanns, Cologne

Klingemann, H-D. (1980) 'Der Wandel des Bildes der FDP in der Bevoelkerung', in L. Albertin (ed.), Politischer Liberalismus in der Bundesrepublik, Vandenhoek & Ruprecht, Gottingen, pp. 125-50

---------- (1984) 'Die Bundestagswahl 1983. Sozialstrukturelle und sozialpsychologische Erklaerunasansaetze', in Berliner Wissen-schaftliche Gesellschaft (ed.) Jahrbuch 1983, Duncker & Humblot, Berlin (forthcoming)

Noelle-Neumann, E. and Piel, E. (eds.) (1980) Die Schweigespirale: Oeffentliche Meinung - Unsere Soziale Haut, Piper, Munich

Pappi, F.U. (1984) 'The West European Party System', West European Politics, 7, 7-26

Pappi, F.U. and Terwey, M. (1982) 'The German Electorate: Old Cleavages and New Political Conflicts', in H. Doering and G. Smith (eds.), Party Government and Political Culture in Western Germany, Macmillan, London, pp. 174-96

Partch, R.D. (1980) 'The transformation of the West German Party System: Patterns of Electoral Change and Consistency', German Studies Review, 85-120

Pedersen, M. (1983) 'Changing Patterns of Electoral Volatility in European Party Systems, 1948-1977: Explorations in Explanation', in H. Daalder and P. Mair (eds.), Western European Party Systems, Sage, Beverly Hills, California, pp. 29-66

Rae, D.W. (1967) The Political Consequences of Electoral Laws, Yale University Press, New Haven

Schindler, P. (1983) Datenhandbuch zur Geschichte des Deutschen Bundestages, 1949 bis 1982, Presse und Informationszentrum des Deutschen Bundestages, Bonn

Shapley, L. and Shubik, M. (1954) 'A method of evaluating the distribution of power in a committee system', American Political Science Review, 47, 787-92

Stinchcombe, A. (1975) 'Social Structure and Politics', in F. Greenstein and N.W. Polsby (eds.), Macropolitical Theory. Handbook of Political Science, Vol.3, Addison-Wesley, Reading, Massachusetts, pp.557-622

Stoess, R. (1983) 'Struktur und Entwicklung des Parteiensystems der Bundesrepublik - Eine Theorie', in R. Stoess (ed.), Parteienhandbuch, Westdeutscher Verlag, Opladen, pp. 17-309

---------- (1983) Parteienhandbuch, vol.1, Westdeutscher Verlag, Opladen

---------- (1984) Parteienhandbuch, vol.2, Westdeutscher Verlag, Opladen

Urwin, D.W. (1974) 'Germany: Continuity and Change in Electoral Politics', in R. Rose (ed.), Electoral Behaviour: A Comparative Handbook, The Free Press, New York, pp.109-70

APPENDIX 1: VOTING INTENTION OF SELECTED SOCIAL GROUPS

The Old Middle Class

	53	61	65	69	72	76	80	83
	%	%	%	%	%	%	%	%
CDU/CSU	34	46	58	50	46	56	43	61
FDP	15	16	13	8	9	13	9	10
SPD	12	9	10	17	28	16	30	19
Other parties	16	2	2	2	2	--	1	4
Non voters, no party mentioned	23	27	17	23	15	15	17	6
N	489	182	170	119	226	203	150	104

The New Middle Class

	53	61	65	69	72	76	80	83
	%	%	%	%	%	%	%	%
CDU/CSU	40	45	47	34	33	39	33	47
FDP	9	10	7	5	8	9	9	6
SPD	20	21	29	41	44	34	41	31
Other parties	11	3	3	3	2	1	3	6
Non voters, no party mentioned	19	21	14	17	13	17	14	10
N	759	325	423	326	700	882	627	429

The Working Class

	53	61	65	69	72	76	80	83
	%	%	%	%	%	%	%	%
CDU/CSU	23	32	34	34	25	33	26	38
FDP	3	3	1	2	3	5	4	3
SPD	36	45	48	48	59	44	49	49
Other parties	13	3	1	2	2	1	1	3
Non voters, no party mentioned	26	17	16	14	11	17	19	7
N	1407	652	609	468	799	691	577	424

Farmers

	53	61	65	69	72	76	80	83
	%	%	%	%	%	%	%	%
CDU/CSU	43	53	62	60	57	49	74	76
FDP	7	11	4	5	6	6	4	5
SPD	6	14	6	8	15	18	15	14
Other parties	19	1	--	5	5	--	--	--
Non voters, no party mentioned	24	21	28	22	17	27	7	5
N	433	132	87	63	87	67	27	42

Respondents not Classifiable by Occupation of Head of Household ('Other')

	53	61	65	69	72	76	80	83
	%	%	%	%	%	%	%	%
CDU/CSU	39	42	45	40	35	33	25	34
FDP	11	7	3	3	6	9	7	1
SPD	14	20	30	36	35	39	37	36
Other parties	11	2	3	1	5	1	8	15
Non voters, no party mentioned	25	29	19	20	19	19	23	14
N	28	163	122	182	240	233	136	85

Union Members

	53	61	65	69	72	76	80	83
	%	%	%	%	%	%	%	%
CDU/CSU	20	--	26	26	22	25	21	32
FDP	4	--	2	5	4	7	6	4
SPD	55	--	58	63	63	55	61	53
Other parties	8	--	3	1	1	1	2	5
Non voters, no party mentioned	13	--	11	5	10	12	10	6
N	359	--	244	146	367	453	333	167

West Germany

Non-Union Members

	53	61	65	69	72	76	80	83
	%	%	%	%	%	%	%	%
CDU/CSU	33	--	47	40	35	42	34	47
FDP	7	--	5	4	6	8	7	5
SPD	20	--	29	35	42	30	37	34
Other parties	15	--	1	2	3	1	3	5
Non voters, no party mentioned	25	--	18	19	14	19	19	9
N	2757	--	1167	1012	1685	1623	1184	913

Catholics

	53	61	65	69	72	76	80	83
	%	%	%	%	%	%	%	%
CDU/CSU	42	55	55	51	43	51	43	59
FDP	4	3	3	2	4	6	6	5
SPD	19	21	24	29	35	27	33	25
Other parties	15	2	2	2	3	1	2	4
Non voters, no party mentioned	20	19	16	16	15	15	16	7
N	1468	691	660	562	975	884	668	504

Protestants

	53	61	65	69	72	76	80	83
	%	%	%	%	%	%	%	%
CDU/CSU	23	27	35	26	24	29	24	35
FDP	10	11	7	5	7	9	7	4
SPD	27	37	41	49	56	42	48	47
Other parties	13	3	1	2	2	1	3	5
Non voters, no party mentioned	27	22	16	18	11	19	18	9
N	1561	697	700	576	977	1044	754	504

Respondents with no Denomination ('Other')

	53	61	65	69	72	76	80	83
	%	%	%	%	%	%	%	%
CDU/CSU	13	21	14	5	13	20	11	19
FDP	3	8	4	10	10	11	9	4
SPD	46	44	57	45	56	48	58	47
Other parties	13	9	4	10	4	5	8	18
Non voters, no party mentioned	25	18	21	30	17	16	14	12
N	87	66	51	20	100	148	97	73

Respondents with Regular Church-going Frequency

	53	61	65	69	72	76	80	83
	%	%	%	%	%	%	%	%
CDU/CSU	49	--	65	61	55	60	61	66
FDP	5	--	2	2	3	6	6	5
SPD	12	--	14	18	23	17	18	18
Other parties	13	--	1	1	2	0	1	1
Non voters, no party mentioned	21	--	18	18	17	17	14	10
N	1184	--	454	317	520	433	288	235

Respondents with Medium Church-going Frequency

	53	61	65	69	72	76	80	83
	%	%	%	%	%	%	%	%
CDU/CSU	24	--	39	35	32	41	33	52
FDP	9	--	7	4	7	8	7	5
SPD	25	--	36	43	46	32	43	35
Other parties	16	--	1	1	2	0	1	2
Non voters, no party mentioned	26	--	17	17	13	19	16	6
N	811	--	503	428	598	539	366	285

Respondents who Rarely or Never go to Church

	53	61	65	69	72	76	80	83
	%	%	%	%	%	%	%	%
CDU/CSU	19	--	26	24	20	28	21	33
FDP	8	--	5	4	7	9	7	5
SPD	36	--	52	51	59	45	50	45
Other parties	13	--	2	4	3	2	4	8
Non voters, no party mentioned	24	--	15	16	11	16	18	9
N	1121	--	446	410	934	1104	864	564

APPENDIX 2: CLASSIFICATION OF SMALL PARTIES

'Left-wing' parties

Kommunistische Partei Deutschlands (KPD); Gesamtdeutsche Volkspartei (GVP); Bund der Deutschen (BdD); Aktion Demokratischer Fortschritt (ADF); Deutsche Kommunistische Partei (DKP); Kommunistische Partei Deutschlands (KPD-ML); Vereinigte Linke (VL); Kommunistischer Bund Westdeutschland (KBW); Gruppe Internationaler Marxisten (GIM); Volksfront (V); Bund Westdeutscher Kommunisten (BWK); Unabhaengige Soziale Demokraten (USD).

'Clerical' parties and parties close to the CDU/CSU

Deutsche Zentrumpartei (DZ); Christliche Volkspartei (CVP); Aktionsgemeinschaft Vierte Partei (AVP).

'Middle class' parties

Deutsche Partei (DP); Radikal-Soziale Freiheitspartei (RSF); Union Deutscher Mittelstandsparteien (UDM); Buergerpartei; Freisoziale Union (FSU).

'Right-wing' parties

Nationaldemokratische Partei Deutschlands (NPD); Aktionsgemeinschaft Unabhaengiger Deutscher (AUD); Unabhaengige Arbeiterpartei (UAP); 5%-Block Partei; Deutsche Gemeinschaft (DG); Deutsche Reichspartei (DRP); Vaterlaendische Union (VU); Dachverband der Nationalen Sammlung (DNS); Europaeische Volksbewegung Deutschlands (EVD); Wirtschaftliche Aufbauvereinigung (WAV); Deutsche Konservative Partei/Deutsche Reichspartei (DKP/DRP).

'Refugee' parties

Gesamtdeutsche Partei (GDP); Gesamtdeutscher Block/Block der Heimatvertriebenen und Entrechteten (GB/BHE).

Regional (separatist) parties

Bayern-Partei (BP); Foederalistische Union (FU); Christliche Bayerische Volkspartei (CBV); Rheinisch-Westfaelische Volkspartei (RWVP); Suedschleswigscher Waehlerverband (SSW).

'European' parties

Europaeische Arbeiterpartei (EAP); Europa-Partei (EP); Europaeische Foederalistische Partei (EFP).

'Ecology' parties

Die Gruenen; Oekologisch-Demokratische Partei (OEDP).

Chapter 10

AUSTRIA

Christian Haerpfer

INTRODUCTION

The Austrian party system in the Second Republic - which came into existence in the aftermath of World War II, more exactly in 1945 - primarily consists of three political groupings. These had emerged from the three traditional political 'laagers' i.e. the Socialists, the Christian-Social camp and the National-Liberals, and have been sitting in parliament ever since 1949.

The most striking feature of party politics in Austria is a strong duopoly of the Socialist Party or SPOe (Sozialistische Partei Oesterreichs) and the conservative People´s Party or OeVP (Oesterreichische Volkspartei). Both had their institutional predecessors in the troubled inter-war period of the First Republic but underwent an ideological rapprochement in the light of the traumatic events preceding 1945. Ever since the mid-1940s the Socialists as well as the Conservatives have been trying to streamline their platforms and party organisation to conform with the ideal-type model of a 'catch-all' party. By cross-national standards, the OeVP´s and the SPOe´s outlook may be likened to that of the CDU and the SPD in Western Germany.

The Liberal Party or FPOe (Freiheitliche Partei Oesterreichs) represents the third but numerically much smaller grouping going back to the third former and equally small laager which had a national-liberal orientation with an emphasis on nationalism. The FPOe´s ideological background is heterogeneous, its electoral asset being an image of protest and dissent because of its role as the permanent party of opposition. In this chapter 'third force parties' are understood to include the FPOe as well as other small parties; the term 'minor parties´ refers to all small groupings except the FPOe. Minor parties have never had any significant impact upon the Austrian party scene. The Communist Party or KPOe (Kommunistische Partei Oesterreichs) held an average of four seats in the Austrian parliament from 1945 to 1959, but no other minor party has succeeded in gaining parliamentary representation.

As far as the social composition of /the three main parties is concerned, class and religious influences are weakening although their effect on Austrian party politics apparently continues to be greater than in other Western nations. During the 1960s and 1970s, the Austrian party system came to be less class-specific, the essentially class-based form of party competition typical of the First Republic being mitigated in the course of ´de-ideologisation´. The SPOe is still the party of the working class; its second stronghold is the civil service. The OeVP draws its support from farmers (who are - unlike in other Western nations - a significant electoral force) as well as from the old middle class and from religiously cross-pressured manual workers. The Austrian party system boasts no single party appealing to a majority of the middle class. The core group of FPOe voters are middle-class people with higher levels of income and education; the FPOe´s supporters are more exclusively middle class than those of the OeVP.

Austria´s electoral system is one of proportional representation. The legal framework for general elections is spelled out in the Austrian Constitution; the Second Republic adopted the 1920/29 Constitution with minor amendments. In 1970 an electoral reform was carried out which involved a structural change of the electoral system, with considerable implications for the party system and its development, by enhancing the degree of representativeness, i.e. the relationship between votes won and seats won. This produced a systematic bonus for the FPOe and a slight advantage for the SPOe.

Allocation of seats in the nine Austrian regions (<u>Bundeslaender</u>) is based on the number of inhabitants recorded at the last census. In the period 1945-70 seats in the first chamber of the Austrian parliament (<u>Nationalrat</u>) numbered 165. This figure was increased to 183 when electoral reform was brought in. The conversion of valid votes into seats takes place in two stages. The first step is the calculation of the amount of basic seats (<u>Grundmandate</u>) for each party according to the Hare System. Originally, that is before 1970, there were 25 constituencies (<u>Wahlkreise</u>) but their number has now been reduced to nine electoral units identical with the nine Austrian regions. The second stage consists in the calculation of the remaining seats (<u>Restmandate</u>) according to the D´Hondt System. The several constituencies are distributed among two constituency pools (<u>Wahlkreisverbaende</u>); the first includes Vienna, Burgenland and Lower Austria, the second covers the remainder of the Austrian territory, i.e. Upper Austria, Styria, Carinthia, Salzburg, Tyrol and Vorarlberg. The Austrian electoral system knows no equivalent to the five per cent threshold that regulates parliamentary access in Western Germany. Parliamentary representation is granted to any party managing to obtain one basic seat. As Austrian electoral history has shown, this regulation makes for a parliamentary threshold well below five per cent.

With respect to levels of electoral participation, Austria ranks second behind the Netherlands. The average level of turnout at general elections from 1945 to 1983 was 94 per cent. Average turnout figures for this period range from 91 (Vienna) to 97 per cent (Styria). In three regions regional laws make voting at general and presidential elections compulsory. Compulsory voting produces very high turnout in the regions of Styria (97 per cent), Vorarlberg (96 per cent) and Tyrol (95 per cent). The Austrian political culture has a strong tendency to regard the act of voting as a duty of every citizen. The sanction for non-voting is a fine of up to 3,000 Austrian schillings but no case is known of a voter having been fined.

A chronology of which parties have been in office so far falls into three separate periods. The era from 1945 to 1966 was that of the Grand Coalition, bringing together the two major parties, the OeVP and the SPOe. The 1966 to 1983 period saw a succession of single-party governments alternating between the OeVP and the SPOe, and since 1983 Austria has had a Social-Liberal coalition of the SPOe and the FPOe (Table 10.1).

The form of government most readily associated with the Austrian party system is the institution of the Grand Coalition, which has left its mark on Austrian domestic politics in a fundamental way.

The predominant features of this period are a balance of power between the two major parties with a slight dominance of the OeVP and a distinctive ´two-and-a-half party system´ with an electorally strong but politically insignificant FPOe and a considerable political influence of the Communist Party until the mid-1950s.

Table 10.1: The Development of the Austrian Party System, 1945-83

Control of Government	VOTES		SEATS	
I Grand Coalition	Mean	s.d.	Mean	s.d.
OeVP-SPOe 1945-66				
OeVP	45.1	2.8	48.3	2.4
SPOe	42.9	2.3	44.8	2.3
FPOe	8.8	2.4	6.3	2.6
KPOe;others	4.7	1.1	2.4	0.5
Rae Index(F)	0.602	0.033	0.560	0.033
II Single Party Government				
OeVP 1966-70				
SPOe 1970-83				
SPOe	48.5	3.5	49.5	2.8
OeVP	44.2	2.5	45.7	3.8
FPOe	5.6	0.3	4.8	1.1
Others	1.7	1.1	-	-
Rae Index(F)	0.564	0.009	0.541	0.008
III Social-Liberal Coalition				
SPOe-FPOe 1983-				
SPOe	47.6		49.2	
OeVP	43.2		44.3	
FPOe	5.0		6.5	
Others	4.1			
Rae Index(F)	0.582		0.558	

The period from 1966 to 1983 is characterised by two-party competition between the Socialists and the Conservatives. The OeVP ruled between 1966 and 1970, but the SPOe was able to form single-party governments from 1970 to 1983. It was in this period that the Austrian party system came closest to a pure two-party system (F=0.564), a fact reinforced by the utter unimportance of minor parties, but it gradually reversed in the wake of

the 1970 electoral reform. The third period began
when the SPOe was finally defeated at the 1983
general election and forced into a coalition with
the Liberals. As this new era of Austrian political
history is only twelve months old, any assessment of
the future prospects of this particular and new form
of goverment is a task for the future.

TRENDS IN VOLATILITY

Net Volatility
     The phenomenon of net volatility is measured by
the ´Pedersen-Index´ (see Pedersen, 1983). This
index can be defined as ´the net change within the
electoral party system resulting from individual
vote transfer´. (Pedersen, 1983, pp.31-2) A
systematic comparison of the varying degrees of
electoral volatility in the European party system
studied by Pedersen produced evidence of the Swiss
and Austrian systems having an extremely low level
of electoral volatility. Austria boasts the highest
degree of electoral stability, the average
volatility index being 3.7 in Pedersen´s study for
the period from 1948 to 1977 and even less (3.2) if
all twelve elections between 1945 and 1983 are taken
into account. Hence, a first over-all glance at
voting behaviour within the framework of the
Austrian party system reveals that net volatility in
Austria is relatively low when compared with that of
other Western nations.
     This basic pattern of electoral stability in
Austria since 1945 is of major importance in the
interpretation of electoral trends and fluctuations.
The occurrence of volatile elections must be analysed against the background of electoral patterns
which are - on the surface at least - characterised
by stability rather than by electoral change.
     As Table 10.2 indicates, Austrian post-war
electoral history can be divided into four different
periods, with either high stability or slight
volatility. The 1945-55 and 1965-70 periods can
aptly be described as periods of relatively volatile
voting behaviour whereas 1955-65 and 1970-80 each
display a high degree of electoral stability. The
decade immediately following World War II was a time
of realignment by which is meant a shift from a
totalitarian regime to a pluralistic ´Western´ party
system rather than a re-organisation of established
party politics. This was bound to produce a series
of political crises reflected in Austrian electoral

Table 10.2: Net Volatility and Swing in the Austrian
          Party System, 1945-83

	Pedersen Index	Swing		Pedersen Index	Swing
1945	-	-	1970	5.1	-4.8
1949	6.0	+0.1	1971	1.8	-1.6
1953	3.6	-3.1	1975	0.4	-0.3
1956	5.5	+1.9	1979	1.3	-0.8
1959	2.9	-1.8	1983	3.0	+2.3
1962	1.5	+1.0			
1966	4.3	+2.2	Mean	3.2	1.8
			Range	0.4-6.0	0.1-4.8

history. Hence, it is not surprising that the 1949 general election shows the greatest net volatility.

This drastic change in party performance was essentially brought about by the enfranchisement of those ten per cent of the electorate representing former members of fascist parties and/or organisations as well as other persons previously associated in one way or another with National Socialism. These voters supported the new VDU (Verband der Unabhaengigen), an institutional predecessor of the FPOe. The volatility index of 6.0 for 1949 is the highest of the Second Republic. The massive influx of new voters is reflected by the fact that the major parties´ share of the vote dropped from 94.4 per cent in 1945 to 82.7 per cent in 1949.

The 3.1 per cent swing in favour of the SPOe and the corresponding high Pedersen index of 3.6 recorded in 1953 signalled the final step towards two-party convergence in the post-war era. The OeVP, within close range of an overall majority (49.8 per cent) at the first general election in 1945, had its share reduced to 44 per cent in 1949. The extensive swing away from the People´s Party in 1953 finally left it with a further diminished vote of 41 per cent. The SPOe on the other hand, starting from a level significantly lower than that of the OeVP, won 44.6 per cent of the vote in 1945. The subsequent swing in favour of the Socialists in 1953 therefore involved two main aspects: first, the extremely low support for the SPOe in 1949 due to the influx of nationalist voters,and secondly the narrow margin, topping the People´s Party by only one per cent (42.1 per cent SPOe versus 41.2 per cent OeVP). The 1956 general election marked the

end of post-war electoral realignment and of a
decade of volatile party loyalties in Austria. The
Pedersen index of 5.5 for 1956 ranks second in
Austria´s electoral history and can be explained by
a significant reduction in support for both minor
parties, the FPOe and the KPOe (Kommunistische
Partei Osterreichs). The FPOe lost almost half of
its supporters, its share of the vote going down
from eleven per cent in the 1940s to 6.5 per cent in
1956.

The Austrian public regarded the KPOe in that
period as the ´party of the Russians´, because
central issues like Marshall aid and the
nationalisation of what formerly were German
industries revealed a coincidence of Soviet and KPOe
policies in opposition to those of the other
Austrian political parties. These perceived close
links between the Austrian Communists and Soviet
troops formed an electoral asset for the KPOe in the
Soviet zone of occupation in Eastern Austria,
because some voters thought life might be easier as
a voter or member of the KPOe. Thus the withdrawal
of Soviet troops from Austrian territory in 1955
promoted the electoral plight of the Austrian
Communist party in 1956 and 1959.

One major outcome of that decade of realignment
was a considerable reinforcement of the duopoly from
83 per cent in the early 1950s to 89 per cent in
1956, a date which ushered in a period of high
electoral stability lasting until 1966. This period
again was largely characterised by three features: a
strong Conservative-Socialist duopoly forming the
basis of the so-called Grand Coalition, a negligible
impact upon the political process by both minor
parties with only ten per cent of the total vote and
a consistent balance of power between the two major
parties. This caused a persistent stalemate between
the OeVP and the SPOe in the period from 1956 to
1966 with a slight edge to the People´s Party but no
single-party rule. While the OeVP gained a small
relative majority at the 1956 and 1962 elections the
Socialists attained a meagre 0.6 per cent lead in
1959 (44.8 per cent SPOe; 44.2 per cent OeVP).
Support for the OeVP ranged between 44 and 46 per
cent, that for the SPOe between 43 and 45 per cent.
Empirical confirmation of this even balance of party
preferences is provided by the swing recorded for
this period which is in line with the long-term
average (1959: -1.8; 1962: +1.0). The apparent
stability of partisan alignments between 1956 and
1966 is reflected by the Pedersen index of 2.9 for

1959 and of 1.5 for 1962.

The second period of volatile voting patterns in Austrian politics was from 1966 to 1970. These years saw the end of the Grand Coalition and the emergence of new forms of government such as single-party governments and, most recently, a coalition bringing together one major and one third force party. Both the 1966 and the 1970 general elections were milestones in Austrian electoral history. The 1966 Pedersen index of 4.3 ranks fourth in the entire period observed, thus pointing to substantial transformations within the electorate. This shift of electoral support furnished the OeVP with an overall majority with 48.3 per cent of the vote and 51.5 per cent of the seats in the lower chamber, re-establishing the record level of parliamentary strength it had held in 1945. The two principal factors behind this high swing (+2.2) were the decrease in support for the Socialists from 43.9 per cent in 1962 to 42.6 per cent in 1966 and, of even more importance, a dramatic rise in the Conservative share of the vote from 45.4 per cent in 1962 to 48.3 per cent in 1966, the year of a crucial structural change. The main reason for the Socialist's bad showing was a fierce and open battle for the party leadership causing a significant number of supporters to lose confidence in the party and leading to the creation of a splinter party, the DFP (Demokratisch Fort-schrittliche Partei). The DFP won almost 4 per cent of the vote in 1966, which did for the SPOe.

The 1966 swing represents the end of the era of the Grand Coalition which lasted from 1945 to 1966. This type of government together with its Austrian forms of political patronage ('Proporzsystem') profoundly influenced the formation and structure of the country's party system and has left deep institutional traces noticeable to this day.

Following the victory of the OeVP in 1966 the political pendulum swung to the other side with a massive rise in popularity of the Socialists at the 1970 general election. Electoral volatility in the period between 1966 and 1970 led to a swing of -4.8 per cent in favour of the SPOe, the biggest swing ever recorded in the Second Republic. Support for the incumbent OeVP went down from more than 48 per cent to below 45 per cent. The SPOe, the clear winner at the 1970 elections, exceeded its level of 42 per cent from the previous elections by six per cent, thus taking 48 per cent of the total vote. The volatile character of the 1970 elections is confirmed by the Pedersen index (5.1) which ranks third in Austria´s history.

The broad conclusions from empirical analysis carried out so far is that the period from 1966 to 1970/71 represents an essential departure from traditional voting practices by the Austrian electorate. Both the high Pedersen index ratings and the extensive swing recorded throughout this critical period indicate a breaking-up of the conventional laager structure assuring electoral stability during the years from the end of World War II to 1966. Party loyalties had been loosening to a considerable extent and strong party identification in the course of political socialisation was increasingly rare. The newly formed floating vote, with no definite party allegiance and voting preferences, came to make up a growing part of the electorate (see Sully, 1981).

The decade covering the years 1970 to 1980 was one of outstanding electoral stability characterised by secure SPOe majorities and Socialist single-party government. The period 1970-83 has also been called the ´Kreisky era´, because of the Socialist chancellor´s dominant role in Austrian political life during these thirteen years. An average of five per cent of the country´s electorate, the so-called ´Kreisky voters´, tended to favour the man rather than the party behind him, thereby forming an additional electoral asset to Socialist cabinets. The immobility shown by the Austrian electorate is reflected by Pedersen values ranging between 0.4 and 1.8. Consequently, the SPOe, having succeeded in increasing their share of the vote from 50.0 per cent in 1971 to 50.4 per cent in 1975, reached an all time high of 51.0 per cent at the 1979 general election.

Thus the new pattern of electoral behaviour determining party competition in 1970 was consolidating during the 1970s. In this decade floating voters seem to have developed and maintained a somewhat reserved preference for the SPOe. In the light of these observations we may assume a partisan dealignment with concurrent voting stability, which may sound paradoxical but will be explained in the course of this chapter.

The most recent general election, held on 24th April 1983, brought about a considerable change in the Austrian picture of party competition at the polls. The creation of two new ecology parties, the VGOe (Vereinte Gruene Oesterreichs) and the ALOe (Alternative Liste Oesterreich), and their contesting of the election produced a Pedersen index of 3.0. At the same time, the duopoly of the vote went down to a level equalling those in the 1950s (90.9 per cent). Overall, the two contenders emerging victorious from this election were the OeVP, enjoying a swing of +2.3 per cent in its favour, and both ecology parties, with a share of three per cent. Only their split into two separate grouping barred the 'Greens' from parliamentary representation. The volatile nature of the 1983 election suggests that both the SPOe and Chancellor Kreisky seem to have lost their ability to attract the majority of the floating vote and that newcomers to the established political scene represent a potential threat to the high stability in electoral behaviour that prevailed throughout the 1970s.

Gross Volatility
     Following the general framework of this book, the analysis of gross volatility in the Austrian party system will concentrate on four major points: OeVP-SPOe switching; the movement between 'third force' parties on the one hand and the major parties on the other; movement involving non-voting; and the effect of the physical replacement of the electorate. This section draws on six pairs of elections for its data base, covering the period 1962 to 1983. Gross volatility before 1962 cannot be assessed, for it was not until the early 1960s that political opinion polls and the collection of panel data were first introduced.
     A first look at the basic pattern of gross volatility in Austria supports the assumption that the country's party system has a considerably higher degree of electoral stability than other Western nations. The proportion of Austrian voters alternating between different parties ranges between four and twelve per cent, which is substantially less than, for example, in Britain, where the same indicator is between 26 and 42 per cent (Crewe, 1981).
     One principal outcome of our quantitative analysis is an analogy between net volatility and gross volatility. All three elections volatile in terms of the Pedersen index, namely 1966, 1970 and 1983, are elections with high rates of individual change (see Table 10.3). These three elections are characterised by an average of ten per cent of the electorate changing their allegiance between successive pairs of elections, the exact gross

273

volatility figures being eleven per cent for 1966
and as much as twelve per cent for 1970, when the
Socialists scored their decisive victory. Throughout the 1970s gross volatility was consistently low,
increasing only marginally from four per cent in
1971 to six per cent in 1979. Owing to the
appearance of the two ecology parties, volatility in
1983 almost reverted to its level in the 1965-70
period.

Table 10.3: Rates of Individual Constancy and Change
Between Each Pair of Consecutive
Elections, 1962-83

	1962-66	1966-70	1970-71	1971-75	1975-79	1979-83
Remained constant by twice	%	%	%	%	%	%
Voting OeVP	43	38	39	39	37	38
Voting SPOe	34	39	45	46	45	42
Voting FPOe	3	3	4	4	5	2
Abstaining	9	8	8	6	7	10
Total Constant	89	88	96	95	94	91
Changed by moving between						
OeVP and SPOe	4	5	2	2	3	3
OeVP/SPOe and FPOe/minor parties	6	6	1	2	1	5
Voting and Abstention	1	1	1	1	2	1
Total Changing	11	12	4	5	6	9
Total	100	100	100	100	100	100

Source: IFES Data Archive.

In the Austrian party system the proportion of
loyal partisanship is comparatively high.
Throughout the 1960s and 1970s about 90 per cent of
the electorate persistently favoured one party, the
climax of electoral stability being reached in 1971,
when 96 per cent of those eligible to vote either
adhered to their previous choice or remained in the
group of non-voters. On the basis of Table 10.3 we
can describe three elections as volatile because
they have a constancy rate five per cent lower than
the others. Thus the labelling of Austrian
elections as volatile elections is a convention to

facilitate a systematic analysis. Nevertheless, constancy rates of around 90 per cent are very high levels of political loyalty. There are three distinctive reasons for this apparent and unusual stability characterising Austrian voting patterns. First and foremost is a marked constancy in people´s loyalty to both major parties; between 77 and 85 per cent of the electorate consistently support the OeVP and the SPOe respectively. A comparison with British standards, where only around 50 per cent of the electorate regularly vote either Conservative or Labour, reveals the enormous benefit that accrues to Austrian parties as a result of this exceptionally high level of voting loyalty. The second reason for electoral stability is the narrow basis of consistent support for the third parliamentary party, the FPOe. Analysis of the Liberal vote in the decade observed demonstrated that regular FPOe voters account for only 50 per cent of the party´s normal share. The other half consists mainly of protest voters expressing their discontent with Austrian party politics and the handling of current affairs by supporting the party of permanent opposition, i.e. the FPOe. In the 1980s this dissenting segment of the population may well withdraw its support from the FPOe and turn to one of the ecology parties showing an even greater degree of independence from the established political process. The Liberals´ participation, since 1983, in the new Socialist-Liberal coalition poses another danger to the FPOe of significant losses among protest voters. The third reason for electoral stability in Austria is the fact that the size of the group of consistent non-voters tends to be unchanging over the years. Consistent abstention ranges between six and ten per cent. During the 1970s non-voting was extremely low, with an average of seven per cent regularly not turning up at the polls. Nevertheless, it is interesting to note that the ten per cent of non-voting recorded at the most recent election in 1983 represented the first double-digit figure of abstention in the entire period observed. The answer to the question of whether this increase in the number of those who prefer to stay away from the polls could be interpreted as a growing disaffection with the present spectrum of party choices will be given in elections to come.

Analysing gross volatility in terms of major party switching, major party - ´third force´ movement and voting versus non-voting leads to clear-cut

results. Alternative voting and non-voting has no
significant impact upon the extent of volatility.
In the period observed only one per cent of the
electorate belonged to that category, except for the
1979 election when two per cent changed between
voting and non-voting. Major party switching is
rare, ranging between two and five per cent of the
vote. However, there is a close link between
volatile election results and voters moving from one
of the major parties to a 'third force' option. In
other words, substantial shifts regularly result
from voters turning their back on both the SPOe and
the OeVP and going for a 'third force' choice or
vice versa. At all three volatile elections in
1966, 1970 and 1983 between five and six per cent of
the electorate changed sides from either the OeVP
and the SPOe to the FPOe, the KPOe, the DFP or the
new ecology parties.

In considering overall volatility in the
Austrian party system it is useful to ask which
components of the floating vote contribute to what
extent to the electoral success or failure of both
major parties, the Socialists and the Conservatives.
Table 10.4 specifies the various components of major
party change in the period 1962-83. The dimensions
distinguished - (1) direct switching (2) circulation
of Liberals (3) participation (4) physical
replacement of the electorate - are controlled for
their direction and extent of impact.
Unfortunately, the circulation of minor party
supporters is not included in this analysis, due to
the lack of reliable data on the subject. Since
major-minor party interaction does, however, play a
crucial role in electoral volatility the explanatory
power of this analysis of different components of
major party change is necessarily somewhat reduced.

Of the six pairs of elections between 1962 and
1983 four swung in favour of the Socialists, the
remaining two saw swings in favour of the
Conservatives. Moreover, it is interesting to note
that three of the elections reviewed indicate a
directional correspondence between individual
components' flow and total net change. This leads
to the assumption that there is a greater degree of
homogeneity in voters' movements at Austrian
elections than there is, in, say, the British party
system, where no election is characterised by a
consistent swing in the same direction at all levels
(Crewe, 1981, p.14). In Austria, such a flow of the
vote occurred at the 1970, 1979 and 1983 elections.
The existence of a consistent pattern of gross

Table 10.4: Components of Major Party Change for Pairs of Successive Elections, 1962-83

	1962-66	1966-70	1970-71
Straight conversion	+2.8	-5.0	-3.2
Circulation of Libs			
Defection to Libs	-0.1)	-0.9)	-0.1)
	+1.1	-1.0	-0.2
Recruitment from Libs	+1.2)	-0.1)	-0.1)
Participation			
Diff. turnout	-2.1)	-1.7)	+0.1)
	-1.6	-0.9	+0.3
Diff. abstention	+0.5)	+0.8)	+0.2)
Replacement of Elect.			
New electors	+1.3)	-0.9)	-0.3)
	+2.5	-1.3	-0.2
Electors died	+1.2)	-0.4)	+0.1)
Total Net Change	+4.8	-8.2	-3.3

Table 10.4: (contd.)

	1971-75	1975-79	1979-83
Straight conversion	-1.2	-1.0	-2.2
Circulation of Libs			
Defection to Libs	-0.3)	-0.2)	-0.2)
	+0.6	-0.4	+0.7
Recruitment from Libs	+0.3)	-0.2)	+0.9)
Participation			
Diff. turnout	-0.4)	-0.5)	0.0)
	-0.1	-0.1	+1.0
Diff. abstention	+0.3)	+0.4)	+1.0)
Replacement of Elect.			
New electors	-0.1)	-1.0)	-0.1)
	+0.2	-0.2	+0.9
Electors died	+0.3)	-0.8)	+1.0)
Total Net Change	-0.5	-1.7	+4.8

Note: + = change in favour of Conservatives (OeVP);
- = change in favour of Labour (SPOe).
Source: As Table 10.3.

volatility at the last two general elections suggests that the homogeneity of voter movement has been increasing over the last eight years. Only one component, straight conversion from one major party to the other, invariably conforms to the direction of overall swing. Hence, in the absence of appropriate information on the circulation of minor party supporters it is of vital importance to the understanding of major party showings to take a look at those voters who alternately favour the OeVP and the SPOe. The weakness of the Liberals´ position stems from their supporters´ lack of firm commitment to this party and readiness to switch to and fro between the FPOe and the Socialists or the Conservatives.

The demographic impact upon electoral volatility is greater than the impact of alternative voting and non-voting. The consistently high level of turnout at Austrian elections - according to an international comparison Austria ranks third in this respect (see Haerpfer, 1983) - allows the group of non-voters to be regarded as a stable electoral force. The demographic factor affects both major parties in different ways. At all elections except one, young people casting their vote for the first time have tended to favour the Socialists. The potential of new voters may therefore be considered a continual electoral asset to the SPOe. The Conservatives, on the other hand, benefit from the disappearance of voters through death.

Bearing in mind the lack of information on the circulation of minor party supporters, the conclusion from this analysis is that the two major parties´ prospects of winning an election increase with their ability to attract additional voters through straight conversion. In other words, the party whose gains exceed its losses with regard to its major opponent is most likely to be ahead at the end of polling day.

SOCIAL STRUCTURE AND ELECTORAL STABILITY

This third section assesses how changes in the Austrian social structure have influenced the relationship between class and party preferences. This empirical analysis of societal change will rest on three quantitative indicators, i.e. the Alford index of class-voting, the Lijphart index of religious voting and the variation explained by social structure variables (R-squared), the latter being derived from a causal model of voting behaviour in Austria.

A look at the parties´ social bases leads one to describe the Austrian party system as two-dimensional, with class and religious differences being by far the most important social-structural influences upon voting behaviour. This is in line with previous research on the social composition of party support in 17 Western nations which found that more than two thirds were two-dimensional (Rose, 1980). However, the paramount influence of class and religion has been declining over the years, a process which seems to have gained momentum during the 1970s. Consequently, all three measures in Table 10.5 indicate a weakening link between social dimensions and party preference. Whereas in 1969 such characteristics as class, religion, income, urban-rural cleavage, education, region, age and sex together still explained one third of the voting variation, their combined impact had declined to 17 per cent of the variance explained by 1981. In a complementary fashion, the Alford index of class voting dropped from its relatively high levels of about 26 at the beginning of the 1970s to a score of 19 in 1981. The same goes for the Lijphart index of religious voting, which declined from 30 in 1969 to 25 in 1981. These trends indicate the continued significance of social-structural influences upon voting, but the close fit between social position and political outlook which used to be typical of the Second Republic has been loosening as a result of a process of dealignment in the course of the 1970s. Hence, we may define the basic electoral pattern prevailing in the 1970s as a partisan dealignment with concurrent voting stability. This ´silent revolution´ within the Austrian electorate was first apparent at the 1981 general election.

The causal model of partisan change in the Austrian party system involves six independent variables: social class, age, income, education, sex and religion. The overall effect of social structure on the floating vote is small. Although there is no homogeneous group responsible for the floating vote, it is possible to produce some evidence of the weak social determinants of electoral volatility. Surprisingly enough, the two-dimentional structure of the Austrian party system does not exist among those who tend to change their party allegiance. Whereas class still exerts the stongest influence on non-aligned voters, religion shows no significant influence in this respect. The three dimensions with a direct and major effect upon the floating vote are social class (Beta: +0.09), age (Beta: -0.08) and education (Beta: 0.06).

Table 10.5: Social Composition of the Vote, 1969-81

	1969	1972	1977	1981
Variation explained by Social structure variables	0.34	0.30	0.19	0.17
Alford Index of Class Voting	26	27	24	19
Lijphart Index of Religious Voting (church attendance)	30	31	26	25

The core group of volatile voting in the Austrian party system is predominantly middle class, making up 35 per cent of the floating potential in 1981. One in every four of middle-class voters has no permanent political alignment and changed his or her party allegiance at least once. Whereas the extent of volatility among middle-class voters remained stable from 1972 to 1981, working-class voters were undergoing a significant process of dealignment. In 1981 almost as many working-class as middle-class voters changed their party choice. Farmers continued to display the greatest degree of electoral stability with 80 per cent supporting the same party. The only social group with an increase in its level of political loyalty were civil servants, among whom the proportion of stable voters rose from 76 per cent in 1972 to 85 per cent in 1981. A breakdown according to income allows a further differentiation of the floating vote. A study by Ernst Gehmacher and the author found that better-paid skilled workers and well-to-do white-collar workers with their personal incomes in the second quartile were especially prone to change their electoral choices on the basis of short-term decisions (Haerpfer and Gehmacher, 1984).
As to the effect of generation and age on electoral volatility, there is a distinctive trend. Party loyalty tends to strengthen with age. Fully 93 per cent of those aged 60 and beyond are loyal voters. Hence the older generation in Austria represents the stabilising force. Conversely, the

volatile segment of the electorate consists primarily of young people aged between 18 and 24. In 1981 as many as 61 per cent of the younger generation had no party ties whatsoever. And it is this non-aligned part of youth that accounts for exactly 50 per cent of the floating vote in the Austrian party system.

There is a positive correlation between a person's educational background and his or her readiness to change party preference. The core group of the floating vote is formed by electors with higher education; in 1981 one third of all well educated people reported a change of partisan choice at least once. Women are traditionally a stabilising force, which is reflected by the fact that 83 per cent of female voters never change their electoral choice, whereas only 73 per cent of male voters are loyal to one party. While religion hardly affects the degree of volatility it is nevertheless fair to say that non-believers are more likely to change their allegiance and that religious voters show a higher degree of political loyalty, with a preference for the Conservatives.

Testing for the effect of socio-economic and socio-cultural dimensions on the stability or variability of partisanship within the Austrian political system demonstrated that there is still a certain time-lag compared with other Western party systems, in that social structure accounts for a higher degree of electoral stability in Austria than elsewhere. Nonetheless, social conditioning of partisan choice became significantly diminished during the 1970s. The proportion of variance explained by social attributes decreased from one third in 1969 to less than one fifth in 1981. The crucial process of political dealignment among significant parts of the post-war generation during the 1970s was disguised by the phenomenon of the 'Kreisky voters' in that period. These non-aligned voters, who represented approximately five per cent of the electorate and exclusively backed the popular chancellor are again 'available' on the political market now that the Kreisky era has come to an end.

The floating vote consists mainly of three social groups: well-to-do employees, better paid skilled workers and young people in some kind of formal education. In addition, these three groups are characterised by a high level of education and a strong male and secular bias. The fact of a whole generation of young Austrians seemingly unwilling to comply with traditional laager thinking and

consequently remaining outside the conventional
system of party loyalties, represents a serious
inroad into the high level of electoral stability
and stable voting patterns of the Second Republic.
Hence the all - important question about Austria´s
political set-up in the 1980s is whether the recent
reinforcement of volatility will lead to the
emergence of a strong fourth party with a
post-materialist platform or, alternatively, to a
more conservative electorate fostered by the
long-term effects of the economic recession
experienced since the mid-1970s.

VOLATILITY AND PARTISAN STABILITY

This concluding section explores the relationship
between the short-term effects of electoral
volatility and the long-term effects of partisan
stability or change by measuring the incidence and
strength of party identification for the years 1972
and 1981. However, it must be noted at this point
that the almost classic concept of ´party
identification´ has not yet found its way into
Austrian political polling (See Budge et al.,
1976), so that research done for this chapter
represents a first attempt to apply the concept to
the Austrian party scene.
     The number of voters reporting a certain
attachment to one of the established parties
declined from 91 per cent in 1972 to 83 per cent in
1981. This exceptionally high level of party
identification in 1972 shows how firmly rooted the
Austrian party system is in people´s minds (see
Table 10.6). In the light of this evidence and
despite its relatively short history by Western
standards the Austrian party system can be looked
upon as a mature and widely accepted reality. The
decline in party allegiance among the electorate as
a whole occurred at all three levels of party
identification in a linear fashion from very strong
to not very strong identifiers, with the share of
affirmative respondents going down by three per cent
in each row. Whereas in 1972 only one in ten voters
had no party identification, the group of
non-identifiers doubled to 17 per cent by 1981.
Hence, the 1981 electorate can be divided into two
distinctive groups, with 83 per cent retaining a
more or less pronounced psychological attachment and
17 per cent reporting no party identification
whatsoever. The overall decline in partisanship is

Table 10.6: The Incidence and Strength of Party
Identification, 1972-1981

	1972 %	1981 %
% with a party identification	91	83
% identify with Con.(OeVP)	30	33
% identify with Lab.(SPOe)	57	47
	87	80
All electors:		
Very strong	33	30
Fairly strong	20	17
Not very strong	25	22
Weak	13	14
No identification	9	17
Conservative identifiers only:		
Very strong	20	22
Fairly strong	23	18
Not very strong	34	30
Weak	23	30
Labour identifiers only:		
Very strong	45	47
Fairly strong	21	21
Not very strong	24	25
Weak	10	7

reflected in a reduction of major party
identification from 87 per cent in 1972 to 80 per
cent in 1981. However, there is no analogy between
the Conservative and Socialist patterns of party
allegiance in the 1970s. The Austrian electorate
became more Conservative, with a rise in OeVP
identification from 30 per cent in 1972 to 33 per
cent in 1981. The share of the electorate
identifying with the Socialists fell sharply from 57
per cent in 1972 to 47 per cent in 1981. Hence, we
may speak of a steady convergence of the Socialist
and Conservative levels of party loyalty with a
continuing advantage for the SPOe. The latter is
partly a result of the SPO´s extremely tight party
organisation which can only be compared with that of
Communist counterparts in single-party governments.
So, when we come to think of the importance of party
membership for election outcomes we must not forget

that 30 per cent of the SPOe´s voters are also members of the party.

If one thinks of the four categories of very strong, fairly strong, not very strong and weak identifiers forming four concentric circles surrounding each party one can detect different tendencies for both major parties. In the period observed, the Socialists were able to increase their core group of staunch supporters by two per cent. In the second and third circles things hardly changed, but at the outer fringe the SPOe lost ground. The OeVP saw similar expansion by two per cent of its core group of confirmed identifiers but suffered substantial losses ranging between four and five per cent in the second and third circles of reported partisanship. However, these losses were again offset by a major influx of intuitive support at the fringe with a seven per cent increase.

Four basic features emerge from this analysis of the incidence and strength of party identification in the Austrian party system. First, and most importantly, Austrian party politics continues to be well established in people´s minds when compared with other Western nations. Secondly, the 1970s can be defined as a period of moderate dealignment of the electorate with eight per cent fewer identifiers. Thirdly, this decline was brought about both by a small growth in Conservative partisanship and a significant reduction in Socialist party allegiance. Finally, the core groups of very strong identifiers in both major parties were expanding. Future success or failure at the polls is going to be decided at the fringe of partisan support.

THE AUSTRIAN PARTY SYSTEM IN THE 1980s

In concluding this analysis of electoral volatility and partisan change two scenarios of the future of the Austrian party system spring to mind. The first suggests a continuation of the process of dealignment of the traditional political spectrum; the second points to a conservative realignment in favour of the OeVP.

One basic assumption about the forthcoming decade is that the SPOe will most probably have lost its appeal to the five per cent of ´Kreisky voters´, a loss severely impairing the party´s prospects of attaining such secure majorities as in the 1971-81 period. So, by 1984 Austria has two major parties

supported by approximately 43 per cent each and a
potential group of volatile voters of at least
eleven per cent. If the OeVP fails to come up with
convincing policy alternatives and an attractive
party leader to match the incumbent Social-Liberal
coalition the emergence of a fourth political force
may well be on the cards. In other words, depending
on the degree of flexibility displayed by the
traditional parties there is going to be more or
less of a chance for a new ecology party to
establish itself on the Austrian party scene. An
indispensable prerequisite for the establishment of
such a 'green' or 'alternative' party is its ability
to create a cohesive and stable party organisation
in order to survive in the long run. However,
recent developments within this emerging fourth
political force indicate a certain proneness to
fractionalism, fierce and almost self-destructive
rows for the party leadership and a rapid turnover
of backers. Hence, the life of a new ecology party
will depend on its organisational strength and skill
in adapting to the specific exigencies of the
Austrian political system. This scenario implies a
further loosening up of conventional party politics
and the establishment of a fourth factor potentially
damaging to the FPOe's parliamentary and political
existence.

A conservative realignment may happen, if the
OeVP succeeds in responding adequately to newly
emerging issues and to demands for a change in key
areas of public policy. This would involve
attracting volatile middle-class groups and
well-to-do skilled workers by a change in economic
policy and appealing to young people by assimilating
post-materialist values. Thus the future structure
and development of the Austrian party system hinges
upon the traditional parties' ability to adapt to
societal change in the closing years of this
century.

FOOTNOTE

The research for this work was supported in part by
the British Council. The data on which the study is
based were obtained from the IFES Data Archive. I
am very grateful for the assistance of Melitta Krcal
in language editing and of Ulrich Frick in data
management. Finally, I wish to thank Ernst
Gehmacher and Franz Birk for their comments and
support.

REFERENCES

Budge, I., I. Crewe and D. Farlie (eds.) (1976) Party Identification and Beyond. Representations of Voting and Party Competition, Wiley, London

Crewe, I. (1981) ´Electoral Volatility in Britain Since 1945´, paper presented at E.C.P.R. joint sessions, Lancaster

Haerpfer, C. (1983) ´Nationalratswahlen und Wahlverhalten 1945-1980' in P. Gerlich and W.C. Mueller (eds), Zwischen Koalition und Konkurrenz. Osterreichs Parteien seit 1945, Braumueller, Vienna

Haerpfer, C. and E. Gehmacher (1984) ´Social Structure and Voting in the Austrian Party System´, Electoral Studies, 3, 1: 25-46

Pedersen, M. (1983) ´Changing Patterns of Electoral Volatility in European Party Systems, 1948-1977: Explorations in Explanation´, in H. Daalder and P. Mair (eds.), Western European Party Systems. Continuity and Change, Sage, London and Beverly Hills, pp. 29-66

Rose, R. (1980) ´Class does not equal Party. The Decline of a Model of British Voting´, Institute for the Study of Public Policy, Occasional Paper No.74, Glasgow

Sully, M.A. (1981) Political Parties in Austria, Hurst, London

Chapter 11

ITALY

Percy Allum and Renato Mannheimer

INTRODUCTION : THE ITALIAN PARTY SYSTEM

The phrase 'electoral volatility' has found its way into the vocabulary of political science in recent years in Italy as elsewhere. It seems to have been introduced in the later 1970s to replace the earlier orthodoxy of 'electoral stability', as an explanation of the electoral changes of the mid-1970s and particularly the Communist advance of 1975-76. However, if discussion of the notion is not without its problems in the general context, one needs to stress that they are compounded in the Italian case. This is due, on the one hand, to the specific character of Italian politics and, on the other, to the kind of material available for analysis and evaluation.

In discussing electoral volatility it is necessary to make a preliminary distinction, the lack of which has been the source of confusion. One must distinguish between the electorate as an institution (i.e. as part of the political system) and the electorate as part of civil society (i.e. as a mass of individual voters, each with his own attitudes, motivations and behaviour patterns). This is because the political system is not an empirical reality but a level of analysis of society. It can be defined as a series of rules and mechanisms for, <u>inter alia</u>, the making of decisions concerning the production and allocation of societal resources. The electorate participates in Western liberal democratic political systems as an aggregate. It is essentially the election result, as translated by the specific electoral system, which is the input of the electorate into the political system, and which the system's rules and mechanisms transform into political actions and decisions; and not the attitudes, motivations and

287

behaviour of the individual electors. The confusions which this distinction seeks to avoid are two-fold. The first is general: that of assuming in analysing individual voting behaviour that one is analysing the political system when, in fact, at best, one is analysing the social context.

The second confusion avoided has a direct bearing on this study; it is, as Parisi has sought repeatedly to stress (Parisi, 1977, 1979, 1980), that volatility at the aggregate level does not automatically mean volatility at the individual voter level, or vice-versa. For example, there can be little doubt that Italian politics was characterised for twenty years by stable parliamentary representation; but that this was based on electoral fluidity and not stability as many analysts claimed. Parisi in his analysis (1979) identified four levels of electoral volatility/stability: 1) parliamentary represen- tation (i.e. the electorate at the level of the political system); 2) the size of the parties' electoral support; 3) the territorial distribution of votes at each election; 4) individual voting behaviour (i.e. attitudes, motivations and decisions of individual voters). It was to overcome confusion about these various levels, and particularly between levels 2 and 4 that the notions of ´net electoral volatility´ (level 2) and ´gross electoral volatility´ (level 4) were introduced. In any event, it is at these two levels, and above all with establishing some quantitative criteria, that this analysis of electoral volatility in Italy is primarily concerned.

Italian Politics
Italian politics has been characterised by a remarkable mixture of continuities and discontinuities.(1) Late national unification in 1861 and consequent continuing widespread regional cleavages together with regime changes have to be offset against the survival of the practices of trasformismo (parliamentary manipulation) and clientelismo (electoral manipulation) on the one hand, and the strength of the Catholic and Socialist mass movements, on the other. In consequence, it is hardly surprising that Italy is often considered to represent today the classic case of the European multi-party system. Nine national parties are represented in Parliament: Leftists, Communists (PCI), Socialists (PSI), Radicals (PR), Social-

Democrats (PSDI), Republicans (PRI), Christian Democrats (DC), Liberals (PLI) and Neo-Fascists (MSI). In addition, a number of regional lists have succeeded in electing MPs as spokesmen for their respective regions.(2) One reason for this proliferation is the electoral system, which is a version of the PR list system for both Houses (with preference votes to decide MPs for the Chamber).(3) Not surprisingly, no single party has succeeded in winning a majority of the popular vote in any post-war election. Thus, government has been by unstable coalition around, and led by, the DC as the largest party. It was centrist (DC, PSDI, PRI and PLI) in the 1950s, then Centre-Left (DC, PSI, PSDI, PRI) in the 1960s and early 1970s. Between 1976 and 1979, a government of national solidarity with external PCI support was formed (the so-called 'historic compromise'), and since 1979 it has been followed by the so-called 'five party coalition' (pentapartito) (DC, PSI, PSDI, PRI, PLI). The most recent novelty has been the formation of non-DC led governments (Spadolini (PRI) 1981-2 and Craxi (PSI) 1983-). Since the fall of fascism, Italy has had no less than 48 different cabinets.

Despite the obvious similarities with the Fourth Republic in France, Italian politics has a number of its own characteristics. In the first place, Italy has been dominated since the war by a Catholic party (DC) which has consistently won around 38 per cent of the vote until 1983 when it slumped to 33 per cent. It has been the major partner in all government coalitions since 1945 and one of the unwritten rules of Italian politics, at least until the 1983 elections, has been the impossibility of forming a cabinet hostile to it. In the second place, the principal opposition party has been the largest Communist party in Western Europe (PCI), which saw its share of the vote rise from 20 per cent in 1946 to almost 35 per cent in 1976 (30 per cent in 1983). It was by origin and definition a revolutionary, working class, anti-system party, and for this reason was forced into opposition during the Cold War and was excluded from power until the late 1970s. The failure of the 'historic compromise' means also that another unwritten rule of Italian politics, the exclusion of the PCI from national power, still survives. In the third place, the other national parties have rarely amassed more than a third of the vote, and so have never been able to provide a valid alternative to the DC. Their greatest aspiration, until very recently, was merely to condition, either singly or as a group, the DC towards a more conservative or a more progressive policy in a particular field, and obtain a cut of the spoils.

TRENDS IN ELECTORAL VOLATILITY

Before examining electoral volatility, it is necessary to say a word about the data available because this is a limiting factor on discussion about Italy. As regards electoral statistics, the Italian authorities make available what is probably the widest range of figures of any Western European country. This wealth of material has stimulated the development of some very sophisticated types of ecological analysis (see, for example, Barbagli et al., 1979). However, electoral results only permit the calculation of net electoral volatility and not gross electoral volatility for which panel survey data are required. As regards the latter, it is not that Italian polls do not exist. Rather panel surveys of vote-switching have been very few and a high level of non-response to questions on political preferences is a general phenomenon of Italian surveys (see Sani, 1975a; 1980). In these circumstances, not only is the material for measuring gross electoral volatility scarce, it has also to be treated with great caution.

Net Electoral Volatility

The first question to consider is the relative size of net electoral volatility in Italy. As in other chapters the measure used here is that proposed by Pedersen (1979). The index values in the Italian case are set out in Table 11.1 and vary from 21.7 for 1946-8 to 4.4 for 1968-72. It will be noted that the early period, 1946-53, had a higher volatility than was typical of the post-war period as a whole.(4) It was clearly the result of the adjustment of the party system to the new political situation created by the fall of fascism and the postwar settlement. What significance are we to give to the mean score of 7.7 with a standard deviation of 2.9? In his classic study, Duverger (1954) suggested that variations which did not exceed five per cent should be considered slight and those falling between five and ten per cent medium (Duverger, 1954, p.302). On this basis, Italy would appear to fall into the medium volatility category.

Moreover, a comparison of Italy´s mean score with those calculated by Pedersen for 13 other Western European countries reveals that it is close to the average. This would seem to confirm that Italy´s net volatility in the postwar period has been in the medium category.

A second question that arises concerns trends: it is difficult to discern anything from the Italian figures for postwar elections, except perhaps a cyclical repetition. This is even truer if we discard the pre-1953 period of postwar Reconstruction because the mean score is reduced to 6.9 and the S.D. more dramatically to 1.8, underlining the general consistency in the size of overall vote movements in the postwar period. In fact, the index scores suggest that elections with greater net volatility follow those with lesser almost alternately.(5) Thus, the Pedersen index does not suggest any trend in volatility since the early 1950s. The fact that net electoral volatility has remained at a similar medium level over time, suggests that it is less the size and more the direction of successive vote movements that is significant in Italian elections.

Given that Pedersen´s index furnishes only limited information on electoral mobility, we have set out a number of other indices in Table 11.1. Compared with the respective indices of the 13 other European countries, they succinctly delineate the Italian situation. Italy displays a high level of electoral fragmentation that changed little over the postwar period. It is among the electorally more fragmented countries of Europe, but is not the most fragmented, being surpassed by the Netherlands and Switzerland. But party support in Italy is more stable and less elastic that that of most other European countries.

Split-ticket voting could furnish a further indication of electoral volatility. Unfortunately, it is a subject that has been almost totally ignored in Italian electoral studies probably because, like abstention, its incidence is assumed to have been very small. However, there are indications that it is a much more common phenomenon than has been generally recognised. Already in 1958, a Doxa national survey found that 31 per cent of respondents believed that Chamber-Senate split-ticket voting took place; and 14 per cent believed that it was common (see Luzatto-Fegis, 1966). More recently, Amyot (1980) has calculated visible split-ticket voting to have been 4.5 per

Table 11.1: Some Indicators of Volatility in Italy, 1946-83

Index of Volatility

1946-48	21.7		1972-76	8.7
1948-53	13.2		1976-79	5.7
1953-58	4.7		1979-83	8.7
1958-63	7.9	Mean	1948-83	7.7
1963-68	8.1		S.D.	2.9
1968-72	4.4	'European'	mean	8.1
			(1948-77)	

Index of Fractionalisation (a)

1946	0.78		1976	0.72
1948	0.66		1979	0.74
1953	0.76		1983	0.78
1958	0.74		Mean	0.74
1963	0.76		S.D.	0.33
1968	0.75	'European' mean		0.7
1972	0.75			

Index of Party Support Variability, 1946-83 (b)

	SD	SD/M		SD	SD/M
DC	3.9	0.10	PLI	1.9	0.46
PCI	4.5	0.17	MSI	2.6	0.36
PSI	3.5	0.27	PR	1.0	0.43
PSDI	1.2	0.43	Mean	2.5	0.30
PRI	1.2	0.43 'European'	mean	2.9	-

Index of Party Support Elasticity 1946-83 (b)

DC	15.6		MSI	3.8
PCI	15.5		PR	2.4
PSI	11.1		PDUP	0.7
PSDI	3.7		Mean	6.0
PRI	3.7	'European' mean		7.8
PLI	5.7			

Notes: (a) Rae's index. (b) Rose and Urwin's indices. 'European' mean refers to the 13 European countries analysed by Pedersen.
Sources: Computation of Italian Electoral Statistics; Novelli (1980, p.247).

cent in 1970, 4.9 per cent in 1976 and 8.3 per cent in 1979 respectively of the DC Regional and Chamber votes. In these circumstances, it is reasonable to suppose that it could involve some 20 per cent of the electorate.(6)

We can conclude this subsection by noting that in a comparative European perspective, net electoral volatility has been moderate in size, electoral fragmentation high and party support more stable and hence more structured. It is this specific combination of moderate net volatility, electoral fragmentation and stable, but unequal, partisan support that explains, in our view, certain characteristics of postwar Italian politics. Small net changes from election to election (whatever the gross movements) effectively meant overall stability of representation. The result was a largely immobile electoral input over a twenty year period during which a whole series of practices, characteristic of postwar Italian politics, matured. But, as Duverger has admonished (1954, p.302), electorates are never totally static and the Italian one, as has been seen, is no exception. Moreover, the cumulative drift from 1946 to 1976 was, as Parisi has argued (1979, p.22), predominantly in one direction - leftward. It is our contention that it was as much this drift as the relatively large Communist advance of 1975-6 that sapped the previous equilibrium, if not the practices, and provoked the (albeit limited) political novelties of recent years.

Gross Electoral Volatility

Three aspects of gross volatility need to be examined. The first, once again, is the size of the phenomenon, i.e. the number of vote-switchers; the second is their socio-demographic characteristics; and the third is the type of vote-switching made.

In attempting to determine the size of vote-switching, we must draw attention to the lack of comparability of much of the survey data (due to differences of questions, type of survey, etc.) which compounds the problems of scarcity and unreliability referred to above. For example, on the one hand, Fabris (1977) reports the results of a Demoskopea national survey of April 1976 in which 57.5 per cent of the respondents claimed they had always voted for the same party, 15.8 per cent that they had switched parties once and 14.3 per cent more than once (but 8.9 per cent had voted only once and 3.5 per cent never). On the other hand, Barnes (1977 p.74, p.187) quotes a CISER national survey of June 1968 in which ´75% of our sample claimed to have always voted for the same party in national elections´, adding a footnote that ´voting continuity is probably greater than that indicated´. Barnes and Sani carried out a national survey in 1972 in which 78 per cent claimed to have always voted for the same party and 86 per cent said that they had voted for the same party in both 1968 and 1972. More recently, a 1983 panel survey (Makno, 1983) suggests that between 30 per cent and 35 per cent are vote-switchers. With regard to Barnes´ figures, it should be pointed out that the percentages were calculated excluding· non-responses which represented about 22 per cent of the sample and there is some evidence (Parisi, 1980, p.25) to suggest that the proportion of vote-switchers is higher among non-respondents than respondents.(7) This would point to a figure of 30 per cent rather than 20 per cent being the proportion of vote-switching in the postwar period.

A partial verification of this figure is provided by the estimates made by the Goodman multiple regression model of electoral mobility (proportion of votes changing parties between two elections) in various cities (see Table 11.2).(8) These vary between 17.8 per cent for Perugia between 1976 and 1979 and 32.1 per cent for Naples between 1979 and 1983. Although incomplete, these figures provoke a number of comments:

(i) that vote-switching of 25 per cent of the electorate is the likely lower limit for Parliamentary elections (as present evidence indicates that a 23 per cent mean for nine cities in 1976-9 represents a collective low whereas the likely upper limit is probably over 30 per cent).
(ii) that the amount of vote-switching in Italy has probably not varied widely over the post-war period, if the historical series for Bologna (see Corbetta and Parisi, 1983) is representative.
(iii) that a certain regional pattern is discernible: the industrial triangle and mainland south seem to experience greater electoral mobility than central Italy, and particularly the so-called ´red belt´.
(iv) that the figures for 1979-83 are higher for all cities than for previous electoral periods, but they are insufficient to confirm an upward trend in electoral volatility. They could just

as likely represent a one-election 'flash' or part of the cyclical pattern identified in the net electoral volatility index.

Table 11.2: Estimates of Electoral Mobility in Italian Cities

---

Bologna

	%		%
1946-48	22.8	1968-72	22.9
1948-53	n.a.	1972-76	23.8
1953-58	21.1	1976-79	18.8
1958-63	25.5	1979-83	25.8
1963-68	22.0		

Other Selected Cities 1976-79

Turin	28.9	Perugia	17.8
Milan	29.3	Naples	32.1
Genoa	21.2	Salerno	29.8
Verona	22.7	Taranto	29.1
Padua	27.5		

Note: The estimates for the cities in the second list are available only for 1976-79.
Sources: Data for Bologna, Turin, Genoa, Padua, Perugia, Salerno and Taranto supplied by P.G. Corbetta and H.M. Schadee of Instituto Cattaneo, Bologna; those for Milan and Naples by ADPSS, Milan.

Assuming that a figure of 25-35 per cent is representative of vote-switching in Italian elections, how does it compare with other European countries? (9) The figures for the countries for which we have seen data indicate that they are very similar, and so the appropriate conclusion would seem to be that gross electoral volatility in Italy, like net electoral volatility, has been near the European average and in any event much greater than the five to six per cent estimated by Galli in 1966 (Galli, 1966, p.128).

The second aspect - the socio-demographic characteristics of vote-switchers - raises in principle fewer problems. All studies concur that Italian vote-switchers have certain characteristics that tend to distinguish them from stable voters (see Sivini, 1966; Fabris, 1977; Martinotti, 1978). These can be summarised by saying that they are found disproportionately among the higher status socio-economic groups, the more educated, the more politicised and the more secularised. The characteristics of vote-switchers found by a 1983 national panel (see Table 11.3) tend to confirm this. However, the panel data do not always confirm what the existing literature suggests. For example, women seem more prone to switch than men in the panel whereas the literature leads one to expect that it would be men; but this may be the result of the 1983 political situation. One question raised by the association of these characteristics is whether age, education or class has the major influence on vote-switching. Since education and class are virtually two faces of the same coin (social position), the problem resolves itself as one between generation and social position. Corbetta (1982) has convincingly shown that in Bologna it is education (and so social position) and not age alone that is the major influence in switching. This does indicate the importance of education as a variable affecting vote-switching, particularly for the younger age-groups; it would appear to coincide with those generations which have benefitted from the expansion of higher education in postwar Italy.

The significance of the profile of Italian vote-switchers outlined above would appear to be its stark contrast with the classic Anglo-American model of the floating voter as particularly likely to be lower class, poorly educated, politically ill-

Table 11.3: Vote-Switching by Socio-demographic Characteristics, Italy, 1983

Sex	%	Class	%
Men	21.2	White Collar	24.5
Women	23.2	Blue Collar	19.0
Age		Size of Commune	
Under 35	26.4	<30,000 inhab.	20.3
35-55	22.0	30-500,000	23.6
Over 55	17.9	Over 500,000	27.6
Education		Index of Church Attachment	
Degree/Upper		Stable Voters	2.7
Secondary	30.0	Vote Switchers	2.4
Lower Second.	26.7	All Voters	2.6

Note: N = 1484. Vote switchers = 22.1% after exclusion of DK, NA, etc.
Source: Makno Panel Survey of May-September, 1983.

-informed and uninvolved. But the profile of well-educated, politically active switchers, if such it really is, is not limited to Italy; it has been found in other continental countries, like Austria and France and the classic Anglo-American model of the uninvolved floating voter is itself under attack in both Britain and America (see Benewick et al., 1969; Dobson and St. Angelo, 1975). The conclusion would appear to be that such a simple creature as the Anglo-American ´floating voter´ never really existed (10) and that vote-switching is a complex phenomenon combining a variety of situations and motivations.

This leads on to a consideration of the third aspect of volatility, namely types of vote-switching and their relative importance. It is generally recognised that gross electoral volatility can be analysed in terms of three component elements: (i) switching between parties; (ii) switching to and from abstention; and (iii) the physical renewal of the electorate. We shall examine component (iii) first, because it represents the major element of structural change in the Italian electorate in the 1970s. It was a particularly important factor in 1975-6, if only because the extension of the suffrage to 18 year-olds coincided with the great postwar advance of the PCI, and has been well documented by Sani (1975b, 1977b) in several articles. He showed that the Italian electorate had a mean growth of 4.8 per cent between elections for the period 1946-72, but in 1972-76 it grew by 9.2 per cent. This represented a net increase of 5.5 million electors, but taking into account, as one must, the 2.5 million who left, the physical renewal of the electorate concerned some one-fifth which is more voters than support the third largest Italian party. Sani further calculated, on the basis of survey evidence, that this renewal was worth some two million of the 3.75 million extra votes won by the Left in the 1976 elections. It can thus be seen that it played a major role in the electoral changes that took place in 1976 and we can safely say that it is unlikely to be repeated, if only because the happy combination (for the Left) of an extension of the suffrage to even younger voters and of such a high proportion of first-time voters oriented to the left (estimated at over 60 per cent) will almost certainly not recur. At present, the Italian electorate grows at the rate of 200-250,000 a year which represents an increase of between 1.0 and 1.5 million electors in the life of a full five year

Parliament, and a turnover of about four million
electors (less than ten per cent) - figures that
will drastically decrease in the late 1980s as the
birthrate has fallen dramatically.

Abstention - the second component of vote-
switching - has never played an important part in
postwar Italian elections. This may be because
voting is officially compulsory.(11) The exceptions
are the last two series of referendums (1978 and
1981) when non-voters and invalid votes together
amounted to about one quarter of the electorate. In
Parliamentary elections, abstention is around ten
per cent of which 6-7 per cent are non-voters and
3-4 per cent spoilt-ballots. Its increase in 1978
was due as much to changes in the law on electoral
registration as to any change in electoral
behaviour. Corbetta and Schadee (1982) conclude
their recent study of abstention in eight major
cities with the assertion that it has neither strong
political nor social connotations. 'The
distribution of the phenomenon leads us to think of
it as resulting more from a situation of generalised
apathy than of explicit protest, and, hence, even in
this case, of marginal political significance.'

The figures of switchers to or from abstention
vary widely. Thus, for example, Parisi claims that
in Bologna switches between parties and abstention
and vice-versa represented 2.6 per cent out of the
25 per cent gross volatility in 1972-6 and 3.2 per
cent out of the 18.8 per cent in 1976-9, while in
Genoa they accounted for 6.7 per cent out of 25.3
per cent gross volatility in 1972-6 and 6.8 per cent
out of 21.2 per cent in 1976-9. On the other hand,
the 1983 national panel indicates a figure of 40 per
cent of all switchers moving between parties and
abstention (i.e. 14 per cent of the 33 per cent of
the sample who switched). It seems fairly clear,
nonetheless, that the major component of
vote-switching is that between parties. In view
of the number of parties contesting elections,
vote-switching between parties in Italy has been
analysed in terms of two types of movement: a)
switching between parties within the same political
area or bloc; and b) that between blocs. These two
types of vote-switching have become the central
elements in two different interpretations of Italian
voting behaviour (see Parisi, 1980). Those who
believed that traditional voting patterns were
breaking down suggested that not only was electoral
volatility on the increase, but that the type of
vote-switching was changing from a predominance of

type a) to that of type b).

We have already noted that evidence in support of a growth in gross volatility is rather thin; the same appears to be the case with vote-switching (see Table 11.4). Indeed, the evidence such as it is (and it is mainly Corbetta's historical series for Bologna) suggests that switching between blocs occurred more frequently in the Cold War 1940s and early 1950s and less during the more 'permissive' 1960s and 1970s. Evidence from Genoa and Verona as well as national surveys, limited to the last decade, confirms that vote-switching between parties in the same bloc has predominated over that between parties in different blocs and there has been no change of direction in this period.

Corbetta has proposed a typology of switchers along the lines of Pulzer, and applied it to a survey of switchers in Bologna (see Corbetta, 1982; Pulzer, 1967). The types are: 1) the 'converted' (those who changed party once and remained faithful to their switch); 2) the 'temporary switchers' (those who switched to another party and then reverted to their original choice); and 3) the 'permanent switchers' (those who had voted for different parties in at least three elections). He found (see Table 11.5) that the 'converted' was the most numerous type, followed by the 'permanent switchers' and, finally, the 'temporary switchers'. Once again we have a situation that apparently contrasts with the Anglo-American situation. What is more surprising, given the changes in the ideological climate and the hypothesis of the growth of a more mobile electorate, was that two-thirds of the 'converted' switched between parties in the same bloc and only a third between blocs. With regard to the 'permanent switchers', the situation was the reverse - 3:1 in favour of switching between blocs. It could be argued that the results reflect the local situation in Bologna, Italy's 'red capital', where the left's ideological hegemony is particularly pervasive. However, there is survey evidence, admittedly indirect, that supports the typology and its results, and suggests that it is probably of more general application in Italy. Thus, a survey carried out in Vicenza in 1980 (Inchiesta University of Turin/CNR, 1980; Allum, 1983) revealed a similar percentage of 'converted' to 'permanent' and 'temporary' switchers. In this case, in a region of Catholic hegemony, not only was it the clerical dimension which discriminated most highly between stable voters and switchers, and between the different types of switchers, but it was reinforced by the Left-Right political dimension, so that switchers were most likely to be found among the 'lay left' identifiers. Unfortunately, the questionnaire did not permit a more detailed analysis of the kind of switches they made.

Table 11.4: Distribution of Within-bloc and Between-bloc Switchers in Selected Cities and National Surveys, Italy, 1946-83

| | Bologna | | | Bologna | |
	Within Blocs %	Between Blocs %		Within Blocs %	Between Blocs %
1946-48	4.3	18.5	1968-72	10.6	12.6
1953-58	8.9	12.2	1972-76	13.0	10.8
1958-63	13.7	11.3	1976-79	9.2	9.2
1963-68	11.9	10.1			

	1972-76 %	1976-79 %
Genoa		
within blocs	12.2	7.9
between blocs	6.4	6.5
Verona		
within blocs	14.9	8.7
between blocs	8.7	7.5
Milan		
within blocs		14.4
between blocs		12.0

	Within blocs %	Between blocs %
Demoskopea-CESPE national survey 1976	10.8	6.2
Makno national panel survey Sept. 1983	8.4	5.7

Note: The difference between the sum of switchers within and between blocs and the total of switchers shown in Table 11.2 is made up of switchers to and from abstention and spoilt ballots.
Sources: Corbetta (1982, p.26); Parisi (1980, p.23); ADPSS, Milan.

The Demoskopea national survey of April 1976 (see Fabris, 1977) also indicated a higher proportion of one-time switchers ('converted') than multiple switchers ('temporary' and 'permanent'), even if the difference was smaller (53 per cent to 47 per cent). What is interesting in this survey is the break-down of the switchers by age-group and occupation: this shows that the 'converted' were recruited in larger numbers from the under 45 age-group, and above all from industrialists, executives and professional men, together with white-collar workers, whereas multiple switchers came disproportionately from shopkeepers as well as from white-collar workers.

Table 11.5: Types of Vote-Switchers in Bologna

	Total %	Within Blocs %	Between Blocs %
'Converted switchers'	60.2	40.7	19.5
'Temporary switchers'	13.5	7.6	5.9
'Permanent switchers'	26.3	6.8	19.5
	100	40.7	44.9

Note: N = 237.
Source: Corbetta (1982, p.29).

This partial data would seem to support Corbetta's analysis that the floating vote in Italy is made up of different types of vote-switchers with different motives, which can be characterised in the contrast between 'changers' (generally politically motivated) and 'waverers' (more apolitical and hesitant). Thus the 'converted' seem to be individuals who start voting in a particular way, like their families perhaps, and after one or two elections experience a conversion, perhaps as a result of political activity, insertion into professional life, etc., and change their allegiance to another party. The 'permanent switchers' move the furthest in political and ideological terms and can clearly be defined as waverers. Paradoxically, at first sight they would seem to come from those groups (shopkeepers, white-collar workers and housewives) whose involvement in politics is low, but this can be explained on the basis of their being carried along on the prevailing tide of opinion. Finally, the 'temporary switchers' are more difficult to typify; they are those who experiment with alternative allegiances, but then return to the party of their first choice, so they would seem to be half 'waverers' and half 'changers'. It has even been suggested that they can be viewed as protest voters making a political protest against a particular action or policy of their national party.

If this outline - and it is only an indication gleaned from the data - is correct it means that not only is vote-switching a much more complex phenomenon in Italy than has so far been recognised, but that a contrast with the Anglo-American studies is inappropriate. A single model, such as the random model of the 'floating voter' of the early Anglo-American studies, is clearly inappropriate for the whole electorate. All European electorates contain low-involvement electors, whose switches in partisan attachment do not bear a meaningful relationship to changes of their vote, as well as involved voters who make deliberate switches based on reflection, albeit in different proportions and at different times. It has been suggested that it is among the waverers that one finds the highest susceptibility to short-term shifts in partisan attitudes, and so they are the most vulnerable to the impact of immediate political circumstances.

A final point concerns the political direction of switching. Given what was said about overall vote movements in the post-war period, it is no surprise that in the Demoskopea national survey of April 1976, of the 47 per cent of the respondents who claimed to know their father's vote and had voted differently, 39 per cent claimed to have moved to the left and only eight per cent to the right. Similarly, in Bologna, according to Corbetta, of the 43 per cent who voted differently from their fathers, 31 per cent voted for a party to the left, and 13 per cent for a party to the right. These surveys elicited voting histories. But according to the 1983 national panel which focussed on switching between 1979 and 1983, the trend to the left seems to have declined: 56 per cent of those who claimed that they had switched parties (excluding those who had switched to or from abstention) said that they had chosen a party more to the left.

Summarising this subsection, we note that gross volatility has probably averaged around 30 per cent of the electorate in postwar elections. Moreover, we have been unable to discern any definite trend to growth. Switchers are disproportionately young people with higher educational qualifications and white-collar occupations. They are more likely to switch between parties in the same political bloc than between parties of different blocs.

Furthermore, there is evidence of the need to differentiate types of switchers: the one-time switcher would seem to be more important numerically and can set a trend, but the ´permanent switcher´ may be more important to a specific election result if only because he moves furthest and so can upset a previous balance between blocs. Finally, if abstention has hitherto contributed little to volatility, the same is not true of the physical renewal of the electorate: it contributed to the leftward trend of successive Italian elections, and was decisive in the change in the balance of forces in the mid-1970s.

EXPLANATIONS

Stability was the key, as we noted at the outset, to the old orthodoxy on Italian voting. Vote-switching was considered minimal and, in any event, unlikely to be sufficient to change the balance of forces between the major Italian parties in the foreseeable future. This view was developed most forcibly by the authors of the Catteneo Institute of Bologna´s major electoral study of the 1960s. The English report (Galli and Prandi, 1970 pp.301, 304) concluded that:

> Catholic and socialist traditions have exerted more influence in determining the attitudes of people than have income levels, party platforms or the party´s ability to protect or further social or economic interests ... Through tradition and organisation these two leading parties have played a decisive role in the electoral unification of the country... this is proof of the superior strength of historical cultural forces over socio-economic changes in determining voting behaviour.

Such a view saw Italian elections not so much as the point at which the parties submitted their programmes to the judgement of the people but rather as a ´rite´ that reconsecrated the party leaders´ own legitimacy (whether to govern or to oppose), the moment when the parties counted their supporters.

The great Communist advance of the mid-1970s undermined the old orthodoxy: either the electorate had become suddenly mobile or an exceptional and unexpected change had occurred. Either way some explanation was required for the sudden break in

electoral stability. It was to meet this challenge
that Parisi and Pasquino (1977) proposed a new model
of voting behaviour which focussed on the
relationship of the voter and his vote, rather than
its immediate partisan orientation, i.e. on the
´why´ and not the ´for whom´. They outlined three
types of vote: 1) the ´opinion vote´, based on a
calculated choice between party programmes and
policies; 2) the ´identity vote´ founded on an
emotional attachment to a party or movement
representing a way of life; 3) the ´exchange vote´,
which was part of a personal service rendered or to
be rendered (cf. the famous <u>clientelismo</u>). The
three types of vote imply different political
strategies and hence tend to relate to different
social groups, depend on different communication
channels and organisational structures and provoke
different consequences in terms of electoral
stability and volatility. If the types are
eminently plausible in theoretical terms, they raise
serious problems of operationalisation for the
authors´ specific hypotheses. These were that the
Italian electorate was experiencing a reduction in
the ´identity vote´, which had tended to be the most
stable, and a corresponding growth in the ´opinion
vote´, which tended to be the most volatile because
of its dependence on immediate political
circumstances. The evidence which they adduce for
this development is again very plausible (the crisis
of the Catholic subculture, mass agrarian exodus,
development of mass media, mass education, etc.),
but external to the vote. The inability to
operationalise the types in such a manner that
changes in voting behaviour can be recognised
empirically, has so far made their hypotheses
unverifiable. Superficially, it might be supposed
that an increase in the ´opinion vote´ translates
itself <u>ipso facto</u> into an increase in volatility,
but they warn against such a naive assumption
because the former does not necessarily mean a
change in the political direction of the vote.
Moreover, the ´exchange vote´ also tends to be
unstable, so how are we to distinguish between the
two in any increase in volatility? Nothing can be
inferred from the electoral figures, although much
might be from the external political situation, but
this is an open question. Finally, they argue
against (and the evidence at present available
seems, as we have seen, to support their contention)
any sudden or substantial growth in electoral
volatility in the postwar period. However, in spite

of their critique of the old orthodoxy, their hypotheses share many common elements: the central role, for example, of the major subcultures as elements of continuity (the bases of the ´identity vote´), the importance of sociological as opposed to political developments in the changes that have taken place, etc.

If Parisi and Pasquino´s typology does not advance, for the present, specific explanation of Italian voting behaviour, it at least has the merit of drawing attention to the plurality, and the complexity, of electoral motives and of voting behaviour patterns. In this context, it is significant that the two major studies of partisan preference both underestimate the plurality of determining factors. Thus, Barnes (1977), on the basis of a Tree Analysis of a 1968 national survey argues that several network ties furnish the basis of partisan preference. He identified three groups. The largest consisted of active middle-class and peasant Catholics; he claimed that it is politically important that it did not decompose into sub-groups with much explanatory power because it was a religious bloc that seemingly rejected the appeal of the left. It became still larger when active Catholic working-class women were included: active Catholic women were strongly anti-left in their preferences, regardless of class. This bloc, which comprised some 42 per cent of party identifiers, gave its vote overwhelmingly to the centre and right. The second group was the leftist bloc which comprised the CGIL-affiliated respondents and accounted for about a quarter of identifiers. Finally, since neither bloc constituted a majority of the population, Barnes identified a third of the population that was not caught up closely in either of the previously identified networks and claimed that this group held the balance in the system. It was amongst this third group that substantial differences in voting patterns, between North and South, between classes, etc., emerged. He concluded his analysis with the contention that religion and social class, which are the two major determinants of political choice in Italy, are not merely psychological objects or sociological categories. ´They involve social networks of organisational ties and face-to-face contacts, as well as conceptual points of orientation´ (p.49). Hence, the determinants of partisanship are largely reinforcing and few people are genuinely cross-pressured. In conclusion, he added a warning: ´Social networks do not explain everything. Not everybody belongs and those who do are integrated in various degrees´ (p.50). Italian reality is too complex to be grasped with a simple formulation; networks are merely points of departure for further analysis.

Sani (1977a), using path analysis techniques on the same data as Barnes, also found that a complex model was required to explain a reasonable proportion of partisan preferences. He tested three complementary models which emphasized: 1) social status, 2) political traditions and 3) organisation networks. No model explained more than ten per cent of the variance by itself. However, he found that if he combined them the proportion of variance explained rose significantly. Thus, if the social status model (even with subjective class identification as an added variable) explained just over five per cent, this rose to eleven per cent adding the major political traditions, and to almost 32 per cent when organisational factors (family affiliation to CGIL and churchgoing) were added. Finally, a general model resulting from the integration of these models, and incorporating an ideological dimension (i.e. the self-location of respondents on the left-right continuum) explained some 57 per cent of the variance. As Sani has observed, what is interesting in the model is the causal paths that link the ten variables used. For example, the influence of the two organisational networks is not fully absorbed by the ideological dimension: CGIL and churchgoing exert a direct influence on partisan preference as well as an indirect one via the ideological dimension. Again, both social status and political traditions exert some, if very modest direct influence. Finally, the ideological position of the individual is not fully explained by the variables that precede it in the general model which means that other, as yet unidentified, factors also contribute to an individual´s ideological positions and through them to partisan preference. Given the complexity of the model, it is not surprising that in subsequent studies Sani (1975a) opted for a simplified version using three composite variables. It explained, on the basis of 1972 data, about a quarter of the variance, two-thirds of which was due to the organisational networks and two per cent and 2.5 per cent respectively to social status and political traditions.

Sociological Factors

Italy experienced a major socio-economic transformation after the war. In 1945 it was a largely agricultural country, but in less than a generation it became an advanced industrial society. Although this development was territorially very uneven, it meant the virtual demise of the peasantry as a major social class and with it a very traditional way of life. The agrarian sector accounted for 42 per cent of the active population in 1951 but only 15 per cent in 1979, while the industrial sector grew to 44 per cent in 1970 and then declined to 38 per cent in 1979. But it was above all the services and tertiary sector, typical of advanced industrial societies, that made the big leap, from 27 per cent to 47 per cent. The virtual disappearance of the peasantry meant a big decline in the self-employed, from 47 per cent to 29 per cent in under twenty years (1956-74). The two socio-professional categories to grow were the white and blue collar workers, the former by 15 per cent and the latter by nearly ten per cent between the 1951 and 1981 censuses (see Sylos-Labini, 1974). These massive social changes were accompanied by a process of secularisation, i.e. a decline in the influence of organised religion, and specifically that of the Catholic Church. This was most visible in the fall in regular churchgoing from over 60 per cent in the mid-1950s to around 30 per cent 20 years later (see Acquaviva, 1971; Parisi, 1978); and a more rapid decline in the Catholic lay organisations, which lost two-thirds of their membership in the 1960s.

The consequences of these changes for partisan preference are shown in Table 11.6. It lists dichotomous party preferences for five key sociological and religious variables for 1958-61 and 1972-6. Three correspond to Rokkan's three major cleavages that succeed pure territoral conflicts: religion (churchgoing), the commodity market (urban/rural) and the labour market (class), while the other two are sex and age. The indices are interesting in confirming, on the one hand, the continuing influence of Rokkan's cleavages, and above all of the religious cleavage, while pointing, on the other, to a significant change of influence between sex and age. The overall pattern is an attenuation of Rokkan's cleavages and sex in the postwar period. This means specifically that if left voting by the working class and even among men has declined, it is above all its expansion among the middle classes (particularly white-collar workers), women and churchgoers that has been important. Recent studies show that the sex differential in partisan voting as well as that among active Catholics has declined in the younger cohorts of voters (Sani, 1977c).

Table 11.6: Voting Indices, Italy 1958-61 and 1972-6

	Class	Church-going	Urban/rural	Age	Sex
1958-61	+20	+46	+12	+5	+22
1972-76	+14	+37	+5	+15	+9
Difference	-7	-9	-7	+10	-13

Note: Calculated according to Alford´s index of class voting and Lijphart´s index of religious voting (see Lijphart, 1971 pp.14-15). We have followed Inglehart´s advice and used the mean of several surveys in our calculation of the percentages.

However, if the socio-economic changes of the last thirty years have been important in undermining the political traditions of partisan preference (it is no coincidence that there is talk of both a Catholic and a Communist crisis in Italy), there is evidence that it did not act directly. Survey data from the mid-1960s suggest that whereas the decline in the partisan differential of churchgoers and non-churchgoers and urban and rural voters has been gradual, that between the classes and the sexes occurred in the later 1960s and early 1970s, i.e. under the impact of the student and worker struggles.(12) We can venture the hypothesis that the experience of these years and the new ideas they engendered and diffused played a significant role. Sani (1975a) reported a significant increase (over 15 per cent) in levels of political interest between 1968 and 1972.(13)

Ideological Factors
It would be surprising if ideological factors were unimportant in determining partisan preference in Italy. In the first place, a plurality of parties, each claiming to represent a distinct ideological position, is present in the Italian

Parliament. In the second place, the major cleavage is as much cultural as sociological (i.e. religion). In the third place, we should note the importance of the ideological dimension of left-right self-location in increasing the explanatory power of Sani's general path analysis model. It confirmed what Barnes had conclusively shown (Barnes, 1971; cf. Daalder, 1983), namely that the left-right continuum is a meaningful concept for a large section of the population. This being the case, we can examine patterns over time (see Table 11.7).(14) These show 1) that the ordering of subgroups of partisans has remained substantially unchanged over all surveys; 2) that there are natural quantitative breaks indicating political groups or blocs: the left (PCI/PSI) the centre (PSDI/PRI/DC/PCI) and the right (MSI-Italian Social Movement); and 3) there was a small, but perceptible, shrinkage in the mean left-right self-placement between supporters of the major parties (PCI and DC) between 1968 and 1981.

Table 11.7: Mean Self-Location of Different Groups of Italian Partisans on Left-Right Continuum, 1968-81

Partisan preference	1968	1972	1976	1981
PCI	17	20	25	23
PSI	33)	36	37	35
PSDI	)	47	48)	51
PRI	45	53	)	49
DC	56	55	59	57
PLI	72	58	65	66
MSI	80	80	83	79

Sources: Sani (1977c, p.102); Daalder (1983, p.227).

However, despite the plurality of parties with proclaimed ideological bases, the fact that one dimension, the left-right continuum, is able to place them all suggests that one ideological cleavage overrides all others and has structured them in the post-war period. It is clear from only a casual acquaintance with postwar Italian politics that this is anti-communism, not only because it has been a permanent theme of postwar elections, but also because, as Sani (1975a) has shown, it is a powerful predictor of partisan preference. He outlined four components: (i) Communism as a threat to democracy; (ii) Communism as responsible for political violence; (iii) Communism as Soviet (i.e. foreign); (iv) Communism as incompatible with Catholicism in a Catholic country, and has indicated that the components overlap only to a limited extent, thus suggesting that they represent different grounds for rejecting Communism by different groups. All evidence available (Daalder, 1983; Putnam et al., 1981) indicates that there has been an attenuation of this cleavage in all four components. We have set out in Table 11.8 evidence for the ideological component - a decline of 24 per cent in the number seeing an incompatibility between Communism and Catholicism over the twenty years from 1953 to 1974. Nonetheless, the cleavage still remains important, particularly inside the political blocs, even if it is less solid that it once was. Thus in 1974 a majority of DC supporters still believed in the impossibility of a good Catholic being a good Communist. Interestingly enough it was the sympathisers with the lay centre parties who had changed their views most radically over this question, thus supporting Sani's contention that anti-communism has multiple elements. This said, it is worth noting that in two surveys (Luzatto-

Table 11.8: Responses on the Compatibility Between Communism and Catholicism in Italy

Can a good Catholic be a good Communist?

	1953 %	1963 %	1974 %
Yes	21	28	45
No	67	56	41
DK	12	16	14
Total	100	100	100

	1974						
	PCI %	PSI %	PSDI %	PRI %	DC %	PLI %	MSI %
Yes	72	58	47	63	27	33	24
No	23	31	48	31	60	61	69
DK	5	11	5	6	13	6	7
Total	100	100	100	100	100	100	100

Source: P-P. Luzzatto-Fegis (1966, pp.1059-61, 1302-5); Bollettino DOXA, n.14, 30 July 1974, p.116.

Fegis, 1966; Marradi, 1974) (carried out in 1958 and 1972) which asked whether the clergy had the right to intervene in politics, the rise from 54 per cent to 72 per cent in the majority opposed to such intervention was largely due to a change of heart by DC sympathisers, (a rise from 37 per cent to 61 per cent). The change in attitude to domestic party politics of the Postconciliar Church was almost certainly responsible for this. Finally, it should be added that the development and activity of the Italian Feminist Movement (See Cantarow, 1976), together with the emergence of womens´ and family issues - divorce, family law reform, abortion - at the centre of the political debate (including two major Referendums in 1974 and 1981) in the last 15 years, has clearly played a major part in changing women´s traditional partisan attitudes and predisposing the younger generation more towards the left.

Government Performance

The Italian electorate´s satisfaction with government performance and the functioning of the State has traditionally been low. It is not surprising, therefore, that Italy has regularly figured in last place in the Eurobarometer survey results over the last decade: the proportion of those satisfied with the functioning of democracy has oscillated between 14 and 27 per cent (with between 1 and 3 per cent very satisfied); and the proportion dissatisfied has ranged between 72 per cent and 83 per cent.(15) Doxa surveys (16) on the functioning of the State in the 1970s tell the same story (2-5 per cent thought it functioned well; over 80 per cent badly; and 6-12 per cent neither). They further suggest a qualitative worsening of the situation at the beginning of 1970s, as figures for a 1967 survey were: 22 per cent well, 35 per cent badly, 22 per cent neither.

It is difficult to know what role, if any, the attitudes revealed in these figures played in the partisan changes in the mid-1970s. It is generally believed that assessment of government performance plays little part in voting choice: scandals and public disapproval (which surveys regularly reveal) so it is argued, have been continuous throughout the postwar period, and their effect on the operation of government and politicians slight. Certainly the partisan changes of the mid-1970s would go some way to explain the apparent contradiction in the surveys between the sweeping condemnation of the operation of the State and the democratic system and the belief of 40 per cent of respondents who regularly claim that they can bring about changes by personal political action.

The burden of the argument in this subsection is that the factors traditionally associated with electoral stability in Italy (the socio-demographic cleavages and ideological polarisation) have become attenuated, and this, in theory, predisposes the electorate to greater volatility. But it is not possible to affirm with certainty that this has happened. In the first place, it seems, as we have endeavoured to document, that volatility was always greater in the past than academic opinion was prepared hitherto to allow. In the second place, although volatility was higher in the last (and two of the last three) elections, we cannot be sure that Italy is entering a phase of greater volatility. The volatility of the 1983 elections (even taken with those of 1976) may yet be a 'flash' phenomenon. Time alone will show.

ELECTORAL VOLATILITY AND THE PARTY SYSTEM : SOME CONCLUSIONS

Italy is generally considered to be a country of intense partisanship. This assessment is, however, open to question. The evidence - Almond and Verba's (1963) data on Christian Democrats' hostility to marriage with Communists and Socialists and Sani's (1975a) survey evidence that a sizeable percentage of respondents would not vote for certain parties in any circumstances - is not altogether convincing. For example, there is the awkward fact that vote-switching between parties in opposed ideological blocs was greater during the Cold War, when there was Papal excommunication of Catholics voting for the left, than in the 1970s when ideological promiscuity was greater. Unfortunately, data on the intensity of partisan attachment in Italy is lacking.

Despite the superficial complexity of Italian party politics, the electoral history of post-war Italy has been relatively straightforward. It was marked almost at the outset by an orienting election, that of 1948 in the midst of the Cold War, which substantially aligned the majority of the electorate to the right of centre. Over the next two decades, moderate net volatility was accompanied

by a small, but regular leftward drift. In this
perspective the 1976 election can be seen as a
realigning election that failed. For while it is
true that the extension of the electorate to include
18-21 year old voters increased the left´s advance,
it is also true that Italy´s PR electoral system
frustrated the formation of any effective
alternative government. The ´historic compromise´
which some saw as a form of ´consociational
government´ (Graziano, 1979) to manage the new
situation created by the election, was rapidly and
effectively undermined by a combination of foreign
pressure (from the USA, IMF and EEC), political
terrorism and internal manoeuvres. Since then,
Italy has known five years of increasingly aimless
government. Political disenchantment and frustra-
tion have begun to gather, as can be seen in the
growth of abstention and spoilt ballots, as well as
increasing fragmentation of the vote at the expense
of the two major parties in the last two elections.

Major electoral changes are more often the
response of the electorate to changes in the
political system than vice-versa. The
deteriorioration of the Italian political system and
above all its incapacity to deal successfully with
the worsening economic crisis has led to proposals
for constitutional changes. Athough their content
is not yet clear, it seems certain to include a
change in the electoral law (the adoption of a
system with a five per cent threshold similar to
West Germany seems the favourite), and should this
happen it is evident that this will have a major
effect on the party system and partisan
representation, and indeed more political
significance than the almost forty years of
electoral fluctuations that preceded it.

FOOTNOTES

1. For details of historical background and
further references see Allum (1973) and Rusconi and
Scamuzzi (1981).
2. Represented in the 1983 Parliament by the
Sudtirloer Volkspartei, Union Valdotaine, Partito
Sardo d´Azione and Liga Veneta.
3. For details of the Italian electoral system
see Seton-Watson (1983) and Lanchester (1981). The
voters not only choose a list but also have the
opportunity of indicating (either by name or list
number) their preference for a number of candidates

(the number being determined by constituency size: maximum four). The successful candidates in each list are those who receive the highest number of preference votes in proportion to the number of seats allocated to the list in each constituency. This means that there are two contests going on at each election: 1) for the party list, and 2) for the preference vote. The importance of the latter is that it can reverse the tendency of the list system to give preference to the party programme over the personality of the candidates.

4. Following Pedersen we excluded 1946-48 from our calculations of the mean and standard deviation of volatility scores. Moreover, our calculations include two further elections (1979 and 1983) as well as a different mode of calculating gains and losses which explain why our indices differ slightly from his.

5. Naturally this also depends on the change in the number of parties taking part in the elections and their splits. As Novelli has shown (1980, p.243), by aggregating the parties in four blocs (left, centre, right and others) the volatility index declines regularly, except for the 1976 election (in which the 18-21 years olds voted for the first time).

6. In a recent survey (1980) carried out in Milan, 22.2% of the respondents declared that they had voted differently for the Chamber and the Senate. See Comune di Milano, Instituto Superiore di Sociologia (1982).

7. Furthermore, the proportion of vote-switchers is also underestimated among respondents because they tend to rationalise their earlier votes: see Himmelweit et al. (1978).

8. For technical details of this model see Goodman (1959). For specific techniques applied in the model of Italian data see Barbagli (1979) and Micheli (1976).

9. Vote switching averaged a little over 30% in the United Kingdom for the five elections from 1959-74. For single elections it was 25% in Sweden (1960); 26% in Holland (1970); 27% in Norway (1965); and 34% in West Germany (1969). See I. Budge and D. Farlie (1977) quoted in Barbagli et al. (1979, p.118).

10. A point of view expressed as long ago as 1967 by Pulzer (1967, p.40).

11. The legal penalty for non-voting is to have one´s name posted outside the Town Hall in his commune of residence and to have one´s ´certificate

of good conduct' stamped, but these provisions have never been applied. (See Seton-Watson, 1983, p.111). Hence the obligation to vote would appear to be largely moral; and the fact that abstention is now a politically sanctioned form of behaviour can be deduced from the fact that the Radical Party openly campaigned for it in the June 1983 general election.

12. Our calculations of CISER surveys of 1964 and 1986, and Demoskopea survey of 1970.

13. This higher level of participation seems to have continued; see the figures for the 1970s in Inglehart (1981).

14. This continuum was constructed by asking sympathisers of the various parties to place themselves on a scale 1 to 100, Left to Right.

15. Eurobarometer, no. 17, March/June 1982, pp.10, 21A.

16. Bollettino DOXA, 5-6, March 1981, p. 42.

REFERENCES.

Acquaviva, S.S. (1971) L'eclisse del Sacro Nella Civilta Industriale, 3rd ed., Comunita, Milan
Allum, P.A. (1973) Italy: Republic Without Government?, Weidenfeld & Nicolson, London
----------(1983) 'Clericali o Conservatori? I Valori Politici dei Democristiani Vicentini Agli Inizi Degli Anni Ottanta', Schema, 11-12 :39-54
Almond, G.A.and S. Verba, (1963) The Civic Culture, Princeton University Press, Princeton
Amyot, G.G. (1980) 'Voto giovanile e voto differenziato nelle ultime elezioni italiane: uno confutazione di alcuni tesi', Rivista Italiana di Scienza Politica, 3:471-83
Barbagli, M., P. Corbetta, A. Parisi and H. Schadee (1979) Fluidita Elettorale e Classi Sociali in Italia, Il Mulino, Bologna
Barnes, S.H. (1971) 'Left, Right and the Italian Voter', Comparative Political Studies, 4, 2 :157-76
---------- (1977) Representation in Italy, Chicago University Press, Chicago
Benewick, R. et al. (1969) 'The Floating Voter and the Liberal View of Representation', Political Studies, XVII:179-95
Budge, I. and D. Farlie (1977) Voting and Party Competition, Wiley, London
Cantarow, E. (1976) 'Abortion and Feminism in Italy: Women Against Church and State', Radical America 10, 6:8-27

Comune di Milano Instituto Superiore di Sociologia (1982) I Bilanci Sociali de Area, mimeo, Milan

Corbetta, P.G. (1982) 'La Mobilata Settorale a Bologna nel Dopoguerra e Sue Caratteristiche Individuali', in F. Anderlini et al. Comportamento Elettorale: Citta e Territorio, CLEUB, Bologna

Corbetta, P. and M. Schadee (1982) 'Le Caratteristiche Sociali e Politiche dell 'Astensionismo Elettorale in Italia', Il Politico, anno XLVII, 4:661-86

Corbetta, P.G. and A. Parisi (1983) Struttura e Tipologia delle Elezioni in Italia: 1946-1983, Fondazione Feltrinelli, Milan, mimeo

Daalder,I.H. (1983) 'The Italian Party System in Transition: The End of Polarised Pluralism', West European Politics, 6, 3:216-36

Dobson, D. and D. St. Angelo (1975) 'Party Identification and the Floating Voter: Some Dynamics', American Political Science Review, LXlX: 481-90

Duverger, M. (1954) Political Parties, Methuen, London. (Originally Les Partis Politiques, A. Colin, Paris, 1951)

Fabris, G-P. (1977) Il Comportamento Politico degli Italiani, F.Angeli, Milan

Galli, G. (1966) Il Bipartitismo Imperfetto, Il Mulino, Bologna

Galli, G, and A. Prandi (1970) Patterns of Political Participation in Italy, Yale University Press, New Haven

Goodman, L.A. (1959) 'Some Alternatives to Ecological Correlation', American Journal of Sociology, LXIV,6 : 610-15.

Graziano, L. (1979) 'Compromesso Storico e Democrazia Consociativa: Verso una "Nuova Democrazia"' in L Graziano and S. Tarrow (eds.), La Crisi Italiani, Vol. 2, Einaudi, Turin

Himmelweit, H. et al. (1978) 'Memory for Past Vote: Implications of a Study of Bias in Recall', British Journal of Political Science, 8: 365-76

Inchiesta Universita di Torino/CNR (1980) 'I Cettadini e l'Amministrazione Locale guigno 1980, Citta Campione, Vicenza'

Inglehart, M.L. (1981) 'Political Interest and West European Women', Comparative Political Studies, 14, 3: 299-326

Lanchester, F. (1981) Sistemi Elettorali e Forme di Governo, Il Mulino, Bologna

Lijphart, A. (1971) Class Voting and Religious Voting in European Democracies, University of Strathclyde, Occasional Paper No.8, Glasgow

Luzatto-Fegis, P-P. (1966) Il Volto Sconosciuto dell'Italia 1956-1965, Guiffre Editore, Milan

----------(1983) in Bollettino DOXA, 9 June, 1983

Makno (1983) Sondaggio, September, mimeo

Marradi, A. (1974) 'Analisi del Referendum sul Divorzio' Rivista Italiana di Scienza Politica, Anno 4, 3

Martinotti, G. (1978) 'Le Tendenze dell 'Elettorato' in A. Martinelli and G.F. Pasquino (eds.), La Politica nell 'Italia Che Cambia, Feltrinelli, Milan

Micheli, G.A. (1976) 'Il Comportamento Individuelle nell 'analisi Sociologica del Dato Aggregato', Giornale degli Economisti, XXXV, 7-8: 429-48

Novelli, S. (1980) 'Elezioni stabilita e sistema politico in Italia', Studi di Sociologia, 3: 233-56

Parisi, A. (1978) 'Tra Ripresa Ecclesiastica vs Eclissi della Secolarizziane', Citta e Regione, Anno 4: 39-42

---------(1979) in Barbagli, et al., Fluidita Elettorale e Classi Sociali in Italia, Il Mulino, Bologna

-------- (1980) 'Mobilita non significa movimento' in A. Parisi (ed.), Mobilita Senza Movimento, le Elezioni del 3 guigno, 1979, Il Mulino, Bologna

Parisi, A and G.F. Pasquino (1977) 'Relazioni partiti-elettori e tipi di voto', in A. Parisi and G.F. Pasquino (eds.), Continuita e Mutamento Elettorale in Italia, Il Mulino, Bologna

Pedersen, M. (1979) 'The Dynamics of European Party Systems: Changing Patterns of Electoral Volatility', European Journal of Political Research, 7, 1: 1-27

Pulzer, P. (1967) Political Representation and Elections in Britain, Allen & Unwin, London

Putnam, R., R. Leonardi, and R.Y. Nanetti (1981) 'Polarization and Depolarization in Italian Politics', paper delivered to American Political Science Association, New York, September, 1981

Rusconi, G.E. and S. Scamuzzi (1981) 'Italy Today: An Eccentric Society?', Current Sociology/La Sociologie Contemporaire, 29, 1: 1-204

Sani, G. (1975a) ´Mass-Level Response to Party Strategy´ in D.L.M. Blockmer and S.G. Tarrow (eds.), Communism in Italy and France, Princeton University Press, Princeton

--------(1975b) ´Ricambia Elettorale e Identificazioni Politiche: Verso un ´Egemonia dell Sinistre´, Rivista Italiana di Scienza Politica, Anno V, 3: 515-44

--------(1977a) ´Fattori Determinanti delle Preferenze Politiche in Italia´, Rivista Italiana di Scienza Politica, Anno 3, 1: 129-43

--------(1977b) ´Le Elezioni degli anni Settanta: Terremato e Evoluzione?, in A Parisi and G.F. Pasquino (eds.) Continuita e Mutamento Elettorale in Italia, Il Mulino, Bologna

--------(1977c) ´The Italian Electorate in the Mid 1970s; Beyond Tradition?´, in H.R. Penniman (ed.), Italy at the Polls: the Parliamentary Elections of 1976, American Enterprise Institute, Washington D.C., pp.81-122

--------(1980) ´Political Culture in Italy; Continuity and Change´ in G.A. Almond and S. Verba (eds.), The Civic Culture Revisited, Little, Brown, Boston

Seton-Watson, C. (1983) ´Italy´ in V. Bogdanor and D. Butler (eds.), Democracy and Elections, Cambridge University Press, Cambridge

Sivini, G. (1966) ´I Mutamenti di Voto e l´interesse Politico´, Quaderni di Sociologia, 15, 3-4: 310-32

Sylos-Labini, P. (1974) Saggio Sulle Classi Sociali, Laterza, Bari

Chapter 12

BELGIUM

Anthony Mughan

INTRODUCTION

The rise of several new, mainly regional-linguistic, parties and the formal division of established parties along linguistic lines has transformed the traditional Belgian party system and made it immensely more complex in the course of the last two decades. Given this, it seems best to adopt a chronological approach in describing how the party system has evolved to reach its present form.

For almost seventy years after independence in 1830, national political life was dominated by the profound conflict between the clerical Catholic and anti-clerical Liberal parties. During this period, these two parties monopolised the government of the country and ´...the differences between them revolved almost entirely around the role of the Catholic Church in the state. The two parties were otherwise agreed on all questions concerning the social and economic order of the country. For both, the state must ´laisser faire et laisser passer´ (Delsinne, 1955, p.17). By the turn of the century, however, rapid and intensive industrialisation had helped to undermine the Catholic and Liberal political power monopoly as well as the unanimity of the Catholic Party´s commitment to unbridled economic liberalism, the catalyst for both developments being the emergence of a ´constitutional´ socialist movement whose immediate and overriding goal was the attainment of universal suffrage. Although qualified by plural voting, this goal was achieved, at least for men, in 1893 and, contesting its first election the following year, the Belgian Workers´ Party (Parti Ouvrier Belge-POB) won 28 of the 152 seats in the Chamber of Deputies; the Liberals won only 20.

The POB´s success served to reinforce many

319

Catholics in their conviction that their party's social and economic principles had to be moderated if more Catholic workers were not to be lost to the secular and anti-clerical socialist movement. This line of argument crystallised in the 1890s with the emergence of a minority christian democratic wing within the Catholic Party. The 1894 election also served to raise in Catholic and Liberal eyes the spectre of an impending socialist parliamentary majority and thereby brought these two parties round to the POB's long-advocated view that the extant majoritarian electoral system should be replaced by one based on proportional representation (PR). The precise form of PR eventually adopted in 1899 was the d'Hondt system and its implementation did much to eliminate the discrepancy between popular votes and parliamentary seats that had benefitted the Catholic Party more than the Liberal Party whose vote was relatively widely dispersed. The accompanying electoral law also stipulated that voting should be compulsory and that the ratio of representatives to residents should not exceed one to 40,000, which meant over the long term that more seats had to be created as the male population grew in size. With the enfranchisement of women in 1948, however, the number of seats was fixed permanently at 212 in 1949 and these are now redistributed within three years of each decennial census to take account of population movement and demographic change (Gilissen, 1958; Hill, 1974, pp.52-9).

The electoral system itself, in contrast, has remained unchanged to this day. The same cannot be said for the party system, however. From the outset, all three traditional parties comprised elements from each of the country's linguistic communities, Dutch-speakers in Flanders and French-speakers in both Wallonia and Brussels. Equally, all three of them actively sought to channel and stifle the nascent conflict between these communities in the interests of party and national unity. Nonetheless, Flemish discontent escalated in the inter-war years with the result that Flemish nationalists emerged on the electoral scene for the first time and gradually increased their share of the popular vote until it reached just over eight per cent in 1939. Their rise was then halted, at least in the short term, by the Second World War and German occupation (Hojer, 1946).

The party system that emerged after the war bore little resemblance to its predecessor. In an

effort to remedy the party fragmentation and
parliamentary ´immobilisme´ of the inter-war period,
the two largest of the traditional parties sought to
moderate their ideological stance and broaden their
electoral appeal. The Catholic Party transformed
itself into the deconfessionalised and christian
democratic Social Christian Party (Parti Social
Chretien-PSC) and the POB became the more social
democratic and less stridently anti-clerical Belgian
Socialist Party (Parti Socialiste Belge-PSB). The
Liberal Party followed suit only in 1961 when it
dropped its anti-clericalism to become the Party of
Liberty and Progress (Parti de la Liberte et du
Progres-PLP). But these changes notwithstanding,
all three parties remained unequivocally unitarist
in terms both of their own internal structure and
their preference for the structure of the Belgian
state (see, for example, Mughan, 1982). The only
other significant electoral force in the late 1940s
was the Communist Party (Parti Communiste de
Belgique - Kommunistische Partij van Belgie or
PCB-KPB) which enjoyed unprecedented success at the
polls and was also unequivocally unitarist.

Thus, the predominant view in the immediate
post-war period was that Flemish nationalism was not
only an illegitimate . phenomenon, but also a
transitory one since it was largely a function of
the very difficult economic circumstances of the
1930s. In the event, however, this diagnosis of the
´problem´ soon proved to have been misguided. Table
12.1 documents the extent of this self-deception.
The Flemish movement re-emerged in the early 1950s
and its parliamentary arm, the Volksunie (VU)
rapidly increased its share of the vote over the
course of the 1960s to reach a peak of just more
than eleven per cent in 1971. The integrity of the
unitary state was placed under still greater strain
when French-speakers´ distaste for Flemish
nationalism was itself translated into the creation
of two new parties of regional defence, the Walloon
Rally (Rassemblement Wallon-RW) and the
Brussels-based Democratic Francophone Front (Front
Democratique des Francophones-FDF). Also advocating
federalism, these two parties contested their first
election in 1965 as separate parties, but as an
alliance thereafter; their joint vote also peaked
at a little over eleven per cent in 1971.

Nor did the fragmentation of the Belgian party
system cease with the emergence and growth of these
new regional parties. Instead, as well as
encouraging the emergence of new parties, the ever-

Table 12.1: Results of Elections for the Belgian Chamber of Deputies, 1949-81

	1949 %	1950 %	1954 %	1958 %	1961 %	1965 %
CVP-PSC	43.6	47.7	41.1	46.7	41.5	34.5
PS-VS	29.8	35.5	38.7	37.1	36.7	28.3
PVV-PLP	15.3	12.0	12.9	11.8	12.3	21.6
PCB-KPS	7.5	4.7	3.6	1.9	3.1	4.6
VU	2.1	--	2.2	2.0	3.5	6.7
RW	--	--	--	--	--	1.0
FDF	--	--	--	--	--	1.3
Others	1.7	0.1	1.5	0.5	2.9	2.0

Table 12.1:(contd.)

	1968 %	1971 %	1974 %	1977 %	1978 %	1981 %
CVP	22.3	21.9	23.3	26.2	26.0	19.7
PSC	9.4	8.2	9.1	9.8	10.1	6.7
PS-VS	28.0	27.2	26.6	26.9	--	--
VS	--	--	--	--	12.4	12.6
PS					13.0	12.6
PVV-PLP	20.9	--	--	--	--	--
PVV	--	9.5	10.4	8.5	10.3	13.1
PLP	--	5.6	4.8	5.9	5.3	8.2*
PL	--	1.6	1.2	1.1	0.7	--
PCB-KPS	3.3	3.1	3.2	2.7	3.3	2.3
VU	9.8	11.1	10.2	10.0	7.0	9.9
RW	3.4	6.7	5.9	3.0	2.9	1.9
FDF	2.5	4.5	3.8	4.3	4.3	2.4
VIBI	--	--	--	--	1.4	1.1
UDRT-RAD					0.9	2.7
Agalev-Ecolo	--	--	--	--	0.1	4.4
Others	0.4	0.6	1.5	1.6	2.3	2.4

Note: * This is the percentage for the PRL, which is an alliance of the Brussels and Walloon Liberal parties that was formed in 1979.
Sources: Dewachter and Clijsters (1982, pp.194-95); Mackie and Rose (1982 p.333).

increasing tension between the language communities worked to sever the unity of the three traditional parties. The first of them to succumb to this tension was the PSC, which, in explicit recognition of its linguistic duality, changed its title to

Christelijke Volkspartij-Parti Social Chretien (CVP-PSC) immediately prior to the 1968 election. Furthermore, its two linguistic wings presented their own lists of candidates in that election and the party then adopted a confederal structure in 1969. Since then its wings have operated as separate and autonomous parties. The PLP and PSB took a little longer to follow this same pattern. While signs of it were apparent in the late 1960s, the formal linguistic division of these parties did not take place until the 1970s. Of the two, it was the PLP that was first to succumb when, in 1972, it became the Partij voor Vrijheid en Vooruitgang - Parti de la Liberte et du Progres (PVV-PLP). Then only a year later, the PLP´s Brussels´ wing (PL) split from its Walloon counterpart and their alliance was reconstituted only in 1979 when the French-speaking party was renamed the Parti Reformateur Liberal (PRL). The PSB´s division was relatively straightforward; it became the Parti Socialiste - Vlaamse Socialisten (PS-VS) just before the 1978 election and has remained so since then.

Linguistic tensions may have brought formal division in their wake, but they failed to alter the fundamental ideological stance of the CVP-PSC, PS-VS or PVV-PRL. To be sure, their respective linguistic wings now tailor their electoral appeals and governmental actions to their regional clienteles, yet their traditional ideological goals continue to dominate in both these areas. Indeed, it is perhaps this continuity coupled with a preoccupation with the relatively new and intractable ´community problem´ that allowed two more new parties to arise outside this three-dimensional cleavage structure and gain parliamentary representation in one or both of the 1978 and 1981 elections. The first is the single-issue, anti-tax Democratic Union for the Respect of Labour (Union Democratique pour le Respect du Travail - Respect voor Arbeid en Demokratie - UDRT-RAD) which won a little less than one per cent of the vote and one seat in 1978 and almost three per cent of the vote and four seats in 1981. Support for the second party, the Ecologists (Agaleve-Ecolo), grew even more rapidly. From virtually no votes and no seats in its first election in 1978, it won 4.5 per cent of the vote and four seats in 1981. The only other party to win parliamentary representation during this period of fragmentation was the ultra-radical offshoot of the Flemish nationalist VU, the Vlaamsche Blok (VlBl), which first appeared in 1978 and won more than 1.5

per cent of the vote and one seat, with a similar performance in 1981.(1)

In more general terms, however, the most noteworthy feature of Table 12.1 is its failure to point to a secular trend in volatility over the period of this analysis. Rather, the party system appears to have gone through two distinct phases in the post-war era. The first phase, which lasted until 1965, is characterised by the electoral dominance of the traditional parties and the CVP-PSC and PS-VS in particular. Then, in a second phase brought on by the politicisation of the language cleavage, this dominance was eroded and the linguistic parties established themselves as institutional features of the party landscape. Stated differently, the party system lurched from one status quo to another between, roughly speaking, the 1950s and the 1970s.

At the governmental level, by contrast, there is no similar transition, at least with regard to the party composition of governments. Their aggregate electoral decline notwithstanding, the CVP-PSC, PS-VS and PVV-PRL have continued to dominate this aspect of political life. There have been twelve parliamentary elections since 1949 and, including the CVP-PSC-PVV-PRL coalition that was formed after the 1981 election, 25 governments have held office. Either as unified parties or, more recently as coalitions of autonomous linguistic wings, the traditional parties have dominated every one of these governments. The CVP-PSC has participated in all but one of them and headed 23; the PS-VS has been in 13 and provided two Prime Ministers; the PVV-PRL has had eleven stints in office but no Premiers. Further highlighting their domination is the fact that no other party came to form even part of a governing coalition until late 1974 when the RW joined the incumbent government and remained in it for only four months. The VU and FDF also subsequently enjoyed a period in office as part of the two coalitions that governed Belgium between June 1977 and January 1980. The VU resigned after the first ten months of this period though the FDF remained in office for all of it. No other party has served in office since 1949 (see Dewachter and Clijsters, 1982).

TRENDS IN ELECTORAL VOLATILITY

As explained in the introductory chapter,

electoral volatility can be conceptualised in either
net or gross terms. Briefly, net volatility is an
aggregate-level phenomenon and gross volatility is
an individual-level one. But before either can be
examined in the specific context of Belgium two
methodological issues need to be referred to. The
first concerns the boundaries of the time period to
be covered, especially in the more extensive net
volatility analysis, and the second the
identification of the individual parties around
which the analysis revolves.

The time period issue is easily dealt with.
Pedersen (1979, p.5) begins his comparative net
volatility analysis with 1948 for the good reason of
´the highly irregular character of the elections
immediately after the Second World War´.
Accentuating the appropriateness of this same year
as a starting point for this single-country analysis
is the added reason that Belgian women were
enfranchised in 1948 so that to include the 1946
election would risk distorting the overall
volatility picture by investing it with a
potentially abnormal baseline.

The party identity issue is more difficult if
only because it involves two decisions. The first
concerns the criterion of selection into the party
population and in particular it raises the question
of how the proliferation of minor parties is to be
handled. Since there is a number of such parties in
Belgium, it was decided not to treat them all as
separate entities in the volatility calculations.
Instead, only those having won parliamentary
representation at some point between 1949 and 1981
are treated as separate parties; all have been
mentioned in the introduction. Parties winning
votes but not seats are aggregated into a single
´other´ category. The second decision is not so
easily resolved since it involves the question of
whether the linguistic wings of the traditional
parties are to be treated as separate entities after
their formal break-up or whether they are to
continue to be aggregated into a single party.
There is no easy answer to this question, but two
considerations lead this analysis to treat them as
single parties throughout the 1949-81 period.
Firstly, this ensures continuity and hence the
direct comparability of the volatility measure over
time. Secondly, net electoral volatility is a
measure of aggregate change in party support, and
since the linguistic wings of each traditional party
do not compete directly against each other for votes

to treat them as separate entities would bias any
measure of volatility.(2)

With this methodological backround and using
the Pedersen index, Table 12.2 presents the net
volatility scores for each pair of elections and for
different combinations of time periods. The index
values presented are calculated from the figures in
Table 12.1, the only qualification being that,
although presented separately, the vote shares of
the linguistic wing of each traditional party as
well as those of the RW and FDF are aggregated
before computing the index.

Table 12.2: Net Volatility in Belgian Elections,
1949-1981

Elections	Index	Elections	Index
1949-50	9.8	1968-71	6.8
1950-54	7.7	1971-74	3.3
1954-58	5.6	1974-77	4.0
1958-61	5.6	1977-78	4.6
1961-65	15.2	1978-81	12.5
1965-68	6.7		
Means			
1949-61	7.2	1949-61	7.2
1961-81	7.6	1961-71	9.6
		1971-81	6.1

Taking elections in pairs, Table 12.2 shows
that with a mean of 7.4 volatility has been fairly
uniform except for three peaks in the 1950, 1965 and
1981 elections. On inspecting the preceding Table
12.1, however, an interesting and important
difference between the first of these peaks and the
last two comes to light. Essentially the 1950
figure appears to be largely the outcome of vote
switching between the extant parties while the 1965
and 1981 peaks are more clearly associated with
either the appearance of new parties or the rapid
growth of parties that had emerged on to the
electoral scene in the previous election (1961 and
1978 respectively). This difference will be
accounted for presently, but its current importance
is twofold. On the one hand, it alerts us to the
need to take account of the politicisation of the
linguistic cleavage in the mid-1960s in our overview
of the volatility of Belgium's electorate, and on

the other it raises the question of whether the 1965 and 1981 elections are as similar in their long-term implications for the shape of the country's party system as they are in net volatility scores. This question will be addressed in the next section of this chapter.

For the moment, however, my concern is to present a general volatility picture that takes into account the emergence and polarisation of the conflict between the Dutch- and French-speaking communities, a conflict that has fundamentally transformed the character of political life in Belgium. It might seem best to take this into account by simply dividing the whole period into two, the first running from 1949 to 1961 and covering the situation without polarised linguistic parties contesting elections and the second, spanning 1961 to 1981, covering the era in which the 'community problem' dominates the political agenda. Making this division produces unexpected results. Given that the latter period saw the emergence of several new parties and substantial and sustained vote losses for the CVP-PSC and PS-VS, we might reasonably have expected it to be characterised by higher rates of volatility. In fact, however, there is little difference between the two periods; their mean volatility scores are 7.2 and 7.6 respectively (Table 12.2).

But this similarity is easily explained. Belgium's experience of linguistic conflict should itself be subdivided into two stages, the first of which involves the escalation of the conflict and the second its institutionalisation. Escalation proceeded unchecked throughout the latter half of the 1960s and the period is characterised by a failure on the part of the leaders of the traditional parties to respond effectively so as to pre-empt the appeal of the linguistic parties whose vote share was growing at their expense. The institutionalisation period stretches from 1971 to 1981 and in it the traditional parties enacted a series of institutional and constitutional reforms, most notably the 'federalisation' of the hitherto highly centralised and unitary state, in an effort to undercut support for the linguistic parties and return to the political status quo ante (Mughan, 1983). The recalculation of the volatility scores attests to the appropriateness of this threefold division insofar as the 1960s can be seen to be a period of substantially increased volatility, whereas the 1970s are even less volatile on average than the 1950s (see Table 12.2).

EXPLANATIONS

Yet, while interesting in itself, to note this changing pattern of net volatility is to explain it only in the limited sense of inferring that elite actions influence individual voting patterns. It tells us nothing, however, about the precise mix of, and reasons for, the individual decisions and behaviours that combine to produce the overall net volatility picture. It is entirely possible, for example, that lower net volatility may be associated with higher gross volatility. Individual changes may simply come closer to cancelling each other out in the aggregate despite their being more extensive in terms of the proportion of the electorate involved. An analysis of the pattern of gross volatility is a necessary prerequisite, therefore, of a real understanding of changes in the balance of support in the larger party system. But there are problems in doing such an analysis in the specific context of Belgium.

The most serious and severe of these problems is a shortage of relevant data. Put simply, sample survey research, of the academic or commercial variety, has only recently taken root in Belgium. No reliable survey data are available for the time period from 1949 to 1961. The situation is a little better for 1961-71 since a number of sociologists did carry out an academic survey of the electorate in 1968 (Delruelle et al., 1970). Unfortunately, however, the data from this survey are not available for secondary analysis so that only its reported findings can be used here. The 1971-81 period is the best endowed of all with survey data since a cross-sectional survey was conducted in 1975 and an ongoing panel study undertaken in 1978. Nonetheless the only data that I have at my disposal for secondary analysis are from the 1975 survey, although the directors of the panel study have kindly made available to me a number of cross-tabulations. (3)

The second and related problem concerns the content of the various surveys and it is that they display a marked lack of continuity in their respective constituent questions. The 1968 survey, for example, was carried out by sociologists and thus shows a different emphasis from the other two, which are more social psychological in their orientation. Indeed, only the former's investigation of the relationship between respondents' social characteristics and voting choice is comparable with the findings of the later surveys. Similarly, the 1975 survey is the only one of the three to contain information on party identification. In short, the three surveys together offer at best limited opportunities for longitudinal comparison, particularly in the areas of partisanship and issue voting.

With these provisos in mind, we turn to the interpretation of the net volatility scores presented in Table 12.2. Whilst a total absence of individual level data means that the 1950 volatility peak cannot be explained definitively, it does seem entirely likely that it represents the electoral culmination of a very contentious and emotional issue that had dominated Belgian politics for several years, namely the question of Leopold III's return to the throne

When the Germans occupied Belgium at the outbreak of World War II, Leopold decided not to accompany his government into exile. With liberation, he was not invited to return to the throne since the government now deemed his war-time actions to have rendered him 'unfit to rule'. Leopold was supported by Social Christians and opposed by Liberals and Socialists, and neither side abandoned its intransigence so that a referendum was eventually called in 1950 to decide the issue. A 57.5 per cent majority voted for Leopold's return, but the Liberal party then withdrew from the governing coalition in the apparent hope that an anti-Leopold government would be returned in the ensuing election. This action only inflamed the situation and the conflict became even more polarised with the result that the only single-party (CVP-PSC) government since the advent of universal male suffrage in 1919 was returned. Amid disorder and street violence, however, Leopold eventually abdicated in favour of his son (Arango, 1961).

The 'Royal Question', then, appears to have been the cause of a substantial increase in electoral volatility but it represented no more than a passing interruption to the normal pattern of party politics. The main argument of this chapter, however, is that this same conclusion does not apply to the next upsurge in volatility in 1965. Instead, the 1965 election is properly regarded as a watershed election in Belgian politics since it

marks the long-term redefinition of the parameters
of the traditional party system. Moreover, the
level of volatility may have been of similar
magnitude in the 1981 election, but, as in 1950, it
was volatility of a qualitatively different kind in
that it represents the effects of short-term forces
rather than long-term ones. In other words, the
volatility of 1981 is more akin to that of 1950 than
that of 1965 in that it represents change within,
rather than of, the parameters of the prevailing
party system.

The most suitable starting point for this
argument is the developments preceding the
politicisation of the language cleavage. In a
nutshell, the evidence that we have suggests that
the far-reaching changes of the mid- to late-1960s
were facilitated by a combination of political
developments and social and economic change that
served to weaken the traditionally close
relationship between the dominant CVP-PSC and PS-VS
and their religion- and class-based support groups.
It is generally accepted, for example, that the
1958 all-party agreement (Pacte Scolaire) on the
long-standing and very divisive question of state
subsidies to Catholic schools helped substantially
to take the religious issue out of politics and that
this particlarly hurt the CVP-PSC because it
allowed many Catholic Flemings to vote in accordance
with their linguistic rather than their religious
sentiments. There is also evidence of the growing
secularisation of the Belgian population prior to
the mid-1960s, which could only undermine further
the electoral importance of the religious cleavage
(see CRISP, 1974). Indeed, this trend is perhaps
best illustrated by the decision of the Liberal
party in 1965 to disavow its traditional
anti-clericalism which it perceived to be
electorally counter-productive. Finally, the rapid
economic decline, in both absolute and relative
terms, of the PS-VS´s regional stronghold, Wallonia,
helped to undermine that party´s standing in the
region. Indeed, it was from within the socialist
movement that the more radical and regionally
conscious Walloon nationalist movement emerged in
the early 1960s (Fitzmaurice, 1983, ch.3).

Against this background of the gradual erosion
of the social underpinning of the traditional party
system, linguistic polarisation reached new heights
in 1968 and precipitated the fall of the incumbent
government. Table 12.3 indicates that the
consequent election was characterised by a very high

level of gross volatility and that a feature of this
volatility is a clear and coherent pattern
indicating the emergence of a permanent clientele
for the parvenu linguistic parties.(4) In the first
place, the latters´ 1965 voters were far more
faithful in 1968 than the voters for the traditional
parties. Furthermore, instead of being random with
regard to the destination of their changed votes,
the infidelity of both traditional and ´other´ party
voters was cumulatively and disproportionately
beneficial to the linguistic parties. Of course,
the Liberals also substantially improved their vote
share in the 1965 and 1968 elections, but the table
clearly shows that this improvement was largely the
result of defections that probably accrued to them
because they were the only traditional party to take
an unequivocally unitarist stance in this period.
The essential fragility of Liberal support is
further suggested by its being the least successful
of all the named parties in retaining its previous
voters.

In sum, then, the linguistic parties were able
both to retain their previous support and to attract
voters away from other parties. When taken in
conjunction with the fact that the defining social
characteristic of 1968 linguistic party voters is
their youth, these achievements inevitably suggest
the conclusion that the 1968 election was the
culmination of a realignment of partisanship away
from the traditional parties, particularly the
CVP-PSC and PS-VS. The persistence of similar
levels of support for the linguistic parties in
later elections further suggests that this
realignment was consolidated as their supporters
aged.(5)

Since the 1975 survey investigated the
phenomenon of party identification in Belgium, it is
possible to offer evidence, albeit no more than
cross-sectional, in support of this conclusion of
realignment and its consolidation. To argue for
consolidation is minimally to argue that linguistic
and traditional party identifiers do not differ
substantially in their strength of partisanship.
If, however, such were not the case, party
identification theory would lead us to expect the
difference to manifest itself most immediately in a)
a less strongly held partisanship among linguistic
party identifiers and b) a greater tendency to
defect at the polls on their part.

With regard to the first of these potential
differences, Table 12.4 indicates that in fact there

Table 12.3: Individual Vote Switching, 1965-68 and 1978-81

	Vote in 1965						
	PSC	PSB	PLP	RW-FDF	VU	OTHERS	NV
Vote 1968	%	%	%	%	%	%	%
PSC	82.7	3.2	6.1	3.2	4.5	--	n/a
PSB	1.7	82.5	1.6	--	1.8	4.9	n/a
PLP	4.6	3.8	77.5	6.5	3.6	4.9	n/a
RW-FDF	1.6	6.1	9.1	87.1	--	12.2	n/a
VU	6.6	1.5	2.5	--	88.2	--	n/a
OTHERS	--	0.2	--	--	--	68.3	n/a
NV	2.8	2.6	3.2	3.2	1.8	9.8	n/a
(N)	(1159)	(868)	(561)	(31)	(110)	(41)	

Table 12.3: (contd.)

	Vote in 1978						
	PSC	PSB	PLP	RW-FDF	VU	OTHERS	NV
Vote 1981	%	%	%	%	%	%	%
PSC	58.0	5.9	9.6	5.1	10.6	5.1	12.1
PSB	5.8	73.9	5.3	13.7	4.7	25.3	19.8
PLP	14.8	8.0	72.2	19.7	8.2	7.6	24.1
RW-FDF	1.1	0.8	1.1	41.0	-	8.9	3.4
VU	9.3	2.9	3.7	-	70.6	1.3	8.6
OTHERS	8.8	5.5	6.4	17.9	5.9	45.6	18.9
NV	2.2	2.9	1.6	2.6	-	6.3	12.9
(N)	(452)	(238)	(187)	(117)	(85)	(79)	(116)

Notes: The old names of the traditional parties are used to label the tables for reasons of space and clarity of presentation. The category ´NV´ signifies ´no vote´ and comprises those respondents spoiling their ballot, casting a blank vote or not going to the polls. The 1965-68 figures are calculated from Delruelle et al. (1970) p.109 where unfortunately the 1968 vote of 1965 non-voters is not given. Percentages in the table do not always add to 100 because of rounding.

Belgium

Table 12.4: Intensity and Distribution of Identification by Party

	Party Identification					
	CVP-PSC	PS-VS	PVV-PRL	FDF	RW	VU
Intensity						
Mean Sympathy Score	77.2	79.7	76.0	79.8	78.7	80.4
Distribution						
% in first quartile	1.4	0.9	0.7	4.3	3.1	–
% in second quartile	7.9	6.9	10.3	4.3	3.1	6.4
% in third quartile	33.3	28.0	35.9	25.6	37.5	34.9
% in fourth quartile	57.4	64.2	53.1	65.8	56.3	58.7
(N)	(291)	(218)	(145)	(117)	(32)	(63)

Note: The question on party identification was, 'By means of the thermometer (0= no sympathy, 100= a lot of sympathy) that you have already used, please indicate the degree of sympathy you feel for the party that you have just mentioned (i.e. the party to which the respondent "normally feels closest")'.

is little difference in the strength of identification across the individual traditional and linguistic parties. Indeed, perhaps unexpectedly, the difference that there is favours the latter group whose mean score is 79.6 as compared with 77.6 for the traditional parties. Mean scores can be misleading, however, since they tell us nothing about the distribution of partisan intensity within each group of identifiers. It could be argued, for example, that the relative newness and evangelical character of the linguistic parties leads to their identifiers falling at one or other extreme of identification, whereas the distribution among traditional identifiers is likely to be more normal in shape. But the bottom section of Table 12.4 highlights the futility of taking this line of reasoning any further. Again, the striking feature is the overall similarity of the distributions across all six parties; there may be some differences in individual quartiles, but these are marginal and just about balance out on the whole.

Much the same conclusion as to the essential

similarity of the groups of party identifiers follows from an examination of the second potential dimension of difference between them, their rate of voting defection. Table 12.5 details by party the relationship between partisanship and vote in the 1974 election, as well as for the time of the survey. In the latter case, the linguistic parties are unfortunately and inextricably grouped into a single category in the survey itself.

At first glance, the immediately striking feature of this table is the relative infidelity of RW and VU identifiers in 1974. Too much should not be read into this, however, since it is likely to be a function, in part at least, of the small number of cases especially in the RW partisan category. Certainly the strength of the identification-vote relationship among linguistic party identifiers as a whole in 1975 suggests the appropriateness of opting for the conservative conclusion that there was little difference between traditional and linguistic parties in terms of voting defections among their partisans.

Table 12.5: The Voting Fidelity of Party Identifiers

P.I.	% faithful at polls 1974 %	(N)	P.I.	% faithful in vote intention 1975 %	(N)
CVP-PSC	77.1	(236)	CVP-PSC	72.8	(213)
PS-VS	71.8	(177)	PS-VS	72.8	(145)
PVV-PRL	68.1	(113)	PVV-PRL	64.5	(53)
FDF	78.3	(92)	FDF/RW/ VU	69.5	(51)
RW	50.0	(22)			
VU	63.5	(52)			

Although not in itself conclusive, then, the available evidence strongly indicates that the 1968 election marked the consolidation of a realignment of partisan support whose principal facilitating conditions were, in the short term, the crisis atmosphere that pervaded this particular election and, in the long term, the declining salience of the two cleavages, religion and class, that underpinned the traditional party system. The subsequent government-initiated linguistic reforms, further- more, did not allow the traditional parties to regain their lost electoral ground because the

'community problem' was only one of the reasons for
their losses. Their more fundamental problem was
that not only were their 'core' support groups
becoming smaller, but also they were becoming less
loyal at the polls. Thus, for example, the
proportion of practising Catholics in the electorate
fell from 57.6 per cent in 1968 to 53.9 per cent ten
years later. Over this same period there was an
even sharper drop, from 58.7 per cent to 50.1 per
cent in the proportion of this ever smaller group
voting for the CVP-PSC.(6)

The picture that emerges, therefore, is one of
a party system whose 'mould' had been broken by
virtue of the institutionalisation of the language
cleavage. Belgians were now in a position to be
able to vote on the basis of their linguistic, as
well as religious and class priorities so that,
other things being equal, they could only be
expected to become less volatile in their voting
habits. Thus it is that the 1971-74, 1974-77 and
1977-78 pairs of elections are characterised by the
lowest levels of net volatility in the whole 1948-81
period (see Table 12.2). What is more, these low
levels of net volatility appear to have been matched
by low levels of gross volatility (compare Tables
12.3 and 12.6).

One problem with this conclusion, however,
would appear to be the level of volatility between
the 1978 and 1981 elections, which is reminiscent of
that found between 1965 and 1968 and thus might be
taken to bode another realignment. But closer
inspection indicates that there is little evidence
for such speculation. Instead, the 1978-81
volatility would seem to be better explained by a
change in the balance of cleavage salience, which
itself is probably most accurately seen as being a
function of the severe economic crisis that beset
Belgium in the late 1980s (see Macmullen, 1982;
Mughan, 1983). The initial evidence in favour of
this explanation comes once again from the behaviour
of practising Catholics. Between 1968 and 1978,
this group became less loyal to the other two
traditional parties as well as to the CVP-PSC; the
proportion voting for the PS-VS fell from 15.3 per
cent to 8.6 per cent. The importance of this is
that it indicates that while the religious cleavage
may have become less salient, its economic
counterpart at least became no more salient. If it
had, we would expect some Catholic support to have
flowed to one or other of the two traditional
parties that are most different in economic

philosophy, the collectivist PS-VS and individualist
PVV-PRL. But there was such a transfer of support
between the 1978 and 1981 elections. In 1981, the
proportion of practising Catholics who voted for the
CVP-PSC declined to 38.5 per cent, compared with
50.1 per cent in 1978, whereas the proportion voting
for the PS-VS increased marginally by 2.1 points and
the proportion voting PVV-PRL more than doubled to
reach 17.6 per cent. In short, at least among
practising Catholics, the 1981 election was marked
by the increased salience of the economic cleavage
and, more specifically, by a strong display of
preference for the PVV-PRL´s proposed solutions to
the country´s severe and worsening economic
problems.

Table 12.6: Individual Vote Switching 1977-78

	Vote 1977						
	PSC	PSB	PLP	RW-FDF	VU	OTHER	NV
Vote 1978	%	%	%	%	%	%	%
PSC	90.8	2.6	2.2	1.7	6.7	8.5	9.3
PSB	0.6	86.5	1.3	1.7	3.8	2.4	3.0
PLP	2.3	3.5	87.2	1.7	4.2	2.4	2.5
RW-FDF	0.4	2.9	2.5	87.9	--	1.2	0.5
VU	1.2	--	1.6	--	70.8	--	1.9
OTHER	2.2	1.7	1.2	4.3	13.8	81.7	5.7
NV	2.4	2.8	4.0	2.6	0.8	3.7	77.1
(N)	(1124)	(652)	(445)	(231)	(240)	(82)	(367)

Note: Percentages do not always add to 100 because
of rounding.

Moreover, an examination of the overall pattern
of vote switching between these two elections
strongly suggests that this conclusion can be
generalised to the Belgian electorate as a whole
(see Table 12.3). Of the six categories of 1978
voter, it is only in the smallest of them that the
Liberals are not the principal beneficiary of voting
changes in 1981. But too much should not be read
into this Liberal ´victory´ since, whatever the
precise reason or mix of reasons for the party´s
good fortunes in 1981, the weight of the evidence is
that, as in the 1960s, the upsurge in its vote
represents a transitory phenomenon rather than an
incipient realignment in its favour. On the one
hand, its support shows the same fragility as in the

1960s in the sense that, at least in relative terms, the upsurge in its vote continues to rest more on attracting defectors than on retaining previous support. The experience of the linguistic parties, however, indicates that realignment requires a strong performance on both these dimensions.(7) On the other hand, if it is indeed economic crisis that is responsible for the improved Liberal performance, it too is likely to be a transitory phenomenon whose passage will lead to a decline in Liberal support. And even if it is not transitory, the PVV-PRL´s policy of austerity will presumably cost it votes in future elections. Again, the linguistic parties are not as prey to such problems since their appeal rests on long-standing divisions in Belgian society that successive governments have still not managed to resolve. The odds are, therefore, that as short-term forces acting on the Belgian electorate change, the balance of cleavage salience will also alter and votes will flow from the PVV-PRL as readily as they flowed to it.

ELECTORAL VOLATILITY AND THE PARTY SYSTEM

On the basis of admittedly patchy and incomplete evidence, this chapter has tried to demonstrate that, under the impulsion of both social structural change and the politicisation of the language cleavage in the 1960s, the pattern of electoral volatility in Belgium moved from being characterised by relatively marginal variations in the fortunes of the Social Christian, Socialist and Liberal parties to the consolidation of a realignment of support away from the first two of these parties in particular. This realignment, however, has not been sufficiently pronounced to weaken the traditional parties´ long-standing hold on governmental office. But it has established a ´new´ party system in which language has joined class and religion in enjoying institutionalised expression. Developments since then have only emphasised that this party system is not a transitory phenomenon, but is here to stay.

The low levels of both gross and net volatility that followed this re-definition of the parameters of the party system might easily be interpreted as stability that derives from the crystallisation of a closer bond between various social groups and the wider range of parties to which they can now give their support. This interpretation is tenable, however, only if one ignores the fact that the institutionalisation of the linguistic cleavage was both cause and consequence of the weakening bond between social groups and political parties in Belgium. The extent of this process did not become apparent until the 1981 election because it was only then that short-term forces, in this case economic crisis, were strong enough to upset an equilibrium that was based on the primacy of linguistic conflict. What happened in 1981 was that language failed to dominate voting choice to the extent that it had done in previous elections. In the longer term, the greater salience of the economic cleavage in this election suggests that language has become a cleavage ´just like the others´ in the sense that its salience is a matter of circumstance rather than preordainment.

The essence of the change that has taken place is that, as in many other Western democracies, the Belgian electorate has become less unquestioningly tied to political parties as it has become more instrumental and short-term in its political expectations and behaviour. In the absence of sharp, short-term stimuli, like economic crisis, it will in all probability continue to display low levels of volatility because the linguistic fragmentation of the party system has meant that its long-term linguistic and class priorities in particular can now be satisfied by a single party. It would be mistaken, however, to interpret this stability as indicating voter docility or unquestioning loyalty. The parameters of the party system may well have been re-defined for the forseeable future, but the outcome of the 1981 election clearly demonstrated that the fortunes of individual parties can vary considerably within the parameters. It would appear, therefore, that the art of winning elections revolves less and less around the mobilisation of traditional group loyalties and more and more around the creation and exploitation of short-term electoral advantage, whether it be in the form of candidates, manipulation of the economy or whatever. This de-emphasis of party loyalty, in turn, can only serve to make the task of governing in a fragmented multi-party system like Belgium even more difficult than it already is.

FOOTNOTES

* The research on which this chapter is based was sponsored by the Nuffield Foundation. I would like to thank the editors of the book and Andre-Paul Frognier for their help with, and comments on, an earlier draft. The Belgian Archive for the Social Sciences kindly made the 1975 survey 'Le Citoyen Belge dans le Systeme Politique', available to me for secondary analysis.

1. Developments in the party system are analysed more fully in Fitzmaurice (1983, ch.5).
2. It is worth mentioning that treating the linguistic wings as separate parties increases the net volatility scores only a little. The overall mean, for example, increases from 7.4 to 7.6. I might add that the linguistic wings of each traditional party do each present candidates in Brussels, but these do not compete for the same votes since they are oriented towards different linguistic groups.
3. The 1975 survey was conducted by Andre-Paul Frognier who then joined forces with Nicole Delruelle-Vosswinkel to undertake the 1978 panel study. See Delruelle-Vosswinkel and Frognier (1980; 1981; 1982).
4. Table 12.3 has been constructed with a view to throwing some light on the pattern of individual vote changing in Belgium over the period for which suitable data are available. It is, however, a table that should be interpreted with a degree of circumspection since only its 1978/81 data are drawn from a panel study covering the two time points; the 1965 and 1977 votes are based on respondents' recall of their voting choice in an election held a year or more prior to the survey. The need for circumspection should not be exaggerated, however, since the argument to be developed in this chapter rests on general trends rather than on specific patterns of inter-party vote switching.
5. There was no partisanship question in the 1968 survey, but for information on the relationship between age and linguistic party voting see Delruelle et al. (1970, pp.84-86).
6. The religiosity and voting data for 1978 come from Delruelle et al. (1970, p.50). It was not possible to construct a similar longitudinal analysis for class groups since there is no subjective class identification question in the 1978 panel study and over half the respondents in this

same study did not volunteer their occupation.

7. A comprehensive comparison of the patterns of vote switching in the two pairs of elections would also examine the fortunes of the parties in the 'Other' category. But it is not possible to do this either individually or collectively because of the small number of respondents in this category; it is only 41 in the 1965-68 pair, for example. The upshot is that it is impossible even to conjecture with any confidence on the future of the new parties of 1978 and 1981, the UDRT-RAD and Agalev-Ecolo. What is noticeable from Table 12.3, however, is that the 'Other' parties collectively retained less than 50 per cent of their 1978 voters in 1981, which suggests that their electoral future is not as secure as the linguistic parties' turned out to be after the 1968 election.

REFERENCES

Arango, E.R. (1961) Leopold III and the Belgian Royal Question, John Hopkins University Press, Baltimore

CRISP (1974) 'L'Evolution du "Monde Catholique" Depuis 1968: Le Devenir de la Pratique Religieuse', Courrier Hebdomadaire du CRISP no. 664 (5 decembre)

Delruelle, N., R. Evalenko, and Fraeys (1970) Le Comportement Politique des Electeurs Belges, Editions de Sociologie, Bruxelles

Delruelle-Vosswinkel, N. and A. Frognier (1980) 'L'Opinion Publique et les Problemes Communautaires (I)', Courrier Hebdomadaire du CRISP no. 880 (9 mai)

---------- (1981) 'L'Opinion Publique et les Problemes Communautaires (II)', Courrier Hebdomadaire du CRISP nos. 927-28 (3 juillet)

---------- (1982) 'L'Opinion Publique et les Problemes Cummunautaires (III)', Courrier Hebdomaire du CRISP no 966 (11 juin)

Delsinne, L. (1955) Le Parti Ouvrier Belge des Origines a 1894, Renaissance du Livre,Bruxelles

Dewachter, W. and E. Clijsters, (1982) 'Belgium: Political Stability Despite Coalition Crises' in E. Browne, and J. Dreijmanis (eds.), Government Coalitions in Western Democracies, Longmans, London pp.187-216

Fitzmaurice, J. (1983) The Politics of Belgium: Crisis and Compromise in a Plural Society, Hurst, London

Gilissen, J. (1958) Le Regime Representatif en Belge Depuis 1790, Renaissance du Livre, Bruxelles

Hill, K. (1974) 'Belgium' in R. Rose, (ed.), Electoral Behavior: A Comparative Handbook, Free Press, New York pp.29-108

Hojer, C. (1946) Le Regime Parliamentaire Belge de 1918 a 1940, Almqvist & Wiksells Boktryckeri, Uppsala

Mackie, T. and R. Rose (1982) 'General Elections in Western Nations During 1981', European Journal of Political Research, 10, 133-40

Macmullen, A. (1982) 'The Belgian General Election of 1981: Economic Polarisation in a Multi-Party System', Parliamentary Affairs, 35, pp. 193-200

Mughan, A. (1982a) 'The Belgian General Election of 1981: The Primacy of the Economic', West European Poltics, 5, pp.298-304

---------- (1982b) 'The failure of Conservative politics in Belgium', in Z. Layton-Henry (ed.), Conservative Politics in Western Europe, Macmillan, London

---------- (1983) 'Accommodation or Defusion in the Management of Linguistic Conflict in Belgium?', Political Studies, 31, pp.434-51

Pedersen, M. (1979) 'The Dynamics of European Party Systems: Changing Patterns of Electoral Volatility', European Journal of Political Research, 7, pp.1-27

Chapter 13

THE NETHERLANDS

C. van der Eijk and B. Niemoller

INTRODUCTION

Of all direct elections which are regularly held in the Netherlands, those for the Second Chamber of Parliament are the most important. In this analysis, therefore, we will disregard elections for local, provincial or European parliaments, all of which are generally considered as politically less important.(1)

The electoral system in the Netherlands is relatively simple. All citizens of a certain age are eligible to vote. Voters do not have to register as the government maintains a universal registration system. Each voter casts one vote and, for all practical purposes the country as a whole forms one constituency. The age limit has been lowered twice since 1945. Originally electors had to be at least 23 years old but this was reduced to 21 years in 1967 and to 18 years in 1972.

From the introduction of universal suffrage in the 1917-1919 period to 1970 voting was compulsory in the Netherlands. Since 1970, however, non-voting has been a legitimate option for electors.

The ballot contains the names of candidates competing for seats, grouped into party lists. Although voters are allowed to vote for any candidate on the list, most people vote for a party rather than for a specific person; they do so by voting for the first candidate of a party list. Seats are allocated according to the principle of proportional representation, and the threshold for representation is equal to the electoral quotient (number of valid votes divided by number of seats). Until 1956 the Second Chamber consisted of 100 representatives; thereafter it was enlarged to 150, thus effectively lowering the threshold for obtaining at least one seat to 0.67 per cent of the valid vote. The order of the candidates on the party list (specified by the parties themselves) determines which persons are elected. If a large number of voters cast their vote for a specific candidate,(s)he can be elected irrespective of the rank on the list, but very few members of parliament have ever been elected by such preferential votes.

Owing to the low threshold for gaining representation there has always been a relatively large number of parties winning seats in parliament. Of all parties which at one time or other since 1945 have been represented in the Second Chamber, there are five whose origins are to be found in the social cleavages which dominated Dutch politics during the last quarter of the nineteenth century and the beginning of the twentieth: religion and class (see Daalder, 1976; Lijphart, 1974, 1975; Lipschits, 1977):

- the christian-democratic parties, KVP (Roman Catholic), CHU (Dutch Reformed) and ARP (Calvinist), which in 1977 merged into CDA, at first only on the ballot but later also with respect to their party organisations;
- the labour party, PvdA (Social Democratic);
- the liberal party, VVD, which contains strong conservative overtones making it comparable to the British Conservative party.

Owing to their size, these parties have dominated parliamentary politics and coalition formation in the entire post-war period. In addition a large number of 'minor' parties have been represented in parliament. Some of these have occupied seats since long before the war, but most of them have sprung up since the late 1950s. These minor parties are:

- a leftist-liberal party, D'66, which started in 1966 on a platform of constitutional reform but which soon afterwards discarded this ambition and developed as a left-liberal, pragmatic political party;
- various small left wing parties, communists (CPN), pacifists (PSP), radicals (PPR);
- secular right parties, the short lived shop-keepers' party (NMP), the farmers' party (BP, rather populist and at times poujadist in character, gradually becoming more extreme right wing) and the Centrumpartij (CP, which is actually not centrist at all, but extremely right-wing,

propagating thinly veiled racist policies);
- various orthodox religious parties, all right wing
in socio-economic matters: SGP, GPV, RPF (all
three calvinist), RKPN (orthodox Roman Catholic);
- a 'centre' party, DS'70, which is difficult to
characterise, as is attested to by Lijphart's
comment that '...(it) is a socialist party albeit
a rather conservative one' (Lijphart, 1974,
p.263);
- minor christian-democratic parties, the KNP (a
temporary right-wing secession from the Roman
Catholic KVP) and, since 1982, the EVP (a
left-wing split-off from the christian-democratic
CDA).

If we want to portray all these parties in one
overall picture, we can do so provisionally along a
left-right dimension. This is possible, not only
because we agree with Daudt (1982) that this
distinction is the most fundamental one in Dutch

Figure 13.1: A Classification of Dutch Parties

LEFT	1. Extreme Left	CPN PSP
	2. Left	PvdA PPR
	3. Centre Left	D'66 DS'70 EVP
	4. Christian Democratic (Centre Right)	KVP ARP CHU CDA KNP
	5. Secular Right	VVD NMP BP
	6. Orthodox Religious	SGP GPV RPF RKPN
RIGHT	7. Ultra Right	CP

politics, but also because the (socio-economic) left-right distinction coincides to a considerable extent with that between religious and secular parties (Van der Eijk and Niemoller, 1983a, pp.225-55). All left of centre parties are secular while right of centre we find religious as well as secular parties. Figure 13.1 provides a first summary of the Dutch party system. From this figure no conclusions should be drawn as to how far apart the various groups of parties are in relation to each other. The main purpose of the figure is to facilitate a first understanding of the Dutch party system, to which refinements and qualifications can be added later.(2)

Since no single party has ever even come close to a majority of seats in the Second Chamber, governments are necessarily of the coalition-type. In other words, voters elect a parliament, not a government. Negotiations between party elites determine both the party composition and the policy programme of coalitions (see De Swaan, 1973 ; Andeweg et al., 1980). The position of the christian democrats between labour (PvdA) and liberals (VVD), and the numerical importance of the five major parties (three since the christian democratic merger in 1977) explains why since 1946 all cabinet coalitions have been composed of christian democrats with labour and liberals as alternating coalition partners. Since the early 1970s various other parties have participated in coalitions as well: DS´70, PPR and D´66. Table 13.1 lists the composition of the various cabinets which have governed since 1946. This table shows that, with the exception of the 1948-51 period, labour and liberals are incompatible coalition partners. Furthermore, there is a striking contrast between the pre- and post-1959 period. In the earlier period, the labour party (PvdA) took part in government for 13 straight years. In the later period (25 years to date) labour participation in coalitions has been the exception rather than the rule. According to Daudt (1982) this is due to the greater ideological similarity between christian democrats and liberals than between the former and labour. In his view, the christian democrats will only opt to govern with labour if there is an ´urgent necessity´ to do so, either because there is no other viable majority in parliament or because it is required for the legitimisation of government policy in ´abnormal´ situations (such as the post-war period of simultaneous economic reconstruction, decolonisation and Cold War). Finally, Table 13.1 demonstrates that the set of parties relevant for coalition formation is restricted for the entire post-war period. Not surprisingly, this relates to the sizes of the parties concerned.

Table 13.1: Party Composition of Dutch Coalition Cabinets since 1946

		Parties in the Coalition					
Period	Name	PvdA	KVP	CHU	ARP	VVD	Others
1946-48	Beel I	+	*	–	–	–	–
1948-51	Drees I	*	+	+	+	+	–
1951-52	Drees II	*	+	+	–	+	–
1952-56	Drees III	*	+	+	+	+	–
1956-58	Drees IV	*	+	+	+	+	–
1958-59	Beel II	–	*	+	+	–	–
1959-63	De Quay	–	*	+	+	+	–
1963-65	Marijnen	–	*	+	+	+	–
1965-66	Cals	+	*	–	+	–	–
1966-67	Zijlstra	–	*	–	+	–	–
1967-71	DeJong	–	*	+	+	+	–
1971-72	Biesheuvel I	–	+	+	*	+	DS70
1972-73	Biesheuvel II	–	+	+	*	+	–
1973-77	Den Uyl	*	+	–	+	–	D66,PPR
			CDA				
1977-81	Van Agt I	–	*			+	–
1981-82	Van Agt II	+	*			–	D66
1982-82	Van Agt III	–	*			–	D66
1983-	Lubbers	–	*			+	–

Notes: – = not included; + = included; * = included, party of prime minister. The periods shown are from installation to installation of succeeding cabinet. These periods include the cabinet´s existence as a caretaker government after having submitted its resignation (either because of parliamentary elections or a government crisis). Cabinets have traditionally been named after the prime minister.

TRENDS IN NET VOLATILITY

The first post-war elections for the Second Chamber were held in 1946 and the most recent ones

are those of 1982. Table 13.2 summarises the shares
of the vote obtained by the parties which gained
representation at some point in this period.
Looking at the various parties a number of
observations can be made:

- the christian democratic parties, KVP, ARP and
  CHU, which commanded roughly half of the total
  valid vote from 1945 to 1963, have suffered a
  continuous loss of votes since the mid-1960s. The
  speed of this decline has levelled off since
  approximately 1972, but even the merger into a
  single party, the CDA, only temporarily arrested
  the downward slide.
- the labour party (PvdA) has experienced marked
  fluctuations in its share of the vote.
  Approximately one third of the vote seems to be a
  kind of ´natural´ ceiling for this party. The
  exceptionally favourable 1977 results have not
  been emulated since then. More than other large
  parties, the PvdA seems to be subject to large
  fluctuations which occur during the entire
  post-war period.
- the liberals (VVD) have experienced a steady
  growth in their share of the vote since 1946.
  Starting in the early 1970s this increase has
  accelerated dramatically.
- some of the new parties of the 1960s seem to have
  followed a rather short-lived ´rise, shine and
  decline´ pattern; a very promising result
  (approximately five per cent of the vote) is
  obtained but this level is not maintained for even
  two consecutive elections. This pattern seems to
  characterise the PPR, DS´70 and the BP alike. The
  NMP and RKPN have never even been shining, but
  just reached a seat because of the extremely low
  threshold. Even D´66, which has obtained more
  than four per cent of the vote in all
  parliamentary elections since 1967 and a memorable
  eleven per cent in 1981, has not yet been able to
  establish itself permanently as an influential
  tendance in Dutch politics.(3) A number of small
  parties, CPN, PSP, SGP, GPV, appear to be a
  permanent feature of the Dutch political scene.
  Notwithstanding some fluctuations in their support
  (most notably for the extreme left parties), their
  position in parliament remains (numerically) of
  only marginal significance.
- Even after the obligation to appear at the polling
  station was rescinded, turnout in national
  elections remains high. Research into non-voting

strongly suggests, however, that the effects of
turnout on parties´ strength is extremely limited
(Schmidt, 1981; 1983).

As can be ascertained from Table 13.2 no
significant changes occurred during the period
1946-63 as far as the combined share of the vote of
the five potential coalition parties are concerned
(PvdA, KVP, CHU, ARP, VVD). During the mid-1960s,
however, this stability broke down. Even earlier,
from 1959 onwards, each election brought one or more
new parties into parliament. In 1959 it was the
pacifists, in 1963 the farmers´ party and the
orthodox GPV, in 1967 D´66, in 1971 the radical
party (PPR), DS´70 and the shopkeepers´ party (NMP),
in 1972 the fundamentalist Roman Catholic RKPN, in
1981 a third orthodox calvinist party, the RPF, and
finally in 1982 the christian democratic splinter

Table 13.2: Share of Valid Votes Obtained by Parties
in Elections for Second Chamber,
Netherlands, 1945-82

	1946 %	1948 %	1952 %	1956 %	1959 %	1963 %
CPN	10.6	7.7	6.2	4.8	2.4	2.8
PSP	*	*	*	*	1.8	3.0
PvdA	28.3	25.6	29.0	32.7	30.3	28.0
PPR	*	*	*	*	*	*
D66	*	*	*	*	*	*
DS70	*	*	*	*	*	*
EVP	*	*	*	*	*	*
CDA	(51.6)	(53.4)	(48.9)	(50.0)	(49.1)	(49.2)
KVP	30.8	31.0	28.7	31.7	31.6	31.9
KNP	*	1.3	2.7	*	*	*
CHU	7.9	9.2	8.9	8.4	8.1	8.6
ARP	12.9	13.2	11.3	9.9	9.4	8.7
VVD	6.4	8.0	8.8	8.8	12.2	10.3
NMP	*	*	*	*	*	*
BP	*	*	*	*	−	2.1
SGP	2.1	2.4	2.4	2.3	2.2	2.3
GPV	*	*	−	−	−	0.8
RKPN	*	*	*	*	*	*
RPF	*	*	*	*	*	*
CP	*	*	*	*	*	*
Others	1.0	1.6	2.0	1.4	2.0	1.5
T´out	93.1	93.7	95.0	95.5	05.6	95.1

Notes: See second part of Table.

Table 13.2: (contd.)

	1967 %	1971 %	1972 %	1977 %	1981 %	1982 %
CPN	3.6	3.9	4.5	1.7	2.1	1.8
PSP	2.9	1.4	1.5	0.9	2.1	2.3
PvdA	23.5	24.7	27.4	33.8	28.3	30.4
PPR	*	1.8	4.8	1.7	2.0	1.6
D´66	4.5	6.8	4.2	5.4	11.1	4.3
DS70	*	5.3	4.1	0.7	–	–
EVP	*	*	*	*	–	0.7
CDA	(44.5)	(36.8)	(31.3)	31.9	30.8	29.3
KVP	26.5	21.9	17.7	*	*	*
KNP	*	*	*	*	*	*
CHU	8.1	6.3	4.8	*	*	*
ARP	9.9	8.6	8.8	*	*	*
VVD	10.7	10.4	14.4	17.9	17.3	23.1
NMP	*	1.5	–	–	*	*
BP	4.7	1.1	1.9	0.8	–	–
SGP	2.0	2.3	2.2	2.1	2.0	1.9
GPV	0.9	1.6	1.8	1.0	0.8	0.8
RKPN	*	*	0.9	–	–	–
RPF	*	*	*	–	1.2	1.5
CP	*	*	*	*	–	0.8
Others	1.0	1.6	2.0	1.4	2.0	1.5
T´out	94.9	79.1	83.5	88.0	87.0	80.6

Notes: *= party did not participate; - = party did not receive enough votes for a seat. The percentage for ´CDA´ from 1946 to 1972 is fictitious and given only for comparative purposes. The CDA did not exist at that time and the figure given is the sum of KVP, CHU and ARP. In 1946 the VVD was still called the Partij van de Vrijheid (PvdV - Freedom Party). ´Others´ includes all parties which did not obtain any seats.
Source: Netherlands Central Bureau of Statistics, Election Statistics.

EVP and the ultra right-wing Centrumparty (CP). This proliferation of parties in parliament has been modified to some extent by the disappearance of NMP, RKPN, BP and DS´70 and by the merger of KVP, ARP and CHU into CDA.

In addition to the eruption of new parties, the period since the mid-1960s has seen the sharp decline of the christian democrats, the ascent of the liberals and a large number of fleeting successes for ´flash´ parties. Evidently, then, at some time during the mid-1960s the party system entered a state of flux which lasted at least until 1972, after which some stabilisation seems to have taken place. The relative pace of all these fluctuations is neatly summarised in Table 13.3 by the Pedersen index (Pedersen, 1979) which measures net inter-party traffic from election to election. Although this index reflects the total of changes in party strengths (i.e. roughly the percentage of seats changing party in the Second Chamber) it cannot be interpreted as an unequivocal measure of political instability. The index does not distinguish between situations where all existing parties contribute to its value roughly equally and those where its value is largely determined by heavy gains and losses affecting only a few parties. Even more importantly, it does not distinguish situations where only certain kinds of party (e.g. leftish parties, confessional parties or coalition parties) gain votes (or lose them) at the expense of the others, and situations where gains or losses cut through such categorisations. The former case would generally be considered a much more dramatic case of instability than the second. Consequently the value of the index by itself is not very informative about changes in power relations in parliament in a multi-party system such as the Netherlands.

Table 13.3: Pedersen Index of Volatility, Netherlands

1946-48	5.6	1967-71	13.4
1948-52	6.0	1971-72	12.2
1952-56	6.7	1972-77	12.7
1956-59	5.8	1977-81	9.1
1959-63	5.4	1981-82	9.9
1963-67	10.8		

Source: As for Table 13.2.

EXPLANATIONS OF VOLATILITY: SOCIAL SEGMENTATION

One of the most popular perspectives on Dutch politics is offered by a social segmentation or ´pillarisation´ paradigm. The most eloquent description and explanation of the consequences of social segmentation in the Netherlands have been given by Lijphart (1968, 1975). Religious and, to a to a lesser extent, class cleavages in Dutch society define subcultures which structure social and political life. These pillars provide their clientele with their own news media, schools, labour unions, professional and recreational organisations, and political parties. The antagonism between the various subcultures is assumed to be strong and this, in conjunction with various forms of social control, accounts also for electors voting according to the subculture or pillar to which they belong. With respect to electoral behaviour this pillarisation perspective implies that the major relevant distinctions among voters are religious in nature and delineate four groups: Roman Catholics, Dutch Reformeds, Calvinists and non-religious voters. The first three groups are assumed to vote for the political party representing their respective pillar (KVP, CHU, and ARP) and it is only for non-religious voters that class is said to be important. The lower class is supposed to be organised in a social democratic pillar and to vote for its political party, the PvdA, and the middle class, although less firmly pillarised, is surmised to be the natural constituency of the liberals (VVD).

With respect to elections up to 1963, the social segmentation perspective appears to be reasonably adequate as a description of the party preferences and voting behaviour of the electorate. On each of the (few) occasions that surveys were held in that period it was found that in particular the Catholic, the Calvinist and the secular lower class segments voted in overwhelming majorities according to the theory and that overall at least some 65 to 70 per cent of the electorate behaved as expected.(4)

The pillarisation paradigm which sees party choice as being to a large extent ´predestined´ by the social segment to which voters belong, leads to an emphasis on social change in the explanation of variations of election results. Social change which would result in shifts in the numerical strength of the various social segments would, ceteris paribus, automatically lead to shifts in the electoral strength of political parties. In this respect three kinds of social change are of particular interest. First, changes in the relative size of the various religious denominations and of the secular segment of society. Second, changes in the society´s socio-economic and occupational structure which might possibly affect the potential basis of the labour and liberal parties. Finally, and possibly overlapping with the other two, generational change might be relevant, that is, the passing away of older generations of voters and the influx of new generations. We will investigate whether or not these kinds of social change can explain (part of) the electoral changes described in Tables 13.2 and 13.3.

Religious Change
     Both census and survey data show a noticeable increase in the proportion of secular voters since about 1960. According to the 1947 census, this group comprised 17.0 per cent of the population; in the 1960 census and the 1971 census (the most recent one in the Netherlands) 18.3 per cent and 23.6 per cent respectively were classified as secular. The various denominational groups lost, therefore, some five to six per cent in their share of the electorate between 1960 and 1971.(5) In the same period, however, the confessional parties (christian democratic plus orthodox parties) lost some eleven per cent of the national vote. The conclusion is obvious. Secularisation can at most account for only part of the electoral decline of the confessional parties. Any attempt to sketch a more complete picture of the mechanisms involved in this decline has to consider the diminished strength of pillarisation.
     In Table 13.4 we report the voting behaviour over time of religious and secular voters. For brevity we do not present the distinctions between Catholic, Dutch Reformed and Calvinist denominations (which together account for more than 95 per cent of all religious people); it should be kept in mind, however, that the pillarisation model would predict all of them to vote for religious parties. Table 13.4 demonstrates several points worth noting:

- secular voters hardly support confessional parties at all, neither in the pre-1967 period of stability nor in the post-1967 period of extensive electoral change.
- religious voters´ support for confessional parties has diminished dramatically since the early 1960s. This phenomenon can be referred to as depillarisation, i.e. the weakening of the behavioural consequences of voters´ belonging to particular segments of society. The process of depillarisation took place in the period between

1963 and 1971; from the early 1970s support for
confessional parties from religious voters did not
decrease systematically any further but varied
slightly, probably because of election-specific
factors.
- religious voters tend to turn out to vote in
higher proportions than secular voters. This
difference has slightly mitigated the confessional
parties' decline in electoral strength.

Table 13.4: Religion and Voting Behaviour in Elections for Second Chamber

	Religious Voters		
	vote for confessio- nal party %	vote for secular party %	do not vote %
1963 and earlier (estimate)	70	25	5
1967	55	38	7
1971	45	37	18
1972	42	47	10
1977	47	43	10
1981	50	44	5
1982	41	48	11
	Secular Voters		
1963 and earlier (estimate)	3	92	5
1967	4	88	8
1971	4	74	22
1972	3	84	13
1977	6	80	14
1981	5	87	9
1982	4	85	11

Source: Van der Eijk and Niemoller (1983c).

Elsewhere it has been demonstrated that the
process of depillarisation can partly (but not
completely) be accounted for by diminishing
religious orthodoxy and declining church attendance
(Andeweg, 1982; Van der Eijk and Niemoller, 1983c).
Interesting as this may be, it does not alter the
conclusion that the principle of pillarisation,
according to which membership of a denomination
automatically entails voting for its associated
party, has weakened considerably.
    In conclusion, we can state that the losses of

the confessional parties can only partly be explained by the shrinking segment of religious voters. At least of equal importance is the process of depillarisation, which undermines not only the electoral strength of confessional parties but also the relevance of a social segmentation perspective on Dutch politics.

Socio-economic change

In the period since the Second World War Dutch society has changed profoundly. The occupational structure has changed by the decline of agricultural employment and the growth of initially industrial, but subsequently tertiary employment from which, according to many theorists, a new class of white collar workers has emanated. At the same time, the average level of formal education has increased greatly, a large amount of intergenerational social mobility (predominantly upward) can be observed, and urbanisation increased progressively. Social changes such as these have frequently been hypothesised to be related to various kinds of electoral change, although little agreement exists among theorists as to what the effects of these developments would be. In the Netherlands, as in many other Western countries, socio-economic characteristics are invariably found to correlate with party choice. The idea that such variables would therefore be useful in explaining electoral change is, in view of the literature, tempting but in our opinion often also rather naive. Quite often there is a stark contrast between the speed and direction of electoral change on the one hand and of social development on the other. Most socio-economic changes are of a relatively long-term and unidirectional nature, whereas the parties assumed to be affected by them often experience large and abrupt alternating gains and losses within a time span so short that most social conditions are constant rather than variable.

Andeweg (1982) has investigated in depth whether or not the following phenomena can explain electoral change: the changing class structure, the rise of the new middle class, social mobility, increases in education, (sub)urbanisation and individual geographical mobility. He summarised his results as follows (Andeweg, 1982, pp.121-22):

the association between socio-economic background variables and voting behaviour, well established in international research, could easily be seen in our data. Electoral change, however, does not appear to be related to any of these socio-economic characteristics. Electoral change is not confined to, nor even particularly strong among, the new middle class, the socially or geographically mobile, the better educated, or the urbanized. The original associations between social position and party choice persisted, only at another level...the growth of some social classes or other socio-economic categories of voters at the expense of others, has not contributed to the changes in the election results in a significant measure.

The pillarisation paradigm which predicts the (secular) lower class to vote for labour and the (secular) higher class for the liberals appears to be unfruitful not only because it only partially fits the situation at any particular moment. More important is its inability to explain electoral change and its inability to explain the emergence of, and incorporate in the theory the position of, a large number of new parties which cannot readily be associated with any one social segment.

Generational Change

Owing to factors such as birth and death, immigration and emigration, the composition of the electorate changes continually. Such changes, consisting mainly of demographic throughput of birth cohorts or 'generations', may alter the relative strength of various segments thus leading to electoral change (ceteris paribus). Previous sections have indicated that changes in social segmentation are of only small consequence for electoral change. A second way in which the replacement of 'generations' may contribute to electoral change is that the new voters flowing into the electorate do not behave according to the pillarisation theory, while the (dwindling) group of older voters continue to do so. This would imply that electoral change can to a significant extent be ascribed to demographic metabolism. Empirical evidence, however, leads us to discard this explanation. Elsewhere we have analysed electoral changes from 1963 to 1981 in great detail and concluded that the effects of inflow and outflow of voters are greatly overshadowed by the net results of individual vote changing among those who are eligible to vote at the elections which are being compared (Van der Eijk and Niemoller, 1983a, pp.41-82). This is not to imply that generational replacement is of no importance at all; at times it does significantly reinforce or counteract the effect of individual changes in the 'durable' electorate. The political preferences of the inflow and outflow of the electorate are, however, not sufficiently different from the rest to allow attributing electoral change to replacement (see also Andeweg, 1982, pp.130-67).

Conclusions on Social Segmentation

Pillarisation appears to describe Dutch politics and the behaviour of voters adequately up to 1963 but only a small part of the changes which have occurred since then in the electoral strength of the various parties can be explained by processes compatible with the social segmentation perspective. The decline of the religious parties can partly be attributed to the shrinking size of the major denominations. A large part of the decline of these parties, and virtually all of the changing electoral fortunes of the secular parties appears, however, to be uniform across all segments of society. The result, is, of course, that pillarisation describes voters' behaviour in the 1980s much less adequately than in earlier times. To assess which perspective, if any, can be put in its place, we will first have to turn to individual vote changing.

TRENDS IN INDIVIDUAL VOLATILITY

So far we have considered only net change, i.e. the differences between various election results. Since individual changes in party choice may cancel out when aggregated, the percentage of electors who change their party choice will at least attain the value of the Pedersen index, and will usually be considerably higher. In this section we will consider individual change in electoral behaviour in an effort to interpret the electoral changes since 1967.

It is impossible to reconstruct for the entire post-war period how many of those who are eligible to vote in each of two consecutive elections change their electoral behaviour. This is partly due to the lack of survey data which are indispensable in this respect, but also to the fact that indicating vote changing is usually only possible by comparing current behaviour with respondents´ own recall of previous behaviour. Such recall data have been demonstrated to be notoriously untrustworthy and, among other things, to underestimate considerably the number of vote changers (Van der Eijk and Niemoller, 1979; 1983a, pp.107-45).

Fortunately, a few panel studies are available since the early 1970s from which the following estimates of changing and stable voters in the elections shown have been derived.(6)

- 1971-1972: 63% stable, 37% changing
- 1972-1977: 61% stable, 39% changing
- 1981-1982: 72% stable, 28% changing.

The stable voters comprise party-loyal voters and a small group of stable non-voters, the latter acounting for one to four per cent for these pairs of elections. The changing voters are also of different kinds; party switchers and changers to and from voting. In the three pairs of elections 26 per cent, 30 per cent and 19 per cent were switchers. These percentages are indeed considerably higher than the values of the Pedersen index (see Table 13.3). The amount of individual change increases even further when we compare voters´ behaviour across three different elections (1971-1972-1977): only 49 per cent are stable and 51 per cent change in one way or another. The latter figure includes only six per cent where the instability is solely due to changing to or from abstention, the remaining 45 per cent involves party switching. If we look not only at the actual voting behaviour of our panel respondents, but also at their vote intention at various other times (this panel has been interviewed six times in the course of eight years) it turns out that the group of voters who can be considered as staunch party loyalists is very small indeed - somewhere around one third of all voters.(7) The stability of voters´ behaviour thus appears to be considerably less than it appears to be when only pairs of elections are compared by means of recall data. In view of this, one can doubt whether traditionally popular research which aims to discover differences in social-structural and psychological characteristics between stable and changing voters makes much sense. To exaggerate a little, every voter is a potential vote changer. Our own research regarding individual vote changing in the parliamentary elections of 1971, 1972, 1977 and 1981 confirms these doubts: stable voters, party changers and occasional voters are hardly distinguishable with respect to many characteristics often thought to be of importance (Van der Eijk and Niemoller, 1983a, pp.147-92).(8)

EXPLANATIONS

Partisanship

When, as in our case, the most obvious social-structural and psychological characteristics appear to be unrelated to individual vote changing, and when such changes are more common than not, it is obvious that sociological approaches (of which the social segmentation perspective is a prominent one) are unrewarding in explaining voters´ behaviour over time. Alternatively, one might attempt to apply the Michigan School´s social psychological model, according to which voters support the party they identify with, unless they are temporarily distracted by powerful short-term factors embodied in (election specific) candidates and issues. In such a perspective electoral change would be the result of short-term factors and of shifts in the overall level, strength and direction of long-term partisan commitments. Such a perspective would be appealing, particularly because it has been demonstrated repeatedly that ´party identification´ is germane to party choice. Still, this approach has run into considerable difficulty in the Netherlands. Thomassen (1976) concludes from an analysis of panel data that party identification is less rather than more stable than vote preference and that there is strong evidence that such identification is not, as it was supposed to be, causally prior to the vote. Subsequent panel data have strongly confirmed that party identification is highly unstable.

Table 13.5 reports party identification in two different panel studies, and how stable this attach--ment is over time. These data show that party identification is extremely unstable, not only in a six-year, but also in a five-month interval.(9)

This instability appears to originate to a large extent from the fact that the conceptualisation of party identification and hence also the commonly used survey questions allow the respondent to identify with only one party, while many Dutch voters, when given the opportunity to do so, claim to ´identify´ with more than one party at

Table 13.5: Number of Identifiers for Various Parties and Individual Stability of Identification

	1971-72-77 panel			Identical
	1971	1972	1977	All 3 Times
No identification	108	95	69	16
PvdA	108	116	146	69
D´66	41	24	29	5
CDA	157	136	168	91
VVD	46	58	70	28
Other Parties	49	80	27	10
Total	509	509	509	219 (=43%)

Source: See second part of Table.

Table 13.5:(contd.)

	Feb.-Apr.-June 1981 panel			Identical
	Feb. 1981	Apr. 1981	June 1981	All 3 Times
No identification	523	516	418	170
PvdA	302	302	310	180
D´66	151	154	171	72
CDA	376	369	395	244
VVD	150	168	189	93
Other Parties	118	111	137	63
Total	1620	1620	1620	822 (=51%)

Source: Van der Eijk and Niemoller, 1983a, pp.330-31.

the same time (see Table 13.6).(10) Whatever else these data may indicate, it is obvious that in the Netherlands questions intended to measure party identification do not tap the kind of long-term feelings of ego involvement with a party which were conceptualised by the Michigan School. Consequently, the potential of theories which involve party identification in the explanation of electoral change appears to be very limited.

Table 13.6: Frequency of Multiple Party Identification by Strength of Identification With First Party Mentioned
(Feb. 1981)

	0 parties	1 party	2 parties	3+ parties	Total
No identi-fication	100%	–	–	–	100 (N=455)
Leaner	–	51%	43%	6%	100 (N=526)
Adherent	–	57%	32%	1%	100 (N=253)
Convinced Adherent	–	62%	31%	7%	100 (N=318)
Total	29%	39%	26%	5%	100 (N=1552)

Source: Van der Eijk and Niemoller (1983a) p.337.

A spatial perspective

So far we have dealt with a social segmentation perspective to account for (net) electoral change, and with common sociological and social-psychological approaches to explain individual vote changing. None of these turned out to be particularly apposite for the Dutch situation. All these approaches have in common that they leave out politics: political parties are regarded as just being different from one another without any attention to what these differences are. The implication of this is that no distinction is being made between, on the one hand, vote changing between relatively similar parties such as, for instance, the PvdA (labour) and the PPR (radical) and, on the other hand, changing between very dissimilar parties such as the CPN (communists) and the VVD (liberals). To arrive at statements about the (dis)similarity of parties with respect to each other a model of the party system is required. Such a model should preferably a) incorporate voters´ perceptions of political parties, as it has to be utilised in the analysis of electoral change, b) allow in a simple way for the derivation of testable propositions regarding voters´ behaviour, c) be compatible with the results of related previous research, d) allow the possibility of empirical repudiation of its central tenets, and finally e) link up with models and theories of other political phenomena, such as coalition formation, parliamentary decision making, party competition and the generation and development of political issues. Elsewhere we have argued extensively that the most promising model in this respect consists of a one-dimensional ideological space which can be described by the polar constructs left and right (Van der Eijk and Niemoller, 1983a, pp. 193-225). It can be demonstrated that such a space can be validly operationalised by means of ordinary left-right rating scales (Van der Eijk and Niemoller 1983, pp.229-47; 1983d, pp.9-11, 16-21).

The concept of an ideological space, in which political parties as well as voters can be located, offers analytical and descriptive possibilities which lead to a new perspective on electoral change. Before outlining this perspective, we will first analyse the relevance of this space for electoral behaviour. If left-right ideology were of importance to voters, their behaviour should conform to the smallest distance hypothesis, which maintains that the majority of voters will vote for the party which they perceive as being closest to them in this space.(11) Table 13.7 reports an empirical test of this hypothesis for the 1981 and 1982 elections.

The data in Table 13.7 show that some 60 per cent of the voters behave according to the smallest distance hyothesis. In each year, 16 per cent voted at least two positions more distant than the party closest to them; their behaviour is not in accordance with the hypothesis. The results are indeterminate for some 24 per cent of the voters who deviated only one position from the smallest distance hypothesis. This deviation may conceivably result from a theoretically permissible reason or from measurement inaccuracies caused by the coarseness of the ten point scale. However the heavy preponderance of confirmatory (60 per cent) as opposed to disconfirmatory cases (17 per cent) attests to the relevance of the left-right dimension in modelling voting behaviour.

More research will be needed to establish in which proportions the deviations from voting according to smallest distance can be attributed to rational ideological voting not resulting in smallest distance, to voting on the basis of political ends which are not adequately represented or summarised in one's ideological (left-right) stance, to voting on the basis of non-political

Table 13.7: Test of the Smallest Distance Hypothesis
for the 1981 and 1982 Elections

% voting for party x position(s) more distant	1981	1982
	%	%
0 (closest party)	61.0	59.1
1 more	23.0	24.9
2 more	9.9	9.4
3 more	3.6	2.9
4 more	1.2	2.0
5 more	0.9	0.9
6 more	0.3	0.4
7 more	0.1	0.3
8 more	–	–
9 more	–	0.1
Total	100	100
(N)	(1020)	(997)

Note: Cases are included only where party choice is
known and the party voted for is included in the
list of parties to be rated on the left-right scale.
Positions relate to a 10-point scale.
Source: Dutch Parliamentary Election Panel Study,
1981-82.

ends (such as, for instance, religion), or to
capricious voting not motivated by any particular
ends at all. At present we can only check whether
or not various subgroups in the electorate differ
from each other in the preponderance of smallest
distance voting. To the extent that such groups
would share choice-directing ends which are not
incorporated in the left-right continuum, we expect
them to fall significantly below the overall level
of Downsian voting. We performed such analyses for
the following variables: electoral cohort (a rough
indicator for age and life cycle), education, social
class, sex, and religion. In none of these cases
were any significant differences found. It is
particularly relevant to note that religious and
secular voters do not differ from each other. The
implication of this is that to the extent that
religious voters would be motivated to express their
confession in the vote, this does not run counter to
their ideological stance.

Ideological Competition and Electoral Change

The behaviour-directing effect of left-right ideology, as demonstrated in the preceding paragraph by means of the test of the smallest distance hypothesis, allows a party competition perspective on electoral change. Such a viewpoint has been proposed by Downs (1957), albeit in a purely theoretical way. In our case, we can support its plausibility by various kinds of empirical data but since systematic empirical research is very recent, it is not yet possible to test all implications of a party competition model nor to employ it in the analysis of electoral change over any extended period of time. This perspective includes the following notions.

Elections are viewed in more or less the same way as economic markets. Parties act as suppliers, voters as consumers of political goods, i.e. policies. Parties compete for power, i.e votes, voters support the party which will provide them the policies they desire. Parties as well as voters are supposed to behave rationally in the economic sense of the word. In order to do so, parties must have an idea of what voters want and voters must have a perception of what parties offer. For various reasons, most notably uncertainty and information cost, these mutual perceptions cannot be cast in terms of all potential issues one can think of, but have to be expressed in terms of overarching and summarising ideologies. Rationality of parties´ and voters´ behaviour depends upon the predictability of each other´s ideological preferences and platforms, hence both kinds of actors should display a reasonable measure of (at least medium-term) stability in their ideological positions. This condition is well fulfilled in the Netherlands. The positions of political parties on the ideological left-right continuum are reasonably stable, as is displayed by Figure 13.2 which shows the averages of the perceptions of the larger parties, plus a few of the smaller ones since 1968.(12) Voters also appear to be quite stable in their own ideological positions; in the 1981-1982 panel study voters have at four different times been requested to locate themselves on a left-right scale. These panel data fit models of extremely high latent stability, as we have demonstrated elsewhere by means of LISREL (Van der Eijk and Niemoller, 1983, pp.20-1).

Electoral change is effected in this perspective as a consequence of various possible circumstances:

Figure 13.2: Positions of Dutch Parties on a Left-
Right Continuum, 1968-82

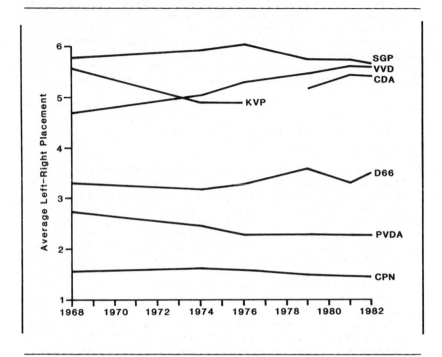

1. Parties' positions on the left-right continuum
   change somewhat as a result of their own
   behaviour in parliament, coalition politics,
   policy proposals, etc. Many of the changes in
   Figure 13.2 fit extremely well the verbal
   accounts of recent political history as provided
   by political commentators as well as parties'
   parliamentary voting records. For electoral
   change it is of no consequence whether or not
   such changes have been the effect of
   market-orientated rationality on behalf of the
   parties, or whether or not such strategic
   attempts to obtain a 'better' position succeed
   owing to variations in skill and resources. The
   important point is that when parties' positions
   change, the effect in terms of votes may be
   considerable when voters act according to
   smallest distance. This is especially the case
   in a multi-party system where large groups of

voters are located approximately halfway between parties, and even more when in some cases parties are exceedingly close together on the left-right dimension. The empirical corrollary of this mechanism is embodied in the distance reduction hypothesis, which maintains that party switching by voters will tend to reduce their distance with respect to the perceived position of the parties they consecutively vote for. Although relevant data are still scarce, our analyses so far indicate that considerably more often than not party switching does indeed effect such a reduction (see Van der Eijk and Niemoller, 1983a, pp.283-94; 1983d, pp. 25-6).

2. Voters´ positions may change, especially over longer periods of time, as a result of learning from experience, changes in personal conditions, changes of opinion due to political argument and debate, etc. Changes of voters´ positions may result in their switching parties in order to remain voting according to smallest distance (as in the distance reduction hypothesis mentioned above). With respect to election results, changes in the ideological distribution of the electorate are of particular importance as they affect each party´s ´share of the market´. Changes in distribution may be the result of individual change, as well as of the differential effects of inflow and outflow of the electorate. Little research has yet been done in this area.

3. Electoral change may be the effect of factors other than parties´ and voters´ ideological positions. First of all, secondary motivations for party choice do exist and have to exert their influence when a voter has to choose one party from several which are perceived as equally proximal. Such other motivational factors may explain party switching which conforms to the limitations of ideology without being directed by it (owing to local independence). Second, competing motivations for party choice may exist in the form of factors which are not incorporated in ideological perceptions or self-definitions. In this respect one can think of short-term factors such as issues and candidates in the Michigan-model, or even long-term factors other than ideology which may determine party choice for (obviously limited) groups of voters.

It is obvious that an ideological-competition approach to explaining electoral change fits the Dutch situation in the 1980s imperfectly. Not all voters elect the party most proximal to them, and not all party switching serves as distance reduction. For a small segment of the electorate ideology will probably play no role at all as they are unable to locate themselves and even a limited number of parties in left-right terms. On the other hand, the available data clearly suggest that ideological perceptions are not figments of a theorist's imagination but important cognitive instruments with a strong behaviour- directing effect.

ELECTORAL VOLATILITY AND THE PARTY SYSTEM

This chapter is not the most appropriate place to draw a fully fledged comparison of the explan--atory power of the social segmentation and ideo--logical competition perspectives on electoral changes. In the 1980s both would yield useful but imperfect predictions and how well they would perform would to some extent depend on ad hoc decisions with respect to the operationalisation and handling of missing data. For a number of reasons, we consider at present the ideological competition model to be the most fruitful, even if its explanatory power would be only marginally better than that of the social segmentation perspective:

- virtually none of the political parties which have emerged since the 1960s fit easily into a pillarisation perspective as they cannot be identified, or even linked with any particular subculture in society. Furthermore, the earlier existing separate subcultures have to a large extent disintegrated and lost many of their own subcultural organisations.
- as the analyses discussed in the preceding paragraphs demonstrate, the fit of the social segmentation model is only static. At any one time a (larger or smaller) group of voters behaves as predicted. The fit in a dynamic sense is very poor, however: relevant social changes appear to a large extent unrelated to electoral change. The ideological competition perspective appeared to be much more promising in this respect.
- only the ideological competition perspective allows for an intelligible interpretation of the

otherwise puzzling evidence with respect to 'party identification' in the Netherlands. Voters appear to identify with ideologies, not with parties per se. In a system with ten to 15 parties, some of these will be very similar in ideological position, allowing voters to claim to 'identify' with each of them. Multiple identifications indeed occur predominantly between parties which are very close in ideological position (Van der Eijk and Niemoller, 1983a, pp.324-47).

- the ideological competition perspective allows empirical research on elections to interlock with research on related political phenomena, while the social segmentation perspective does not. Coalition formation cannot easily be explained from pillarisation (Daudt, 1982, pp.8-9), but fits very well in a left-right perspective (de Swaan, 1973). The same can be said about roll-call behaviour in the Second Chamber (Wolters, 1984), and issue formation.

To the extent that the social segmentation perspective is appropriate for the period up to the early 1960s, its declining relevance since 1967 and the emergence of ideological voting testify to the political emancipation of individual citizens who can now choose, rather than be predestined by social position. Elections have evolved from social-accounting systems which register the size of social segments, to mechanisms for aggregating individual choice into social choice. Simultaneously, political parties have changed from noncompetitive to competitive.

What does all this mean for the future? First of all, the emancipation of the individual voter makes a return to the highly stable 1940s and 1950s extremely unlikely. Electoral change is here to stay. Second, in view of the apparent stability of ideological self-definitions of voters it is not very likely that the distribution of parliamentary power over the ideological continuum will change drastically from one election to the next. This does not, of course, preclude considerable changes in the fortunes of the various separate parties. Third, as entry-costs are low, a steady flow of new parties can be expected, occasionally acquiring one or even a few seats. Their success may very well depend upon their skill and ability to attract voters on grounds other than ideology. The odds of permanently succeeding in this way appear small, however, in view of the stake which most of the already existing parties have in the existing definition of what the principal political controversies are and in view of the ability of the left-right dimension to structure and incorporate newly emerging issues. Finally, with respect to the major parties as of today, important changes in their respective strengths may occur as their ideological ordering changes. The steady move rightwards of the CDA bodes ill for them (see Figure 13.2). Not only can this party expect further secularisation to diminish its share of the vote but they also deprive themselves of a competitive position on the ideological spectrum by moving closely to the (secular) VVD (liberals). In addition, they risk being passed on the left by the VVD (which in its turn hardly has to modify its position to accomplish this), which would not only leave the CDA without their former electoral strength, but, even worse, would make them lose their pivotal position in coalition formation. Were that to happen, the dynamics of ideological competition would undoubtedly give rise to another period of heightened electoral change.

FOOTNOTES.

    1. The First Chamber of Parliament is elected by the provincial councils but its political prerogatives are very restricted and it is clearly of secondary importance in the Dutch bicameral system.
    2. For most parties it can be said that they have occupied roughly the same position during the entire period since 1945. For some, however, this is not the case. See later sections of the chapter for the most recent position of these parties.
    3. The stability which is suggested by D'66's shares of the vote in Table 13.2 is to some extent misleading. Provincial and local elections as well as numerous opinion polls show that this party is subject to extreme fluctuations in its support which have threatened its very survival several times.
    4. The success rate of the theory depends slightly upon certain specifications that have to be made, i.e. how to distinguish between secular and religious voters, between lower class and middle class, and how to count cases such as Calvinist voters not voting for the ARP but for orthodox Calvinist parties. The figure of 65 to 70 per cent is derived from our own recalculations of 1956 data

presented by Lijphart (1974).

5. Census figures do not relate to the elect-orate, but to the entire population. Andeweg (1982, p.47) investigated this problem in detail and claims that the census figures are a useful, albeit slightly deflated indication of the electorate as well.

6. These percentages refer to the ´durable electorate´, i.e. those who are eligible to vote in all elections being compared.

7. Due to the general phenomenon that non-voting is under-reported in surveys, it is not possible to assess the size of the groups of permanent non-voters and irregular voters directly. A combination of panel data and analyses of non-voting (Schmidt, 1981, 1983) leads to an impression that roughly 80 to 85 per cent of the electorate can be considered regular voters who (due to forces beyond their control) occasionally fail to turn out. Some 10-15 per cent of voters may be considered to be irregular voters, and some 5 per cent as persistent abstainers.

8. Similar results have been reported by Daudt (1961) for American and British data, and by Kaase (1967) for Germany.

9. The instability of responses on ´identification´ questions occurs at all levels of intensity and can only to a small degree be accounted for by switches to and from the category of ´no identification´.

10. Similar distributions as displayed in Table 13.6 have been observed regularly since 1979, when questions probing for multiple identification were first introduced. For a detailed account of question wording and various kinds of results see Van der Eijk and Niemoller, 1983a, pp. 307-47.

11. This hypothesis is an offshoot from Downs´ (1957) theory on party competition and voter behaviour. The theory allows for voters to deviate from voting according to smallest distance. A review of Downs´ theory, various criticisms levelled against it and its usage in the study of electoral change has been presented by us elsewhere (Van der Eijk and Niemoller, 1983a, pp.196-215, 276-94). All data reported in the text are derived from our more detailed publications (1983a, 1983d).

12. More detailed data with respect to all parties can be found in Van der Eijk and Niemoller (1983d, p.17). We also present data there demonstrating that the stability in average ratings is not solely an aggregation artefact, but that most

individuals´ perceptions of parties are quite stable as well.

REFERENCES.

Andeweg R.B., Th. van der Tak and K. Dittrich (1980) ´Government Formation in the Netherlands´, in R.T. Griffiths (ed.), The Economy and Politics of the Netherlands since 1945, Nijhoff, The Hague, pp.223-49

Andeweg R.B. (1982) Dutch Voters Adrift. On Explanations of Electoral Change - 1963-1977, dissertation, University of Leiden, Leiden

Budge I., I. Crewe and D. Farlie (eds.) (1976) Party Identification and Beyond. Representations of Voting and Party Competition, Wiley, London

Daalder H. (1966) ´The Netherlands: Opposition in a Segmented Society´ in R. Dahl (ed.), Political Oppositions in Western Democracies, Yale University Press, New Haven, pp.188-236

Daudt H. (1961) Floating Voters and the Floating Vote, Stenfert Kroese, Leiden

Downs A. (1957) An Economic Theory of Democracy, Harper & Row, New York

Eggen A.Th.J., C. Van der Eijk and B. Niemoller (eds.) (1981) Kiezen in Nederland, Actaboek, Zoetermeer

Eijk C. Van der, and B. Niemoller (1979) ´Recall accuracy and its determinants´, Acta Politica, 14, 289-342.

---------- (1983a) Electoral Change in the Netherlands. Empirical results and methods of measurement, CT-Press, Amsterdam

---------- (1983b) (eds.) In het spoor van de kiezer. Aspekten van 10 jaar kiezersgedrag, Boom Meppel, Amsterdam

---------- (1983c) ´Stemmen op godsdienstige partijen sinds 1967´, Acta Politica, 18, 169-82

---------- (1983d) ´Ideology, party identification and rational voting in the Netherlands´, Paper presented at Annual Meeting of APSA, Chicago

Eijk C. van der, B. Niemoller and A.Th.J. Eggen (1981) Dutch parliamentary election study 1981 (codebook), Department of Political Science, Amsterdam

Kaase M. (1967) Wechsel von Parteipraeferenzen. Eine Analyse am Beispiel der Bundestagswahl 1961, Anton Hain, Meisenheim am Glan

Lijphart   A .   (1968) Verzuiling,   pacificatie   en
    kentering in de Nederlandse politiek, De Bussy,
    Amsterdam
---------- (1974) 'The Netherlands: Continuity and
    Change in Voting Behaviour' in R. Rose (ed.),
    Electoral Behaviour. A Comparative Handbook,
    Free Press, New York, pp. 227-68
---------- (1975) The Politics of Accommodation -
    Pluralism and Democracy in the Netherlands, 2nd
    edition, University of California Press,
    Berkeley, California
Lipschits   I.   (1977) Politieke   stromingen   in
    Nederland. Inleiding tot de geschiedenis van de
    Nederlandse   politieke   partijen,   Kluwer,
    Deventer
Pedersen M.N. (1979) 'The Dynamics of European Party
    Systems: Changing Patterns of Electoral
    Volatility', European Journal of Political
    Research, 7, 1-26
Schmidt O. (1981) 'Opkomst' in Eggen, Van der Eijk
    and Niemoller (eds.), pp. 42-61
---------- (1983) 'Kiezersopkomst van 1971 tot 1982'
    Acta Politica, 18, 139-55
Swaan A. de (1973) Coalition Theories and Cabinet
    Formations, Elsevier, Amsterdam
Thomassen J.J.A. (1976) 'Party Identification as a
    Cross-National Concept: Its Meaning in the
    Netherlands' in Budge, Crewe and Farlie (eds.),
    pp. 63-79
Wolters M. (1984) Interspace politics, dissertation,
    University of Leiden, Leiden

Chapter 14

DENMARK

Ole Borre

INTRODUCTION

The Danish party system unfolded towards the end of the 19th century as a rough reflection of the class system of its time.(1) It contained a Conservative party for the urban middle class, a Liberal party for the farmers, and a Social Democratic party for the workers. A fourth party, the Radical Liberal, was located between the Liberal and the Social Democratic parties, and included smallholders as well as intellectuals. These four old parties came to dominate the Danish political scene throughout the sweeping economic and social development of the first two-thirds of the present century. From 1929 onward, the Danish public gradually became accustomed to thinking of the country as a welfare society which was built by Social Democratic governments, supported by the Radical Liberal party and resisted - though not attacked - by the Conservative and Liberal opposition parties.

The voting support upholding this balance persisted until 1960. As seen from Table 14.1, the Social Democrats and the Communists together received between 42 and 47 per cent of the votes, but support from the Radical Liberals secured a majority at every election.

In 1960, however, the new left made its entry in the form of the Socialist People's party, and this set the standard of socialist support to almost 50 per cent. From 1966 to 1973 a new political order had appeared in which the Social Democrats and People's Socialists were aligned against Conservatives, Agrarian Liberals and Radical Liberals.

The 1973 election was extremely turbulent. Three new bourgeois parties, the Progressives, the

Table 14.1: Distribution of Vote at Danish General Elections, 1947–84

	1947 %	1950 %	1953 (Apr.) %	1953 (Sep.) %	1957 %	1960 %	1964 %	1966 %	1968 %	1971 %	1973 %	1975 %	1977 %	1979 %	1981 %	1984 %
Soc. Dem.	40.0	39.6	40.4	41.3	39.4	42.1	41.9	38.2	34.2	37.3	25.7	30.0	37.0	38.3	32.9	31.6
Soc. People	—	—	—	—	—	6.1	5.8	10.9	6.1	9.1	6.0	4.9	3.9	5.9	11.3	11.5
Comm.	6.8	4.6	4.8	4.3	3.1	1.1	1.2	0.8	1.0	1.4	3.6	4.2	3.7	1.9	1.1	0.7
Left Soc.	—	—	—	—	—	—	—	—	2.0	1.6	1.5	2.1	2.7	3.7	2.7	2.7
Other Soc.	—	—	—	—	—	—	0.3	—	—	—	—	—	—	0.4	0.2	0.1
Total Soc.	46.8	44.2	45.2	45.6	42.5	49.3	49.2	49.9	43.3	49.4	36.8	41.2	47.3	50.2	48.2	46.6
Con.	12.4	17.8	17.3	16.8	16.6	17.9	20.1	18.7	20.4	16.7	9.1	5.5	8.5	12.5	14.5	23.4
Agrarian Lib.	27.6	21.3	22.1	23.1	25.1	21.1	20.8	19.3	18.6	15.6	12.3	23.3	12.0	12.5	11.3	12.1
Radical Lib.	6.9	8.2	8.6	7.8	7.8	5.8	5.3	7.3	15.0	14.4	11.2	7.1	3.6	5.4	5.1	5.5
Centre Dem.	—	—	—	—	—	—	—	—	—	—	7.8	2.2	6.4	3.2	8.3	4.6
Progress	—	—	—	—	—	—	—	—	—	—	15.9	13.6	14.6	11.0	8.9	3.6
Christ. People	—	—	—	—	—	—	—	—	—	2.0	4.0	5.3	3.4	2.6	2.3	2.7
Inds.	—	—	—	2.7	2.3	3.3	2.5	1.6	0.5	—	—	—	—	—	—	—
Single—Tax	4.5	8.2	5.6	3.5	5.3	2.2	1.3	0.7	0.7	1.7	2.9	1.8	3.3	2.6	1.4	1.5
Lib. Centre	—	—	—	—	—	—	—	2.5	1.3	—	—	—	—	—	—	—
Other Nonsoc.	1.8	0.3	1.2	0.5	0.4	0.4	0.8	—	0.2	0.2	—	—	0.9	—	—	—
Total Nonsoc.	53.2	55.8	54.8	54.4	57.5	50.7	50.8	50.1	56.7	50.6	63.2	58.8	52.7	49.8	51.8	53.4

Note: The Faroe Islands and Greenland are excluded from these figures.

Table 14.2: Seats Won in the Danish Parliament, 1947-84

	1947	1950	1953 Apr.	1953 Sep.	1957	1960	1964	1966	1968	1971	1973	1975	1977	1979	1981	1984
Social Dem.	57	59	61	74	70	76	76	69	62	70	46	53	65	68	59	56
Soc. People	—	—	—	—	—	11	10	20	11	17	11	9	7	11	21	21
Comm.	9	7	7	8	6	—	—	—	—	—	6	7	7	—	—	—
Left Soc.	—	—	—	—	—	—	—	—	4	—	—	4	5	6	5	5
Total Soc.	66	66	68	82	76	87	86	89	77	87	63	73	84	85	85	82
Con.	17	27	26	30	30	32	36	34	37	31	16	10	15	22	26	42
Agrarian Lib.	49	32	33	42	45	38	38	35	34	30	22	42	21	22	20	22
Radical Lib.	10	12	13	14	14	11	10	13	27	27	20	13	6	10	9	10
Center Dem.	—	—	—	—	—	—	—	—	—	—	14	4	11	6	15	8
Progress	—	—	—	—	—	—	—	—	—	—	28	24	26	20	16	6
Christ. People	—	—	—	—	—	—	—	—	—	—	7	9	6	5	4	5
Inds.	—	—	—	—	—	6	5	—	—	—	—	—	—	—	—	—
Single Tax	6	12	9	6	9	—	—	—	—	—	5	—	6	5	—	—
Lib.Centre	—	—	—	—	—	—	—	4	—	—	—	—	—	—	—	—
Total Nonsoc.	82	83	81	92	98	87	89	86	98	88	112	102	91	90	90	93
German min.	—	—	—	1	1	1	—	—	—	—	—	—	—	—	—	—
Faroe Islands	1	1	1	2	2	2	2	2	2	2	2	2	2	2	2	2
Greenland	1	1	1	2	2	2	2	2	2	2	2	2	2	2	2	2
Total	150	151	151	179	179	179	179	179	179	179	179	179	179	179	179	179

Centre Democrats and the Christian People's party entered Parliament backed by 27 per cent of the voters between them. Since then, the Danish parliament has contained an average of ten parties as against the average of six parties during previous election periods.

Table 14.2 indicates the seat division for the same period as Table 14.1. After a revision of the constitution in 1953, the Folketing has 175 members for Denmark proper plus two from the Faroes and two from Greenland. Hence 90 seats are needed for a majority. However, since 1973 no government has been capable of mustering a permanent majority.

It is evident from these tables that the Danish party system has been the subject of increasing volatility from the 1950s to the middle 1970s. I have shown elsewhere by comparison with the other Scandinavian countries that the growth of volatility is the direct or indirect consequence of fragmentation in the party system (Borre 1979, 1980b). However, the experience of the last five years, 1979-1984, leads to a modification of that thesis into an hypothesis about the cyclical or wave-like nature of electoral volatility. Such an hypothesis underlies this chapter.

TRENDS IN ELECTORAL VOLATILITY

Table 14.3 and Figure 14.1 show the increase in electoral support (in per cent of valid votes) for every election, totalled for all parties that increased their support; or the total decrease in support for parties getting reduced support.

It can be seen that volatility, thus computed, rose from a low level of four per cent during the 1950s to a level around ten per cent in the period 1966-71, and peaked dramatically with almost 30 per cent in 1973 as the party system fragmented. Since then it has subsided, first to the 18 per cent level in the elections of 1975 and 1977, and then to the level of 10-12 per cent in the last three elections.

The decline in volatility through the last decade does not signify greater stability on the parliamentary level. A Liberal minority government from 1973 to 1975 was succeeded by Social Democratic minority governments which held out until 1982, but only because it could stage a succession of majority coalitions with various parties from the bourgeois side. For a year, 1978-79, it included ministers of the Liberal party, but in August 1982 it collapsed, as the prospects of new coalitions seemed exhausted. It is perhaps suggestive of the level of parliamentary instability that the present government is composed of four bourgeois parties - the Conservative, Liberal, Centre Democratic and Christian People's parties - who command only around 40 per cent of the seats, and that the latter two of these parties did not enter parliament until 1973.

Table 14.3: Net Volatility at Danish General Elections 1950-84

	Election	Net Volatility	Election	Net Volatility
	1950	10.4	1971	9.5
April	1953	3.2	1973	29.1
Sept.	1953	4.6	1975	17.8
	1957	3.8	1977	18.2
	1960	11.1	1979	11.0
	1964	3.0	1981	12.5
	1966	9.6	1984	10.8
	1968	11.8		

The decline of volatility since 1973 is a consequence of the fact that on the electoral level, the party system has stabilised in its new and fragmented form. The same eleven parties have contested all elections, although occasionally one or two of them have fallen below the two per cent threshold required for representation, and no significant new parties have emerged since 1973. Hence we may speak of the fragmentation of 1973 being followed by a period of realignment, which included the 1975 and 1977 elections. The last three elections, in 1979, 1981, and 1984 have largely led to fluctuations that have been contained within this new political order.

Much of the electoral volatility in Denmark since 1947 results from fragmentations of the party system and subsequent adaptations to the new situation by existing parties. The intrusion of the Socialist People's party alone accounts for about half the volatility in the 1960 and 1966 elections, and the adaptation to this new situation goes far toward explaining the volatility of the 1968 and 1971 elections. In 1973 the greater part of the volatility was caused by the intrusion of two new parties, the Progressive and the Centre Democratic, which obtained 24 per cent of the vote between them.

Figure 14.1: Electoral Volatility at Parliamentary Elections in Denmark Since 1950

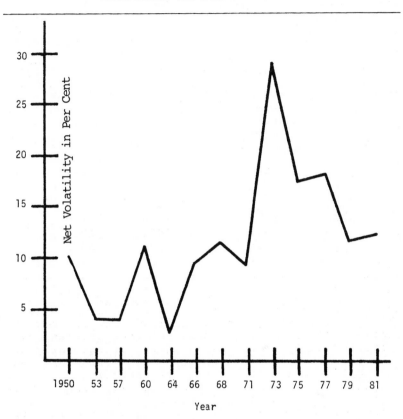

The 1975 and 1977 elections were dominated by attempts to cope with this new situation, and this process seemed to come to an end with the 1979 election. However, due to the greater number of parties, electoral volatility is not likely to decline much below ten per cent even in normal elections under the new party system.

Since the intrusion of new parties appears to be the key to an understanding of much of the volatility we observe, at least in Denmark, it is appropriate to construct a model of fragmentation and its aftermath as a prerequisite for explaining electoral volatility. The model, outlined below, will be called the fragmentation/realignment model, or F/R model for short. In subsequent sections the model will guide the choice of indicators used to illustrate electoral behaviour during the period 1971-81, which includes six elections for which survey data are available.

THE F/R MODEL

The fragmentation/realignment model owes a debt to the late Angus Campbell (1966a, 1966b). With some adjustment his concepts, such as the distinction between maintaining, deviating, and realigning elections, also apply to multiparty systems. But particularly for such systems they need to be supplemented in order to deal with elections in which the elements themselves - that is, the parties - change. The repercussions of major fragmentations of party systems are sometimes so great as to remind one of political revolutions, in which one regime is replaced by another. Hence, another source of inspiration for the F/R model is the cyclical models of revolution devised by Edwards (1927) Pettee (1938) Brinton (1939) and Huntington (1968). In embryonic form, the fragmentation/realignment process may possess some of the same characteristics as the pattern of participation during an institutional breakdown and subsequent emergence of a new political order.

The model posits two phases, a fragmentation phase and a realignment phase. But each of them may stretch over two or even more elections, and it is possible that intermediate elections combine features of both phases. For example, fragmentation may continue on one wing while realignment begins on the other wing of the party system.

Electoral volatility peaks during the fragmentation phase, when the new party or parties break through. Since the old parties do not shift their issue positions or their pattern of coalition in response to the fragmentation, the new parties may continue to gain support and volatility may then be spread over two or three elections in a prolonged fragmentation phase. This is enhanced by a tendency for the new parties to split up after the first fragmentation.

Volatility tends to drop during the realignment phase when the old parties, or at least some of them, take remedial action. When the realignment is over and the new party system is established volatility drops further, although not quite to the level before the fragmentation. This is because the new party system contains more parties than the old and, other things being equal, volatility is greater when the number of parties is larger.

With regard to voter interest, the appearance of a new party, presumably with refreshingly new and simple viewpoints, is likely to create attention in the media and discussion in the electorate. The fragmentation phase will therefore be marked by a rising level of voting turnout. This high level is likely to continue through most of the realignment phase because the older parties engage in a process of shifting issue positions and alliance partners, all of which is certain to give media exposure and arouse interest among the voters.

The voter base of the new party must in the main be sought outside the camps of party identifiers and it will disproportionately consist of young voters and occasional voters. It is possible, however, that during a fragmentation/realignment process the 'floating voter' hypothesis will not hold true as in normal elections. The least involved voters are generally slow to realise that a new party has appeared on the stage and they therefore tend to switch their votes rather unsystematically among the older parties. Also during the ensuing realignment, the least involved are less likely to perceive the change in issue positions and alliance partners in the system, and are, therefore, less likely to respond by switching their votes. It should also be taken into account that the level of education is rising with each new cohort of electors. Young and well-educated voters without firm attachments to the established parties are a great asset for new parties. The issues raised by the new parties are eagerly discussed among the young, and as a result one may find that the highly informed voters are disproportionately attracted to the new parties.

The level of general trust in politics is at a low level prior to fragmentation and continues to fall as established parties are attacked by the leaders of the new parties. The low level of trust signals a feeling that there is no viable alternative within the established party system. Parties may have alternated in government without noticeable effect upon long-standing problems of high priority to the public and voters begin to believe that new leaders and new parties are required. However, political distrust often has a strong expressive component. Once the new leaders have made their way to parliament and it is evident that the other parties are adjusting to the new

situation, political trust slowly begins to rise.
The new party or parties tend to gain votes in significant proportions from several or all of the established parties. Quite often the new party cuts across traditional cleavage lines to generate a new dimension in party preferences, at least temporarily. This is related to the function of the new party as a promoter of an issue or minority group that was neglected by the older party system. Fragmentation may therefore have little to do with opinion changes on existing issues. Such changes would often be contained within the established party system, which was designed to deal with just these older lines of political conflict. Fragmentation is typically nourished by issue positions that are not already monopolised by the older parties. There may have existed a sort of tacit agreement among the leaders of these parties not to bring such issues into the campaign (for example, racial and other minority problems), or the issues may be problems raised by new technology and economic growth (for example, the 'green issues' of the 1970s).

As to the outcome of the realignment, the F/R model is not very determinate. In some cases fragmentation is very short-lived, the new parties disappearing again after a few elections without leaving significant impact on the party system. However, the model was devised to analyse permanent change in which at least one major party was added to the system.

Net and Gross Volatility

The relation between net and gross electoral volatility is a special case of the relation between indicators at the macro level and at the micro level. The absence of net volatility is no guarantee against a high frequency of vote switching, since that switching may cancel out in the total support for each party. However, such borderline cases are rare and in practice one may count on a fair correlation between gross and net volatility, at least compared with other correlations in the field of social science. In Figure 14.2, the lower line represents the net volatility for the elections between 1971 and 1981, repeated from Figure 14.1. The upper line represents gross volatility defined as the per cent of those voting at two successive elections who voted for different parties. For the six elections

Figure 14.2: Gross and Net Partisan Change (Volatility) at Parliamentary Elections, 1971-81

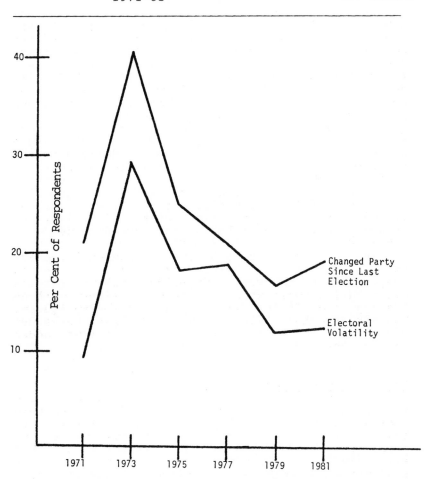

the correlation between the two series is r=0.92, and the regression coefficient indicates that around three quarters of gross vote switching materialises on the macro level as electoral volatility.

It is true that reservations other than those already mentioned may cause errors in projecting from vote switching to electoral volatility. If new generations of voters, and voters switching from non-voting to voting, have other party preferences

than those leaving the electorate, there will be net
volatility without vote switching. Even more
importantly, vote switching that is computed by
means of recall of the respondent´s vote at the
previous election, generally underestimates the
frequency of vote shifts because of respondents´
tendency to distort past party preference in the
direction of present party preference (see Chapter
1 in this volume). Except for 1973, our
information on vote switching is based on recall,
and it is likely that the true points of the upper
graph are therefore somewhat above the ones
displayed.

Nonetheless, Figure 14.2 suggests that
electoral volatility is the outcome of general vote
instability and therefore can be approached by using
indicators commonly employed in survey analysis.

Other Indicators of Volatility

In an attempt to trace the instability to
various components of the decision process going on
among the voters, we may compare the partisan shift
shown in Figure 14.2 with indicators of vacillation
during the campaign in Figure 14.3.

The two graphs show the proportion of
respondents who made their final partisan choice in
the last week of the campaign and the proportion who
considered voting for a different party than the one
they actually voted for. On separate levels, they
follow the indicators of vote change closely and
serve to forecast the approaching storm in 1973.
Also the intermediate level of instability in the
realignment period of 1975-77 is accurately
predicted, but with respect to the confirming
elections of 1979-81 these campaign indicators
suggest that after the volatile period, vote
decisions continue to be made later than under the
old party system. This may be a consequence of the
higher level of fragmentation in the new party
system.

Figure 14.4 deals with indicators of party
identification and the amount of vote defection
among identifiers. It is based on survey questions
asking whether the respondent considered himself or
herself an ´adherent´ of any particular party, and
if not, whether he or she usually felt closer to one
party than to others. Again, the fragmentation of
1973 shows up clearly. But it is interesting that
the level of party identification (upper graph)
already in 1975 returned to its 1971 level of 60 per

Figure 14.3:Indicators of Indecision During Election
Campaigns, 1971-81

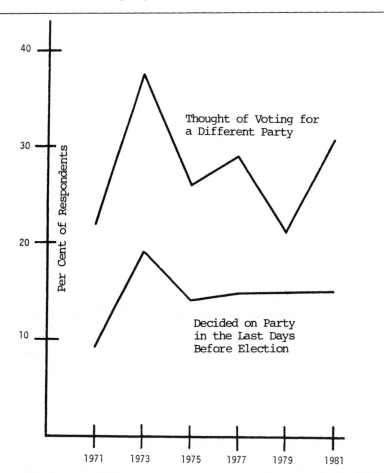

cent and indeed proceeded beyond this level in 1977.
Apparently a camp of 'adherents' quickly formed
around the new or growing parties (see Borre, 1984).
The proportion of defectors among those feeling
'closer' to a particular party (middle line) closely
follows the indicators of campaign vacillation in
Figure 14.3, whereas the proportion of defectors
among the outright 'adherents' (lower line) follows
the indicators of vote instability in Figure 14.2,
suggesting that on this count the 1979 election
meant a return to normality.

Taking stock of the indicators used in this

Figure 14.4: Lack of and Defection from Party Identification at Elections, 1971-79

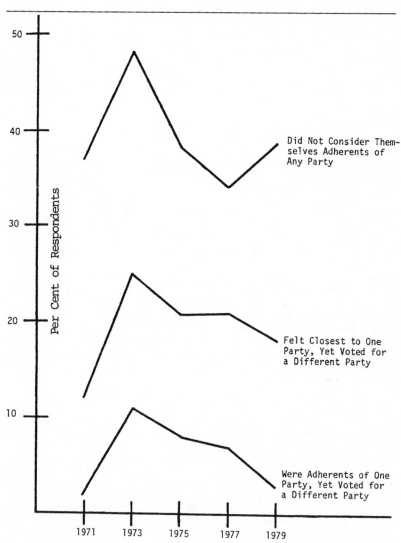

section, we observe that all of the seven indicators of vote instability increased sharply at the fragmenting election of 1973, that all declined at the next election, the early realignment of 1975, and that all but one of them declined further after the realignment in 1979. The exception is the number of respondents who did not identify with any party. With this exception the F/R model has yielded correct predictions. During fragmentation not only did electoral volatility rise sharply but so did a broad range of indicators of voter instability. This is followed by a fairly unstable period of realignment, after which volatility declines as the new party system becomes more or less institutionalised.

The Wave of Participation

It was suggested above that voter involvement in the elections would be abnormally high during the process of fragmentation and realignment of the party system. Such a projection follows from theories of mobilisation of collective action (see, for example, Tilly, 1978). True enough, in the Danish elections of the 1970s, voting turnout rose in 1973 from 87.2 to 88.7 per cent. The next two elections in 1975 and 1977, which we have classified as parts of the realignment phase, also had high turnout, namely 88.2 and 88.7 per cent, respectively. After that, turnout dropped in 1979 to its previous level, 87.2 per cent. The 1981 election had a dramatically low turnout by modern Danish standards, 82.7 per cent, but this may well have been influenced by the fact that a municipal election had been held three weeks earlier, and the news media had criticised this excessive demand upon the voters. In the election of January 1984 turnout rose to 88.4 per cent.

In order to provide other independent tests of the model's projections, we shall look at indicators of voter interest and activity from the series of surveys between 1971 and 1981. First, Figure 14.5 contains measures of the public's exposure to the news media during the election campaigns. In the case of exposure to television and radio, the data points for the period 1971-73 are not directly comparable with those from 1974-81 because the wording of the relevant questions was changed in the 1975 survey. All three, however, exhibit the projected rise in voter interest associated with the fragmentation in 1973. In the case of the exposure to television and radio, the expected decline in 1979 also materialises. The failure of the newspaper exposure to decline significantly in 1979 is probably due to a strike among the typographical workers during the 1977 election campaign, which affected exposure in that year.

Figure 14.5: Media Exposure During Election Campaigns, 1971-81

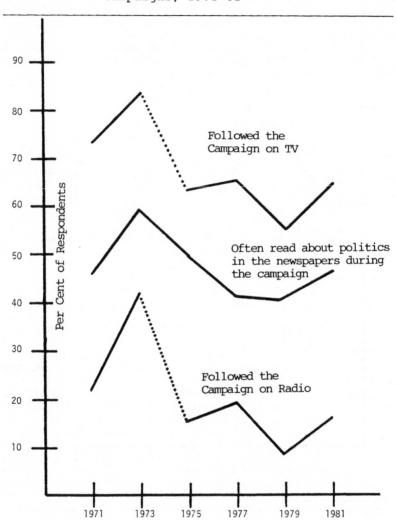

Secondly, the extent of political communication on the personal level can be measured by means of questions asking whether respondents had discussed politics with family, friends, and colleagues. While the amount of family discussion appears to be fairly constant from one election to the next, discussions with friends and colleagues vary strongly. These two indicators are graphed in

Figure 14.6: Political Interest and Discussion During Election Campaigns, 1971–81

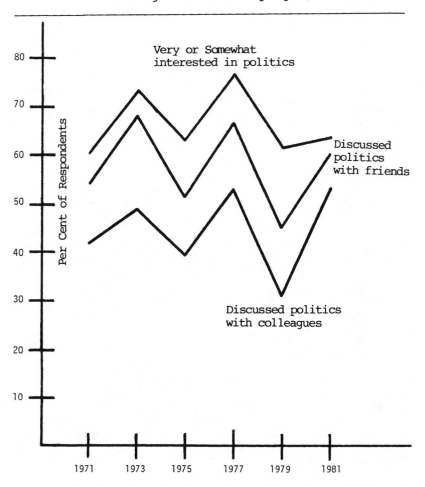

Figure 14.6 along with the per cent of voters who indicated that they were interested in politics.

Again we find that voter interest and activity increased in association with the 1973 fragmentation and decreased in association with the completion of the realignment in 1979. The intermediate election of 1975 appears to have elicited a lower voter interest than the 1977 election, a fact which could also be gathered from the previous figure. The explanation might be that the 1975 election campaign partly coincided with the Christmas-New Year vacation. Concentrating on the changes projected by the F/R model, we observe that all our seven indicators of voter involvement rose at the fragmentation election in 1973 and (with the possible exception of newspaper exposure) dropped after the completed realignment in 1979.

The simultaneous surge of voter participation and vote instability at a particular election, as well as the simultaneous decline in a subsequent low-stimulus election, conforms to the mechanism described in Angus Campbell's (1966a) classic article on 'Surge and Decline'. It arises from the generally higher level of political involvement among party identifiers than among non-identifiers. The latter tend to be partisan 'floaters', who are mobilised only during high-stimulus elections. When outlining the F/R model, we anticipated that a fragmentation election is a special case of a high-stimulus election in which the 'floaters' might include highly involved sections of the electorate. Such an assumption is in accord with studies of collective behaviour, which almost invariably show that new political movements have a high proportion of intellectuals.

Some evidence that this principle applies also to the case of fragmentation of party systems is found in the Danish surveys. Dividing the 1973 sample into three categories according to their media activity, we find that among the most active 35 per cent switched to new parties (Progressive or Centre Democrats) or small parties, while only 17 per cent of the least active did so; the intermediate category had a rate of 26 per cent switching to the new or small parties (see Borre et al., 1976, p.239). However, the media-active were less inclined to switch between the old parties than were the inactive, just as predicted by the floating voter hypothesis. Hence it appears that new or relatively unknown parties rely on the media to such an extent that their new supporters rise above the stalwarts of the old parties in terms of electoral involvement.

The Wave of Distrust in Politics

At the level of voter motivation, a precondition for fragmentation is a high level of discontent with all or both of the established parties. This is a plausible assumption since discontent with one or only some of the parties ordinarily leads to vote shifts toward the remaining parties. A sizeable fraction of the electorate must feel that shifting their vote within the circle of established parties is no solution to their problems. Sympathy with a new party is enhanced by the feeling that there is no consistent response to the electorate's needs within the existing party system. The alternative, a resort to abstention or blank ballots as a protest, is psychologically inconsistent with the mounting tide of voter participation which occurs at the same time. Sometimes, however, a hitherto almost neglected small party scores an electoral triumph (much to the surprise of its leaders) due to its having been neglected or scorned by the other parties for so long that the electorate does not consider it part of 'the establishment'; this can be considered a kind of pseudo-fragmentation of the party system. This occurred in the Danish party system with respect to the Communist party just after the Second World War and the Single-Tax party during the 1950s; and the exodus from the established parties in 1973 favoured not only the two new parties, the Progressives and the Centre Democrats, but also the Communists and Single-Taxers, who had been robbed of their parliamentary representation since 1960, and the Christian People's party, which had tried in vain to overcome the two per cent threshold in 1971.

It is true that discontent may be concentrated on one wing of the party system. The success of the Socialist People's party was strongly influenced by the feeling that neither the Communist party nor the Social Democratic party were in a position to accommodate the sentiment of the New Left. The quarrel among the Socialist parties led to an electoral victory for the bourgeois parties in 1968, and a change of government. But it soon became clear that the bourgeois parties could not agree on a clear alternative to the socialist policies which they had condemned. In this way discontent spread to the entire electorate.

Though in terms of electoral support politics is a zero-sum game, this is not always so in terms of supporting attitudes. The prestige of politics and politicians in general may be lowered causing normlessness among the public and a search for other types of leadership. One is here reminded of the wave of ridicule and scandal in the media, so vividly described by Lyford Edwards to be a precursor of revolution (Edwards, 1927). The data we can present are a much more prosaic and dry expression of the public sentiment. They are based

Figure 14.7: Average Agreement with Three Attitudinal Items Showing Distrust in
Politics, 1971-81

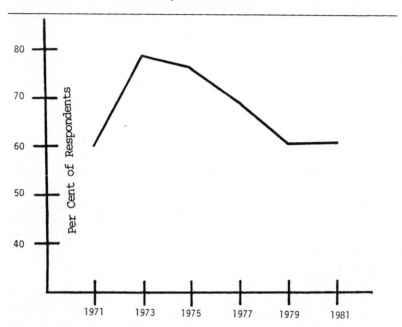

on two attitudinal items on political distrust, or
cynicism, that originated in the Michigan surveys,
and a third indicating a desire for a 'strong
man'.(2) Figure 14.7 displays the average
proportion showing distrust on these three items.
It is seen that the average level rose sharply from
1971 to 1973 and thereafter gradually returned over
the next three elections to its 1971 value. Though
not all distrust items follow exactly the same
course, their average clearly conforms to the
projections of the F/R model.

Also for individual voters, showing political
distrust is correlated with having a stake in
fragmentation. With regard to the 1971-73
situation, it has been shown elsewhere that on five
distrust items the distrust response was correlated
with vote switching from the old bourgeois parties
to the new parties. On four of the five items,
distrust was correlated with voting for the
Progressive party (Rusk and Borre, 1974). The
general character of these findings holds whether or
not one controls for party identification. In an

analysis of the 1971-73 panel, which divided the respondents into the trustful and the distrustful on the basis of their 1971 responses to the above items, it was found that among party identifiers (those calling themselves ´adherents´ of some party), 20 per cent of the distrustful switched to one of the new parties in 1973, as against only eight per cent of the trustful. Among non-identifiers, 47 per cent of the distrustful switched, as against 23 per cent of the trustful (Borre et al., 1976, p.117) That is, lack of party identification and lack of political trust independently of one another caused the voter to join the fragmentation which was to come more than a year later. It seems that political trust operates much like party identification, only for the established party system as a whole. A rise in political distrust consequently means loss of loyalty to the established party system and a willingness to vote for new parties or non-establishment parties.

Issues and Ideology

Fragmentation is usually a result of the injection of new issues into a party system which was organised around a set of older issues. Over a generation, positions on the older issues have become part of political socialisation and a basis for recruitment into the older party organisations. This has made the old system an almost perfect mechanism to absorb shifts in public opinion along the older cleavage line, usually a left-right dimension. Shifts to the left manifested themselves in an increasing vote for left-side parties at the cost of right-side parties and forced the latter to change their position toward a more competitive one. Similarly, shifts to the right brought about a crisis in left-side parties and made them reconsider their position. This process of adaptation might be slow and painful due to the commitment of parties to their older positions. Between 1924 and 1935 the Agrarian Liberal party was slowly drained of around 15 per cent of the Danish electorate, and the Social Democratic party gained a similar per cent of the vote, before the Agrarian Liberals in effect gave up their insistence on economic liberalism and accepted the welfare system. On one hand, one cannot deny that the vote mechanism worked, and yet it would be going too far to say that the losing parties automatically change their positions so as to restore the equilibrium and their own competitive power.

The new issues of the 1960s and 1970s produced ideological confusion in the alignment of the older party system. When the Socialist People´s party presented a left-wing platform which was also opposed to Soviet imperialism and dictatorship, it took the Social Democratic party seven or eight years to realise the danger on its left flank and in the meantime the new party had grown to twelve per cent of the vote establishing itself as the fifth party of the system. Our electoral surveys do not reach back into the 1960s, and hence it is difficult to reconstruct the process of fragmentation and subsequent realignment which took place in connection with the emergence of the New Left in Denmark. But to interpret the electoral change as produced by a straightforward shift to the left in existing ideological attitudes appears much too simple. New issues and priorities, new beliefs about older topics of controversy and spokesmen giving voice to existing beliefs that had somehow been ´homeless´ in the older party system, are all elements of the F/R process.

We are in a better position to study the process with regard to the 1973 debacle. The conventional interpretation of this election is that it constituted a large swing to the right: the Social Democratic party fell from 37.3 to 25.6 per cent of the total vote, and two new parties appeared on the bourgeois side with a total of 23.7 per cent of the vote. Yet this explanation is grossly inadequate. We have already seen that general distrust in politics played a role, and this explains why the established bourgeois parties were unable to exploit a possible shift to the right in ideological opinions. Figure 14.8 shows the average proportion agreeing with four leftist viewpoints which have appeared with identical wording in all the questionnaires since 1971.(3)

This indicator does not show a swing to the right in 1973. On the contrary, agreement with our four leftist statements rose from an average of 55 per cent in 1971 to 61 per cent in 1973. Looking solely at this evidence one might indeed think that left-wing parties stood a very good chance in an election with such change in ideological opinions. Yet it was the new bourgeois parties that made the largest gains in popular support.

The line in Figure 14.8 suggests that the slight shift to the left in 1973 was followed by a

Figure 14.8: Average Agreement with Four Attit-
              tudinal   Items   Showing   Leftist
              Orientation, 1971-81

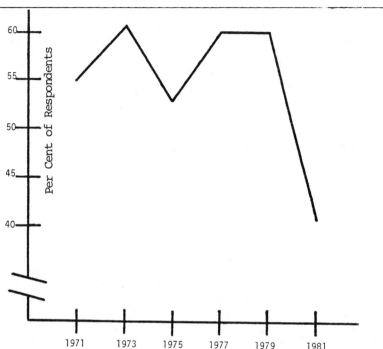

shift to the right in 1975 and a new shift to the
left in 1977. But any of these changes in public
opinion was dwarfed by the shift to the right which
took place in 1981, long after the realignment was
over.   It   appears   that changes in public opinion
have little to do with the magnitude of electoral
volatility or even with the electoral fortunes of
parties on the right and left. This suggests that
most public opinion change takes place within the
partisan camps rather than between them.   Thus the
voters of different parties manage to keep up their
attitudinal distance from one another, which at
least reduces their inclination to switch to other
parties.
     If opinion change goes on within the various
partisan camps, it is certainly also the case that
partisan change often goes on within the various
issue publics, defined as voters with approximately
the same attitudes on a number of issues.   This is
especially so with new parties that are not assoc-

Figure 14.9: Frequency of Inconsistent Party Choice

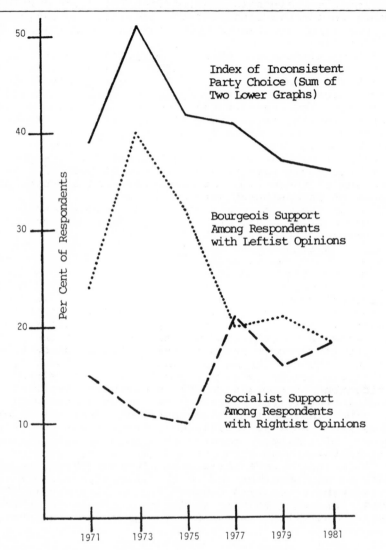

iated with the older issues. A certain ideological
confusion often takes place in connection with the
rise of a new party, in part because the issue or
combination of issues which the new party promotes
have no well-defined location on the older cleavage
line, and in part because the parliamentary
coalitions into which the new party will fit are not

yet clarified. This confusion is likely to diminish
during the realignment period when the older parties
react to the new issue and the possible new patterns
of coalition are tested out in the parliamentary
roll calls.
     To illustrate this we shall utilise the four
attitudinal items of Figure 14.8 for a
classification of our respondents into three
ideological categories: left, centre, and right.(4)
For each of these three ideological categories we
can follow the development of support for different
parties. An extract of this information is
contained in Figure 14.9, which shows support for
socialist parties among voters of the right, support
for bourgeois parties among voters of the left, and
the sum of these two, which may serve as a sort of
index of inconsistent voting.
     As the upper graph shows, this index rose from
39 per cent in 1971 to 51 per cent during the
fragmenting election of 1973. But already at the
first realigning election of 1975, it dropped back
to 42 per cent, and in the course of the three
subsequent elections it dropped further to 36 per
cent. Judging by the two lower graphs, the most
important component in the rise and decline of
inconsistent voting was the ´bridgehead´ which the
bourgeois parties (especially the Progressives)
succeeded in establishing among voters of the left
during the fragmentation in 1973, and its decline
during the realigning 1975 and 1977 elections. But
the latter election also brought about a sizeable
bridgehead of socialist party preference (especially
Social Democratic voters) among voters of the right.
In the last three elections, both partisan sides
have succeeded in maintaining brigeheads of the
order of 20 per cent in the opposing ideological
categories.
     On the face of it, electoral volatility appears
to have much more to do with inconsistent voting
(viz. the similarity between Figure 14.2 and Figure
14.9) than with opinion change on left-right issues.
This illustrates the temporary blurring of cleavage
lines projected in the F/R model.

ELECTORAL VOLATILITY AND THE PARTY SYSTEM

     A wave of electoral volatility and vote
switching, of interest and participation in
elections, of distrust in politics generally, and of
apparent inconsistency between ideology and partisan

choice - all of these features seem to go together when a fragmentation and subsequent realignment of the party system takes place. We have argued that these features are not coincidental but aspects of a particular electoral process, and we have therefore attempted to relate them with one another in a model of electoral change, the F/R model. Danish parliamentary elections between 1971 and 1981 were used to illustrate the operation of that model. Naturally, the usefulness of the model can only be assessed when it has been applied to other settings. In the case of Danish electoral development through the 1960s and 1970s it is plausible to view electoral volatility as chiefly caused by fragmentation of the party system and subsequent adaptation to the situation after the new party or parties were added to the system. In other countries, electoral volatility may primarily take the form of larger fluctuations in support for permanent parties without the triggering impulse of fragmentation. It may also be possible to demonstrate the relation between electoral volatility and social and economic change much more directly than in Denmark, where changes of the party system itself are paramount in the attempts to account for electoral volatility in modern times. We have not touched on, for example, the decline of class voting or the saturation of welfare state politics, in part because their relation with volatility is indirect and somewhat speculative in our case, and in part because such basic and trend-like changes have already been analysed elsewhere.(5) For a broader understanding of change in Danish electoral politics the present chapter should therefore be read in conjunction with these other contributions.

FOOTNOTES

1. A brief history of the party system and the rules of representation can be found in Borre, (1980a).
2. The distrust items read, 'The politicians care too little about the voters' opinions', 'In general we may trust our political leaders to make the right decisions for the country', and 'It would be sensible to let a strong man seize power in a situation of economic crisis'. They called for five-way responses from 'Agree completely' to 'Disagreee completely'. In computing the data

points in Figure 14.7, only the two 'Agree' and the
two 'Disagree' categories were used. Agreement with
the first and third item and disagreement with the
second were considered distrust responses.
    3. The leftist items read, 'The government has
too little control over private investments', 'High
incomes should be taxed more strongly than they are
today', 'In politics one ought to strive to give
everybody the same opportunities, no matter what
their education and occupation are', and 'We should
get out of NATO as soon as possible'. They called
for five-way responses from 'Agree completely' to
'Disagree completely'. In computing the data points
in Figure 14.8, only the two 'Agree' and the two
'Disagree' categories were used.
    4. See note 3. By assigning the values 1 to 5
to the five responses and adding the values for each
respondent, we obtain an index of leftist
orientation ranging from 4 to 20. The left was
defined as scores 4-9, the centre as scores 10-14,
and the right as scores 15-20.
    5. See, in addition to the other cited studies
on Danish voting behaviour, Worre (1980); Borre
(1977, 1979, 1981, 1982); Borre et al.(1983);
Nielsen and Sauerberg (1977a, 1977b).

REFERENCES

Borre, O. (1977) 'Recent Trends in Danish Voting
    Behaviour' in K. Cerny (ed.), Scandinavia at
    the Polls, American Enterprise Institute,
    Washington
--------- (1979) 'Ustabilitet ved parlamentsvalg i
    fire nordiske lande 1950-77' in M. Pedersen
    (ed.), Dansk politik i 1970'erne, Samfunds-
    videnskabeligt Forlag, Kobenhavn
--------- (1980a) 'The Social Bases of Danish
    Electoral Behaviour' in R. Rose (ed.) Electoral
    Participation. A Comparative Analysis, Sage
    Publications, Beverley Hills and London,
    pp.241-51
--------- (1980b) 'Electoral Instability in Four
    Nordic Countries 1950-77', Comparative
    Political Studies, 13, 2, 141-71
--------- (1981) in Partisystemet i oprud, Politica,
    Aarhus
--------- (1982) in D. Anckar et al. Partier,
    ideologier, valjare, Meddelanden fran
    Stiftelsen for Abo Akademis Forskningsinstitut,
    Abo

--------- (1984) ´Critical Forces in Scandinavian Electoral Behaviour´ in P. Beck et al., Critical Electoral Forces, Princeton University Press, Princeton

Borre, O. H.J. Neilsen, S. Sauerberg and T. Worre (1976) Vaelgere i 70erne, Akademisk Forlag, Copenhagen

Borre, O. et al. (1983) Efter vaelgerskredet, Politica, Aarhus

Brinton, C. (1939) The Anatomy of Revolution, Prentice-Hall, New York

Campbell, A. (1966a) ´Surge and Decline: A Study of Electoral Change´ in A. Campbell et al., Elections and the Political Order, Wiley & Sons, New York

--------- (1966b) ´A Classification of Presidential Elections´ in A. Campbell et al., op.cit.

Edwards, L. (1927) The Natural History of Revolution, University of Chicago Press, Chicago

Huntington, S.P. (1968) Political Order in Changing Societies, Yale University Press, New Haven

Neilsen, H.J. and S. Sauerberg (1977a) ´The uncivic culture: attitudes toward the political system in Denmark and vote for the Progress Party´, Scandinavian Political Studies, 12

--------- (1977b) ´The uncivic culture: Communication and the political system in Denmark 1973-75´, Scandinavian Political Studies, 12

Pedersen, M. (1979) ´The Dynamics of European Party Systems: Changing Patterns of Electoral Volatility´, European Journal of Political Research, 9, 1, 1-26

Pettee, G. (1938) The Process of Revolution, Harper, New York

Rusk, J. and O. Borre (1974) ´The Changing Party Space in Danish Voter Perceptions 1971-73´, European Journal of Political Research, 2, 4

Tilly, C. (1978) From Mobilization to Revolution, Addisson-Wesley, Reading, Massachusetts

Worre, T. (1980) ´Class Parties and Class Voting in the Scandinavian Countries´, Scandinavian Political Studies, new series 3, 4

APPENDIX

Survey Indicators of Volatility, Involvement, Attitudes and Partisan Choice at Danish Parliamentary Elections, 1971-81

	1971 %	1973 %	1975 %	1977 %	1979 %	1981 %
Changed party since last election (of those voting at both elections)	21	40	25	21	17	19
Thought of voting for a different party	22	37	26	29	21	31
Decided on party late in campaign	9	19	14	15	15	15
Did not consider self adherent of a party	37	48	38	34	39	–
Felt closest to a party, voted for different party	12	25	21	21	18	–
Adherent of a party, voted for different party	2	11	8	7	3	
Saw all/nearly all parties´ TV broadcasts	(73)	(84)	63	65	55	65
Heard all/nearly all parties´ radio broadcasts	(22)	(42)	16	20	10	17
Often read about politics in press during campaign	46	59	49	42	41	47
Very/somewhat interested in politics	60	73	63	76	61	63
Discussed politics with friends	54	68	51	67	45	60
Discussed politics with colleagues at work	42	49	40	53	31	53
Average agreement with three items showing distrust in politics	60	78	75	68	60	60
Average agreement with four items showing leftist orientation	55	61	53	60	60	41
Bourgeois support with leftist opinion	24	40	32	20	21	19
Socialist support with rightist opinion	15	11	10	21	16	19

Note: Figures in parentheses are not comparable with the other figures.

Chapter 15

CONCLUSION

David Denver

        The approach we have adopted in this book -
considering electoral volatiliy and partisan change
on a country-by-country basis - tends to lead to an
emphasis upon what is peculiar or unique about each
case as it is considered in turn. And, indeed, the
impression to be gained from even a casual perusal
of the individual chapters - despite some common
features and attempted uniformity of treatment - is
one of variety. There are variations in the nature
and extent of data available and hence in
methodological approaches; trends in electoral
volatility do not follow any consistent pattern;
changes in party systems range from minimal to
wholesale; and a variety of explanations has been
put forward to account for the patterns found.
        A concluding chapter might be expected to
'pull all this together'. But if by this is meant
something like 'inferring from the individual
country studies generally applicable statements
about the relationships between social change,
electoral change and party system change', then, as
was suggested in the introductory chapter, such a
task is impossible. Each country considered in the
preceding chapters has a unique combination of
electoral arrangements, governmental institutions
and party system (not to mention wider differences
in social structure, political culture and history)
and these impinge directly upon the processes which
connect change among individual electors and change
in the party system. The result is that patterns of
electoral change and their effects upon party
systems are characterised more by variation across
different political systems than by similarity.
        This is made clear if we attempt to relate the
analysis of trends in the countries which have been
considered in this volume to the model which Ivor

Conclusion

Crewe outlined in the Introduction. This model underlies much discussion of electoral change in Western democracies. Its starting point is changes in the social structure and/or changes in the attitudes and values of citizens (with the implicit suggestion that these two may be connected).

There can be little doubt that in the post-war period all the countries which have been analysed here have experienced rapid and fundamental social changes. There have, of course, been variations in the pace, extent and precise nature of the changes. Simplifying drastically, however, it might be said that typically social change has reflected the 'modernisation' of the societies involved - declines in agricultural and traditional heavy industries; increases in the importance of consumer-oriented industries and the service sector; increasing urbanisation and secularisation; increased social and geographical mobility. As a consequence, traditional class structures and religious commitment have been progressively undermined.

Evidence relating to changes in attitudes and values is rather less clear-cut. This may be because these are, indeed, more resistant to change, but part of the problem here is also that in most countries there is little survey or poll evidence on citizens' attitudes until the 1960s, by which times changes (if such there were) are thought to have been well under way. Even so, many of the authors of the preceding chapters have identified the emergence of a 'counter-culture' in the 1960s which contributed to the raising of new issues in the political sphere - for example, the role of women in society, environmentalism, race and regionalism - issues which cut across the traditional political cleavages of class and religion.

In a broad way, then, it seems fair to suggest that nearly all countries have experienced to some extent the kind of social and cultural changes which might be expected to lead to the second stage in the model - partisan dealignment.

Partisan dealignment is a concept which has both individual-level and aggregate-level strands. At the individual level it refers to a situation in which there is a weakening in the psychological attachment of the voter to his or her party. For a variety of reasons, voters become less committed to 'their' parties. The vote is no longer cast on the basis of traditional loyalty, it is no longer a near-automatic response to the stimulus of an election.

401

Conclusion

This is reflected at the aggregate level where there is a marked decline in the strength of the relationship between social-structural variables and party support. The solidity with which different social groups give their support to one party or another begins to crumble. Both of these features, then - weakening party identification and attenuation of the social group/party link - would indicate a dealigning party system.

Of the 13 systems that have been covered, six offer clear evidence of dealignment during the post-war period - United States, Belgium, The Netherlands, Denmark, Britain and its component part, Scotland. In all these cases the social bases of the established parties have become less firm and (though the evidence on this point is a little more patchy) identification with traditional parties has weakened.

In two cases - Austria and Italy - there is evidence of at least partial dealignment. In the former, in the late 1960s, there was some increase in the ´newly-formed floating vote with no definite party allegiance and voting preferences´ (p.272) and there has been some weakening of the link between class and religion and party support (p.280). The latter phenomenon seems also to have occurred to some degree in Italy (see p.308) and here too there is some evidence of a decline in ´identity voting´ and a growth in ´opinion voting´ (p.304).

In four systems - Canada, Ireland, West Germany and Australia - there is little evidence of partisan dealignment at the aggregate level arising from the socio-cultural changes of the last forty years or so. In the case of Canada we should perhaps say evidence of <u>further</u> dealignment, since the argument put forward by Le Duc (chapter 3) is that Canadian electoral politics is best characterised as an instance of ´stable dealignment´. The relationship between social characteristics and party support in Canada has never been strong and party identification has always been highly unstable. In Ireland, the party system is largely based on political conflicts associated with the gaining of independence rather than on social cleavages so that no weakening of a non-existing relationship can be expected. In this case, however, partisanship appears to be strong and steady. In explaining this, Marsh (chapter 7) refers to the adaptability of the parties and the Single Transferable Vote electoral system, which allows extensive intra-party competition, but confesses that the absence of dealignment remains a puzzle, given that Ireland has been affected by more rapid social change than most Western societies. In Australia there has been some moderation of the link between class and party (pp.89-90). But despite occasional party splits leading to the formation of new parties, there is little evidence of genuine dealignment in Australia. Aitkin (chapter 4) emphasises the electoral system - in which voting is compulsory and the method preferential - as a dampening influence upon change. In West Germany, Klingemann notes a number of factors which have sustained the stability of the party system (p.236) but nonetheless concludes that this stability is ´fragile´. He argues that the traditional cleavage alignments have declined in importance and that there are signs of a move from ´traditional and stable-group politics towards change-prone issue politics´.(pp.252-3)

The only country not so far mentioned is France. Under the Fourth Republic, to 1958, the plethora of parties, their emergence and disappearance, and the continual coalescing and disintegration of groups strongly suggests a dealigned system, although electors were relatively stable in their preferences for, and identified with, the different tendances. Since 1958, however, the institutions of the Fifth Republic appear to have helped to reduce slowly the fissiparous tendencies of French parties and to have encouraged the development of a more bi-polar system. If anything France in the period since 1958 has seen a move towards a stronger partisan alignment rather than dealignment.

Clearly, then, social and attitudinal changes have not automatically given rise to partisan dealignment. While eight of the countries we have covered do show at least some evidence of dealignment, four do not and one (France) appears to have moved in the opposite direction. Moreover, there is no obvious characteristic or set of characteristics which distinguishes the different categories. No group exclusively shares a similar electoral system, or constitutional set-up, for example.

Part of the process of dealignment is the creation of an ever-increasing pool of electors who are detached from traditional party loyalties. Being detached, they are more likely to desert traditional voting habits by switching to other established parties or by supporting newly-emerging parties. Their votes are more likely to be affected by short-term influences. In short, dealigned voters are more likely to be volatile. At the aggregate level this is reflected in higher levels of net volatililty in successive elections. This, in outline, is the argument which underlies the link between partisan dealignment and electoral volatility in the model.

As indicated in the introductory chapter, however, electoral volatility is a complex concept and measuring it is far from straightforward. In particular many of the authors of individual chapters have been at pains to emphasise the fact that individual or gross volatility need not necessarily be reflected in measures of net volatility.

When considering trends in volatility, however, we are inevitably limited to utilising net volatility figures. This is simply because of the non-availability of suitable survey data in the great majority of countries for most of the post-war period. Excluding France, there are net volatility scores in this book for 154 national elections from 1948 onwards. But estimates of gross volatility (based on data of very variable quality) are given (or can be derived from the data) for just 34 of these. For an additional 15 cases, there are estimates of the extent of party switching among those who voted in successive elections. Moreoever, the figures are based on panel surveys in less than half of these 49 cases, the remainder being based on recall.

Analysis of the cases for which data are available suggests three conclusions about the relationship between individual-level and aggregate-level volatility. Firstly, individual volatility is uniformly greater than net volatility. This is not surprising given that movements in one direction are partly cancelled out by movements in the opposite direction and therefore not reflected in the net figure. In addition, the wider definition of gross volatility to include movement to and from abstention, again unsurprisingly, yields larger scores than simple switching between parties in successive elections. These points are illustrated in Table 15.1 which shows the mean and standard deviation for each measure where all three are available and also compares party switching and net volatility in the larger number of cases where this is possible.

Secondly, in most political systems individual volatility, however defined, is greater than commentators used generally to believe. Relying on aggregate statistics only, or on recall of past vote in surveys, commentators had built up a picture of voters as being highly stable in their preferences. But the mean figure for gross volatility suggests turnovers involving a quarter of the electorate and cases involving a third or more are common. When the analysis can be extended to more than two elections by means of panels, the volatility figures are even more striking. This can only in part be explained by increases in the ´real´ level of volatility. So far as one can judge, the level of individual volatility seems, on the whole, to have been seriously underestimated in the past.

Table 15.1: Mean Volatility Scores

	Net Volatility	Gross Volatility	Party Switching
Mean	7.7	25.8	15.2
S.D.	4.6	11.7	7.8
(N)	(34)	(34)	(34)
	Net Volatility	Party Switching	
Mean	8.6	17.3	
S.D.	5.7	8.1	
(N)	(49)	(49)	

Notes: The top set of figures (N=34) refers to cases where some estimate of gross volatility (including movement between voting and non-voting) is available. The lower set (N=49) refers to these plus an additional 15 cases where estimates of party switching only are available.

Thirdly, although it is logically possible that variations in gross volatility may not be reflected in variations in volatility at the aggregate level, the two are in fact significantly related. Using the 34 cases for which both gross and net volatility figures are available yields a correlation coefficient of .600 between the two. The figure for party switching and net volatility is .523 (N=49). Given the cross-national nature of the data and the relative unreliability of some of the estimates, these are quite respectable correlations. Thus, the gross volatility figure for the Australian 1977 election is likely to be a serious underestimate (see Table 4.5, notes) and if this case is excluded the coefficients rise to .623 and .537 respectively.

Conclusion

Similarly, we have already noted that Canada is something of an exceptional case, combining aggregate stability and individual volatility. If the three Canadian elections are also excluded the correlations rise to .732 (N=30) and .591 (N=45). Within individual systems the relationships are very strong. Thus Borre (p.381) gives a figure of .92 for the correlation between party switching and net volatility in Denmark. Austria shows a correlation of .93 between gross and net volatility while the five panel studies of British elections give a figure of .89. Although it is not entirely satisfactory, using aggregate figures to discuss trends in electoral volatility does not, therefore, seem to be an unreasonable procedure.

To some extent, the suggestion of the model that partisan dealignment gives rise to increased electoral volatility is borne out by the data. In those countries where there was no evidence of (further) dealignment at aggregate level (Canada, Australia, West Germany and Ireland), the striking feature of post-war election results is their stability rather than volatility. Variations in volatility seem to be fluctuations around a fairly constant level (especially if the first post-war West German election is excluded from consideration). Indeed, a simple regression of net volatility scores against number of years since 1945 suggests a downward trend in Canada, West Germany and Ireland and the absence of any relationship in Australia (see Table 15.2). The West German figure is heavily affected by the high volatility recorded between the first two post-war elections, which reflected unusual circumstances. But even excluding these, the trend is still gently downwards. Le Duc argues that aggregate stability in Canada is a product of the fact that short-term forces rarely combine in such a way as to favour any one party. When this does happen, Canada's high individual volatililty will produce a comparable net volatility figure. This, presumably, is the explanation for the unusually high aggregate volatility in the 1958 and 1962 Canadian elections. (Le Duc's argument also seems confirmed by the results of the Canadian election of 1984 which was held as this book was going to press. The victory of the Progressive-Conservatives reflects very high net volatility).

The case of France also seems to be consistent with the model. It was suggested above that France has moved from a situation of dealignment to one of

406

alignment. Given this, we would expect volatililty to decrease and, although Grunberg gives no figures in his chapter, Pedersen (1983) does indeed show volatility declining in France from a mean of 21.8 in the period 1948 to 1959 to 11.9 in the 1960s and 10.6 in the 1970s.

In Austria and Italy, which have been described as ´partly dealigned´, the picture is again one of mild fluctuations in a stable situation, after an initial period of readjustment in the first elections after the war. The relatively high levels of volatility recorded in these early elections largely accounts for the fact that in both cases regression analysis suggests a downward trend in volatility over time (Table 15.2). The failure of dealignment to translate into volatility in Austria is explained by Haerpfer (chapter 10) as resulting from a combination of very high turnout and a stable preference on the part of dealigned voters for the SPOe - the ´Kreisky voters´. The implication is that in the post-Kreisky era volatility may well increase. In Italy the process of dealignment has probably not proceeded far enough for any significant impact upon volatility to be discernible.

Table 15.2: Regression Results - Net Volatility and Number of Years since 1945

Country	Constant	Slope	R-squared	N
Australia	5.8	+.02	.001	15
Canada	11.1	-.17	.150	12
Ireland	12.8	-.23	.554	12
West Germany	18.7	-.39	.527	9
Austria	5.3	-.10	.344	11
Italy	15.3	-.28	.399	9
Denmark	3.7	+.33	.279	15
Netherlands	4.8	+.19	.521	11
United States	5.2	+.28	.324	9
Great Britain	2.1	+.20	.370	11
Scotland	0.6	+.33	.691	11
Belgium	8.7	-.06	.024	11

Note: The figures for the United States refer to presidential elections only.

Conclusion

Turning finally to the six systems in which there seems clear evidence of volatility, all have exhibited high levels of volatility at some time in the post-war period, but a common pattern is difficult to detect. In three cases - the United States (presidential elections), Denmark and The Netherlands - a period of relative stabililty was followed by a sharp increase in volatility. This was followed in turn by a reduction in volatility (not as marked in The Netherlands as elsewhere) although levels were still higher than in the pre-volatile period. In all three cases the overall post-war trend is upwards according to regression analysis, although low R2 values for the United States and Denmark indicate considerable variation around that trend.

In Scotland and in Britain as a whole, there is a steady upward trend which has not, so far, shown any signs of coming to an end. The only major deviations in the trend occur in elections which followed very shortly after the previous ones (especially 1966 and October 1974). If these are ignored, then volatility is seen to be rising very steadily.

The case of Belgium is more complex: there seems to be a cyclical pattern with volatility suddenly rising in 1965 only to decline again until the most recent election when another sharp increase in volatility occurred. The effect is that over the post-war period there is no linear trend (Table 15.2).

This description of volatility trends in the 13 democracies covered in this book are, of course, greatly simplified and cannot match the more subtle and detailed discussions given in the individual chapters. What this overview suggests, however, is that there is no simple predictable relationship between partisan dealignment and electoral volatility. While dealignment produces voter instability, this can be contained by the sustained popularity of one party or its leader (Austria); it can result in sudden explosions of volatility (Belgium, Denmark); steady increases in volatility (Britain, Scotland); or wide variations in volatility over time (United States). There is some relationship between dealignment and volatility but the consequences of the former for the latter are unpredictable. The level of volatility in any given election is affected by a host of other short-term factors - the timing of the election, the personalities of candidates/leaders, government performance, media coverage, and so on.

Pedersen (1983) finds support for two hypotheses which help to account for variations in volatility. Firstly, the larger the number of parties contesting an election, the greater the volatility. Secondly, where the number of parties contesting successive elections changes, volatility goes up and down in tandem. These hypotheses clearly relate very directly to the final stage of the model we are discussing - the link between volatility and party system change. Pedersen tends to assume that the causal links between these two all flow in one direction - from the party system to volatility (Pedersen, 1983, p. 60) although he also gives a more qualified and complex interpretation (p. 64).

It seems clear, however, that the two are interactive. In the Introduction Crewe referred to France under the Fourth Republic and The Netherlands as cases where changes in the party system appeared to cause rather than reflect high levels of electoral volatility. Similarly, the SDP in Britain was almost entirely a product of manoeuvering among political elites. However, not all parties are guaranteed electoral support and a place in the system by their mere existence. New parties with no impact are formed constantly; a multiplicity of parties languish on the fringes of politics without ever breaking through (the National Front in Britain, for example); others make an immediate impact (D´66 in The Netherlands); yet others find themselves pitched from long-term obscurity into the forefront of politics (the SNP in Scotland).

If changes at the elite level of the party system are to affect levels of net volatility they must usually strike a chord among electors. If the latter strongly identify with existing parties and are securely bound to them by ties of class or religion then new or established minor parties will have little impact. If, however, voters are dealigned and therefore predisposed to volatile behaviour then this can in turn produce, via elections showing high levels of net volatility, a ´real´ change in the party system. The relationship between volatility and system change is not, then unidirectional but interactive.

In six of the countries we have covered (Australia, Canada, Ireland, Austria, West Germany and Italy) little evidence of increasing dealignment was found and no tendency towards increasing volatility. Even though in some cases conditions

Conclusion

exist which might lead one to expect increased volatility and some of the authors concerned anticipate the possibility of significant developments of this kind in the near future, to date there have been no major changes in the party systems established by the early 1950s.

In France, in contrast, there have been marked changes in the party system since 1958. However, these are very much related to constitutional and institutional changes (although the decline of Communist support is perhaps a contrary example) which have produced declining volatility among voters.

In the six political systems where there is clear evidence of partisan dealignment and high volatility the interaction of these with structural changes in the party systems has produced a variety of effects.

In the United States the party system has remained intact. The major consequence of volatility has been a series of landslide victories for one party or the other in presidential elections as voters react to short-term forces - in particular the personalities of the candidates and the performances of incumbents.

In Britain as a whole and in Scotland, as volatility has increased minor and/or new parties have steadily increased their support. The electoral system has largely prevented this from being translated into changes in party representation in the legislature but the Liberals and the SDP throughout the country and the SNP and Plaid Cymru in their respective nations now appear to be important permanent features of the political landscape - at least in terms of electoral support.

In Denmark, Belgium and The Netherlands, the effects of the interaction of dealignment, volatility and party system changes have been somewhat similar. In each case high volatility in the 1960s and early 1970s was accompanied by a marked fractionalisation of the party system which then stabilised in its new, more fragmented form. The election of 1973 was crucial in Denmark. Three parties - the Progressives, Centre-Democrats and Christian People's - burst upon the scene and have remained important elements without achieving the status of a major party, In Belgium, the Christian People's Party declined and in 1965 the system was transformed| by an upsurge in support for linguistic part|ies. Although the traditional parties continued to dominate government coalitions, the new parties

have consolidated their position electorally
throughout the 1970s. Mughan (chapter 12) concludes
that the high volatility recorded in the most recent
election (1981) is a response to short-term
influences and does not bode a further realignment.
The Netherlands similarly entered a period of flux
in the party system in the 1960s. There was a rash
of new parties some of which rapidly disappeared
(PPR, DS70, BP) while others, such as D´66, claimed
a permanent position in the system - even extending
to membership of governing coalitions. At the same
time the Christian parties were in decline and this
continued even after their merger in 1977.

As before, this overview of the interaction
between electoral volatility and party system change
does scant justice to the subtleties and
complexities explored in the preceding chapters.
Once again, however, the conclusion seems to be that
the effects of the interaction vary between systems.
The nature of the established parties, the electoral
system and the governmental system are only three of
the more obvious variables which are interposed
between increasingly volatile electorates and
changes in party systems.

As I noted at the outset of this chapter and as
Ivor Crewe anticipated in the Introduction, we have
not sought here to derive general statements about
the relationships between social change, electoral
volatility and party system change. Although the
discussion has been based on one simple model and
the book as a whole has sought to provide comparable
treatment of the cases covered, we have been
concerned to emphasise the complexity of the
relationships and the diversity of patterns found in
different countries. The latter arises because,
while all the political systems considered can be
described as ´Western Democracies´, their politics
are conducted within a daunting variety of
historical, cultural and institutional frameworks.

In saying this we are not intending to deny the
possibility of generalising. Clearly the social and
attitudinal changes associated with ´modernising´
societies did begin to affect political life in most
Western democracies from the 1960s onwards. But
because of the differences we have referred to, the
impact and effect of these changes differed also.
In some cases long-stable party systems were
overturned; in some the party system was modified;
in some the system absorbed change and remained
secure. In yet other cases the repercussions of
change have yet to be felt in the political system

Conclusion

and are still working themselves out.
This last point serves as a reminder that we are not dealing here with something static. There is always a forthcoming set of elections and every new election provides a new data-point to be incorporated into the analysis. There can be no ´last word´ on electoral change in Western democracies.

REFERENCE

Pedersen, M. (1983) ´Changing Patterns of Electoral Volatillty in European Party Systems, 1948-1977: Explorations in Explanation´, in H. Daalder and P. Mair (eds.), Western Europe Party Systems, Sage Publications, Beverley Hills, pp. 29-66

Authors Cited in Text

413

Authors Cited

414

Urwin, D.W. 1, 7, 9,
159, 195

Verba, S. 38, 44, 89,
312, 315, 318

Waller, R. 156
Webb, P. 105, 147
Weill, P. 210
Whiteley, P. 134
Whybrow, R. 105, 147
Whyte, J. 184
Wilson, J. 71
Wolters, M. 367
Worre, T. 397

Ysmal, C. 220

Zingale, N.H. 14, 44, 45

INDEX

For ease of reference, and to avoid unnecessary duplication of entries, the index has been produced in alphabetical order of countries.
Where an indexable item appears in a footnote the page reference number is followed by a small ´n´ followed by a footnote number.

Index

Index

DATE DUE
